# GEOGRAPHICAL ESSAYS IN HONOUR
## OF
## K. C. EDWARDS

Photo: *J. Houldgate*

KENNETH CHARLES EDWARDS, C.B.E., M.A., PH.D.(LONDON), F.R.G.S.

# Geographical Essays in Honour

## of

# K. C. Edwards

*Edited by*

R. H. OSBORNE, F. A. BARNES AND J. C. DOORNKAMP

DEPARTMENT OF GEOGRAPHY
UNIVERSITY OF NOTTINGHAM

1970

SBN: 900 57215 9

PRINTED IN GREAT BRITAIN BY
DERRY AND SONS LIMITED · CANAL STREET · NOTTINGHAM

# CONTENTS

CONTENTS—*continued*

# PREFACE

This volume is published to mark the retirement of K. C. Edwards as Professor and Head of the Department of Geography in the University of Nottingham. It has been compiled by three members of the staff of his Department, and every contribution has been provided by a past or present colleague or a former student of his. We have done this in order to signify our respect for him as mentor, guide, teacher and friend. The high esteem in which Professor Edwards is held was evident from the immediate and warm response that we, as editors, received from those who were invited by us to contribute essays. Everyone was anxious to be involved in paying this tribute; so much so that we had to decline, regretfully, a number of offers of contributions.

We have arranged the volume in two parts. The first part contains essays on themes relating to the East Midlands, an area on which Professor Edwards is the acknowledged authority after a lifetime of work and study within it. This part is simultaneously being published as the 1970 issue of *The East Midland Geographer*, which he founded in 1954. The second part is made up of contributions on a wide variety of topics concerning many different areas throughout the world. This diversity in itself reflects the keen interest shown by Professor Edwards in all branches of geography and his acquaintance with many countries and environments.

There are many who would readily acknowledge the early stimulus provided by Professor Edwards in their chosen field and the continuing encouragement that he has given so freely in research and teaching and in other spheres of activity. We offer this volume to him as an expression of the admiration, gratitude and affection of the members of his Department, past and present, knowing that our sentiments will be shared by a great number of others who have known him or worked with him elsewhere.

Our sincere thanks are due to the many sponsors, listed at the end of the volume, who generously made donations to subsidise the cost of production. We are also grateful to the University of Nottingham for making a loan from the Publications Fund; to Mr. M. Cutler for cartographic work; to Miss A. Bosworth and Miss R. Hudson for clerical assistance; to Mr. J. Houldgate and Mr. E. Payne for photography; and to Mr. N. Barker, of Derry and Sons Limited, for his advice and patience.

THE EDITORS

*Nottingham*
*May 1970*

# FOREWORD

Kenneth Charles Edwards was educated at Itchen Grammar School and University College, Southampton, where he took the University of London External B.A. Honours degree in Geography in 1925. In the following year, after obtaining the Cambridge Teaching Diploma, he was appointed by the late Professor H. H. Swinnerton, c.b.e., as Assistant Lecturer in the joint Department of Geology and Geography at University College, Nottingham.

His early duties were very wide and included the teaching not only of these two subjects but also of Education, as well as the supervision of school practice. His students, as a result, were also varied, including Honours undergraduates, graduates training as teachers, students on two-year non-graduate teachers' courses and students of Mining. His typical teaching load was about 30 hours per week. It was during this period that he was called on to develop his undoubted gift of versatility in teaching approach, and this quality of striking the right note and the right level for whatever group he might be teaching has remained with him over the years, to the great benefit of all those whom he has taught. He has also retained an active interest in geographical education at all levels, as shown, for instance, by his long-standing involvement in the work of the training colleges and in the Geographical Association, not least its local branches, especially those in the East Midlands. He also rapidly identified himself with the study of Nottingham and the East Midland region. It is not surprising, therefore, that his M.A. of 1931 should have been concerned with geographical aspects of the origins and growth of the city.

It is 'in the field', perhaps, where K. C. Edwards has always been happiest and where his intellectual and personal impact on individual students has often been greatest. To his skills as a teacher were added other necessary qualities of leadership in the field—good humour, good fellowship and unflagging energy, all of which have persisted unimpaired up to the time of his retirement. In the 1930s he was thus to be found in the forefront of those geographers who were actively promoting field studies and making them an integral part of academic training. Not only did he organise regular courses for his own students in the British Isles, but he also led numerous field parties of students and teachers to various countries on the Continent under the auspices of the Leplay Society Student Group, of which he became Chairman. In all cases the aim was to study in depth a particular area in all its geographical aspects. Nor were the results of field survey discarded once they had served their immediate purpose of training; they were carefully collated and published where possible and, as a result, valuable contributions were made to our stock of geographical knowledge. The areas were chosen with skill and imagination—places offering a variety of geographical phenomena and at the same time lying outside the conventional haunts of the tourist of those days. The visit to Luxembourg, for which he was to develop a special interest in the years to come, was a felicitous substitute for Hungary, which had suddenly become too expensive as a result of the financial crisis of 1931. This active interest in fieldwork was carried over into other spheres, including extra-mural teaching in Nottingham and the East Midlands and the holding of office in the Ramblers' Federation, the Youth Hostels Association and the Nottinghamshire Footpaths Preservation Society. For the latter body he helped in the plotting of footpaths on a six-inch scale. At a later date his years of first-hand contact with the Peak District made him the obvious choice to be the author of Collins '*New Naturalist*' volume on that area.

In 1934 K. C. Edwards became Lecturer in charge of a separate Department of Geography, which, by virtue of necessity and choice respectively, cohabited and collaborated with a separate Department of Geology under Professor Swinnerton; unity thus gave way to partnership. In the 1930s he was already playing an active rôle in the various national geographical bodies, such as the Geographical Association and the newly-formed Institute of British Geographers, of which he was a founder-member. In 1937 he was Local Secretary of Section E (Geography) of the British Association for the Advancement of Science when it held its annual meeting in Nottingham, and he also contributed to the regional survey produced on that occasion. He was Convener for 21 years, from 1937 to 1958, of the Conference of Heads of University Departments of Geography and in that capacity produced a report in 1939 on the nature and extent of laboratory work in Departments of Geography in British and Commonwealth Universities. His interests in planning were foreshadowed by his keen local support for Dudley Stamp's great Land Utilisation Survey and by the fact that he was amongst those geographers who submitted material through the Royal Geographical Society to the 'Barlow' Commission on the Distribution of the Industrial Population.

K. C. Edwards was appointed to a Readership in 1939. The outbreak of the Second World War in the same year inevitably led to a pause in the Department's growth, to staffing difficulties and to an increased teaching load, which now included lecturing to the Forces. Although exempt from military service he 'did his bit' in the Home Guard and the National Fire Service, while for two months at the very beginning of the war he served as Regional Press Relations Officer for the Ministry of Information. Appropriately enough, one of his tasks was essentially Applied Geography—to report on the extent to which the population was adequately covered territorially by the various local newspapers, which were then, of course, important media for wartime instructions to the public.

In several ways the wartime period was remarkably productive. He wrote the Nottinghamshire county report for the Land Utilisation Survey and the Admiralty Handbook on the Grand Duchy of Luxembourg. He was later to receive the Order of the Crown of Oak for his geographical services to that country and in 1947 it was to be the subject of his doctorate. Together with F. A. Wells, later to be Professor of Industrial Economics, he investigated the White Fish Industry for the Nuffield College Social Reconstruction Survey and they also acted as joint advisers for a Civic Survey of Lincoln. Following the creation of the Ministry of Town and Country Planning K. C. Edwards was seconded in 1944 as Regional Research Officer, a post he held until 1946. During these years he did much spadework on the problems of the region and thereby helped to establish the standing of geographers on the post-war planning scene. By its very nature little of his work was published, but one small part was the section on housing in a Ministry of Fuel and Power Report on the North Midland Coalfield.

After the Second World War the need to provide higher education for returning ex-servicemen as well as for an increasing number of applicants from school led to a rapid growth in the size of the Geography Department in the late 1940s. The Department moved in 1947 from cramped quarters shared with Geology in the palatial Trent Building to the temporary, but sturdily-built, huts known to all as the 'cowsheds'. The College received its long-awaited Charter as an independent University in 1948 and in the following year K. C. Edwards was elected to its first Chair of Geography. Meanwhile he had revived his support of fieldwork activities as founding President of the Geographical Field Group, which for over 20 years now has organized field-study parties at home and abroad and published associated geographical reports from its headquarters in the Department of Geography. His planning interests also continued. In 1949 he and F. A. Wells collaborated again, this time on a survey of the Chesterfield region, at the invitation of the constituent local authorities concerned. He was also called on to draft the University's submission to the Schuster Committee on the Qualifications of Planners.

In 1951 K. C. Edwards enjoyed a well-earned break of nearly a year from his Nottingham duties, but this was in no sense a rest, since he went to New Zealand to deputise for K. B. Cumberland, a former student, as Acting Head of the Department at Auckland. The visit to New Zealand stimulated him into founding *The East Midland Geographer* in 1954. The possibility of a regional geographical journal had crossed his mind more than once; and if New Zealand could sustain its own journal, why not the East Midlands of England, with a similar population? Supported in the idea by his colleagues and encouraged ('in a teashop after a meeting of some kind in Lincoln') by Sir Francis Hill, President of the Council of the University, he went ahead. The venture proved a clear success. The journal now has a circulation of about 700 at home and abroad and is still the only regional geographical periodical in England.

By the late 1950s student numbers were beginning to grow again, and since then have risen nearly every year. The Department moved once more in 1960, into a new Education and Social Sciences Building, K. C. Edwards having acted as Chairman of the Committee planning and supervising its construction. At this time (1958–61) he was also first Dean of the newly-established Faculty of Law and Social Sciences, the creation of which he had recommended for several years. In 1959 he was able to renew a pre-war acquaintance with Poland, since in that year the Institute of British Geographers, of which he was then President-elect, received an invitation from the Geographical Institute of the Polish Academy of Sciences to send a delegation of 12 to take part in a joint seminar. This inaugurated a series of joint seminars, held every few years, which have alternated between Poland and Britain, and K. C. Edwards, leader of the British delegation to the first seminar, has taken part in each of them. For his services to Polish–British relations he was awarded the Officer Cross of the Order of Polonia Restituta.

The 1960s were also busy years. With the assistance of other colleagues he was asked to make a private report on the problems of the east Derbyshire coalfield to the County Planning Committee and this was presented in 1963. In 1963 he was also President of the Geographical Association and during his period of office rendered valuable service in supervising the move to a new headquarters. The summer of that year was spent lecturing at Makerere University College, Uganda. In 1964 the award to him by the Royal Geographical Society of the Murchison Grant, for his contributions to regional survey in the East Midlands, happily coincided with the tenth anniversary of the foundation of *The East Midland Geographer* and with the holding in Nottingham, under his Chairmanship, of an Urban Geography Symposium forming part of the 20th Congress of the International Geographical Union. As regards teaching duties he was still entirely responsible until the mid-1960s for four lecture courses per week, three of them being to the third-year students and, in addition, he continued personally to direct the Easter fieldwork for the first year. Indeed, his range of teaching became even wider as a result of the introduction of a taught M.A. in Advanced Regional Studies and of a lecture course on environment to first-year architects. For the Nottingham meeting of the British Association in 1966 he edited the magnificent study of *Nottingham and its region*, to which he himself contributed several chapters and sections. Within a few years of its occupation the Education and Social Sciences Building was already proving inadequate and University Grants Committee (U.G.C.) approval was secured for a separate new building for the Social Sciences. He thus became Chairman, in 1965, of a further building committee, and the Department of Geography duly moved into its present spacious and well-equipped home in 1967.

It was only to be expected that the introduction of a system of regional economic planning by the new government elected in late 1964 should have led to the involvement of K. C. Edwards. Appointed first to the research committee of the Regional Economic Planning Council, he became a full member of that body in 1967. His services to regional planning in the East Midlands were fittingly recognised by the award of the C.B.E. in the New Year honours list of 1970. Within the University he simultaneously championed the cause of planning as an academic discipline and it is largely owing to his advocacy that it was eventually decided to form an independent Institute of Planning Studies on the occasion of a reorganization of the existing Department of Architecture and Civic Planning. Despite his commitments to the Economic Planning Council and his headship of a Department that now had a teaching staff of 12 and an Honours undergraduate population approaching 150, he willingly accepted a further public appointment in 1968 to the Sub-Committee for Social Studies of the U.G.C. In this capacity his experience of guiding two major buildings from design to completion and his long collaboration with other Social Science Departments must surely be of great value.

So far we have spoken of K. C. Edwards' professional geographical career, but the record would not be complete without mention of his other activities. He has never been content to be a passive member of the institution which he has served for over 40 years. For him the University was never to be regarded merely as an employer or a 'flag of convenience', but a fraternity in which all should play a part over and above purely academic duties. From his early participation on the hockey field he has continued to give support to student activities over many years, including those of the Geographical Society, always one of the most active in the Students' Union. Triennial reunion week-ends for old students have been held for many years. It would be impossible to mention the many University committees on which he has served, in addition to being a member of Senate for over 30 years. We should mention, however, his active interest in Adult Education, recently culminating in his Chairmanship of a working party to prepare the University's submission to the Russell Committee on Adult Education. He was also Chairman of the planning committee for a University Club, opened in 1954, and was subsequently its Chairman until 1957, with a further term of office from 1967 to 1969.

He has also taken a keen interest in overseas students, both academically and socially, contributing to the lecture courses for the Certificate and Diploma in English Studies and being a member of the Board of Studies for Overseas Students for very many years. Before the war he was one of the British representatives working for the realization of the International Students' Sanatorium in Switzerland. At this time also he was an active member and sometime Chairman of the University branch of the League of Nations Society. His liberal and international sympathies were also demonstrated during the war when he was a University representative on the Association of University Professors and Lecturers of Allied Countries in Great Britain. This brought him into touch with such well-known figures as Sir Ernest Barker and Gilbert Murray, 'whose steadfast belief in the survival of liberal principles and of European civilization as a whole served as a stimulus and encouragement to many who otherwise could have easily faltered in those dark days'.

Despite his retirement Professor Edwards' work for geography, for education and for planning is clearly not yet done. He still holds two important offices, on the East Midland Economic Planning Council and on the Social Studies Sub-Committee of the U.G.C. He has not yet completed his task of directing the compilation of a National Atlas of Luxembourg, a project which he initiated with the support of a group of scholars in that country. In connection with the World Atlas of Agriculture he is still occupied as Head of the Monograph Department. In retiring not only does he hand on a Department that is physically the envy of many, but also, and more important, a community characterized at all levels by the happy and informal relationships that he has engendered over many years of dedicated service.

It seems incongruous that he should formally retire while still in full command of his formidable and productive energy. We hope that he will have many years of continued activity, in which a reduction of commitments will leave him more time to indulge his appreciation of other pursuits, such as cricket and music. In wishing him happiness in his retirement, we also include Mrs. Edwards, who is known as a gracious hostess to a multitude of students and other visitors and who has given him unobtrusive support in all his work.

\* \* \* \* \*

There are many who would have liked to record their personal tribute to Professor Edwards. We can quote from only a few of the appreciations and reminiscences that reached us. One of his earliest colleagues and closest friends was Professor Neville Scarfe, now Dean of Education at the University of British Columbia, who has sent the following recollections of the early 1930s:

> As a result of my contact with K. C. Edwards in Corsica in 1929, on the occasion of the field visit by the Leplay Society, I was able to pursue work towards a Master's degree, partly by attending Saturday classes at University College, Nottingham . . . . . Luckily in those days I was Geography Master at Bemrose School, Derby, and could, therefore, commute easily . . . . . And so it came about that I was invited on 3rd December 1930 to join the Department of Geology and Geography at University College . . . . . From then on my indebtedness to the wisdom and advice of K. C. Edwards grew continuously until I left . . . . . in the summer of 1935. My four-and-a-half years of association with K.C. were among the happiest of my life, not only because we built together a fine department which soon became autonomous and independent, but because of the life-long friendship which arose therefrom.

Both of us, of course, profited from watching the great teaching skills of Professor H. H. Swinnerton, and from his insight into the value of field study and the use of visual aids in the classroom, but Ken went much further in promoting and developing imaginative new approaches, both in teaching and in field studies. The famous Easter field camps were not only a great enlightenment to students but occasions which gave staff and students lasting bonds of friendship and goodwill. Nowhere have I ever known a happier or friendlier department, nor one in which the quality of scholarship or good humour was higher. Of course, the numbers of students in 1931–35 were not large but it would be hard to find a group where the percentage of those who succeeded subsequently to high office in geography or education has been greater. Nor do I believe one could find a group that has retained such friendly contact with each other for so long . . . . .

Somehow idealism in philosophy was always balanced by direct contact with the reality of field work; intensive periods of serious scholarship were always balanced by humorous interludes which maintained sane perspectives. Throughout it all his warm humanity and kindly concern brought a charm and spontaneity unexcelled elsewhere . . . . . K. C. Edwards' name must go down in the annals of geography in Britain as the pioneer and leader of field studies—the man who kept geographers' feet solidly on the real earth. He believed in intensive depth studies in well-chosen, particular places. He was never an armchair geographer, he was never superficial or unscholarly, he was never a vague theorist—just a great geographer, a great teacher, and a superb colleague.

A colleague during the late 1940s and the 1950s was E. M. Rawstron, now Reader in Economic Geography at Queen Mary College, University of London. For several years after its inception he was responsible for the bulk of the editing of *The East Midland Geographer*. He recalls that:

. . . . . it was a most happy, and at all times encouraging, experience to serve as editor under K.C.'s direction as 'Editor in Chief'. I must, however, admit to my full share of 'sub'-editorial mistakes . . . . . Whomsoever in the Department these lapses most closely affected, they were always quickly forgiven and forgotten, because there was mutual understanding and trust amongst us all in far more important matters than a few typographical errors. Indeed, in every aspect of our work in the Department there was close rapport, for the emphasis was always placed upon strengths rather than weaknesses; K.C. knew the members of his team and how best to manage them. His great achievements as a geographer and East Midlander are equalled by his achievements at a personal level as a senior academic and head of department. Academics are prone to be lone wolves, ill at ease working in a pack, however small it may be. Much, therefore, depends on the leader, and there can have been few heads of department more dependable, encouraging and understanding than K.C.

To speak for K. C. Edwards' public-spirited national work for geography we quote from Professor Alice Garnett, for many years Secretary of the Geographical Association:

K.C. has always been a staunch supporter and leading figure in Geographical Association affairs . . . . . During his year of office as President he gave most generously of his time and energy in helping in the delicate tasks of reorganization and decision-making concerned with the acquisition and redevelopment of new headquarters. His judgment and discernment over a difficult year were invaluable . . . . . He is well known to geographers all over the country as a frequent lecturer at Branch meetings and again shows his generous spirit in finding time to fit in more than most. When, in 1958, we decided to begin the series 'Landscapes through maps' it was to him that we turned as Editor for this important venture. He turned to this Herculean job with characteristic energy and coaxed from authors a splendid series for publication. We were amazed at the speed with which he got this series going. The first publication was on sale early in 1960 and ten years later 12 titles are available and more than 100,000 copies have been sold. This is a truly remarkable achievement, solely due to his splendid endeavour, wisdom and foresight in this editorial capacity . . . . . Through his labours for the G.A. over so many years and in so many ways he has rendered a fine service to the teaching of geography in this country and we owe a very great debt to him.

Marcus Aurelius, in his *Meditations,* considers in turn the teachers of his youth and examines their influence and impact upon him. A colleague and former student of K. C. Edwards concludes this foreword by borrowing a tribute made therein to a Roman tutor whose qualities included:

> kindliness, how to rule a household with paternal authority, . . . . . an unselfconscious dignity, . . . . . and a good-natured patience with amateurs and visionaries. The aptness of his courtesy to each individual lent a charm to his society more potent than any flattery, yet at the same time it exacted the complete respect of all present. His manner, too, of determining and systematizing the essential rules of life was as comprehensive as it was methodical. Never displaying a sign of anger, . . . . . he was at once entirely imperturbable and yet full of kindly affection. His approval was always quietly and undemonstratively expressed, and he never paraded his encyclopaedic knowledge.

THE EDITORS

# PUBLICATIONS OF K. C. EDWARDS

## METHODOLOGY

World geography and the training course, *Geog.* 14 (Summer 1928) 456–457.

*Land, area and region* (Inaugural lecture, University of Nottingham, 1950); also in *Indian Geog. Journ.* (Jubilee Volume, 1951).

Geography in the training college: some observations on the individual study, *Institute of Education Bulletin* (University of Nottingham, May 1956).

The Humboldt and Ritter centenary, *East Mid. Geog.* 2, no. 12 (December 1959) 44–45.

The Mackinder centenary in the East Midlands, *East Mid. Geog.* 2, no. 15 (June 1961) 39–40.

The importance of biogeography, *Geog.* 49 (April 1964) 85–97. (Presidential Address to the Geographical Association).

Geography, review and prospect, *Times Educ. Suppl.* (26th May 1967).

The broadening vista, *Geog.* 52 (July 1967) 245–259. (Joint lecture to Royal Geographical Society, Institute of British Geographers and Geographical Association).

Organization for field work, *Geog. Mag.* 42 (4) (January 1970) 314.

Regional geography, *Geography: an outline for the intending student* (ed. W. G. V. Balchin) (1970) 99–114.

## REGIONAL PLANNING

Housing *and* Housing requirements, *North Midland coalfield: regional survey report* (Ministry of Fuel and Power, H.M.S.O., 1945) 19–25, 41–42.

The East Midlands, *Studies in regional planning* (ed. G. H. J. Daysh) (1949) 133–168.

*A survey of the Chesterfield Region* (with F. A. Wells) (Chesterfield Regional Planning Committee, 1949).

Town and country planning in Britain: background conditions, *The English Midlands: a complex industrial society* (University of Kentucky, Lexington, 1951).

Regional planning in Great Britain, *East Mid. Geog.* 3, no. 23 (June 1965) 353–357.

Regional economic planning in Great Britain, *Symposium on regional planning* (21st Congress of I.G.U., New Delhi, 1968).

## URBAN GEOGRAPHY

The influence of mineral production upon town development in the East Midlands, *Comptes Rendus du 16me Congrès, I.G.U., 1949* (Lisbon, 1951).

Corby—a New Town in the Midlands, *Town Planning Rev.* 22 (July 1951) 122–131.

New Towns in Britain, *Survey* 6 (2) (University of Nottingham, March 1956) 7–19.

Trends in urban expansion, *Adv. of Science* 16 (1959–60) 55–66. (Presidential Address to Section E of British Association for the Advancement of Science).

Trends in central area differentiation, *Proc. I.G.U. Symposium on Urban Geography* (Lund, 1960).

The New Towns of Britain, *Problems of applied geography, Geographical Studies* 25 (Warsaw, 1961) 141–146.

The New Towns of Britain, *Geog.* 49 (July 1964) 279–285.

The problem of small towns in England and Wales, *Problems of applied Geography* 2, *Geographia Polonica* 3 (Warsaw, 1964) 71–78.

Report of the Urban Geography Symposium, *Congress Proceedings, 20th Congress, I.G.U., 1964* (London, 1967) 212–220.

## EAST MIDLANDS AND NOTTINGHAM

Nottingham, *Geog.* 20 (June 1935) 85–96.

The Nottingham and Derby Railway, 1839, *Railway Gazette* (30th June 1939).

Nottingham and its region, The climate of Nottinghamshire, *and* The economic aspects of the Trent, *A scientific survey of Nottingham and district* (ed. H. H. Swinnerton) (British Association for the Advancement of Science, 1937) 25–38, 56–65, 99–101.

*The re-planning of Nottingham* (with F. A. Wells and others) (Nottingham, 1943).

*The Land of Britain, Part 60: Nottinghamshire* (Report of the Land Utilisation Survey of Britain, 1944).

Soils of the East Midlands, *Guide to the geology of the East Midlands* (ed. C. E. Marshall) (University of Nottingham, 1948).

Grimsby and Immingham: a port study, *Tijdschrift Econ. en Soc. Geog.* 42 (December 1951) 382–386.

*Lincoln: a geographical excursion* (Geographical Association, 1953).

Changing geographical patterns in Lincolnshire, *Geog.* 39 (April 1954) 78–90.

The East Midlands: some general considerations, *East Mid. Geog.* 1, no. 1 (June 1954) 3–12.

Some location factors in the development of Nottingham, *East Mid. Geog.* 1, no. 5 (June 1956) 3–9.

East Midlands coal production in relation to Britain's fuel and power problem, *East Mid. Geog.* 1, no. 6 (December 1956) 26–35.

The site and setting of the University of Nottingham, *Ten years a University* (eds. P. R. Mounfield and J. Wakeford) (Nottingham, 1958).

*Nottingham: the planners' legacy* (Town Planning Institute, Nottingham Summer School, 1962).

The East Midlands (chapter 16) *and* Lincolnshire (chapter 17), *Britain: geographical essays* (ed. J. Mitchell) (1962) 287–329.

The Nottingham conurbation, *East Mid. Geog.* 3, no. 18 (December 1962) 63–71.

*Nottingham and its region* (ed.) (British Association for the Advancement of Science, 1966). Also contributions by the editor: Introduction and historical note, 1–7; Economic development: alabaster working (chapter 12) 231–235; Extractive industry (chapter 16) 274–297; Communications (chapter 19) 315–340; The geographical development of Nottingham (chapter 21) 363–404; The Nottingham conurbation (chapter 25) 448–454.

The East Midlands urban region, *East Mid. Geog.* 4, no. 26 (December 1966) 63–71.

A map of Nottingham for 1800, *East Mid. Geog.* 4, no. 32 (December 1969) 478–480.

## LUXEMBOURG

*Luxembourg studies,* Leplay Society Student Group (1933, second edition 1937).

The Luxembourg iron industry, *The Colliery Guardian* (29th September 1933).

Some aspects of the Luxembourg iron industry, *Iron and Coal Trades Review* (29th September 1933).

Fels (Larochette), Besuchs Studie eines Industrie Städtchens (with S. W. Tiller), *Luxemburger Wort* (Luxembourg, 30th November and 1st December 1934).

The relationship between urban and rural settlement in the Grand Duchy of Luxembourg, *Comptes Rendus du Congrès I.G.U., 1938* (Amsterdam, 1938).

La répartition de la population dans le Grand Duché de Luxembourg en 1861 et en 1930, *International Kleingärtnerkongress zu Diekirch* (Luxembourg, 1939).

The iron industry in Luxembourg, *Geog. Journ.* 96 (2) (August 1940) 146–147.

*Luxembourg* (Admiralty Geog. Handbook, Naval Intelligence Division, 1944).

The Sidney Gilchrist Thomas centenary in Luxembourg, *Geog. Journ.* 117 (1) (March 1951) 109–111.

Historical geography of the Luxembourg iron and steel industry, *Trans. Inst. Brit. Geog.* 29 (1961) 1–16. (Presidential Address to the Institute of British Geographers).

Luxembourg: how small can a nation be?, *Northern geographical essays in honour of G. H. J. Daysh* (ed. J. W. House) (1966) 256–267.

The Grand Duchy of Luxembourg, *Problems of smaller territories* (ed. B. Benedict) (1967).

*Luxembourg, the survival of a small nation: a centenary lecture* (University of Nottingham, 1967).

## MISCELLANEOUS

*The ABC of climate* (1929).

Valley settlements in North Tirol, *Geog.* 16 (September 1931) 197–206.

The Nowy Targ basin of the Polish Tatra: its human geography with special reference to the Bukowina district (with N. V. Scarfe and A. E. Moodie), *Scottish Geog. Mag.* 51 (July 1935) 215–228.

Polish geography, *Baltic Studies* 1 (Toruń, 1936).

*Dalarna studies* (Leplay Society Student Group, 1940).

Note on transhumance in Sweden, *Geog.* 27 (June 1942) 67–68.

A note on routes to Russia through Iran, *Geog. Journ.* 99 (1) (January 1942) 44–46.

Soviet northern seaways, *Geog.* 28 (September 1943) 78–85.

The white fish industry: Grimsby and Fleetwood (with F. A. Wells), *Further studies in industrial organisation* (ed. M. P. Fogarty) (1948) 129–145, 157–167.

An early geography of New Zealand, *N.Z. Geog.* 7 (October 1951) 173–174.

A note on the River Trent (3) *and* The Netherlands floods: some further aspects and consequences (8) *in* The storm floods of 1st February 1953, *Geog.* 38 (July 1953) 161–164, 182–187.

The geographical basis of the Benelux Union, *Tijdschrift Econ. en Soc. Geog.* 45 (February 1954) 41–46.

De Britse Eilanden (with E. M. Rawstron), *De wereld waarin wij wonen en werken* (ed. W. E. Boerman), vol. 1, part 3 (Zeist, 1959).

The underground gasification of coal in England, *East Mid. Geog.* 2, no. 11 (June 1959) 30–36.

Geography in Great Britain, 1956–1960 (with G. R. Crone), *Geog. Journ.* 126 (4) (December 1960) 427–441.

*The Peak District* (with H. H. Swinnerton and R. H. Hall) (1962).

## POPULAR

Nottingham's resources and development, *Nottingham Journal Trade Review* (1st January 1935).

Nottingham's communications by road, waterway and rail, *Nottingham Journal Trade Review* (1st January 1936).

The great Trent waterway, *Nottingham Journal Trade Review* (4th January 1937).

Whither Nottingham? Some aspects of the city's growth, *Nottingham Journal Trade Review* (3rd January 1939).

The changing face of Nottinghamshire, *Notts. Countryside* 3 (1) (July 1939) 28–30.

Types of farmland in Nottinghamshire, *Notts. Countryside* 5 (1) (July 1941) 14–15.

The orchard lands of Nottinghamshire, *Notts. Countryside* 6 (1) (July 1942) 8–10.

The foundations of modern agriculture in Nottinghamshire, *Notts. Countryside* 11 (12) (April 1950) 1–3.

Nottingham, Queen of the Midlands, *Geog. Mag.* 38 (5) (September 1965) 329–347.

# THE FOUR HOMES OF THE DEPARTMENT OF GEOGRAPHY
## UNDER THE HEADSHIP OF K. C. EDWARDS

*(A)*   Main (later Trent) Building 1934–1947

In 1928 the Department of Geology and Geography moved from Shakespeare Street
to this building at Highfields (University Park)

*(B)*   Temporary Buildings 1947–1960

*(C)*  Education and Social Sciences Building 1960–1967

*Photos: E. Payne*

*(D)*  New Social Sciences Building 1967–1970

# PART ONE

---

*East Midlands Essays*

# EARLY LEAD SMELTING IN THE PEAK DISTRICT:
# ANOTHER LOOK AT THE EVIDENCE

## G. JOAN FULLER

### INTRODUCTION

The special problems of the historical geographer, trying to establish distribution patterns for times past, become particularly evident when working on a local scale. The geographer investigating present-day phenomena can see for himself what the objects are and where they are located. The historical geographer, after painstaking research, may have to say, 'Don't know'. The ancient lead industry of the Peak provides many examples of the problems which the historical geographer would like to solve. In this brief paper the main aim is to re-examine the evidence provided by Domesday, but it is useful first to look back at earlier evidence.

### THE ROMAN AND ANGLO-SAXON PERIODS

#### Roman

For the Roman era we have good, though limited, evidence of lead smelting. Over 20 lead pigs, nearly a quarter of the Roman pigs recorded as found in Britain, came from Derbyshire, some being discovered on Humberside, and one as far south as Pulborough in Sussex. This evidence suggests the importance of the Peak for lead production. But there are other questions for the historical geographer. When did the industry flourish? Here the evidence, compared with that of the Mendips, is scanty. The only datable inscription comes from Hadrian's reign in the early second century. More important still is the problem of location. Where were the Roman mines and smelting hearths? Roman pigs have been discovered close to the eastern margins of the lead field, from Bradwell in the north, *via* Matlock and Cromford Moors, to Carsington in the south. Does this indicate a widespread distribution of Roman mines and smelting hearths? We cannot be certain about this because archaeological evidence is inconclusive.

There is the further question of mining settlement. Several of the Roman lead pigs have abbreviated inscriptions LVT., LVTVD, or LVTVDARES, deriving, it is thought, from *Lutudarum*. But where and what was *Lutudarum*? No evidence has come to light in Derbyshire of a Roman mining centre like Charterhouse, and experts are divided in their views as to whether *Lutudarum* was a mining centre near Chesterfield, Matlock, or Wirksworth, or a general name for the Derbyshire mining field.

#### Anglo-Saxon

The era of the Dark Ages poses a characteristic problem to the researcher. Is there any evidence of continuity between the lead industry of Romano-Britain in Derbyshire and that of later Anglo-Saxon times? So far there is none, and, with the collapse of civilised life, the market for lead must have disappeared. But, after the coming of Christianity, a few historical records have survived which suggest that the Church was becoming interested in lead for building, because of its durability and weather-proof quality. Amongst these records is a ninth-century one from Repton Abbey in the Vale of Trent. It shows that land at Wirksworth was held by the Abbey, and was leased in A.D. 835 at an annual rent of 300 shillings' worth of lead, to be paid to Archbishop Ceolnoth and his successors and Christchurch, Canterbury.[1] This charter is of special geographical interest, being the first historical record of Wirksworth, the settlement later to become one of the chief centres of the lead industry. Wirksworth, situated on the south–eastern margin of the lead field, lay less than 20 miles north of Repton, and its hinterland included some of the richest mineral veins in the Peak.

The record does not tell us in what form the lead was to be supplied to Canterbury, but it is probable that it would be sheet lead, not pigs. Sheet lead, cast in sand moulds, was convenient for using either flat for roofing, or curved for water pipes or coffins. Clearly, then, Wirksworth in the first half of the ninth century was a centre both for lead mining and smelting. Whether it continued activity after the Danes destroyed Repton Abbey later in the century is not known.

### THE REIGN OF EDWARD THE CONFESSOR

Soon after his accession to the throne, in A.D. 1042, Edward the Confessor began building his great church on Thorney Island, the nucleus of Westminster Abbey. It is recorded that the wooden roof of the central tower was 'well covered with lead'.[2] Unfortunately, there is no mention of the source of this lead, but Domesday evidence suggests a possible connection between the Peak lead industry and Edward the Confessor's Westminster.

The first thing to note is that, in Domesday, Derbyshire is the only county with a record of lead production. While this does not rule out other possible sources, it appears to emphasize the importance of the Derbyshire industry. A second point is that information is given both for 1066 (*Tempus Rex Edwardus*) and 1086, which suggests continuity and a basis of comparison. Domesday records that, in the time of King Edward, the three royal manors of Bakewell, Ashford and Hope returned 'XX lib. and V$\frac{1}{2}$ sestarios mell. and V plaustrata plumbi di L tabulis', i.e. 30 pounds, five-and-a-half sesters of honey, and five cartloads of lead of 50 slabs (each). This record clearly implies lead smelting and casting into sheets suitable for roofing. A yearly total of 250 slabs indicates a large output and, since the manors were royal and the West Minster was still unfinished in 1066, it does seem probable that the cartloads were destined for the king's great church on Thorney Island.

The question of the geographical distribution of lead mining and smelting in 1066 receives little help from Domesday, however, for it makes no mention of either. But, since the lead slabs were part of the joint render of three manors, it is reasonable to suppose that each returned a quota derived from its own mines and smelting hearths. We may say, therefore, that lead mining was being carried on in the north of the lead field within the manor of Hope, and more centrally around the Wye Valley in the manors of Ashford and Bakewell (Figure 1). The Peak mineral veins, however, outcrop only on the Carboniferous Limestone, and, since these three settlements were situated in the Limestone Shale valleys below the upland, it is not likely that their inhabitants were the chief lead miners.

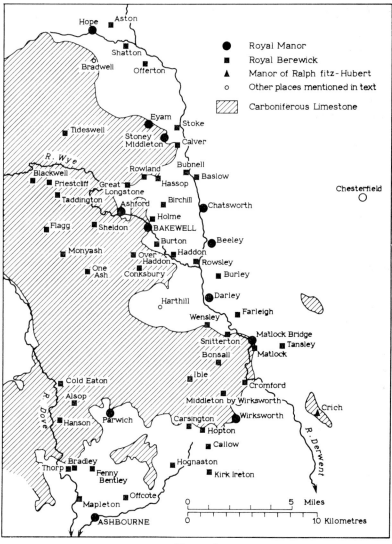

FIGURE 1
The Peak District: royal manors and berewicks recorded in Domesday

In fact, the manorial lands at this time were very extensive, including large areas of the limestone upland which were subsequently divided into separate manors. In 1066 the upland was a pioneer fringe, and the three Domesday manors included no less than 27 berewicks, many of which had been established where a water supply was found available within the upland. Mineral veins outcropping in the waste would readily be discovered and exploited from such berewicks as Tideswell, Monyash, and Sheldon. Here and elsewhere lead ore, at this early stage, could be got by shallow surface workings which followed the lines of the principal veins or 'rakes' in a general east–west direction. From these small-scale workings

3

ore would be carried to smelting hearths on hillsides, probably in the vicinity of Hope, Ashford and Bakewell. Thus, brief as it is, the evidence for 1066 establishes that lead smelting was important on the royal manors of High Peak.

## Domesday (1086)

A comparison between the 1066 and 1086 data for lead is difficult because the records deal with different items. For 1086 the Domesday clerks recorded not *tabulae* but *plumbariae*, viz.:

Ashford Manor with 12 berewicks had one *plumbaria*
Bakewell Manor with eight berewicks had one *plumbaria*
Matlock Bridge Manor with six berewicks had one *plumbaria*
Wirksworth Manor with seven berewicks had three *plumbariae*
Crich Manor had one *plumbaria*

We now come to the main issue. What was a *plumbaria*? According to the *Revised medieval Latin word-list*,[3] a *plumbaria* is a lead mine; it was also translated as such in the *Domesday geography of Northern England*.[4] There is nothing unexpected in this. Almost without exception twentieth-century writers on Domesday or on lead mining have translated *plumbariae* as lead mines. An exception can be made for the historian H. R. Loyn, for he refers to *plumbariae* without translation, leaving the question open.[5] More significantly, two works just published by authorities on Peak lead mining suggest that the *plumbariae* might be smelting works rather than mines.[6, 7] It is clearly useful, therefore, to take another look at the evidence.

### *Domesday vocabulary*

The Domesday vocabulary as related to mineral and other workings is the first evidence to consider. A basic difficulty facing the Domesday translators is the paucity of references to minerals and related works, but, few though they are, they contain one or two useful clues. As Table I shows, the Domesday clerks had a word for 'mines', as shown in the reference to an iron mine in the Welsh borderland manor of Rhuddlan. It therefore is reasonable to suppose that if the clerks recorded an iron mine in the Welsh borderland as *mineria ferri*, they would similarly record a lead mine in a neighbouring county as *mineria plumbi*. The second clue is of the type we associate with the 11-plus examination. Of the three 'aria' words, two (*ferraria* and *ollaria*) are translated as processing works of some sort. *Plumbaria* as 'lead mine' is odd-man-out, but if it were translated as 'lead works' it would come into line with the others.

TABLE I
Domesday words relating to the mining and processing of minerals

| Name | Translation | Reference |
|---|---|---|
| Ferraria | Iron works | H. C. Darby, *Domesday geography of eastern England* (1952) 84 |
| Ferraria | Smithy, forge | R. E. Latham, *Revised medieval Latin word-list* (1965) 189 |
| Mineria ferri | Iron mine | H. C. Darby and I. S. Maxwell (eds.), *Domesday geography of Northern England* (1962) 388–389 (Rhuddlan) |
| Ollaria | Pottery | R. E. Latham, *op. cit.* (1965) 322 |
| Plumbaria | Lead mine | H. C. Darby and I. S. Maxwell (eds.), *op. cit.* (1962) 323–324 |

4

TABLE II

Translations of *plumbaria*, 1788–1968

| Date | Author or translator | Reference | Translation of plumbaria |
|------|---------------------|-----------|--------------------------|
| 1788 | Robert Kelham | *Domesday Book illustrated,* 297 | Plummer's shop or perhaps lead mine |
| 1789 | James Pilkington | *A view of the present state of Derbyshire* 1, 100 | Lead mine |
| 1817 | Daniel Lysons | *Magna Britannia Vol. 5, Derbyshire,* CXCIV | Lead mine |
| 1833 | Sir Henry Ellis | *Introduction and indexes to Domesday* 1, 138 | Lead works |
| 1880 | A. H. Stokes | Lead and lead mining in Derbyshire, *Transactions of Chesterfield and Derbyshire Institute of Mining, Civil and Mechanical Engineers* 8 (1880) 143 | Lead works |
| 1886 | J. P. Yeatman | *Feudal history of the county of Derbyshire* 1, 27 | Lead works |
| 1887 | W. de Gray Birch | *Domesday Book,* 276 | Lead mine |
| 1905 | F. H. Stenton | *Victoria County History of Derbyshire* 1, 316 | Lead works |
| | F. H. Stenton | *Op. cit.,* 330 | Lead mine |
| 1906 | Adolphus Ballard | *The Domesday inquest,* 182 | Lead mines |
| 1907 | J. H. Lander and C. H. Vellacott | *Victoria County History of Derbyshire* 2, 323 | Lead mine |
| 1923 | L. F. Salzman | *English industries of the Middle Ages,* 42 | Lead mine |
| 1962 | H. R. Loyn | *Anglo-Saxon England and the Norman Conquest,* 103 | Not translated |
| 1963 | H. C. Darby and I. S. Maxwell (eds.) | *Domesday geography of Northern England,* 323–324 | Lead mine |
| 1963 | R. Welldon Finn | *An introduction to the Domesday Book,* 203 | Lead mine |
| 1965 | R. E. Latham | *Revised medieval Latin word-list,* 356 | Lead mine |
| 1965 | Arthur Raistrick and Bernard Jennings | *A history of lead mining in the Pennines,* 22 | Lead mine |
| 1968 | William Rees | *Industry before the Industrial Revolution,* 46–47 | Lead mine |
| 1968 | J. H. Rieuwerts | *Lead mining in the Peak District,* 9 | Lead smelter |

In fact, in a number of nineteenth-century works on Domesday, the word *plumbaria* was translated as 'lead works', and it is interesting, therefore, to trace the course of its translation from the beginning. A chronological list (Table II) shows that the translation of *plumbaria* has varied from time to time. In the late eighteenth and early nineteenth centuries, 'lead mine' was the accepted translation. Then in 1833 came Sir Henry Ellis's authoritative *Introduction and indexes to Domesday,* in which *plumbariae* was translated as lead works. Writers in the later nineteenth century varied between the two meanings, but none discussed alternatives. Are we to conclude, therefore, that the two terms were synonymous? This seems unlikely. Then, as now, lead works were processing plants, usually smelters.

In 1905 the publication of the first volume of the *Victoria County History of Derbyshire* included an introduction to, and translation of, the Domesday text by the young F. H. Stenton. In his introduction Stenton referred to the Domesday lead works,[8] thus following Sir Henry Ellis. But in his subsequent translation of the text, *plumbariae* is translated as lead mines.[9] Was Stenton, therefore, in two minds about the significance of the word? It is unfortunate that he did not comment on it, and it may be that he did not fully recognise the problem. Then, two years later, the second volume of the *Victoria County History of Derbyshire* appeared, including Lander and Vellacott's learned article on the lead industry, an article which has become a standard reference.[10] It is especially significant, therefore, that they followed Stenton's translation of *plumbaria* as 'lead mine'. Subsequently almost all writers have accepted this meaning, apparently without question. But, as we have seen, the Domesday clerks had a word for 'mine' which they could have used in the Derbyshire folios. Exchequer clerks were certainly using this word 70 years later, in Henry II's reign, when a Pipe Roll of 2 Henry II records 'In defectu minarie plumbi £18'.[11] Surely it seems unlikely that the Domesday clerks could choose between two possible names for a lead mine, and yet have none for a lead-smelting works, which was a more important economic unit.

## Manorial rights

So far the argument has been concerned with problems of translation. But there are other approaches to the question of the *plumbariae*. One of these also relates to the Domesday text, and arises from the matter of manorial rights in early medieval times. It is well established by historians that, in this period, corn mills usually belonged to the lord of the manor, providing him with a valuable source of revenue. Frequently also the lord's oven was another monopoly,[12] and in some manors the work of the smith was under the direct authority of the lord and was linked with a particular holding.[13] Now there is substantial evidence that a similar state of affairs regarding lead smelting prevailed in the Peak during early medieval times and in certain manors persisted into the modern period. As John Farey explained:

> The miners within the manors of Haddon and Hartle [Harthill] were restricted by the custom of those manors from smelting their lead, but at the lord's hearth, which occasioned the Duke of Rutland to maintain one of the old hearths at the north–west end of Great Rowsley village, long after they had been elsewhere disused.[14]

This hearth was finally pulled down about 1780. There is documentary evidence even later of smelting at the 'Lord's cupola' in Middleton Dale, part of the manor of Stoney Middleton in High Peak.[15] These two examples are probably the last remnants of a more general prerogative prevailing in early medieval times, as stated by Farey:

> Anciently, it seems, that the Crown claimed the right of smelting all the lead ore which was obtained in the King's Field, and took toll or duty from it.[16]

It therefore seems reasonable to conclude that, at the time of Domesday, lead smelting works in the Peak, like corn mills, belonged to the manorial lord and yielded him revenue. In Domesday the number of corn mills recorded for the Peak in 1086 is small, as is the number of *plumbariae*. And only in two royal manors possessing corn mills do we find records also of *plumbariae*. They appear as follows:

> In Ashford with its berewicks . . . . . there [is] 1 mill [rendering] 12 pence, and the site of 1 mill, and 1 plumbaria . . . . . In Bakewell with its 8 berewicks . . . . . there is 1 mill [worth] 16 shillings and 8 pence and 1 plumbaria.

We see, then, that in the Domesday text the records of the manorial mill and its annual return are followed immediately by the record of the *plumbaria*. This does suggest that it was the manorial lead-smelting hearth which was being listed, since it was the smelting hearth and not the lead mine which was the lord's monopoly.

## Lead output

Another approach to the problem of the Domesday *plumbariae* relates to output, and here we are faced with the difficulty of comparing the production of 250 slabs of lead in 1066 with the list of *plumbariae* in 1086 unaccompanied by any mention of production. As has been said, the 1066 yield of cast lead was large and was probably the joint yield of three royal manors. Of these manors, two, Ashford and Bakewell, were recorded also in 1086, each having one *plumbaria*. Now, if we take it that the *plumbaria* was merely a lead mine, we must conclude that the production of cast lead had declined to insignificance. The point is that the small surface workings characteristic of early times probably yielded little individually but, spread over the rich field on the eastern side of the Carboniferous Limestone upland, the total production of ore for a manorial smelting-hearth might have been substantial. This would provide a significant potential source of revenue for the Domesday record to note.

Another reference to Derbyshire lead production about this time lends support to the notion that the lead output was indeed of some importance. The *Inquisitio Eliensis,* a survey, bearing some relation to Domesday, of the lands belonging to Ely Abbey, contains an isolated reference to Peak lead quite out of context amongst the returns of abbey estates.[17] This note states:

> A carretata [fodder] of Peak lead contains 24 fotinels; every fotinel is of 70 pounds . . . . . the London carretata is heavier than that by 420 pounds by the lesser hundred.

This meant that the Derbyshire fodder weighed 1,680 pounds and the London fodder 2,100 pounds.[18] This may be the first reference to the 'fodder' which subsequently became the accepted measure for smelted lead. The note by the clerk of Ely Abbey may possibly relate to Abbey purchases of lead for roofing, etc., and it suggests that Ely looked to the Peak for supplies and that the Peak was producing substantially in the Norman period. The output of seven mines would not suffice for this, but seven manorial smelting hearths might well do so.

## Inquisition of Ashbourne

It may be of some value to approach the problem of the Domesday *plumbaria* retrospectively, looking at it in the light of evidence established at the Inquisition of Ashbourne, held in A.D. 1288 to determine the rights and customs of Peak lead miners on the royal lands known as the King's Field.[19] At this inquisition, the mining customs were said to have been handed down from 'time out of mind', a conventional phrase we now know to have implied existence as early as 1189, the first year of Richard I's reign.[20] Such customs may have originated much earlier, possibly as far back as Anglo-Saxon times. They make it clear that, far from mining being a matter of a few manorial mines owned by the lord, Peak mines were numerous and belonged to their peasant owners as long as they were worked. It seems highly probable that this was the characteristic pattern of development from Anglo-Saxon times onward. It was the best means of ensuring lead production in a pioneer fringe area, and the crown gained revenue thereby as well as a supply of lead for building. In such a context it is difficult to see Domesday's seven *plumbariae* as seven manorial mines, but reasonable to think of them as manorial smelting hearths, all on crown manors except for Crich, which was outside the King's Field.

## Conclusion

This argument has been concerned with the nature of the evidence on lead provided by Domesday; and the fact that it has emerged as a research topic is sufficient to demonstrate one of the special problems of the historical geographer. But, having reached the conclusion that the *plumbariae* of Domesday were lead smelters, the geographer then wants to know where, precisely, they were located. The answer, as yet, can only be 'Don't know'.

## NOTES

[1] W. DE GRAY BIRCH, *Cartularum Saxonicum* 1 (1885) 597.
[2] R.'A. BROWN, H. M. COLVIN, and A. J. TAYLOR, *History of the king's works* 1 (1963) 15.
[3] R. E. LATHAM, *Revised medieval Latin word-list* (1965) 356.
[4] *Domesday geography of Northern England* (eds. H. C. Darby and I. S. Maxwell) (1962) 323–324.
[5] H. R. LOYN, *Anglo-Saxon England and the Norman Conquest* (1962) 103.
[6] *Lead mining in the Peak District* (eds. T. D. Ford and J. H. Rieuwerts) (1968) 9.
[7] NELLIE KIRKHAM, *Derbyshire lead mining through the centuries* (1968) 99.
[8] F. H. STENTON, Introduction to the Derbyshire Domesday, *Victoria County History of Derbyshire* 1 (1905) 316.
[9] *Idem*, Text of the Derbyshire Domesday, *Victoria County History of Derbyshire* 1 (1905) 330.
[10] J. H. LANDER and C. H. VELLACOTT, *Victoria County History of Derbyshire* 2 (1907) 323–349.
[11] Pipe Rolls of 2–3–4 Henry II (1930 edition) 38.
[12] H. S. BENNETT, *Life on the English manor* (1937) 129.
[13] G. C. HOMANS, *English villages of the thirteenth century* (1942) 286.
[14] JOHN FAREY, *General view of the agriculture and minerals of Derbyshire* 1 (1811) 384–385.
[15] DERBYSHIRE RECORD OFFICE, *Brooke-Taylor archives*.
[16] JOHN FAREY, *op. cit.*, 384.
[17] N. E. S. A. HAMILTON, *Inquisitio Comitatus Cantabrigiensis and Inquisitio Eliensis* (1876) 191.
[18] S. O. ADDY, Derbyshire lead weights, *Journal of Derbyshire Archaeological and Natural History Society* 46 (1924) 108.
[19] J. H. LANDER and C. H. VELLACOTT, *op. cit.* (1907) 326.
[20] G. W. KEETON, *The Norman Conquest and the Common Law* (1966) 204.

# FRINGE EXPANSION AND SUBURBANIZATION AROUND NOTTINGHAM: A METROPOLITAN AREA APPROACH

## J. A. GIGGS

A considerable amount of attention has been paid to the 'metropolitan' form of community organization since R. D. McKenzie identified its major structural attributes and formative forces.[1] Most of this research has been undertaken by authorities in the U.S.A. and this, perhaps, led Schnore to claim, in a review of the literature,[2] that 'metropolitan development can best be conceived as a new form of urban growth especially characteristic of twentieth century America'.[3] In a subsequent paper[4] he recognized that research by Kingsley Davis and others had revealed the existence of metropolitan development on a world-wide scale. It was noted, however, that these studies

> deal primarily with population aggregation, with special emphasis upon levels of metropolitanization and rates of metropolitan growth . . . . . there are fewer examples of frontal assaults upon problems of spatial structure.[5]

The purposes of this paper, therefore, are twofold: firstly to outline the spatial structure of the metropolitan community of Nottingham, specifically summarising certain aspects of its recent population growth and decentralization and summarising the current residential distribution of the population according to social class; secondly, to distinguish the specific types of suburban sub-centres which have emerged in the south-east sector of the metropolitan rural ring, outlining their present functional and morphological attributes.

### THE SPATIAL STRUCTURE OF THE NOTTINGHAM METROPOLITAN AREA

Explanatory models of the 'closed' metropolitan community usually involve the recognition of three distinct, but interdependent, sub-areas which are variously defined as 'rings', 'zones' or 'belts'. This procedure has been adopted here, and three rings of Nottingham's metropolitan area, embracing an area of 335 square miles (868 square kilometres), have been identified and selected for analysis. The areal components of these rings have been determined by the configuration of the existing administrative units and are shown in Figure 1.

*Inner ring*

The central city, consisting of Nottingham County Borough, and comprising 8.5 per cent of the metropolitan area.

*Intermediate ring*

The urban ring, or urban fringe, consisting of the five adjoining Urban Districts, and collectively comprising 10.2 per cent of the total metropolitan area.

*Outer ring*

The inner-rural or suburban ring, consisting of 126 census Enumeration Districts with populations dependent to a greater extent upon the urban centres of the inner and intermediate rings than upon other, outlying, urban centres. In the inner rural ring, as defined here, over 50 per cent of the working population which commutes outside each Enumeration District goes to work in the central city or the urban ring.[6] These Enumeration Districts make up the entire Rural Districts of Basford and Bingham, together with the western part of Southwell Rural District. Collectively they account for 81.3 per cent of the metropolitan area, as defined here.

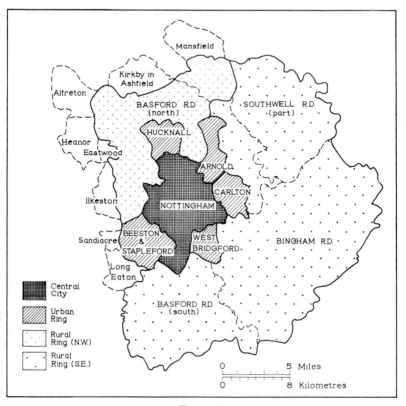

FIGURE 1

Administrative composition of Nottingham 'metropolitan area'

A cluster analysis, using the 15 variables listed in Table IV for the 126 Enumeration Districts revealed two distinct sectors within the rural ring. One is located north and west of the city and was extensively built up and industrialized in the nineteenth century; the other is located east and south of the city and is still relatively undeveloped. These two sectors are treated separately in the following analysis. Beyond the outer ring lies a belt of satellite towns (almost continuous to the north and west of the city) and rural settlements which have progressively more tenuous affiliations with Nottingham. This peripheral zone has not been included in the present study.

*Metropolitan growth and decentralization, 1931–68*

Using census data one is able to document the timing and extent of population growth and outward shifts in the metropolitan area since 1931.[7] Two phases have been identified, the first lasting from 1931 to 1951, thus

10

according broadly with the house-building boom of the 1930s,[8] World War II and the period of building restrictions, which ended in 1948. The second phase dates from 1951 and spans the period when the forces which create metropolitan areas have been able to reassert themselves under conditions of increasing affluence and personal mobility, although land-use planning controls have restricted the scale and location of development.

Table I contains the basic demographic data for the entire metropolitan area and its constituent parts. From Part A it can be seen that the population of the whole metropolitan area has grown substantially over the entire period under review, but that the 1951–68 rate of growth is smaller than that for 1931–51, even when allowance is made for the difference in length of period. Analysis of the differential growth rates (Part B) reveals considerable internal variations. Between 1931 and 1951 ring growth was already three times as high as that in the central city. Within the metropolitan rings urban growth greatly exceeded rural growth and the rate for the north–west rural sector was five times that in the south–east sector. During the post-1951 phase the situation has changed remarkably. The central city has declined in population and the greatest percentage increases have been recorded in the rural ring, chiefly in the south–east sector.

TABLE I

Population changes within metropolitan area, 1931–68 [9]

| | *A*<br>*Population (thousands)* | | | *B*<br>*Per cent change* | |
| --- | --- | --- | --- | --- | --- |
| | *1931* | *1951* | *1968* | *1931–51* | *1951–68* |
| Total metropolitan area .. | 452.4 | 537.5 | 611.6 | 18.8 | 13.7 |
| Central city .. .. | 276.2 | 308.2 | 305.2 | 11.1 | −1.1 |
| Rings .. .. | 176.2 | 229.3 | 306.4 | 33.2 | 33.6 |
| Urban .. .. | 105.6 | 152.1 | 190.8 | 44.0 | 25.4 |
| Rural .. .. | 70.6 | 77.2 | 115.6 | 9.3 | 49.7 |
| North–west .. | 27.2 | 32.1 | 39.1 | 18.4 | 21.4 |
| South–east .. | 43.4 | 45.1 | 76.5 | 3.7 | 69.6 |

| | *C*<br>*Per cent share of*<br>*total growth* | | *D*<br>*Per cent distribution of*<br>*total metropolitan area population* | | |
| --- | --- | --- | --- | --- | --- |
| | *1931–51* | *1951–68* | *1931* | *1951* | *1968* |
| Total metropolitan area .. | 100.0 | 100.0 | 100.0 | 100.0 | 100.0 |
| Central city .. .. | 37.1 | 0.0 | 61.2 | 57.3 | 49.9 |
| Rings .. .. | 62.9 | 100.0 | 38.8 | 42.7 | 50.1 |
| Urban .. .. | 55.0 | 52.2 | 23.3 | 28.2 | 31.1 |
| Rural .. .. | 7.9 | 47.8 | 15.5 | 14.5 | 19.0 |
| North–west .. | 5.9 | 5.3 | 5.9 | 6.2 | 6.5 |
| South–east .. | 2.0 | 42.8 | 9.6 | 8.3 | 12.5 |

Part C of Table I shows the shares of the total metropolitan growth going to the centre and the rings. The central city gained 37.1 per cent of the total growth between 1931 and 1951 and none of the increase thereafter. The urban ring accounted for most of the growth during both phases, but the south–east sector of the rural ring has made substantial gains since 1951. The results of these outward shifts are summarized in Part D, which

11

shows the proportions of the population of the total metropolitan area contained in the three rings for 1931, 1951 and 1968. As a result of differential growth over the period under review the central city's share of the total metropolitan area population has fallen from almost two-thirds to less than a half.

The above findings reveal that the Nottingham metropolitan area displayed characteristics similar to those of metropolitan areas in the U.S.A. If, however, we accept Schnore's suggestion that 'In a rough sense . . . . . decentralization is an index of the maturity of metropolitan areas', then it is apparent that in Nottingham the process of decentralization is less marked and that the current (1968) level of decentralization is comparable with that found in the U.S.A. in 1960.[10]

The explanation for the process of slow central-city population growth between 1931 and 1951 and the subsequent absolute decline can largely be found in the progressive diminution in the area available for house building and in the failure of the city to annex the surrounding urban areas.[11] In addition, many city residents have moved out to the rings, where they have been joined by migrants into the region who have settled directly in the rings. Unfortunately, detailed evidence showing the relative contributions of natural increase and net migration to the differential growth of the three rings is not available. The limited evidence which exists is summarized in Table II.

TABLE II

Components of population change, 1951–61 and 1961–66 (per cent)[12]

|  | 1951–61 | | 1961–66 |
|---|---|---|---|
|  | *Natural increase* | *Net in-migration* | *Gross in-migration* |
| Total metropolitan area .. | 4.1 | +0.3 | 14 2 |
| Central city .. .. | 1.3 | −6.1 | 9.1 |
| Rings .. .. .. | 7.7 | +7.3 | 18.3 |
| Urban .. .. | 7.8 | +5.1 | 14.1 |
| Rural .. .. | 6.2 | +12.9 | 25.2 |
| North–west .. | — | — | 16.0 |
| South–east .. | — | — | 29.2 |

Research into the causes of metropolitan growth and decentralization in the U.S.A. suggest that the spatial changes follow economic and technological changes at both national and regional levels.[13] The most significant formative factor has undoubtedly been the rising level of *per capita* real income since the beginning of the century.[14] The most important results of this trend have been the increasing freedom apparent in the selection of places of residence, made possible by greatly increased mobility[15] and expenditure on private means of transport.[16] At the regional level continuous road improvements since the early 1930s have also enhanced mobility.[17]

Although the development of the Nottingham metropolitan area resembles that of its North American counterparts in many respects, there are also important differences. In the U.S.A. decentralization of most land uses has proceeded apace,[18] whereas in Nottingham the process has been restricted almost exclusively to residential land use. Businessmen and industrialists have not joined the flight to the suburbs, generally preferring traditional, central-city locations for their concerns.[19] Since 1960, however, a small, but growing, number of firms have moved out from the central city to sites in the urban ring.[20]

A further distinction relates to the importance of planning controls, which have operated in this country in a fashion not found in the U.S.A. Both the scope and scale of decentralization have been retarded by successive constraints which have been applied by planning authorities. The most important of these have been the Town and Country Planning Act (1947) and the Green Belt Plan (initiated in 1955 but effectively applied in Nottinghamshire since 1961). Their influence can be gauged from the fact that planning permission was refused for 8,748 houses in the south–east rural ring between 1961 and 1968. Had this permission been granted, the population in this sector would now be approximately 35 per cent greater (roughly 27,000 persons).[21]

## The socio-economic structure

The cumulative effects of economic and technological developments during the period under review have been non-residential expansion in the central city and residential growth in the rings. The demographic spatial shifts summarized in Tables I and II have thus resulted in an increasing separation of home and work place. Table III reveals that the residential

TABLE III

Social and economic characteristics, 1951 and 1966 (per cent of ring totals)[22]

|  | Social classes I/II | | Households with car | Owner-occupied dwellings | Exclusive use of all household amenities |
|---|---|---|---|---|---|
|  | *1951* | *1966* | *1966* | *1966* | *1966* |
| Total metropolitan area .. | 13.8 | 14.0 | 43.1 | 41.2 | 71.1 |
| Central city .. .. | 13.3 | 10.4 | 34.0 | 27.1 | 59.1 |
| Rings .. .. | 16.0 | 17.5 | 54.2 | 55.3 | 80.0 |
| Urban .. .. | 19.8 | 16.6 | 51.3 | 56.2 | 81.0 |
| Rural .. .. | 3.7 | 18.6 | 58.2 | 52.1 | 77.1 |
| North–west .. | — | 12.3 | 51.1 | 50.4 | 69.2 |
| South–east .. | — | 21.8 | 62.4 | 56.3 | 81.3 |

distribution of metropolitan dwellers exhibits a pattern found in many other studies.[23] There has been increasing polarization of social classes over time, with the upper classes shifting from central to peripheral locations. The four socio-economic indices reveal that the metropolitan area is highly structured with respect to social class and standards of living. There is, in all four cases, a regular gradient with respect to the central city, and the south–east sector of the rural ring emerges as the most favoured region in the entire metropolitan area.

THE GROWTH AND FUNCTIONS OF SUBURBS IN THE SOUTH–EAST RURAL RING

In the post-1951 period, therefore, population decentralization has proceeded rapidly. In the urban ring the pattern of development has been one of typical peripheral growth. In the rural ring, however, the emergent physical pattern has been very different. Population increase has not been uniform over the region but has been concentrated into a small number of parishes. Thus in the south–east sector 97 per cent of the total population growth was recorded in only 22 out of 78 parishes and seven of these accounted for 79 per cent of the growth. The period has thus witnessed the emergence of large, residential, non-agricultural settlements, which U.S. demographers classify as suburbs.

The number and sizes of suburbs with populations over 1,000 have consequently changed considerably. In 1951 there were 14 suburbs with populations ranging between 1,000 and 5,000, compared with 12 in 1931. By 1968 the number in this size range had risen to 17 and a further six places had populations of between 5,000 and 10,000.[24] It is thus apparent that the greatest changes have occurred since 1951, although expansion in the area has been deliberately restricted and localized since 1947. If the estimated populations affected by planning application refusals is added to the existing suburbs then the suburbanization which would have occurred in 1968 would have been substantially greater, for the number of suburbs with populations of 1,000 to 5,000 and 5,000 to 10,000 would have been 26 and eight respectively, and two places would have had populations of 10,000 to 15,000.

Figure 2(A) summarizes the post-1951 growth in population in the south–east sector of the rural ring. It reveals that the greatest increases occurred in a ring of suburbs fringing the urban ring. Figure 2(B) presents the parish population for 1968, graded according to size. The largest suburbs are again to be found adjacent to the urban ring.

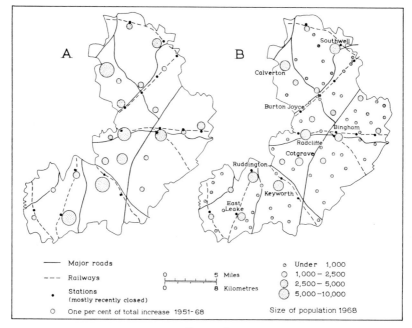

FIGURE 2

Population of south–eastern rural ring

A   Distribution of percentage population increase, 1951–68
B   Size of parish populations, 1968

14

A cluster analysis of the 78 parishes in the sector, involving 15 variables, revealed that the parishes were not homogeneous, but that there were significant differences in their social and economic characteristics. Four distinct sets of parishes emerged. Sets 1 to 3 have been classed as suburbs and their major traits are summarized in Table IV.

TABLE IV

Social and economic characteristics of suburbs, south–east sector[25]

| | | Type of suburb | | |
| --- | --- | --- | --- | --- |
| | | Employing | Residential | |
| | | | Large | Small |
| A | *Population growth* | | | |
| | 1  Average increase, 1931–51 | 15 | 32 | 44 |
| | 2  Average increase, 1951–68 | 510 | 99 | 32 |
| | 3  Per cent places declining, 1951–68 | — | — | 30 |
| | 4  Per cent in-migrant, 1961–66 | 34 | 32 | 25 |
| B | 5  Per cent aged 0–14 | 36 | 23 | 23 |
| C | *Housing characteristics* | | | |
| | 6  Per cent owner-occupied, 1966 | 21 | 60 | 51 |
| | 7  Per cent all amenities, 1966 | 88 | 82 | 79 |
| D | *Socio-economic status* | | | |
| | 8  Per cent social classes I-II, 1966 | 10 | 24 | 18 |
| E | *Employment* | | | |
| | 9  Per cent in mining, 1966 | 81 | 3 | 4 |
| | 10  Per cent in agriculture, 1966 | 3 | 3 | 7 |
| F | *Workplace, mode of travel* | | | |
| | 11  Per cent work in other Local Government Area, 1966 | 38 | 56 | 36 |
| | 12  Per cent work in central city and urban ring, 1966 | 34 | 46 | 24 |
| | 13  Per cent travel by car | 13 | 25 | 19 |
| G | *Mobility* | | | |
| | 14  Per cent households with car, 1966 | 56 | 66 | 77 |
| H | *Dependency* | | | |
| | 15  Worker/non-worker ratio, 1966 | 1 : 2.44 | 1 : 2.25 | 1 : 1.99 |
| *Number of suburbs* | | **2** | **10** | **11** |

*Set 1: modern mining settlements (employing suburbs)*

There were only two in 1968: Cotgrave and Calverton, with populations of 3,624 and 6,671 respectively. They are principally mining settlements and are akin to the older employing satellites located to the north and west of the city (Figure 1). They do, however, have important secondary residential (i.e. commuter) and service functions.

*Set 2: large residential suburbs*

There were 10 in 1968, with populations ranging between 3,208 and 8,383. Formerly villages, they have become bedroom suburbs, housing labour for the central city and urban ring. Secondary rural service and minor industrial functions are also in evidence.

15

## Set 3: small residential suburbs

There were 11 in 1968, with populations ranging between 1,026 and 2,103. Their functions duplicate those found in set 2, albeit on a much more modest scale.

## Set 4: small villages

There were 55 in 1968, with populations ranging between 37 and 996. The 1966 10 per cent sample census data is too inaccurate to attempt to generalize concerning their functional attributes. Some of these settlements are still essentially rural service centres, others are small suburbs, but most are small communities with a substantial agricultural element.

The pattern summarized briefly above reflects the operation of post-war planning policy. In 1947 the rural areas of the county were surveyed and

> A hierarchy of settlements was decided upon, so that future population growth would be channelled to those villages with existing or proposed facilities for shopping, social activities and medical services.[26]

Three tiers were selected; tiers one and two (i.e. sets 1 to 3 above) were to be provided with residences for workers in the central city and urban ring, also for the coal- and gypsum-mining industries, together with service functions for the surrounding rural areas. The third and lowest tier (set 4) would consist of unmodified villages.

The limited number of settlements designated as growth points were granted 'white envelopes' into which they could expand, within the Green Belt. The selection and subsequent timing, rate and scale of residential development in these settlements have been dictated to a large extent by the existence of adequate water and sewage facilities. Most of the approved residential development in the area consists of large council or private estates, which place heavy demands upon village service systems. Consequently, the region has witnessed bursts of residential building, successively at Radcliffe, Ruddington, Keyworth, Bingham and, currently, at East Leake. These developments have been presaged by extensive improvements in the sewage plant of each village.

TABLE V

Selected functions for employing and residential suburbs, 1941 and 1969 [27]

| Functions | Employing | | | | Large residential | | | |
| | Calverton | | Cotgrave | | Bingham | | Keyworth | |
| | 1941 | 1969 | 1941 | 1969 | 1941 | 1969 | 1941 | 1969 |
|---|---|---|---|---|---|---|---|---|
| Retailing | 21 | 41 | 7 | 24 | 50 | 51 | 15 | 43 |
| Post Office | 1 | 1 | 1 | 2 | 1 | 1 | 1 | 2 |
| Banks .. | 0 | 1 | 0 | 1 | 1 | 3 | 0 | 2 |
| Car sales/service | 0 | 4 | 0 | 2 | 1 | 3 | 0 | 2 |
| Industry | 6 | 10 | 4 | 9 | 10 | 12 | 7 | 8 |
| Social (commercial and other clubs) | 2 | 13 | 4 | 10 | 10 | 15 | 1 | 9 |
| Doctor, etc. | 0 | 5 | 0 | 4 | 3 | 4 | 1 | 4 |
| Social services* .. | 0 | 3 | 0 | 2 | 0 | 4 | 0 | 3 |
| Infant school | 2 | 5 | 1 | 3 | 2 | 4 | 1 | 3 |
| Secondary school | 0 | 1 | 0 | 0 | 0 | 1 | 0 | 1 |

*Includes health centres, fire and police stations, and libraries

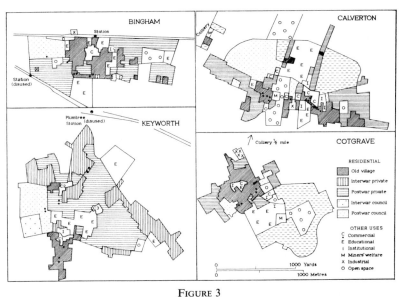

FIGURE 3

Growth of selected villages in rural ring

The cumulative effects of the recent functional development of these new suburbs is exemplified by the experience of four cases, as shown in Table V. In every case the functional status of these settlements has been enhanced and diversified to accommodate the needs of their growing populations and those of the surrounding rural areas. Recent changes in the morphology of these four villages are shown in Figure 3. Although the original villages differed in form they have all been extensively modified by suburban growth. In Dobriner's words, they are 'sacked villages'.[28] The major residential tracts of the suburbs—old village, private housing, council estates and miners' estates—are all clearly segregated, with the private estates generally located closest to the old village cores. Large planned tracts are given over to commercial, educational and institutional uses. In most cases these sub-regions have been located near the centre of each suburb, linking the old village with modern residential tracts.

## NOTES

[1] R. D. McKenzie, *The metropolitan community* (New York, 1933).

[2] Cited in: L. F. Schnore, *The urban scene* (New York, 1965) 43.

[3] *Ibid.,* 80.

[4] L. F. Schnore, Urban form: the case of the metropolitan community, *Urban life and form* (ed. W. Z. Hirsch) (New York, 1963) 167–197.

[5] Examples of areal research outside the U.S.A. are: L. F. Schnore, Metropolitan growth in the United Kingdom, *Economic Geography* 38 (1962) 215–233; and R. E. Pahl, *Urbs in rure* (London, 1965).

[6] The source of this information was a special tabulation of the 1966 census, kindly provided by the County Planning Officer.

[7] Although the local administrative areas were modified after 1931 a special set of supplementary census volumes were published for the new areas, using the 1931 data.

[8] K. C. Edwards, The geographical development of Nottingham, *Nottingham and its region* (ed. K. C. Edwards) (Nottingham, 1966) 374–377.

[9] *Sources:* County Census Reports, Nottinghamshire, 1931 and 1951; Registrar General's Estimates, 1968.

[10] L. F. SCHNORE, *op. cit.,* 72.

[11] Minor annexations occurred during the 1930s (Bilborough and Wollaton) and in 1951 (Clifton). In consequence the process of population decline in the city was retarded for several decades, since large housing estates were built in these areas.

[12] The data for the rural rings for the period 1951–61 do not include the western part of Southwell Rural District, since information was available only for entire Rural Districts. *Sources:* R. H. OSBORNE, *Atlas of population change in the East Midland counties, 1951–61* (Department of Geography, University of Nottingham, 1966); Registrar General's Estimates, 1968.

[13] R. D. MCKENZIE, *op. cit.*

[14] The national income *per capita*, at 1913 prices, rose from £50 in 1931 to £92 in 1966: P. DEANE and W. A. COLE, *British economic growth: 1688–1959* (Cambridge, 1964), App. III, Table 90. Figures for 1966 were calculated from: *National income and expenditure* (Board of Trade, 1968).

[15] The number of private cars in the U.K. rose from 1.2 million in 1931 to 9.5 million in 1966.

[16] In 1967 the national consumer expenditure on private motoring was 8.1 per cent of total expenditure, compared with 2.9 per cent in 1938.

[17] B. J. TURTON, The changing transport geography of the East Midlands, *East Midland Geographer* 4 (1969) 387–399.

[18] For example, see: J. GOTTMAN and R. A. HARPER, *Metropolis on the move* (New York, 1967).

[19] Information supplied by the officers of the Nottingham City and County Planning Departments.

[20] Most of the established and new firms which have moved out are located on the Trent floodplain, between the city and Beeston, for example Boots' new office complex. A notable addition to the retail structure of the urban ring is the Gem Supercentre at West Bridgford. This is a single-storey shopping centre under one roof, with 70,000 square feet of selling space and parking facilities for 1,000 cars.

[21] NOTTINGHAMSHIRE COUNTY PLANNING DEPARTMENT, *Rural Nottinghamshire* 1 and 4 (1967 and 1969).

[22] *County Census Report, Nottinghamshire* (1951). The figure for the rural ring in 1951 excludes the western portion of Southwell R.D. The 1966 data were abstracted from the Special Census Tabulation held by the City and County Planning Officers.

[23] For example: L. F. SCHNORE, *op. cit.*

[24] *County Census Report, Nottinghamshire,* 1931 and 1951; and *Registrar General's Estimates* (1968). The information relating to planning refusals was provided by officers of the County planning office.

[25] *County Census Report, Nottinghamshire,* 1951; and *Special Census Tabulations,* 1966.

[26] NOTTINGHAMSHIRE COUNTY PLANNING DEPARTMENT, *op. cit.,* 1, 3.

[27] Data for 1941 were abstracted from *Kelly's Commercial Directory* (1941). Data for 1969 were obtained during fieldwork.

[28] N. M. DOBRINER, *Class in suburbia* (Englewood-Cliffs, New Jersey, 1963).

# CHANGES IN THE SPIT AT GIBRALTAR POINT, LINCOLNSHIRE, 1951 to 1969

CUCHLAINE A. M. KING

## INTRODUCTION

In 1957 an account was published of the development of the spit at Gibraltar Point,[1] based on surveys covering the previous six years. The surveys have since been continued over a further 12 years, giving a continuous record that covers more than 17 years. It seems appropriate now to review the whole series of observations and to relate the changes recorded to the processes that bring them about.

Before the more recent observations are considered, the earlier results should be reviewed briefly. The spit prolongs the north–south coast where it turns sharply westwards into the embayment of the Wash. It is a small spit, and was only just over 1,800 feet long when first surveyed in 1951. C. Kidson[2] commented upon its small size, which can be accounted for by the general pattern of coastal change on this coast of accretion, which extends for about three miles from the southern end of Skegness to Gibraltar Point. Along this stretch of coast there are a number of different environments that depend on the dominance of different formative processes.

Offshore sand banks formed by the tidal streams play an important part in determining the details of the pattern of accretion on the foreshore, which in turn is closely related to the development of the spit. The offshore banks form between the interdigitating ebb and flood tidal stream channels along which sediment is carried in the direction of the residual of the tidal streams.[3] This sediment is eventually brought to the foreshore where it can be deposited by the waves, which are the dominant agents on the beach. The sediment is built up into beach ridges on those parts of the beach where there is a surfeit of material reaching the foreshore. These beach ridges move landwards up the beach under the influence of the waves as they diverge slightly from the coast in an offshore direction southwards, and move bodily southwards with the general direction of wave transport along the coast.[4] As they approach the upper beach they may become stabilised through the growth of further ridges to seaward which allows wind-blown sand to accumulate upon them round sand-loving vegetation. They then form foredunes, separated from the coast by muddy strips of salt marsh. Thus an eastward outgrowth of the coast is brought about in the area where most material is reaching the foreshore.

Records of past changes in the offshore banks indicate that their movement is associated with the changing pattern of accumulation along this stretch of coast. There is also evidence of the varying position of maximum accretion in the pattern of dune ridges that is revealed on vertical aerial photographs of the area. The spit is intimately associated with the pattern of accumulation, for it represents its southward extension, being built from the material that passes southwards from the growing ness of sandy foredunes. Therefore, as soon as a new major ness of accumulation starts to develop a new spit starts to form at its southern end and the present spit is only one of a series of such features that have developed during the

19

last few centuries. Such a former spit was illustrated on Armstrong's map of Lincolnshire, drawn in 1779.

Occasional storms also leave their marks on the coast by breaking through old dune ridges and spreading sand over the marsh deposits behind the dunes. One such storm preceded the initiation of the present spit's formation in 1922, when the tip of the main eastern dune ridge was pierced and sand washed over the mature marsh that had formed in its shelter. Since that date further dune ridges have developed on the foreshore eastward of the main eastern dune ridge, and it is from the southern end of these ridges that the present spit extends. In its shelter the new marsh is developing.

## OBSERVED CHANGES IN SPIT MORPHOLOGY

The spit is linked to the dune ridge by a broad low proximal section, across which sand is washed into the new marsh at very high tide. At its distal end the spit is higher and narrower. The distal end has been surveyed by plane table on 20 occasions between May 1951 and May 1969, mostly in the late spring, with the assistance of undergraduate students specialising in geomorphology at Nottingham. The surveys record the area of the spit above each one-foot contour from 10 feet O.D. (Liverpool) and the position of the contours relative to fixed posts. The relevant data are assembled in Table I. The areas above the various contours have been used to calculate the volume of the spit above the 10 feet contour. The table also records the length of the spit at the different levels, and the horizontal movement of the crest of the spit at the site of the fixed posts.

TABLE I

Measurement of spit growth

| Date | Highest point, feet | Volume, 1,000 cubic feet | Area in 1,000 square feet | | | | | Horizontal movement of crest, feet | Length in feet from fixed pegs | | |
|---|---|---|---|---|---|---|---|---|---|---|---|
| | | | Above 10 feet | Above 11 feet | Above 12 feet | Above 13 feet | Above 14 feet | | To 10 feet | To 11 feet | To 12 feet |
| May 1951 | 12.8 | 105.9 | 128.5 | 44.3 | 6.7 | 0 | 0 | | | | |
| Aug. 1951 | 12.95 | | | 46.3 | 9.9 | 0 | 0 | | | | |
| April 1952 | 11.9 | 123.6 | 187.9 | 45.8 | 0 | 0 | 0 | | | | |
| Aug. 1952 | 11.7 | 120 | 207.2 | 43.8 | 0 | 0 | 0 | 0 | 240 | 120 | |
| April 1953 | 12.5 | 168.6 | 179.3 | 78.5 | 8.3 | 0 | 0 | 10 | 460 | 300 | 130 |
| April 1954 | 11.9 | | | 60.7 | 0 | 0 | 0 | 20 | 620 | 160 | |
| June 1955 | 11.9 | 243.6 | 329.7 | 100.3 | 0 | 0 | 0 | 20 | 570 | 220 | |
| April 1957 | 12 | 303.8 | 289.8 | 153.6 | 7.1 | 0 | 0 | 20 | 630 | 550 | 400 |
| May 1958 | 11.4 | | 298.6 | 153.1 | 0 | 0 | 0 | 0 | 610 | 430 | |
| Nov. 1958 | 12 | 244.6 | 266.3 | 116.5 | 1.6 | 0 | 0 | −20 | 570 | 390 | 40 |
| May 1959 | 13.16 | 295.6 | 256.3 | 128.6 | 52.8 | 4.9 | 0 | 0 | 720 | 710 | 540 |
| May 1960 | 12.44 | 289.9 | 238.1 | 144.9 | 36.1 | 0 | 0 | 50 | 620 | 440 | 280 |
| June 1961 | 13.16 | 356.4 | 217.3 | 157.1 | 103.6 | 11.6 | 0 | 60 | 800 | 780 | 600 |
| May 1962 | 13.07 | 348.7 | 250.0 | 155.4 | 87.2 | 13.0 | 0 | 110 | 760 | 480 | 350 |
| April 1963 | 13 | 339.3 | 266.7 | 143.1 | 89.3 | 6.9 | 0 | 170 | 560 | 460 | 390 |
| April 1964 | 12.6 | 457.4 | 389.0 | 203.0 | 107.0 | 0 | 0 | 150 | 990 | 590 | 320 |
| May 1966 | 13.59 | 511.4 | 260.0 | 206.0 | 173.0 | 140.0 | 0 | 150 | 940 | 920 | 910 |
| April 1967 | 14.23 | 483.0 | 226.5 | 176.0 | 136.5 | 58.8 | 15.6 | 180 | 830 | 810 | 790 |
| April 1968 | 15.12 | 514.0 | 279.0 | 189.5 | 123.4 | 60.2 | 25.1 | 190 | 760 | 740 | 720 |
| May 1969 | 14.26 | 436.5 | 229.1 | 163.7 | 130.0 | 74.5 | 0.3 | 210 | 820 | 790 | 716 |

## Changes in the spit at Gibraltar Point, Lincolnshire, 1951 to 1969

During the years over which measurements have been made the distal end of the spit has moved a considerable distance westwards. This movement has been such that one fixed post which was originally on the landward side of the spit was buried by its landward movement and then later reappeared on its seaward side. New fixed posts have had to be put on the spit crest. The trends of the changes of the various measurements throughout the period are shown in Figure 1.

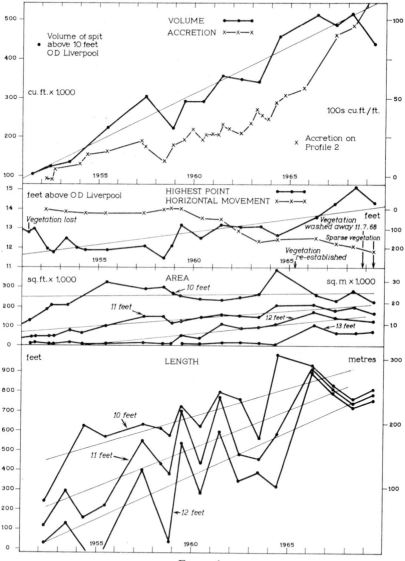

FIGURE 1

Trends of changes in the volume, area, length, height and horizontal movement of the spit at Gibraltar Point

Accretion on profile 2 is also shown. The trend lines have been calculated and their equations are given in Table 2. Measurements refer to the distal end beyond the line marking the top margin of Figure 2

21

The trend equations have been calculated for most of the changes shown in Figure 1. The equations are given in Table II. The trend equation is given in the form $Y = a + bX$. $a$ is given by $\Sigma Y/n$, and $b$ is given by $\Sigma XY/\Sigma X^2$, where X refers to the years numbered from the central year of the sequence, with negative values for the first half and positive values for the second half. The values for the $a$ coefficient in the equation give the mean value for the variable in the middle of the period, which was mid-1960. The $b$ coefficient gives the rate of change in the variable annually, as the trends have been calculated for the annual values. For the years 1956 and 1965, when observations were not made, interpolated values have been used. This method of trend analysis provides least square best fit trend lines, which have been entered on Figure 1.

TABLE II

Trends of spit growth and profile accretion

| | Trend equation | | |
|---|---|---|---|
| | *1952–68* | | *1951–69* |
| Spit maximum height | $Y = 12.8 + 0.154 X$ | | $Y = 12.85 + 0.134 X$ |
| *Spit length* | | | |
| at 10 feet .. | $Y = 686 + 30 \quad X$ | | |
| at 11 feet .. | $Y = 525 + 40 \quad X$ | | |
| at 12 feet .. | $Y = 383 + 47.5 \quad X$ | | $Y = 384 \quad + 46.8 \quad X$ |
| *Spit area* | | | |
| above 10 feet .. | $Y = 269 + 2.26 X$ | | $Y = 259 + 1.56 X$ |
| above 11 feet .. | $Y = 143 + 8.75 X$ | | $Y = 139 + 8.07 X$ |
| above 12 feet .. | $Y = 62 + 11.6 X$ | | $Y = 62.3 + 9.9 X$ |
| *Spit volume* | | | |
| above 10 feet .. | $Y = 315 + 24.9 X$ | | $Y = 310 + 24.4 X$ |

Profile accretion 1953–69:
Profile 1 $Y = -1 + 43.42 X$
Profile 2 $Y = 826 + 114.68 X$
Profile 4 $Y = 1504 + 190.71 X$

All the trend coefficients given in Table II are positive, which indicates that the spit has been gaining in height, length, area and volume throughout the period of detailed surveys. The increase in height has not been uniform, but has occurred in steps. After being relatively high in level when surveys began, with vegetation growing on its crest, the spit was lowered, to reach a minimum elevation in 1958. Subsequently, it has increased in height, rapidly at first and then more slowly until a rapid upward growth started again in 1964. Small amounts of vegetation have been recorded on the spit each year since 1965; and all vegetation was washed from the spit during a very high tide on 11th July 1968.

The increase in height has been more rapid than the increase in area above 10 feet, which has been very slow, amounting to a mean of only 1.56 × 1,000 square feet. The increases in the areas above 11 and 12 feet have been faster and by 1966 there was a substantial area above 13 feet. There is a close correlation between the area above 11 feet and the volume of the spit, which has increased fairly steadily during the period of observation. The difference between the calculated trend value and the measured surveyed value has a mean of 22.8 × 1,000 cubic feet. This shows that material has been reaching the spit at a fairly constant rate, with rather more than the mean amount arriving during the periods 1955 to 1957, and 1964 to 1966, and slightly less than the mean amount in the intervening periods.

The actual form of the spit, however, as indicated by its length and shape, has varied considerably more. The trend lines for the length of the spit show that the higher contours have lengthened more rapidly than the lower,

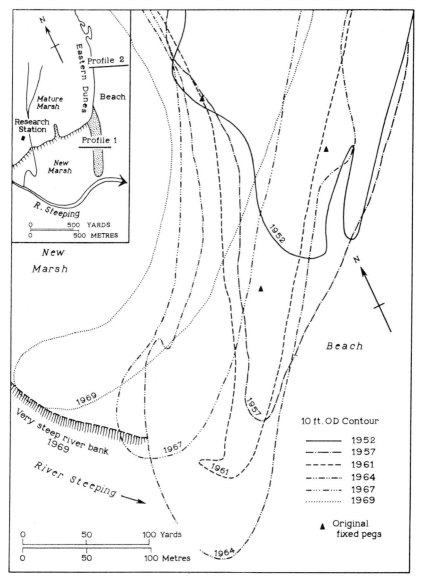

FIGURE 2

Selected 10-foot contours, surveyed in 1952, 1957, 1961, 1964, 1967 and 1969, to illustrate the changing form and position of the spit at Gibraltar Point

in the same way as the area. But there has been a much greater oscillation in the length of the distal portion and steepness of the distal point of the spit. The mean variation of the length at 11 feet from the trend value is 115.6 feet, and there have been rapid oscillations above and below the mean trend value. In general the three contours have varied together, and the trend lines approach each other towards the end of the period, reflecting an increase in the steepness of the distal end of the spit. During the three years 1965–68 the tip of the spit was very steep and was reduced steadily in length. This was caused by the swinging of a meander of the Steeping river across the marsh behind the spit until it actively eroded the distal tip of the spit. The river has now cut through the beach direct to the sea, washing the distal tip of the spit as it flows past. This reduction of length was more than compensated for by an increase in the height and area of the spit at the upper levels, so that the volume continued its upward trend until 1969, when the spit was lower and narrower once more.

The earlier extensions of the spit marked the arrival of ridges from the north and contractions with their passage further south. During these oscillations the spit varied in shape as indicated by the examples of its morphology, shown in Figure 2. At times the spit has had a recurved end, but at other times it has had a simpler form. The recurves probably form during periods of strong easterly winds, which at high tide can move material west from the tip of the spit.

## THE NATURE OF THE SEDIMENT

The spit is formed predominantly of sand, but it also includes some shingle, while mud accumulates on the new marsh in its shelter and on the lower foreshore of the beach in front of it. Samples of sediment have been collected from the spit and along the neighbouring beach profiles. The details of the graphic moment measures[5] for these samples are given in Table III, and Figure 3 illustrates some points concerning the characteristics of the sediments.

TABLE III

Sediment samples, graphic moment measures
(all values in Ø units)

|  | *Mean* | *Sorting* | *Skewness* | *Kurtosis* | *Median* |
|---|---|---|---|---|---|
| *Profile 1* |  |  |  |  |  |
| Seaward side spit crest | 1.89 | 0.755 | −0.77 | 1.34 | 2.16 |
| Swash slope | 2.14 | 0.67 | −0.74 | 2.24 | 2.27 |
| Lower beach below swash slope | 2.29 | 0 395 | −0.05 | 1.52 | 2.30 |
| Low water beach level | 5.07 | 2 03 | +1.04 | 1.51 | 4.12 |
| *Profile 2* |  |  |  |  |  |
| Dune crest with vegetation | 1.55 | 0.80 | −0.445 | 1.45 | 1.85 |
| Beach ridge no vegetation | 1.13 | 1.34 | −0.55 | 0.815 | 1.70 |
| Top of swash slope | 1.98 | 0.45 | −0.30 | 1.04 | 2.07 |
| Seaward ridge (landward side) | 1.81 | 1.23 | −0 83 | 1.50 | 1.85 |
| Seaward ridge (seaward side) | 1.85 | 1.09 | −0 59 | 2.74 | 2.13 |
| Muddy runnel (landward side) | 3 31 | 2 00 | +0.77 | 1.52 | 2 40 |
| Muddy runnel (seaward side) | 4.36 | 2 285 | +0 46 | 0.54 | 3.60 |

The sediments fall into three groups, on the basis of their characteristic moment measures. The first group comprises those sediments characteristic of the ridge crests, dune ridges and the spit crest. These are distinctly coarser than those of the other groups, less well sorted and with a stronger negative skewness, indicating a tail of coarse particles. These characteristics result from the fact that the sediment is brought by wave action, which can move the coarser particles to the ridge crests, where they accumulate amongst a considerable amount of finer wind-blown material. The lag deposit of coarser material gives the negative skewness and the large mean value.

The sample from the spit crest is less coarse than those from the other ridge crests because the shingle on the spit was not included in the sample. However, this shingle has been separately analysed for roundness, using stones with a mean length of 40 centimetres, which is characteristic of those on the spit crest. The mean roundness of the stones, using Cailleux's roundness index,[6] is 320, with a standard deviation of 125. The histogram of the distribution is shown in Figure 3. There are a number of very well rounded pebbles that are far-travelled erratics, derived from the till exposed on the foreshore to the north at Ingoldmells and Sutton-on-Sea and possibly also from further north, in Holderness. The pebbles of lower roundness, of which there are a fair number, are angular pieces of flint that have been shattered fairly recently by frost action. They also must have been largely derived from the drift, although some could have been brought down by the River Steeping or be material used in temporary sea defences in 1953. The pebbles are not as well rounded as many beach shingle stones, probably owing to the relatively weak wave action on this coast, which is protected from the most violent wave action by offshore sand banks, which dry out at low water.

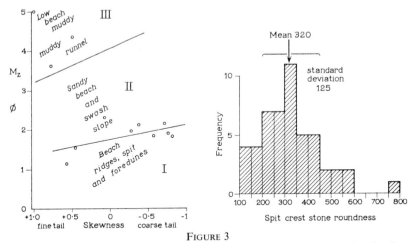

FIGURE 3

The graphic mean and skewness of the sediments at Gibraltar Point, showing the three main sediment groups

The histogram of the roundness of the pebbles on the spit crest is shown

The second group of sediments are those from the swash slope and sandy beach. They are intermediate in size, consisting of pure sand, with a mean size of about 2 ∅.[7] They are better sorted and still have a negative skewness, but rather smaller than that of the first group. This signifies the sorting effect of sustained wave action which has removed the finer particles that cannot settle in the vigorous environment in which they accumulated.

The third group includes those sediments that have collected in the quietest conditions in the runnels, protected from waves by the beach ridges, and on the lower foreshore, which is protected from wave action at low water by the drying banks offshore. These sediments have a positive skewness and are much finer than those in the more vigorous environment. Their sorting is poorer than that of the swash slope samples, as revealed by the bimodal nature of the curves, which include both a silt and clay fraction and a sand fraction.

### ACCRETION ON THE FORESHORE

The intimate relationships between the build-up of the spit and the accretion on the foreshore to the north depends on the fact that material is supplied to the spit from the beach to the north by wave action. The trend in the accretion on the foreshore and its relationship to the form of the beach profile will, therefore, be discussed briefly. The trend of accretion of material on three of a series of long-surveyed profiles down the beach is shown in Figure 4. Profile 1 runs seaward from the crest of the spit; profile 2 lies about half a mile to the north; and profile 4 is at the southern end of Skegness in the zone where accretion is at a maximum at present. A new ness of foredunes and marsh slacks has developed in this area.

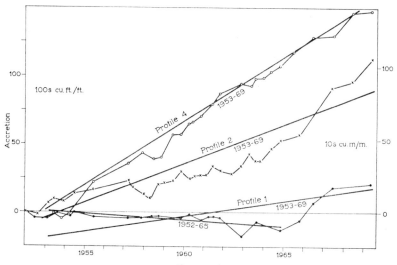

FIGURE 4

Trends of accretion on profiles 1, 2 and 4 for the period from 1953 to 1969. The trend lines have been inserted

The trend lines in Figure 4 show that profile 4 has gained a large amount of material, and profile 2 a smaller amount, but profile 1 has gained relatively little, an upward trend starting there only in 1966. The ridges are highest on profile 4 (Figure 5), and lowest on profile 1. This relationship is probably a consequence of the action of the waves, which are attempting to build up a gradient suitable to their size on an overall gradient that is flatter than the equilibrium swash slope gradient. The more material there is on the beach, the flatter the overall gradient, and hence the larger the size of the ridges built by wave action.

26

The relationship between the size of ridge and the amount of accretion is shown in Figure 5, on which the three profiles are differentiated by distinctive symbols. The regression lines for the three individual profiles are shown, together with that for the combined data, derived by analysis of co-variance. This technique allows the ridge height and amount of accretion to be correlated at the same time as variation due to the three different profiles is controlled. The co-variance test also allows the interaction between the three profiles to be assessed. If the interaction is not significant then the three profiles can be pooled to give a stronger correlation between the two variables.

Theoretically, as mentioned above, a correlation between the amount of accretion and the ridge size is to be expected. The mean ridge size differs between the three profiles; it is 4.4 feet on profile 4, 1.9 feet on profile 2 and 1.45 feet on profile 1. The mean accretion is $16.2 \times 10^5$ cubic feet/feet on profile 4, 9.7 on profile 2, and only 2.4 on profile 1. There is a fairly strong correlation between ridge height and accretion on profiles 4 and 2, the coefficient of correlation, $r$, having values of 0.747 and 0.754 for profiles 2 and 4 respectively. The correlation for profile 1 is not significant.

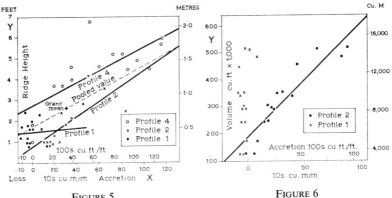

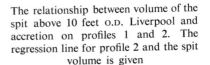

| FIGURE 5 | FIGURE 6 |
|---|---|
| The relationship between ridge height and accretion on profiles 1, 2 and 4. The regression lines have been calculated by analysis of co-variance, which provides the pooled regression line | The relationship between volume of the spit above 10 feet O.D. Liverpool and accretion on profiles 1 and 2. The regression line for profile 2 and the spit volume is given |

When the three sets of data are combined, controlling for the three profiles, the amount of variation in the data that is explained increases from about 50 per cent to about 80 per cent, taking the ridge height as the dependent variable that is explained in terms of accretion on the foreshore. The increase in percentage of variation explained is due to the control of the difference between the ridge heights on the different profiles. Both profiles react in the same way to accretion, but the ridges are higher on profile 4. This greater height is explained by the coarser grade of sand on profile 4 (mean 1.35 ∅) as compared with that on profile 2 (mean 2.27 ∅). The coarser sand requires a steeper equilibrium gradient and hence a higher ridge.

The development of the large ridges is the result of continued accretion of sand on the foreshore, and as the ridges become stabilised so the coast builds out eastwards. Some of the sand is, however, transmitted southwards along the coast, and this sand goes in part to build up the spit.

## THE RELATION BETWEEN THE ACCRETION ON THE SPIT AND THE FORESHORE

The regular landward movement of the ridges on the foreshore indicates that movement southwards along this stretch of coast is also fairly regular. In order to establish the source of material building up the spit, the accretion on profile 1, in front of the spit, and profile 2, a little to the north, were correlated with the volume of the spit. The relationship between these variables is shown in Figure 6, which makes it clear that there is no significant correlation between the amount of sand on profile 1 and the changing volume of the spit. These ridges on profile 1 have never exceeded 2.5 feet in height and have never been large enough to provide protection to the spit, which, with only brief exceptions when minor ridges lay in front of it, has always been fronted by a steep swash slope.

However, Figure 6 shows that a much closer relationship exists between the volume of the spit and the accretion on profile 2. The correlation coefficient of 0.90 is a value that explains 80.8 per cent of the variability of the spit volume in terms of the amount of material reaching profile 2. The regression equation is $Y = 174.1 + 0.20 X$, where Y is the spit volume and X is the accretion on profile 2. The reason for this relationship must be the southward transfer of material from profile 2 to the spit by wave action. It seems that most of the material moving south from profile 2 has been carried to the spit and not to the foreshore in front of it where profile 1 lies. This means that the material must move along the highest part of the foreshore and not along the ridges on profile 2, which run out on to the lower part of profile 1, where relatively little additional sand has been received until the last year or two of observations. The movement must, therefore, be accomplished by the waves at high tide. At such times the depth of the water offshore is at its greatest so that wave refraction will be less effective than at other times and the waves will approach the shore most obliquely and hence have their maximum capacity for longshore transport of material.

One note of caution should be added. There is a danger of auto-correlation in relating two time series of the type correlated in this instance, when the individual observations are not necessarily independent of those preceding and following them. The relationship can be demonstrated, but the connection may be the result of auto-correlation, rather than being a true causal relationship. In view of the close proximity of the two areas and the southerly movement of material, it seems likely that here the relationship is one of genuine cause and effect.

### CONCLUSION

In an earlier paper[8] it was suggested that the spit in this vicinity would undergo a cyclic development related to the formation of the nesses of accumulation that are in turn related to the pattern of tidal offshore banks and their migration. The present spit has been shown to have been in the early stage of development throughout the period of detailed surveys, as it has been gaining material at a fairly steady rate. It has regained its former height, and vegetation has become re-established on its crest. However, it has moved over 200 feet bodily inland during the last 10 years and its distal end is now being eroded by the meander swing of the River Steeping, which made a permanent break through the foreshore to establish a new channel for the tidal flow up and down the river in the early summer of 1968. But, because the spit receives most of its material from the north, changes that are taking place at its southern end may not much affect its volume, although they are changing its morphology as indicated by the rapid swing inland of its distal tip between 1968 and 1969. The development of recurves could well be associated with changes on the foreshore near the distal end, where erosion would allow more effective waves to reach this point from the deeper water offshore.

The continued westward transgression of the spit over the New Marsh was also predicted in 1961.[9] A break-through of the River Steeping was also suggested as the possible cause of erosion at the distal end of the spit. Both of these possibilities have in fact occurred and the developing hook at the end of the spit, shown in the latest outline in Figure 2, may be fulfilling predictions made earlier.

Ultimately it is the major accretion that is proceeding to the north that is more likely to set a limit to the growth of the spit. When the ness has built out sufficiently far to divert material further offshore along the beach, then the spit is likely to be starved of sand and to become static as another spit develops seawards of it. There is some indication that this change is already beginning. In 1969 profile 2 had a large volume of accretion, and the beach ridge near the top of the profile is clearly becoming stabilised, for it now supports vegetation, and dune formation is beginning upon it. This development will prevent the passage of material southwards on the upper beach as this is raised above the effective level of the waves at high tide. The recent growth on the lower foreshore at profile 1, which for a long time was very static and muddy, suggests that much sand is now moving along shore at a lower level on the beach, rather than to the spit, the growth of which was reduced between 1968 and 1969.

The spit in fact is an ephemeral feature on this coast, which is building out eastwards rapidly as a result of beach ridge growth, following the accretion of sand determined by the pattern of tidal streams. The beach ridges in turn develop into dune ridges, separated by elongated marsh slacks, formed from the mud-filled beach runnels, At any one time a spit will be likely to prolong the outermost stabilised beach ridge which is being converted into foredunes. The speed with which these changes take place means that repeated surveys of the type carried out annually at Gibraltar Point provide data for a useful quantitative study of the particular coastal processes involved.

## NOTES

[1] F. A. BARNES and C. A. M. KING, The spit at Gibraltar Point, Lincolnshire, *East Midland Geographer* No. 8 (1957) 22–31.

[2] C. KIDSON, Movement of beach material on the east coast of England, *East Midland Geographer* No. 16 (1961) 3–16.

[3] C. A. M. KING, The character of the offshore zone and its relation to the foreshore at Gibraltar Point, Lincolnshire, *East Midland Geographer* No. 21 (1964) 230–243.

[4] C. A. M. KING and F. A. BARNES, Changes in the configuration of the intertidal beach zone of part of the Lincolnshire coast since 1951, *Zeit. für Geomorph.* NF8 (1964) 105*–126*.

[5] Graphic moment measures, as devised by: R. L. FOLK and W. C. WARD, Brazos River Bar: a study in the significance of grain size parameters, *Jour. Sed. Petrol.* 27 (1957) 3–26; are found from percentile readings on the cumulative frequency graph as follows:

Mean $\quad\quad M_z = \dfrac{\emptyset_{16} + \emptyset_{50} + \emptyset_{84}}{3}$

Median $\quad\quad M_{d\emptyset} = \emptyset_{50}$

Sorting $\quad\quad \sigma_1 = \left(\dfrac{\emptyset_{84} - \emptyset_{16}}{4}\right) + \left(\dfrac{\emptyset_{95} - \emptyset_5}{6.6}\right)$

Skewness $\quad Sk_1 = \left(\dfrac{\emptyset_{16} + \emptyset_{84} - 2\emptyset_{50}}{2(\emptyset_{84} - \emptyset_{16})}\right) + \left(\dfrac{\emptyset_5 + \emptyset_{95} - 2\emptyset_{50}}{2(\emptyset_{95} - \emptyset_5)}\right)$

Kurtosis $\quad K_g = \dfrac{\emptyset_{95} - \emptyset_5}{2.44(\emptyset_{75} - \emptyset_{25})}$

[6] Cailleux's roundness index, R, is found by $R = \dfrac{2r}{a} \times 1000$, r = minimum radius of curvature in principle plane and *a* is length of long axis of stone.

[7] $\emptyset$ units provide a logarithmic size scale. $\emptyset = -\log_2$ millimetres. Coarse sediment has a negative value and the finer the sediment size the larger the $\emptyset$ value, for example:

$\quad\quad -1\,\emptyset = 2$ millimetres
$\quad\quad\ \ \ 0\,\emptyset = 1$ millimetre
$\quad\quad +1\,\emptyset = 0.5$ millimetre
$\quad\quad +4\,\emptyset = 0.0625$ millimetre

[8] F. A. BARNES and C. A. M. KING, *op. cit.* (1957).

[9] F. A. BARNES and C. A. M. KING, Salt marsh development at Gibraltar Point, Lincolnshire, *East Midland Geographer* No. 15 (1964) 30.

# THE GEOGRAPHICAL EFFECTS OF THE LAWS OF SETTLEMENT IN NOTTINGHAMSHIRE: AN ANALYSIS OF FRANCIS HOWELL'S REPORT, 1848

D. R. MILLS

## INTRODUCTION

On the whole, geographers have not paid much systematic attention to the influence of institutional factors on the evolution of settlement patterns. One exception is the reference by K. C. Edwards to the relationship between great houses and landscape features in the Dukeries.[1] Also in Nottinghamshire, his colleague J. D. Chambers was one of the first regional historians to relate social structure to enclosure history and poor law policy.[2] Enclosure history has long been of interest to geographers for its contribution to landscape evolution. On the other hand, poor law policy has been very largely overlooked. This is, therefore, an appropriate opportunity to bring forward some neglected evidence collected in Nottinghamshire by Francis Howell in 1848.

In the 1840s the poor law system was still adjusting to the tremendous changes brought about by the Poor Law Amendment Act of 1834, which had bound townships together in unions equipped with central workhouses. The townships, however, still remained financially responsible for their own poor. Moreover, Parliament's intention that the vast majority of destitute persons should be put in the workhouses failed to become a reality even in the 1840s. One reason for this failure was the fact that a labourer remained the financial responsibility of his native township, at least in theory, even if he settled permanently in a far distant part of the country. Thus, in two most important respects the 1834 Act left untouched the traditional way of administering poor relief.

The tradition that every person belonged to one place, which was responsible for his well-being, had grown up in the Middle Ages, when it was part of an insurance that the ploughs of a village would always have a ready supply of labour. As the economy became increasingly market-oriented and industrialized, this tradition became a restriction on the necessary free movement of labour. The settlement laws of 1662 were a formal recognition of the problem, in that they required townships exporting labourers to issue them with certificates promising maintenance in their home townships should they fall destitute in the places which received them. Thus mobility was permitted, but the theory of belonging remained in force. Unfortunately, good labourers were less likely than inefficient ones to be given the freedom to migrate. This is one of the reasons why there was large-scale evasion of the settlement laws. Indeed, as time went by it became easier to gain a new legal 'settlement' in a place other than one's native township.[3]

There was one way in particular of avoiding the tiresome business of recalling destitute persons to their 'home' township, which was known as 'non-resident relief'. In other words, it was cheaper to send money to the destitute to be spent where they were living. This was obviously not an

easy procedure to administer with care. Moreover, it enabled a whole class
of paupers to get relief without going to a workhouse, in defiance of the
main provision of the 1834 Act. The Poor Law Board were naturally
concerned to block the loophole and one of their first measures was to
find out the total number of persons in receipt of non-resident relief on
Lady Day, 1846. In the whole of England and Wales it came to the very
substantial figure of 82,249.[4]

## THE SITUATION IN 1848

Thus we come to the immediate reason for Francis Howell's fieldwork:
to investigate the effects of the Acts of 1846 and 1847. Sir James Graham's
Act, following up the Lady Day tally,

> made persons who had been resident five years wholly irremovable; widows,
> resident when their husbands died, irremovable in the first twelvemonths of
> widowhood; and persons chargeable only through temporary sickness and
> accident irremovable.[5]

After a period of confusion, during which it was decided that the Act had
retrospective effect, there was a flood of applications for relief from persons
who had hitherto held back, for fear of being removed to their 'home'
township and thence to the workhouse.

As will be shown below, this flood did not affect all townships equally.
The afflicted places set up a great outcry of injustice, which led to the
passing of Bodkin's Act. This placed *on the unions* financial responsibility
for the wandering poor and also the cost of relieving unsettled persons
chargeable to the poor rate by virtue of sickness and accident.[6] This Act
made the first breach in the principle of financing poor relief through
township rates and it spread a fraction of the costs evenly on all townships,
in proportion to their rateable value. But it was not sufficient to stem the
complaints and Sir Charles Buller, President of the Poor Law Board, was
now convinced of the need for an inquiry. Thus Howell and his colleagues
were dispatched into the country.[7]

## OPEN AND CLOSED VILLAGES

Earlier reports on poor law matters had already recorded a piece of
terminology important at this point, i.e. the distinction between close and
open townships. Close, or closed, townships were those in which one large
proprietor, or a small number of large proprietors, controlled cottage
accommodation in order to keep down the poor rates, which fell mainly
on their own tenant farmers. Although rural population generally rose
rapidly between about 1750 and 1850, the closed villages were often marked
off from their neighbours by a relatively stable level of population. In some
instances, houses were actually demolished to reduce the labouring
population, for example at Ossington.[8] Moreover, the landlords and their
tenants and bailiffs took precautions to remove 'bad characters' from their
villages. Howell described how Lord Manvers cleared out a gang of
burglars from Laxton by pulling down cottages; and reported the
complaints of open villages that they were worried about the type of
labourers who came to them, quite as much as the number.[9]

Open townships were those of mixed ownership, especially where the
presence of a large number of small owners effectively prevented the
imposition of a restrictive policy. These villages grew rapidly in the century
up to 1850, with uncontrolled expansion of the labour force, both native

and immigrant, in farming and often in domestic industries or coal-mining. Some of the small proprietors willingly sold land for building purposes to small bricklayers and carpenters, who ran up mean tenements to let at high rents.[10] These stood in contrast to the modest but sound cottage accommodation in the closed (estate) villages, of which Perlethorpe and Budby are two of the best examples in Nottinghamshire. They are still worth a visit today.

As population pressure and poor law problems mounted, the plight of the open villages became quite remarkable. Sir James Graham's Act had caused a sudden increase in the already high poor rates in these villages. For example, in Radford the total expenditure on the poor went up from £1,981 in 1844 to £5,504 in 1848. At Sutton-in-Ashfield, during the first quarter of 1848, the overseers spent £698 on their own poor, £141 on the newly irremovable poor, and £125 on behalf of the union, under Mr. Bodkin's Act of 1847. At Newark, it was reckoned that the Act of 1846 threw 100 to 120 extra families onto the parish.[11]

### GEOGRAPHICAL ANALYSIS OF HOWELL'S DATA

In the course of his journeys round the county Howell recorded the status of about 125 villages, in terms of open or closed, either directly or by such strong implication that little doubt is left. The distribution of these places is shown in Figure 1. He did not visit the entire territory of Nottinghamshire, the areas north of Retford and in the far south of the county being the principal exceptions. On the other hand, the shape of Poor Law Union boundaries led him occasionally into surrounding counties. Within the areas visited there are gaps in the record, the significance of which would concern local researchers, but they do not disturb the firmness of the general conclusions reached in this paper. On the whole, it is reasonable to assume that Howell was more consistent in recording closed than open villages. After all, he was collecting information about places and proprietors who were shirking their responsibilities to the country. A comparison with Leicestershire also confirms this impression, for in that county closed villages were less numerous than open villages, while the list derived from Howell's report consists approximately of 50 per cent of each kind.

The implication of Figure 1 is that virtually the whole of the county was affected by the operation of the laws of settlement in some way or other. Open and closed villages were to be found in all the major physical divisions of Nottinghamshire, and the coalfield, the hosiery and lace districts, and even towns up to the size of Nottingham, were all caught up in the effects of this institutional factor. It is beyond the scope of this paper to attempt to measure these effects, as compared with the effects of many other factors, such as the history of settlement, soil fertility, husbandry practices, the availability of raw materials, the impact of industrialization on the region, demographic factors, transport networks and the distribution of land and capital among social classes. A comprehensive survey of mid-nineteenth-century Leicestershire, however, indicates that the administration of the poor law, linked with patterns of land-ownership, was a sufficiently important factor to demand attention in other parts of the country.[12]

In addition to his information on open and closed villages, Howell also reported on daily journeys between them, unfortunately without stating how many men were involved. From other evidence,[13] however, it is reasonable to assume that the numbers were significant in relation to the total labour force. The patterns of movement shown on the maps indicate that a broad distinction can be made between the mainly industrial areas around Nottingham and Mansfield, on the one hand, and the largely agricultural remainder of the county on the other. The relative absence of

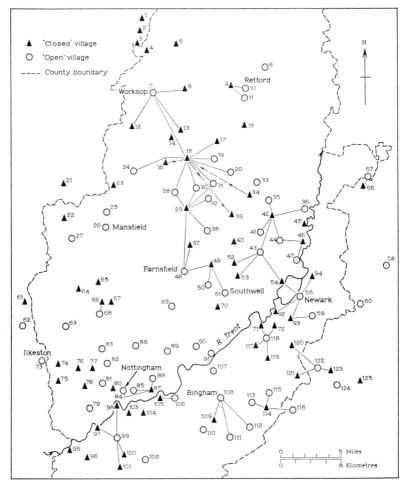

FIGURE 1

Open and closed villages in Nottinghamshire, as classified in Howell's report (1848)

*Notes:* Closed villages printed in *italics* in the following list of places

Nos. 16, 19 and 20 interpolated from *Stanhope's Report of 1867*

The lines indicate daily movement of labourers from open villages to farms in closed villages

The three arrows indicate the direction of movement in cases where Stanhope reported movement between pairs of villages both classified as closed villages by Howell (15, 16, 34, 39)

Budby (16) was one of the estate settlements for Thoresby Park (15)

—*Fig. 1 continued on p. 35*

# The geographical effects of the laws of settlement in Nottinghamshire

—*Fig. 1 continued from p.* 34

| No. | Place | No. | Place |
|---|---|---|---|
| 1 | *Firbeck* ⎫ | 64 | *Annesley* |
| 2 | *Letwell* ⎬ Yorkshire | 65 | *Newstead* |
| 3 | *Gildingwells* ⎭ | 66 | *Linby* |
| 4 | *Wallingwells* | 67 | *Papplewick* |
| 5 | *Hodsock* | 68 | Hucknall Torkard |
| 6 | Clarborough | 69 | Oxton |
| 7 | *Worksop* | 70 | *Halloughton* |
| 8 | *Osberton* | 71 | *East Stoke* |
| 9 | *Babworth* | 72 | *Thorpe* |
| 10 | East Retford | 73 | Ilkeston (Derbyshire) |
| 11 | Ordsall | 74 | *Cossall* |
| 12 | *Welbeck* | 75 | *Trowell* |
| 13 | *Clumber* | 76 | *Strelley* |
| 14 | *Carburton* | 77 | *Bilborough* |
| 15 | *Thoresby Park* and *Perlethorpe* | 78 | *Wollaton* |
| 16 | *Budby* | 79 | Beeston |
| 17 | Bothamsall | 80 | *Nottingham Park* |
| 18 | *Gamston* | 81 | Radford |
| 19 | Walesby | 82 | Basford |
| 20 | Kirton | 83 | Bulwell |
| 21 | *Glapwell* (Derbyshire) | 84 | Nottingham |
| 22 | *Teversal* | 85 | Sneinton |
| 23 | *Sookholme* | 86 | Arnold |
| 24 | Warsop | 87 | *Colwick* |
| 25 | Mansfield Woodhouse | 88 | Carlton |
| 26 | Mansfield | 89 | Lambley |
| 27 | Sutton-in-Ashfield | 90 | Lowdham |
| 28 | Edwinstowe | 91 | Caythorpe |
| 29 | *Rufford Abbey* | 92 | *Farndon* |
| 30 | Ollerton | 93 | *Hawton* |
| 31 | Boughton | 94 | *Winthorpe* |
| 32 | Wellow | 95 | *Thrumpton* |
| 33 | Egmanton | 96 | *Gotham* |
| 34 | *Laxton* | 97 | *Clifton* |
| 35 | Moorhouse | 98 | *Wilford* |
| 36 | Sutton-on-Trent | 99 | Ruddington |
| 37 | *Bilsthorpe* | 100 | *Bradmore* |
| 38 | Eakring | 101 | *Bunny* |
| 39 | *Kneesall* | 102 | Keyworth |
| 40 | *Maplebeck* | 103 | *West Bridgford* |
| 41 | Norwell Woodhouse | 104 | *Gamston* |
| 42 | *Ossington* | 105 | *Holme Pierrepont* |
| 43 | Caunton | 106 | Radcliffe |
| 44 | Norwell | 107 | East Bridgford |
| 45 | *Carlton-on-Trent* | 108 | Bingham |
| 46 | *Cromwell* | 109 | *Tythby* |
| 47 | North Muskham | 110 | Cropwell Bishop |
| 48 | Farnsfield | 111 | Langar |
| 49 | *Kirklington* | 112 | Granby |
| 50 | Hallam | 113 | Whatton |
| 51 | Southwell | 114 | *Elton* |
| 52 | *Winkburn* | 115 | Orston |
| 53 | *Hockerton* | 116 | Bottesford (Leicestershire) |
| 54 | *Kelham* | 117 | *Syerston* |
| 55 | Newark | 118 | Elston |
| 56 | *Swinethorpe* (Lincolnshire) | 119 | *Sibthorpe* |
| 57 | Harby | 120 | *Cotham* |
| 58 | Bassingham (Lincolnshire) | 121 | *Staunton* |
| 59 | Balderton | 122 | Long Bennington ⎫ |
| 60 | Beckingham (Lincolnshire) | 123 | *Westborough* ⎬ Lincolnshire |
| 61 | *Codnor Park* ⎫ Derbyshire | 124 | Foston |
| 62 | Heanor ⎭ | 125 | *Marston* ⎭ |
| 63 | Greasley | | |

*Baston* and *Lostford*, in Basford Union, not located; also St. John's, in Worksop Union
 (possibly St. John Throapham, in Laughton-en-le-Morthen, West Riding)

movement around Nottingham cannot have been due to any lack of closed villages. There was, for example, a block of them lying to the west of the city (Nottingham Park, Wollaton, Bilborough, Strelley, Trowell and Cossall). We should also note that agricultural labourers went out each day from Nottingham, Sneinton and Carlton to the estate of Mr. Masters at Colwick. In the district as a whole, however, the principal occupations were in coal-mining and textiles, where the circumstances were different from those obtaining in agriculture.

In mining a large proportion of the capital came from landed proprietors and their lessees, who were in the habit of building cottage accommodation for miners near the pit-head. They took care not to allow this type of settlement into the central parts of their estates, where the great house, the park and the game lay undisturbed.[14] In the hosiery industry the capital came from the urban hosiers and the rural middle class, who were strongest in the open villages. As the industry grew it absorbed the natural increase of population in these villages. As it was excluded from the closed villages, it was inevitable that their population levels would remain relatively stable.[15] Thus mining villages drew on the surplus labour of the surrounding districts, the hosiery villages supported their own population by industrial expansion, and in the agricultural areas the demand for extra labour was often met by daily journeys to work. These are very broad generalizations, but they are supported by other evidence, especially by analysis of some 1851 enumerations in Leicestershire.[16]

The large proprietors and their tenants in the closed townships were much more aware of the burden of the poor rate than many of the tradesmen in open villages and towns, because it fell very heavily on agricultural property. What is more, they were able to do something about it. Despite the inconvenience of having a large part of their labour force resident at a distance from their farms, many proprietors and farmers held back from building cottages at the very time when the new methods in arable agriculture had increased the numbers of labourers required per unit area. The network of daily journeys to work in the agricultural districts will come as a surprise to many town-bound car-borne commuters of today. The morning movement was outwards from the market towns and big villages into the thinly-populated large estates. Distances of up to six miles each way were not uncommon, mostly on foot, but sometimes on donkeys. The network was particularly well developed in certain parts of the Dukeries, where the new methods of farming had made it possible to exploit the light sandy soils on a much more intensive basis.

The maps may also be interpreted in terms of social networks. For example, men from Worksop worked on the Thoresby estate alongside men from Kneesall and Laxton, their homes being separated by a distance of 12 miles. Men who lived in Ollerton had a network of personal contacts stretching from Osberton in the north to Farnsfield and Southwell in the south. This is rather different from the townsman's traditional view of the rustic labourer, living and working in one spot all his life. News of good and bad employers would spread very quickly through these channels, which help to explain the relatively rapid turnover of the agricultural work force noticed by the writer in other investigations.[17] By comparison, the men who broke away from the land to become miners or stockingers could live stable lives in a much more self-contained community, usually a town or a large village.

## ACTION FOLLOWING THE REPORTS OF 1848

Howell, of course, was chiefly concerned to establish the degree to which Sir James Graham's Act had placed an unfair burden on the open townships. Some places, such as East Retford, reported that they had been relieved by Mr. Bodkin's Act and now had no complaints to make.[18] But majority opinion was in favour of a union rating for all poor law purposes. Other reporters passed up much the same message. Thus, in 1848 another Act added to the union's account all 'persons rendered irremovable by reason of five years' residence.'[19] This measure, supported by rising prosperity, satisfied public opinion, but it was not regarded as sufficient by a body of poor law specialists, who kept up pressure for fundamental changes. These came in the '60s, when an Act of 1861 made three years instead of five the qualifying period for irremovability, and at the same time altered the principle of payment into a union by a township from one based on pauperism to one based on rateable value. In 1865 a further Act completed the process by making the union the sole unit of administration.[20] These Acts came at the height of the high farming period and, therefore, too late to prevent the operation of the settlement laws from having a long-term influence on the distribution of population and the character of places. In the country areas many of the closed villages of 1848 have remained much smaller than their neighbours. The Park and West Bridgford are high-quality residental areas today partly because of their earlier history as closed villages adjacent to Nottingham.

In a report written in 1867 the Hon. Edward Stanhope described the still-continuing movement of labourers each day to work on the Thoresby estate:

> Many of the servants and labourers immediately connected with the establishment, such as stablemen, porters, masons, carpenters, etc., live in the park and at Budby, about one mile from Thoresby; others come from Edwinstowe (2¾ miles), Boughton (3), Walesby (2¾), Kirton (3½), Ollerton (2½), Bothamsall (2¾), Warsop (5), Laxton (6), and Kneesall (6). Those from the latter places take lodgings near at hand during the week at 3d. a night, and go home on Saturday night. Some of the others, and old men, have donkeys, which they are allowed to depasture in the park; as a matter of course, having to walk a long distance not only interferes with their work, but (to use a common expression) takes the steel out of them.[21]

It is interesting to notice that Laxton and Kneesall both had the characteristics of closed villages in Howell's day. Another change in status, this time the other way round, was recorded by Mellors,[22] when he described how the stockingers were turned out of Papplewick and Linby in the 1840s:

> At Linby the expulsion of the framework knitters caused a diminution of the population from 515 to 271. In other words, the poor were practically driven to live in Hucknall Torkard, and labourers and farm workers had to walk the distance night and morning . . . . . Now look at the revenge Time brings. There was sixty years of occupation, and then the people are expelled, lest they should burden the land and lessen its value. Nearly all the parish [Papplewick] belonged to one owner, doubtless a very good landlord, and his will was, of course, paramount. Hucknall, on the other hand, was an open parish, with a number of freeholders, and there have always been the means of obtaining allotments, or of purchasing land. The value of the land continued to increase in Hucknall because of the growth of population and industry.
>
> For a rural walk, however, commend me to Papplewick . . . . .

37

## NOTES

[1] K. C. EDWARDS, *The land of Britain, part 60: Nottinghamshire* (1944) 499–501.

[2] J. D. CHAMBERS, *Nottinghamshire in the eighteenth century* (1932, republished 1966), particularly 142, 152, 168, 172, 266–267.

[3] This passage is based mainly on: A. REDFORD, *Labour migration in England, 1800–1850* (1926); T. MACKAY, *A history of the English poor law* (1899), especially vol. 3, 340–364; and S. WEBB and B. WEBB, *English poor law history, part II: the last hundred years* (1929), especially 419–434.

[4] T. MACKAY, *op. cit.,* 350.

[5] *Ibid.,* 351. The Act was 9 and 10 Vic., c. 66, 1846.

[6] *Ibid.,* 352. The Act was 10 and 11 Vic., c. 110, 1847.

[7] Their work is contained in *Reports to the Poor Law Board on the operation of the laws of settlement and removal of the poor,* presented to both Houses, 1850. There is a copy in Nottingham University Library. The reports also covered Suffolk, Norfolk, Essex, Reading Union of Berkshire, Surrey, Sussex, Dorset, Hampshire, Somerset, Bedfordshire, Berkshire, Buckinghamshire, Oxfordshire, and Northumberland. Mr. P. Grey of Bedford College of Education is working on Bedfordshire.

[8] *Op. cit.,* 132.

[9] *Op. cit.,* 130–131.

[10] *Op. cit.,* 129.

[11] *Op. cit.,* 126, 138–139. It is interesting to notice that 1847 was the only year in which there was a nationwide collection of parochial data on poor rates: *Return showing population, annual value of property, expenditure, rate in the pound, total number of paupers relieved* (B.P.P., 1847–48), 735, LIII, 11.

[12] D. R. MILLS, The social geography of rural Leicestershire in the mid-nineteenth century, *Rural history and population change* (provisional title) (ed. E. A. Wrigley) (Weidenfeld and Nicolson, expected early 1972). This monograph also contains a summary of the writer's other work in this field.

[13] J. A. SHEPPARD, East Yorkshire's agricultural labour force in the mid-nineteenth century, *Agr. Hist. Rev.* 9 (1961) 43–54.

[14] Based on fieldwork and D. R. MILLS, *op. cit.*

[15] D. R. MILLS, *op. cit.,* and D. M. SMITH, The British hosiery industry at the middle of the nineteenth century, *Trans. Inst. Br. Geogrs.* 32 (1963) 131–136.

[16] C. T. SMITH, Population, *Victoria County History of Leicestershire* III (1955) 151.

[17] D. R. MILLS, *op. cit.*; investigations into family history; the records of hiring fairs; and in novels of the period, especially those of Thomas Hardy.

[18] Howell's Report, 142.

[19] T. MACKAY, *op. cit.,* 354. The Act was 11 and 12 Vic., c. 110, 1848.

[20] T. MACKAY, *op. cit.,* 355–356. These Acts were 24 and 25 Vic., c. 55, 1861; and the Union Chargeability Act, 28 and 29 Vic., c. 79, 1865.

[21] *Commission on the employment of children, young persons and women in agriculture* (B.P.P., 1868), appendix to part 1 of the first report.

[22] R. MELLORS, *In and about Nottinghamshire* (Nottingham, 1908) 326–327.

# A GENERAL VIEW OF POPULATION CHANGE IN THE MIDDLE TRENT COUNTIES, 1801-1861

R. H. OSBORNE

## INTRODUCTION

Derbyshire, Leicestershire and Nottinghamshire may conveniently be termed the Middle Trent counties. With the chief exception of north Derbyshire they are drained largely by the middle section of the Trent and its tributaries (Figure 1), the main valleys also being economically significant as intercommunicating routeways for roads and railways and, formerly, for canals. The three large county towns and neighbouring smaller towns, including those situated on the two coalfields of east Derbyshire–Nottinghamshire and south Derbyshire–Leicestershire, constitute the loosely-knit urban and industrial heartland of the East Midlands. A particular coherence is imparted by the long-established 'hosiery' or knitwear industry, which has shown a high degree of national concentration in the three counties for well over 200 years.

The aim of this essentially cartographical study is to show how the distribution of population recorded in the first census, taken in 1801, underwent considerable changes during the years up to 1861, and also broadly to relate these changes to contemporary economic factors.[1] The period chosen enables a contrast to be made between the widespread growth of the population in the early nineteenth century and the prevalence of rural decline that had established itself by the middle of the century. In several ways, moreover, the 1850s and 1860s mark an important stage in the area's economic development, as will be indicated later. The changes are analysed in three 20-year periods with the aid of detailed maps compiled from the census returns. The adjoining Burton-on-Trent salient of Staffordshire is also shown.

## DISTRIBUTION OF POPULATION IN 1801

Today the population of the Middle Trent counties is over 2.5 millions. In 1801 it was less than half a million (Table I). Its distribution is shown in Figure 2, where the symbols correspond to communities rated separately for Poor Law purposes and thus returned separately in the census. In most instances they were later to become known as civil parishes. The map also offers a very generalized view of the settlement pattern, although it must be remembered that the symbols often relate to more than one village or hamlet. Despite modifications over time it is still possible to appreciate the greater density of settlement on the lowland areas that had occurred as a result of the Anglian and Danish colonization. Here soils developed chiefly on Keuper Marl, Lower Lias clay, or Boulder Clay overlying these, had been particularly favourable to agricultural settlement (Figure 1). By contrast settlement was still sparse in areas of less favourable environment, notably Sherwood (Bunter Sandstone) and the high gritstone moors of the Peak District and the East Moor, although neighbouring areas on the shales were better populated. On the Carboniferous Limestone and the Coal Measures agriculture had for centuries been supplemented by the local and intermittent exploitation of lead and coal respectively.

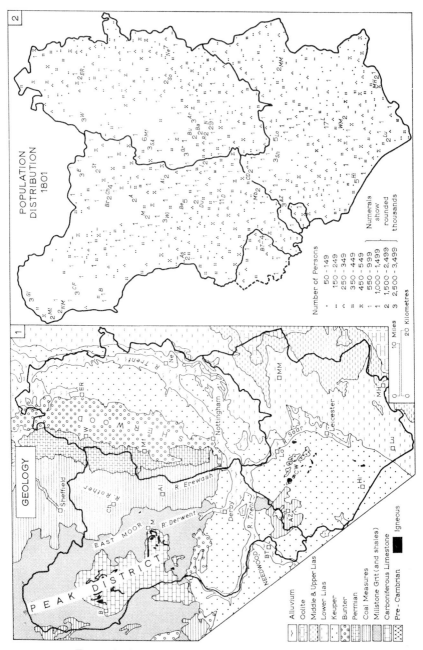

FIGURE 1—Solid geology (generalized) of the Middle Trent
*Note:* Boulder Clay covers large parts of Leicestershire and south Nottinghamshire.
County boundaries, 1961.   CW—Charnwood

FIGURE 2—Population distribution, 1801, in the Middle Trent
*Note:* County boundaries *c.* 1890.   (See p. 49 for key to places)

During the eighteenth century significant changes in the pattern of peopling were already occurring as a result of industrial expansion. The domestic framework-knitting industry had established itself in numerous places within an area stretching from beyond Matlock and Mansfield in the north to Hinckley and Lutterworth in the south. Yarn was provided by the silk-throwing industry, chiefly located at Derby, where water power had been successfully applied by 1720, and by water-powered cotton mills, mostly in the Derwent basin, dating from Arkwright's venture at Cromford, near Matlock, in 1771. Leicester provided worsted yarn. By the end of the eighteenth century the machine-lace industry was developing in the Nottingham area as a technological offshoot of framework knitting. Water-powered cotton spinning had also developed in the north–west of Derbyshire using head-streams of the Mersey. Here also Buxton was developing as a fashionable spa. In the coalfield areas the output of coal and iron was growing rapidly in the closing decades of the century, assisted by the access to wider markets now being provided by canals and tramways. In the agricultural sphere the enclosure, by individual Acts of Parliaments, of common arable fields and pastures, where these still existed, and residual areas of 'waste' was accompanied by changes in organization, techniques and output, but little is known about the demographic effects.

Over half the population still lived in communities of under 1,000 persons (Table II), some of which were already engaging in non-agricultural activities to an important extent, especially in the framework-knitting belt, which also embraced the main coalfield, and in the Peak District. A further 27 per cent were living in large villages and small towns of 1,000 to 5,000, most of which were concerned with industry, mining or tertiary functions, but only 17 per cent were living in the towns of over 5,000. These were Derby, Hinckley, Leicester, Mansfield, Newark and Nottingham. Belper and Loughborough had over 4,500.

## POPULATION CHANGE, 1801–61

*1801–21*

During this period the population of England and Wales grew by 35 per cent and that of the three counties by 33 per cent (Table I). Figure 3a shows the pattern of relative change. Areas growing by over 40 per cent were thus growing at well above national and regional rates and it must, therefore, be assumed either that their rate of natural increase was high or that they were areas of net in-migration, or both. Areas growing by between 25 and 40 per cent may probably be regarded as areas where natural increase was broadly retained, while those failing to achieve 25 per cent experienced either a low rate of natural increase or net out-migration, or both. The pattern displayed in Figure 3a obviously depends not only on the adoption of these simple categories of change but also on the great variation in the areas and shapes of the civil parishes. Nevertheless it is clear that large parts of the Middle Trent approached, equalled or exceeded the national and regional rates of change.

Growth appears to have been slowest in those agricultural lowland areas where alternative occupations were fewest, i.e. eastern Nottinghamshire and Leicestershire and south–western Leicestershire and Derbyshire, but in none of these areas was there complete uniformity. Enclosure of the 'waste' accounts for some high rates of increase in the Peak District, the

41

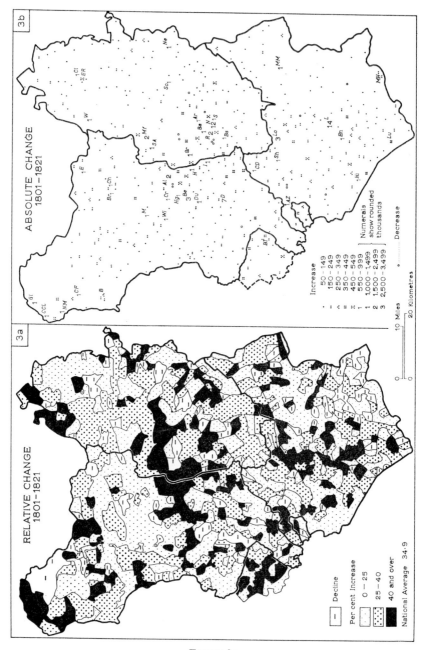

FIGURE 3a
Relative population change, 1801–21, in the Middle Trent

FIGURE 3b
Absolute population change, 1801–21, in the Middle Trent

north of Nottinghamshire, Sherwood, Charnwood and Needwood, although in the former area cotton-spinning must be taken into account. In central Leicestershire the broad central hosiery belt emerges as a zone of average and above-average growth. Some high rates of growth also occurred to the north in the adjoining hosiery belt of Derbyshire and Nottinghamshire, but here cotton-spinning in the Derwent valley and increasing exploitation of the coalfield were locally more important. Rapid growth in this southern part of the coalfield (Erewash valley district) may be contrasted with relatively slow growth in the north (Rother basin). The reason may be that the former enjoyed good waterway links with the expanding markets of the three county towns and the South.

Widespread rural depopulation and concentrated urbanization were the two most striking features of the changing geography of England's population during the nineteenth century, but in the period 1801–21 the former had not yet become serious in the Middle Trent. Population declines were recorded at only just over 100 places (about one-third of them containing less than 100 persons) out of a total number of well over 900, and very few of the declines exceeded 50 persons (Figures 3a and 3b). It must be added, however, that the early census returns are known to have been somewhat unreliable in spite of retrospective corrections made in 1851.

Enclosure has sometimes been blamed for causing rural depopulation at this time. In the Middle Trent, however, enclosure of the common arable fields and pastures had already been largely completed by 1801, although a time-lag should be allowed for in considering possible effects. The present writer has thus tried to relate population change between 1801 and 1821 with enclosure occurring between 1790 and 1820, which affected nearly 200 places.[2] Over a third of these were known to have important non-agricultural activities and even if they are excluded it appears that a large majority of the remainder increased in population by 20 per cent or more, even though stagnation or decline sometimes occurred in one of the two decades. Where large areas of waste were enclosed increases often exceeded 40 per cent. Only about 20 to 25 places experiencing enclosure could be found amongst the 100 or so that declined in this period and in any case several of them had other non-agricultural activities.[3] Thus even where enclosure had recently occurred there was no necessary accompaniment of population decline, or even of very slow growth.[4] In this period, as in others, it is difficult to account for unusual population changes in small communities in the absence of precise details of their demographic and economic structure, although it is true that the census sometimes offers a reason.[5]

Figure 3b, using the same method of representation as Figure 2, shows the absolute changes in this period and reinforces the impression of widespread growth, even though increases of less than 50 are not plotted. Nevertheless several leading areas of expansion may be discerned. These were the three county towns, sustained by their various textile interests to a large extent; the new cotton-manufacturing centres of Derbyshire, i.e. Belper and Duffield (then including Milford) in the Derwent valley and the Glossop–New Mills group in the north-west; and the Erewash coal and iron district, including Alfreton, Heage, Heanor, Ilkeston and Greasley. Growth in the south Derbyshire–Leicestershire coalfield was not yet particularly impressive, although it should be observed that the western

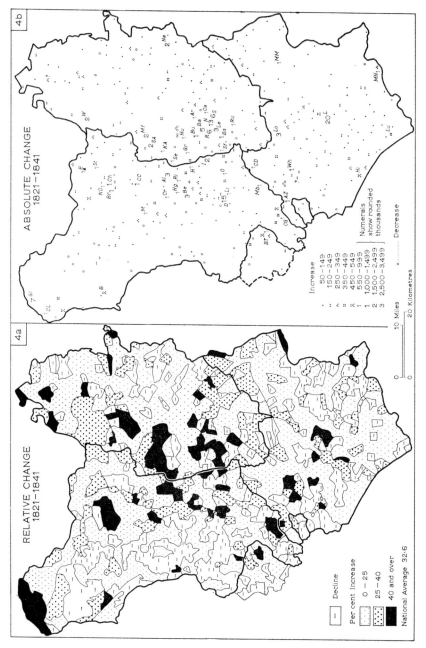

FIGURE 4a
Relative population change, 1821–41, in the Middle Trent

FIGURE 4b
Absolute population change, 1821–41, in the Middle Trent

44

part of Ashby parish included mining settlements. Amongst the other towns Loughborough and Melton Mowbray are noteworthy, expansion, according to the census, being due to the lace industry at the former and to fox-hunting and its labour requirements at the latter. Framework-knitting towns and villages usually showed brisk growth.

## 1821–41

Between 1821 and 1841 the national rate of growth continued at about one-third, but only Nottinghamshire maintained parity, assisted no doubt by the spectacular lace boom of the 1820s in Nottingham and district. Relatively few rural communities now achieved an increase of 25 per cent and the number of declines was much higher (Figure 4a). The apparent disequilibrium between the changing distribution of employment opportunities, favouring manufacturing towns and coalfields, and that of a rapidly-growing population still showing a strong rural and agricultural bias was thus becoming acute. It is possible that by the end of the period the impact of the rigorous new Poor Law was to speed up the developing process of migration from agriculture and depressed forms of rural employment.

Urban growth was chiefly confined to the same places as before, i.e. the three county towns, the two cotton areas and the Erewash coal and iron district (Figure 4b). Growth at Nottingham was scarcely greater in this period than in the previous one, largely owing to the acute shortage of building land. There was thus much growth in adjoining Sneinton and the industrial villages of the Leen valley to the north–west. In the Rother basin railway development at the very end of the period was beginning to foster increased activity in coal and iron, as is shown particularly by the growth of the new town of Clay Cross. Increased activity is also indicated on the south Derbyshire–Leicestershire field, including the concealed area to the south–east, where the new town of Coalville was beginning to develop at the junction of four parishes, including Whitwick. By contrast towns and villages engaging in framework-knitting grew only very moderately and some declined in the second decade. The industry had been in a depressed, over-crowded condition for most of the century, but the 1830s were a particularly critical time, even in the absence of any threat from steam power, and a Royal Commission of enquiry was appointed in the early 1840s. In the Peak District lead-mining was now declining at a number of places, owing partly to exhaustion and partly to the effect of cheaper imports. Migration from rural areas thus involved not only those engaged in agriculture but also those in framework-knitting and lead-mining.

## 1841–61

The national rate of growth fell to about one-quarter and thus the categories have been adjusted in the relative-change map to take account of this (Figure 5a). Of the three counties only Derbyshire, with its rapidly-expanding coalfield, came near to matching the national rate, and Leicestershire, the county most committed to hosiery and agriculture, grew by only 10 per cent. The census of 1861 reveals, as might be expected, that all three counties had been losing population through migration and that the greatest absolute and relative loss was from Leicestershire (Table III).[6]

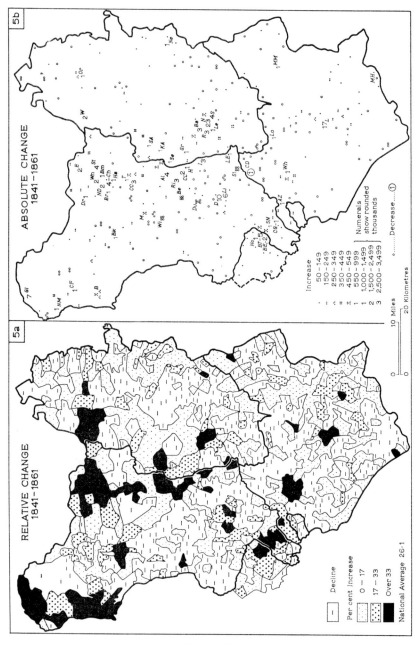

FIGURE 5a
Relative population change, 1841–61, in the Middle Trent

FIGURE 5b
Absolute population change, 1841–61, in the Middle Trent

Rural depopulation was widespread now, declines of more than 50 persons were much more numerous, and few areas achieved a growth rate of even one-sixth (17 per cent). Urban expansion again showed a similar pattern (Figure 5b). Derby's railway suburb of Litchurch had now become important, while in the Nottingham area the city reasserted its growth *vis-à-vis* the satellite industrial villages as a result of the long-awaited release of the common fields for building. At Leicester, with, as yet, no major industry except hosiery, growth was smaller than in 1821–41. Expansion was again prominent on the coalfields. The market town of Worksop had now become a coal-mining centre with the sinking of one of the first pits on the concealed coalfield of Nottinghamshire. Railway development and a central location were now enabling Burton-on-Trent, with its highly-suitable water supplies, to develop as a great Victorian brewing centre. There was further expansion in the Glossop cotton district, although Mellor declined. There were also declines in the Derwent valley cotton district, partly due, however, to the collapse of the accompanying silk hosiery industry. Stagnation or decline was typical of most hosiery towns and villages, and their plight is well-documented in the minutes of evidence to the Royal Commission.[7] The present author has calculated that, out of the 67 places declining in 1851–61 that had achieved a population of over 1,000 by 1851, 44 were framework-knitting centres, including places as large as Belper, Loughborough, Mansfield and Sutton-in-Ashfield. Out of 42 declining in the first decade 26 were framework-knitting centres, including Hinckley. The other places were very varied and included cotton-spinning villages, lead-mining centres and small moribund market towns. Census comments on declines in the smaller villages mention emigration and the migration of agricultural labourers into the manufacturing or (coal) mining districts, together with depression in framework knitting, the failure of lead mines and the stoppage of cotton mills.

CONCLUSION

The year 1861 is a convenient year at which to conclude this general survey of population change. The change from a situation showing a considerable degree of stability to one of extreme contrasts is well-demonstrated by the three pairs of maps. Within a context of rapid growth, falling, nevertheless, below the national average (Table I), much redistribution had taken place, achieved partly by migration and partly, it must be assumed, by variations in local rates of natural increase, themselves necessarily affected by migration through the transfer of reproductive capacity. Redistribution, it should be noted, involved not only a change in the geographical pattern, but also a change in the numbers and proportions living in the different categories of community size (Table II).

The 1850s and 1860s also broadly coincide with several new developments in the economic evolution of the Middle Trent, especially the growth of coal-mining on the concealed coalfield of Nottinghamshire and of wholesale footwear manufacture in Leicestershire. Also, the hosiery industry was now being successfully converted to a steam-power basis, with a tendency, at least initially, to localization in the larger towns. Conversion had begun before 1820 in lace but only now was nearing completion.[8] Conversion had also been proceeding in cotton, and the

TABLE I
Population growth, 1801–61

| Year | Derbyshire | | Leicestershire | | Nottinghamshire | | Total | | Burton-on-Trent area, Staffordshire | | England and Wales |
|---|---|---|---|---|---|---|---|---|---|---|---|
| | Thousand | Percentage increase | Thousand | Percentage increase | Thousand | Percentage increase | Thousand | Percentage increase | Thousand | Percentage increase | Percentage increase |
| 1801 .. | 162 | — | 130 | — | 140 | — | 432 | — | 11.3 | — | — |
| 1821 .. | 214 | 36.2 | 174 | 33.7 | 187 | 33.1 | 575 | 33.1 | 14.5 | 28.6 | 34.9 |
| 1841 .. | 272 | 27.1 | 216 | 24.1 | 250 | 33.7 | 738 | 28.3 | 16.6 | 14.7 | 32.6 |
| 1861 .. | 339 | 24.7 | 237 | 10.0 | 294 | 17.6 | 871 | 18.0 | 24.9 | 49.6 | 26.1 |
| 1801–61 | 178 | 110.0 | 107 | 82.5 | 154 | 109.4 | 439 | 101.5 | 13.6 | 120.6 | 125.7 |

TABLE II
Population structure by community size, 1801–61

| Year and community size | Derbyshire | | Leicestershire | | Nottinghamshire | | Total | | Burton-on-Trent area, Staffordshire | |
|---|---|---|---|---|---|---|---|---|---|---|
| | Thousand | Percentage | Thousand | Percentage | Thousand | Percentage | Thousand | Percentage | Thousand | Percentage |
| *1801* | | | | | | | | | | |
| Below 1,000 .. | 91 | 56.3 | 78 | 59.8 | 71 | 50.5 | 240 | 55.4 | 5.3 | 47.0 |
| 1,000 to 5,000 .. | 60 | 37.0 | 30 | 23.3 | 28 | 19.8 | 118 | 27.3 | 6.0 | 53.0 |
| 5,000 and over .. | 11 | 6.7 | 22 | 17.0 | 42 | 29.7 | 75 | 17.3 | — | — |
| *1861* | | | | | | | | | | |
| Below 1,000 .. | 89 | 26.2 | 84 | 35.4 | 72 | 24.7 | 245 | 28.2 | 5.5 | 22.2 |
| 1,000 to 5,000 .. | 126 | 37.1 | 62 | 26.0 | 60 | 20.5 | 248 | 28.4 | 9.8 | 39.5 |
| 5,000 and over .. | 125 | 36.7 | 92 | 38.6 | 161 | 54.9 | 378 | 43.4 | 9.5 | 38.3 |

TABLE III
Net migration balances, 1861

| Year | Derbyshire | | Leicestershire | | Nottinghamshire | | Total | | Burton-on-Trent area, Staffordshire | |
|---|---|---|---|---|---|---|---|---|---|---|
| | Net migration (thousand) | Percentage | Net migration (thousand) | Percentage | Net migration (thousand) | Percentage | Net migration (thousand) | Percentage | Net migration (thousand) | Percentage |
| 1861* .. | −18.1 | −5.2 | −30.4 | −11.5 | −13.7 | −4.5 | −62.3 | −6.8 | n.a. | |
| 1841–61† .. | −9.4 | −3.9 | −32.6 | −14.8 | −18.1 | −6.7 | −60.0 | −8.2 | +3.3 | +11.4 |

*In-migrant natives of other English or Welsh counties minus out-migrant natives of named county, as percentage of all natives of named county enumerated in England and Wales in 1861

†Total increase between 1841 and 1861 minus natural increase, as percentage of 1841 population

*Note:* Registration Counties, not counties proper, and Burton Registration District (including a large part of south Derbyshire). Percentage rates of natural increase were, respectively, 26.5, 25.0, 26.3 and 30.8

KEY TO PLACES IN FIGURES 2 TO 5

A—Ashover, Al—Alfreton, Ar—Arnold, As—Ashbourne, AZ—Ashby-de-la-Zouch, B—Buxton, Ba—Basford, Be—Belper, Bk—Bakewell, Bm—Brimington, Br—Brampton, Bs—Beeston, Bu—Bulwell, BE—Burton Extra, BT—Burton-on-Trent, Ca—Carlton, Ch—Chesterfield, Cl—Clarborough, Cr—Crich, CC—Clay Cross, (CCL—(Charlesworth), Chisworth and Ludworth (1801–41), CD—Castle Donington, CF—Chapel-en-le-Frith, CG—Church Gresley, CL—Codnor and Loscoe (1841–61), D—Derby, Dr—Dronfield, Du—Duffield, E—Eckington, En—Enderby, ER—East Retford, Gl—Glossop, Gr—Greasley, H—Heanor, Ha—Hasland, Hg—Heage, Hi—Hinckley, Ho—Horninglow, Hu—Hucknall, I—Ilkeston, KA—Kirkby-in-Ashfield, L—Leicester, Le—Lenton, Li—Litchurch, Lo—Loughborough, Lu—Lutterworth, LE—Long Eaton, M—Melbourne, Mb—Melbourne, Mf—Mansfield, Ml—Mellor, MH—Market Harborough, MM—Melton Mowbray, N—Nottingham, Ne—Newark, ND—Newbold and Dunston, NM—New Mills, O—Ockbrook, Or—Ordsall, R—Radford, Ri—Ripley, Ru—Ruddington, S—Sneinton, Se—Selston, Sf—Stapleford, Sh—Shepshed, Sl—Shardlow, So—Southwell, St—Staveley, SA—Sutton-in-Ashfield, SN—Stanton and Newhall, T—Tupton, W—Worksop, Wh—Whitwick, Wi—Wirksworth, Wn—Whittington, WM—Wigston Magna, WN—Worthington and Newbold

'cotton famine' of the 1860s, resulting from the American Civil War, was to lead to further closures in an industry that had already shed a number of small country mills. In the field of transport the main outline of the railway network had been established and the canals were redundant to a large extent.[9]

The changes in the geography of population revealed through the nineteenth-century census are, indeed, a striking witness to the economic, social and demographic turbulence occurring during the main formative period of modern urban and industrial England. In this context we must agree with Walter Gerard in Disraeli's novel of the times, *Sybil or The Two Nations,* that 'the Population Returns of this country are very instructive reading'.

## NOTES

[1] The general economic development of the three counties is described in their respective *Victoria County History*. Geographical articles dealing with particular activities include: G. J. FULLER, Lead-mining in Derbyshire in the mid-nineteenth century, *East Midland Geographer* 3 (1965) 373–393; D. M. SMITH, The cotton industry in the East Midlands, *Geography* 47 (1962) 256–269; D. M. SMITH, The silk industry of the East Midlands, *East Midland Geographer* 3 (1962) 20–31; D. M. SMITH, The British hosiery industry at the middle of the nineteenth century, *Institute of British Geographers, Transactions and Papers* 32 (1963) 125–142; K. WARREN, The Derbyshire iron industry since 1780, *East Midland Geographer* 2, no. 16 (1961) 17–33. See also: F. C. COUZENS, Distribution of population of the mid-Derwent basin since the Industrial Revolution, *Geography* 26 (1941) 31–38.

[2] Lists of enclosures, with dates, are given in: J. D. CHAMBERS, *Nottinghamshire in the eighteenth century* (1932) 333–353; J. C. COX, *Three centuries of Derbyshire annals* 2 (1890) 305–325; J. THIRSK, in *Victoria County History of Leicestershire* (ed. W. G. Hoskins and R. A. McKinley) 2 (1954) 260–264.

[3] The chief remaining places are: Chaddesden, Egginton, Etwall (near Derby); Barlborough (north–east Derbyshire); Bringhurst (including Drayton and Easton Magna), East Langton, Tur Langton, Slawston (south–east Leicestershire); Annesley, Tollerton (near Nottingham), Eaton, Headon (near East Retford) (but Headon's decline was in the first decade, a few years before enclosure).

[4] After a similar examination of the evidence, C. T. SMITH found that 'Over much of Leicestershire inclosure had no apparent effect on population at the end of the 18th and in the early 19th century', *Victoria County History of Leicestershire* (ed. W. G. Hoskins and R. A. McKinley) 3 (1955) 148.

[5] The decline of villages near Nottingham particularly exemplifies the problem of explanation at the local level. Enclosure occurred in four of them; coal-mining, framework-knitting or cotton-spinning were represented in several; all had rapidly-expanding neighbours; and, perhaps more significantly, nearly all were 'closed' villages (see D. R. MILLS, pp. 31–38 in this publication). Only in one instance, Wollaton, does the census give a reason—the demolition of houses. Apart from that at Wollaton the only other large declines were at Coleorton, a mining village on the Leicestershire coalfield, and at Pentrich, near Ripley. At the former the census cites 'the demolition of a number of houses and the removal of a Poor House', while at the latter there was retaliation for the 'Derbyshire Insurrection' of 1817 'in consequence of which the Duke of Devonshire's agents destroyed many of the houses'.

[6] The civil registration of births and deaths was introduced in 1837. For the period 1801 to 1841 totals of baptisms and burials were returned by the clergy, but they were admitted to be unreliable as a measure of births and deaths. P. DEANE and W. A. COLE have adjusted them in order to calculate 'highly tentative' estimates of county net migration for 1801–31. The balances for the Middle Trent are: Derbyshire −25,500, Leicestershire −6,000, Nottinghamshire −9,900; *British economic growth, 1688–1959: trends and structure* (1964) 106 et seq.

7 Report of the Commissioner appointed to inquire into the condition of the framework knitters, *British Parliamentary Papers* XV (1845). The minutes of evidence also contain a full analysis of the geographical distribution of frames by W. Felkin.

8 The census of 1861 cites 'the introduction of machinery in the stocking industry' (presumably steam-driven?) and 'the introduction of steam-power in the lace factories' for migration from Earl Shilton (Leicestershire) and Stapleford (Nottinghamshire) respectively.

9 The decline at the canal port of Shardlow was attributed by the census to 'the carrying trade . . . . . having been diverted by the Midland Counties Railway'. Several other waterside villages were similarly affected, for example neighbouring Aston and the lower Trent port of West Stockwith.

# LAND OWNERSHIP AND URBAN GROWTH
# IN SCUNTHORPE

### D. C. D. POCOCK

The influence of land ownership on urban growth is in general a neglected aspect of urban geography. This paper is an assessment of the relative importance of this factor with respect to the present morphology of Scunthorpe. The town is essentially a creation of the last 100 years, being the urban response to the rediscovery and exploitation of the Lower Lias or Frodingham ironstone.[1] Although the present borough and built-up area enclose five former villages, the urban form has to a large extent evolved from only two of them—Scunthorpe, in particular, and Ashby. The differential growth rates of the five original villages are in large measure attributable to differences in land ownership. Table I shows the population of the five townships (subsequently parishes) from the beginning of industrial growth until administrative amalgamation in 1918 to form an Urban District. When the first ironworks was opened in 1864 the area had a population of some 1,400 but by the time of amalgamation this had risen to 25,000. It has subsequently risen to 67,000 within unchanged boundaries. The Urban District became a Municipal Borough in 1936.

TABLE I

Population of Crosby, Scunthorpe, Frodingham, Brumby and Ashby parishes, 1851–1918

|            | 1851  | 1861  | 1871  | 1881   | 1891  | 1901   | 1911   | 1918   |
|------------|-------|-------|-------|--------|-------|--------|--------|--------|
| Crosby     | 236   | 235   | 288   | 304    | 299   | 364    | 3,339  | 5,575  |
| Scunthorpe | 303   | 368   | 701   | 2,126  | 3,481 | 6,750  | 10,171 | 12,312 |
| Frodingham | 113   | 113   | 577   | 1,306* | 1,384 | 1,369  | 1,734  | 1,750* |
| Brumby     | 159   | 204   | 178   | 560*   | 756   | 904    | 1,197  | 2,004* |
| Ashby      | 456   | 503   | 669   | 1,462  | 1,634 | 1,843  | 3,237  | 3,735  |
| TOTAL      | 1,267 | 1,423 | 2,413 | 5,758  | 7,573 | 11,232 | 20,580 | 25,376 |

*The 1881 Census figures for Frodingham and Brumby parishes, 1,663 and 203 respectively, are almost certainly incorrect, probably through the inclusion of the New Brumby population within Frodingham parish. (Acknowledged in communication to author from General Register Office, A.R.C./I.C. 5/2, 12th February 1963.) The 1918 *Inquiry's* composite figure for Brumby and Frodingham Urban District has been derived on the basis of 1911 and 1921 Census figures.

*Source:* Census volumes 1851–1911; 1918 from *Minutes of inquiry into proposed amalgamation, 1918* (1918).

The growth of the built-up area shows the early and continuous expansion of Scunthorpe itself (Figure 1A). The adjacent parish to the north, Crosby, showed no response until the turn of the century, while southwards the small and delayed population rises in Frodingham and Brumby were on two entirely new sites at some distance from the ancient village (New Frodingham and New Brumby). In the extreme south there has been a continuous expansion outwards from the village of Ashby. The built-up area as a whole has coalesced only since the last war and now occupies the west–central third of the administrative area. Thus its present form can only be appreciated through a retrospective study of a century of growth.

## GENERAL FACTORS RESTRICTING DIRECTION OF GROWTH

Some general restrictive forces on urban growth, given the present site, are shown on Figure 1B. The whole of the eastern half of the borough was originally floored with Frodingham ironstone, so that the likelihood of widespread residential development in this section may be considered as small. The ore was discovered on Scunthorpe common, half a mile to the east of the village, on the estate of Charles Winn. Under Winn's initiative ore extraction began at the point of discovery and was worked systematically both north and south.[2] Progress was rapid, as the initial workings often involved only the top layers. Moreover, the early emergence of smelting works made particular sections doubly unsuited to housing. The first six works were all sited by Winn on the east commons adjacent to the quarries and near to the west–east railway.

The ancient villages, then, were located to the windward of the works, which were deliberately sited on their raw material. Moreover, apart from a few houses adjacent to four of the ironworks,[3] the first residential development away from the villages was also located well clear of the workings—Winn's New Frodingham and nearby New Brumby, established by Lord Beauchamp. (While the latter consists of normal bye-law housing and is distinguished today only by street names, the uniform design and compact layout of New Frodingham is not without charm.) The overlap of ferruginous beds with the residential area that does occur represents buildings in existence before the discovery or exact extent of the ore was known, notably around Scunthorpe; building on land after ironstone extraction, confined to an area south of the railway; or, lastly, deliberate sterilising of the westernmost acres, which consisted of thin basal layers, the top and middle beds of the deposit having been denuded through the easterly dip of the strata.

Westwards from the ironstone bed the gentle, dry dip slope of the Lower Lias offered no physical barrier until the low but uninterrupted escarpment of the Trent Cliff was reached. This may be deemed, at least during the early phases, as a potential barrier to growth. Expansion southwards was restricted from the outset by the course of the railway, with only two crossings in the central and eastern part of the present borough. In the eastern half the built-up area was further disrupted in the interwar years by the creation of extensive marshalling yards parallel to the main line. Another barrier, although less serious, was the construction of the A.18 trunk road as a town by-pass in 1933.

## EFFECT OF PARISH BOUNDARIES AND LAND OWNERSHIP

The old township or parish boundaries, aligned west–east and enclosing narrow elongated strips, have been an important element in the development of urban form. Scunthorpe and Frodingham townships were particularly elongated, being under a quarter of a mile in width for most of their five-mile length. This restrictive influence on the growth of the progressive settlement, Scunthorpe, was visible by the 1880s, by which time the built-up area had spread from the village core to the parish's north and south boundaries. Confined between its narrow boundaries and adjoined on the east by the industrial area, Scunthorpe was forced to expand westwards for the next three decades. After the turn of the century, the Sheffield family released the adjacent part of Crosby parish for residential

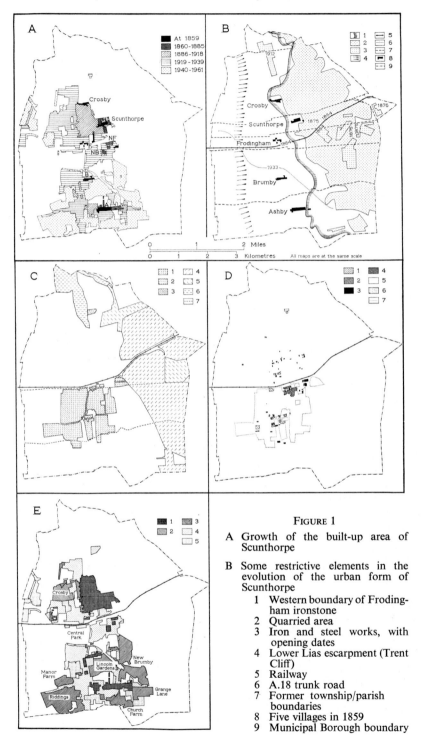

FIGURE 1

A Growth of the built-up area of Scunthorpe

B Some restrictive elements in the evolution of the urban form of Scunthorpe
  1 Western boundary of Frodingham ironstone
  2 Quarried area
  3 Iron and steel works, with opening dates
  4 Lower Lias escarpment (Trent Cliff)
  5 Railway
  6 A.18 trunk road
  7 Former township/parish boundaries
  8 Five villages in 1859
  9 Municipal Borough boundary

—*continued on p. 55*

purposes, but southwards Frodingham remained 'closed' until amalgamation. Moreover, the latter's councillors remained strongly opposed to any co-operation with Scunthorpe until the principal landowners and ironmasters were united over the request by the war-time Ministry of Munitions for a large increase in steel production.[4]

To some extent the pattern of township or parish boundaries coincided with the more detailed mosaic presented by individual land ownership. Figure 2 gives an approximate indication of land ownership prior to ironworking. The basic source for the map is enclosure maps, although for Brumby the tithe maps have been used.[5] Additional sources are particularly relevant in Crosby, where, after enclosure and prior to iron-working, large areas were acquired by the Sheffield family from Healey, a former lord of the manor.[6] Clearly, large proportions of the five townships belonged to four families; this is given on a numerical basis in Table II (see note to key). Overall, the combined acreage listed is equivalent to 67 per cent of the total area awarded at enclosure.

TABLE II

Distribution of acreages belonging to lords of the manor in the five townships of the Scunthorpe area prior to ironworking

| | *Sir R. Sheffield* | *C. Winn* | *Lord Beauchamp* | *W. Skipworth* |
|---|---|---|---|---|
| Crosby .. | 759¾ | — | — | — |
| Scunthorpe .. | ¼ | 293½ | 25½ | — |
| Frodingham .. | — | 500¾ | 77¾ | — |
| Brumby .. | — | 1,045¼ | 1,501 | — |
| Ashby .. | — | — | — | 648¼ |
| TOTAL .. | 760 | 1,839½ | 1,604½ | 648¼ |

Note that, except for Brumby, the figures relate to land awarded at enclosure and therefore understate the total holdings. Figures for Gunness have been omitted from Scunthorpe and Frodingham

*Sources:* Enclosure Awards for Crosby (1812), Scunthorpe and Frodingham (1833), Ashby (1809); Tithe Apportionment for Brumby (1844), T.R.O. 20/58.

—*continued from p.* 54

C  Maximum extent of land ownership by iron and steel companies in Scunthorpe M.B.

Land acquired for residential purposes:

1  Frodingham Estate Company  3  John Lysaght's
2  Richard Thomas and Co.

Land currently owned for industrial purposes:

4  United Steel Co. Ltd.  6  John Lysaght's
5  Richard Thomas and Baldwins Ltd.  7  Former parish boundary of Brumby

D  Company housing in Scunthorpe M.B.
1  Appleby-Frodingham Steel Co. houses
2  North Lincolnshire Iron Co.
3  Richard Thomas and Co. (houses purchased)
4  Richard Thomas and Co. (houses erected by Redbourn Village Society)
5  John Brown and Co.
6  John Lysaght's
7  Boundary of Frodingham Estate Co. and Richard Thomas and Co. land at maximum extent

E  Types of residential development in Scunthorpe M.B.
1  Existing in 1918  4  Private, inter-war
2  Local authority, inter-war  5  Private, post-war
3  Local authority, post-war

FIGURE 2

Land ownership in five townships of the Scunthorpe area prior to iron-working

Land belonging to lords of manor is shaded:
1   Sir R. Sheffield
2   C. Winn
3   Lord Beauchamp
4   W. Skipworth

*Sources:* Enclosures Awards for Ashby (1809), Crosby (1812), Scunthorpe and Frodingham (1833); Tithe Apportionment for Brumby (1844); plan of Scunthorpe village (1850); information from Messrs. Lawrence, Graham and Co., solicitors to Conesby Investment Co. Ltd.

Further details of ownership of the newly enclosed land—or tithe land for Brumby—are given in Table III. Of the two centres which responded to the advent of industry in the second half of last century, Ashby shows the highest number of owners and smallest proportion of land owned by the lord of the manor. Although Scunthorpe has the next lowest proportion belonging to the leading land-owner and the smallest average parcel size, the figures do not strongly differentiate the township. Further evidence is gained, however, if attention is turned from the townships as a whole to land division within the more detailed confines of the villages (Figure 3).

Here, Scunthorpe and Ashby clearly had the largest number of owners and holdings within the villages. Moreover, if it is assumed that land belonging to the lords of the manor was a restrictive factor regarding growth potential, then the number of separate parcels not held by the chief land owner is perhaps the most significant column in Table IV. Scunthorpe and Ashby are again pre-eminent. In Scunthorpe it may be noted that the earliest industry-based urban growth did, in fact, take place on land other than that belonging to the lord of the manor—on land parcels sold by Parkinson, at first to the north–west of Market Hill (Chapel Street, Church Street, Providence Place) and then in the opposite direction along South Sand Field Road (Manley Street). Up to the time of amalgamation very little of the extensive growth of Scunthorpe was on land owned by Winn, whose particular contribution remained the detached settlement of New Frodingham. Apart from the legacy of the proportion of dwellings dating

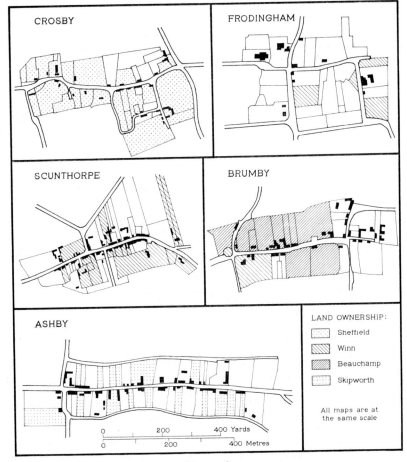

FIGURE 3

Land ownership within five villages of the Scunthorpe area prior to iron-working
Land belonging to lord of manor in each village is shaded

*Source:* As Figure 2

from this early period, the detailed effect of land-ownership on the present morphology is seen most clearly along the former southern boundary of Scunthorpe parish to the south of Mary Street. Here a uniform area of bye-law Victorian terracing adjoins modern development or open space.

TABLE III

Some aspects of land ownership in the five townships of the Scunthorpe area prior to iron-working

| | Acreage involved | | No. of owners | Average parcel size (acres) | Acreage to largest owner (per cent) |
|---|---|---|---|---|---|
| | No. | Per cent | | | |
| Crosby .. | 1,066 | 34 | 14 | 41 | 71 |
| Scunthorpe | 607 | 59 | 13 | 8 | 48 |
| Frodingham | 735 | 72 | 7 | 24½ | 68 |
| Brumby .. | 2,986 | All | 15 | 12 | 50 |
| Ashby .. | 1,874 | 85 | 19 | 22½ | 35 |

Notes: (a) Except for Brumby, where tithe records are used, figures relate to land awarded at enclosure;
(b) acreages of highways, drains, pits are omitted;
(c) figures for Gunness are omitted from Scunthorpe and Frodingham.

Source: As Table II.

TABLE IV

Some aspects of land ownership within the five villages of the Scunthorpe area prior to iron-working

| | No. of owners | No. of parcels | No. of parcels not belonging to lord of manor |
|---|---|---|---|
| Crosby .. .. | 7? | 34 | 9 |
| Scunthorpe .. | 10 | 43 | 24 |
| Frodingham .. | 8 | 16 | 11 |
| Brumby .. .. | 7 | 25 | 16 |
| Ashby .. .. | 13 | 42 | 25 |

Sources: As Table II, plus plan of village of Scunthorpe, 1 inch : 1 chain 1850 (Appleby Estates Office; copy in Scunthorpe Museum); information from Messrs. Lawrence, Graham and Co., solicitors to Conesby Investment Co. Ltd.

The position and form of the present commercial centres also stem from initial differences and policies of land ownership. Parish totals for numbers of shops highlight the inert response of Crosby (until 1900) and Frodingham and Brumby to the large population influx to the district (Table V). By contrast, Scunthorpe, in particular, and the more distant Ashby immediately responded by adding to their small commercial roles and thereby laid the basis for the two major shopping centres in the present borough. Both are entirely linear in form and extend west–east through the centre of their former parishes. The nature of the progressive extension of shopping premises westwards for half a mile along Scunthorpe High Street can be clearly recognised today, for many of the facades barely conceal their conversion from former residences.

58

TABLE V

The number of shops in the five parishes in the Scunthorpe area, 1861–1918

|  | *1861* | *1885* | *1905* | *1918* |
|---|---|---|---|---|
| Crosby .. | 2 | 1 | 7 | 67 |
| Scunthorpe .. | 5 | 50 | 173 | 275 |
| Frodingham .. | 2 | 9 | 4 | 6 |
| Brumby .. | 2 | 7 | 13 | 17 |
| Ashby .. | 9 | 16 | 37 | 51 |
| TOTAL .. | 20 | 83 | 234 | 416 |

*Source: Kelly's* directories for relevant years

## CHANGES SINCE 1918

The question of land ownership was revised to some extent after the First World War, when large parts of the Winn (now Lord St. Oswald) and Beauchamp estates were acquired by the various steel companies for residential purposes. The Frodingham Estate Company, formed in 1918 by collaboration of four works[7] for the purpose of erecting a garden city, purchased 445 acres, while Richard Thomas and Company acquired a further 330 acres. The remaining company, John Lysaght's, purchased 27 acres adjacent to its works for its own model village (Figure 1C).[8]

However, the potential of the new ownership lay largely unrealised and the visible legacy has been one of detail rather than general form. Of the housing erected by five separate companies (Figure 1D and Table VI), only the compact development of the Redbourn Village Society to the west of New Brumby is sufficiently extensive to provide a recognisable quarter; even this represents but one-fifth of the projected layout. The remainder are scattered in small or even individual lots. Nevertheless, two broad influences of the new ownership on urban form are worthy of note.

TABLE VI

House completions by iron and steel companies within Scunthorpe in the interwar years

| Company | Houses | Year of erection |
|---|---|---|
| Richard Thomas .. .. | 238 | 1919–22 |
| John Brown .. .. | 63 | 1919–21 |
| Frodingham Iron and Steel .. | 63 | 1918–37 |
| John Lysaght's .. .. | 10 | 1920–22 |
| North Lincolnshire Iron .. | 7 | 1925 |
| Appleby Iron .. .. | 4 | 1918 |

*Source:* Company records

Firstly, land to the south of Brumby Hall which was allocated by the Frodingham Estate Company as playing fields for company employees was the indirect beginning of a central park. (The corporation purchased 29 acres for this purpose in this undeveloped central area in 1937.) Secondly, with the cessation of its own housing programme, the Estate Company has influenced the distribution of housing types since 1922 by a discriminatory manner in disposing of its land.[9] As a result, in 1961 only in two small sections of the original area purchased by the company is local-authority housing to be found (compare Figure 1D and 1E).[10] In contrast, a third of the area acquired by Richard Thomas is now covered by local-authority housing, the bulk of which forms the large Lincoln Gardens estate.

The contribution of town planning to urban form has become increasingly evident since the 1947 Act, although its foundations were laid in the inter-war period. The newly formed Urban District passed a resolution to prepare a town-planning scheme in 1920, and an outline plan covering the town and an equivalent area outside its boundaries was prepared by Abercrombie and Johnson within a few months. Although the partnership between council and consultants was relatively short-lived,[11] several of the latter's recommendations can be recognised in the present town.[12] These include the joining of the separate northern and southern parts of the town by extensive development in Frodingham and Brumby, the creation of a civic centre in the central area and a careful development along the western scarp face. In detail the eastern part of the corporation's Crosby estate, with its heavy and, at times, classical design, is the tangible contribution of Sir Patrick Abercrombie.[13]

TABLE VII

Population changes within Scunthorpe, 1918–61

| Ward | Approximate former equivalent | 1918 | 1939 | 1961 |
|---|---|---|---|---|
| Crosby, Park | Crosby | 5,500 | 12,000 | 11,189 |
| West, Town, East | Scunthorpe | 12,300 | 14,200 | 13,146 |
| Brumby, Frodingham | Brumby, Frodingham | 3,600 | 11,500 | 21,358 |
| Ashby | Ashby | 3,700 | 6,200 | 21,631 |
| | TOTAL | 25,100 | 43,900 | 67,324 |

*Source:* See Table I

The population growth in the central and southern portion of the borough since 1918 is summarised in Table VII, where the wards have been combined to approximate to the former parish divisions. The figures may be compared, therefore, with those up to 1918 in Table I. Integration of the residential area to the south of the railway has been aided by extensive local-authority housing, which has accounted for three-quarters of post-war construction, compared with one-quarter between the wars (Figure 1E). The overall urban form, therefore, is increasingly becoming that as planned by the county and borough authorities.[14] The present town, however, still clearly reveals, both in general outline and in detail, numerous instances of its polynuclear origin and differential rates of growth. And, as has been shown, its present form can only be fully appreciated by due consideration of former land ownership and its effects.

NOTES

[1] D. C. D. POCOCK, Iron and steel at Scunthorpe, *East Midland Geographer* 3 (1963) 124–138.

[2] D. C. D. POCOCK, Stages in the development of the Frodingham ironstone field, *Trans. Inst. Br. Geogr.* 35 (1964) 105–118.

[3] Appleby Ironworks, 20; North Lincoln, 20; Redbourn, 12; Trent Ironworks 6.

4 D. C. D. Pocock   Scunthorpe and Frodingham: early struggles in civic history *Appleby-Frodingham News* 16 (March 1963) 33–40.

5 Ashby was enclosed in 1801–09  Crosby in 1807–12  Frodingham and Scunthorpe in 1831–34, but the area about about Brumby village was enclosed at a much earlier, but unrecorded, date. The moors to the west and the commons to the east of Brumby remained unenclosed until 1871 and 1875 respectively, although in fact a notice of intention had been served in 1836.

6 Lincolnshire Archives Office, *Sheffield Deposit*, A/46/2, A/46/3.

7 The four companies were the Appleby, Frodingham, North Lincolnshire and John Brown.

8 Borough Engineer's Department, *John Lysaght's Model Village Plan* (1910), Drc. 25H.

9 'More land could no doubt have been sold . . . . . but the policy has been to keep up the value, particularly of certain areas, and so keep these neighbourhoods more select', Frodingham Estate Co. Ltd. (typescript, 1936) 5.

10 The sale of 60 acres to the corporation in 1960 for the Westcliff estate has slightly altered the pattern, but there remains the legacy of the greater portion. In the interwar period, despite tentative moves by the local authority to purchase between 50 and 150 acres in 1921, sales to the council up to 1938 were confined to land required for road widening or construction and for the central park. See Frodingham Estate Co. Ltd.

11 The parting came after a prolonged disagreement, which ended in the work being transferred to the town's Engineer's Department. See Scunthorpe and Frodingham U.D.C., *Minutes of Town Planning Committee 1920–30*, 1–91.

12 See Scunthorpe and Frodingham U.D.C., Development plan and town planning scheme, *Minutes of Town Planning Committee 1920–30*, op. cit. 10–24; and Scunthorpe and Frodingham U.D.C., *Town Planning Scheme Map*, six inches : one mile (n.d., 1925?) in Borough Engineer's Department.

13 See Brocklesby and Marchment for P. Abercrombie, *Crosby Housing Scheme for Scunthorpe and Frodingham U.D.C.* (1920), 1 : 1,250 plan in Borough Museum.

14 See Lindsey County Council, *County Development Plan, Report of the Survey: Scunthorpe and Brigg* (1953), and *First Quinquennial Review: Scunthorpe and Brigg* (draft 1962).

61

# COASTAL EVOLUTION IN NORTH-EAST LINCOLNSHIRE

## D. N. ROBINSON

'The only way to learn a place like this,' he shouted, 'is to see it at low water. The banks are dry then and the channels plain.'[1]

### INTRODUCTION

The key to the coastal evolution of north–east Lincolnshire is on the foreshore, an area of saltings and beach ridges which can be up to two miles wide at low spring tides. Basically it is a coast of accretion between the protected cliffs of Cleethorpes and the concrete-clad dunes of Mablethorpe, and a wide foreshore is its distinguishing feature. The greatest accretion has been during the last 700 years, particularly since the disappearance of the offshore barrier of glacial drift islets in the stormy thirteenth century.[2] The results of this accretion have been utilised by man for salt-making, for pasturing and for reclamation.

The evolution of the coastline from the Iron Age will be traced, but first it is necessary to appreciate that during the Last Glaciation ice reached its maximum extent just over the eastern Interglacial cliff of the Wolds.[3] The retreat and re-advance stages left a cover of drift on the chalk platform, in front of the cliff, which is now 60 to 90 feet below the present surface. The area of hummocky drift is usually known as the Middle Marsh, and its limit is approximately marked by the 25-foot contour. There is a significant break of slope at 22 feet O.D., but it is suggested that this break is a result of a marine transgression which took place between 7000 and 5000 B.C.[4] The flat silts (the Outmarsh) are the result of post-glacial deposition in the shelter of the offshore barrier[5] and, together with a considerable thickness of coastal sands (40 feet or more), completely mask the hummocky features of the drift.

### IRON AGE TO 1200 A.D.

In Iron Age and Roman times it is likely that there was an extensive area of saltmarshes, sand and mud flats along a coastline running approximately along a line through Humberston, Tetney, the Theddlethorpes and Mablethorpe. Undoubtedly salt-making took place among the shallows and creeks within the shelter of the offshore barrier. A Roman Salters' Way from Lincoln reached the coast at Beacon Hill and Romano–British pottery of the kind associated with salt-making has been found at Acre Bridge, Conisholme and Marsh Chapel Ings. Subsidence in the post-Roman period led to the erosion of Holderness and to the acceleration of erosion of the protective coastal barrier. The deposition of this eroded material onto the coast of north–east Lincolnshire more than compensated for the effects of subsidence. When the Anglo-Saxons arrived the coast probably consisted of the tidal saltmarsh-fringed estuaries of the Lud, Waithe Beck and other streams, up which the invaders would be attracted to establish their settlements, as at Alvingham, North Cockerington and Fulstow on the boulder clay edge. As the ratio of sinking to silting swung further in favour of silting on this coast, saltmarshes developed further and outfalls became divided and choked with mud.

As the saltmarshes became suitable for depasturing cattle or sheep, a sea dyke was built in sections from North Coates to North and South Somercotes and to Skidbrooke/Saltfleet. These very names suggest huts or cottages (cotes) erected on the dyke, which in summer were occupied by those tending the grazing animals.[6] Also the great common pasture of Fulstow was called 'la Sumerette'.[7] By the eleventh century the marshland between the parent villages and the sea dyke had been reclaimed, and the line of settlements on the dyke—North Coates, Marsh Chapel, Wragholme, Grainthorpe, Conisholme, North and South Somercotes and Skidbrooke— were developing as daughter settlements from North Thoresby, Fulstow, the Covenhams, Yarburgh, Alvingham and (North) Cockerington. All are mentioned in the Domesday Book except North Coates (earliest reference 1115 A.D.), Marsh Chapel (formerly Foulestowemersch and not a separate parish until the fifteenth century)[8] and Conisholme (earliest reference 1195 A.D.). It is also worth noting the fragmentation of Saltfleetby into St. Peter, St. Clement and All Saints, and Theddlethorpe into All Saints and St. Helen with the development of grazing on the reclaimed Outmarsh.

The road B 1198 follows the line of the old sea dyke, to the west are flat silts and to the east are hummocky saltern mounds created by salt-workings recorded in Domesday.[9] Saltfleet is not mentioned as a settlement, but three havens are given—Salfluet, Mare and Suine. The first and third are Saltfleet Haven and Swine Dyke (in Grainthorpe); Mare lay between them, on the North Somercotes/South Somercotes boundary.[10] In other words, they lay on three distributaries of the River Lud.

## THE STORMY CENTURIES

Historical evidence, especially that amassed by Owen,[11] indicates that the late twelfth century to early fourteenth century was a very stormy period, with severe marine inundations on the Lincolnshire coast. The occurrence of storms, the final destruction of the offshore barrier, greater erosion of Holderness and the re-sorting of sea-bed glacial sands would result in storm beaches. On these blown sand would accumulate to form the basis for the Somercotes Warren, which extends, narrowing south–eastwards, towards Mablethorpe North End, and for the old dune line from Cleethorpes to Humberston Wadhouse. Some of these dunes now rise to 50 feet. It seems doubtful whether the storm beach line from Humberston to Somercotes was ever continuous, as suggested by Reid;[12] in any case his 'fluviatile warp' can be shown to be man-made waste tips of salterns. What is certain is that the stormy centuries disrupted outfalls, interfered with the manufacture of salt and buried areas of saltmarsh beneath the storm beaches. Mare Haven fell into disuse, a 'port' at North Coates became silted up in 1274,[13] and the Withern Eau was diverted into Saltfleet Haven before 1347 to help scour out the channel and because of the silting up of its own outfall.[14]

## ACCRETION AND SALTMAKING

After the stormy centuries there was a period of steady accretion over the next 300 years, during which the saltmaking industry flourished. The results of this industry can be seen in the clustered masses of irregularly-shaped mounds from Low Farm, Tetney, to Porter's Marsh, North Somercotes. These mounds, which are up to 20 feet high, are readily identified on aerial photographs and relate to the 'round groundes' or 'maures' as shown on Haiwarde's map of Fulstow–Marsh Chapel of 1595.[15] This not only gives information about saltmaking, but shows the limit of The Salt Marshes ('called the Fittyes which are alway is drouned at Spring Tydes')[16] and the line of 'deade lowe water'. The latter indicates that by that time the present low-water mark had been reached. Since then accretion has heightened the beach to its present wide, plateau form.

The sandy shore of north–east Lincolnshire was ideal for saltmaking. After high spring tides the sandy silt of the upper shore would have a high salt content. This silt or muldefang was scraped up and placed in a trench or kinch. Water was added, which carried off the deposited salt into a wooden receptacle. This strong brine was then boiled over turf or coal fires. The de-salted muldefang was thrown onto a waste heap and so the maures grew in size.[17] It is likely that peat or turf was obtained from the fen, and later coal would be imported into Suine Haven (where the name Coal Shore Lane still exists). As the saltmarsh grew outwards and it became necessary to move the processing point nearer the source of silt, new maures would be built up.

Between Tetney Lock and Grainthorpe salterns form a zone about one-and-a-half miles wide. The volume of these mounds, which largely represents silt taken from the back of the foreshore, is a clear indication of a high rate of accretion.

RECLAMATIONS

Up to the seventeenth century the saltmarshes surrounding the saltern mounds were used for grazing sheep and may have been ripe for reclamation, but saltmaking was clearly more profitable. Although the salt industry suffered a severe blow from the great flood of 1571,[18] it declined rapidly as a result of imported Bay salt[19] and the raising of reclamation banks in the 1630s. In September 1632 Endymion Porter, a London courtier, decided to adventure in drainage. He was granted about 1,000 acres of saltmarsh in North Somercotes, and by spring 1638 the first 500 acres were inned and embanked and ready for cultivation. This ambitious project would have entailed a sea bank some five miles in length, part of which forms the present headland from Donna Nook to Stonebridge. In the 1640s the commoners seized the land and broke down the banks.[20] A new sea bank was built in 1702,[21] but the great August flood of 1744 broke the bank in places.[22] The areas reclaimed are still known as Porter's Marsh and Fivehundred Acres, the latter showing the small divisions as allotted to the commoners. When the Seven Towns South Eau was diverted into Somercotes Haven from its easterly outfall, as shown by Armstrong (1778), is not known. Also by 1638 a bank extending out to the present headland of Horse Shoe Point enclosing 600 acres in the parishes of North Coates and Marsh Chapel had been raised and the saltern mounds or saltcoteholmes were under pasture.[23]

The next surge of reclamation activity came in the second half of the eighteenth century. Work began on the Louth Navigation Canal in 1765; it was opened from Tetney Lock to Firebeacon in 1767 and to Louth in 1770. Four hundred acres in Grainthorpe parish were added to the north–west of Porter's Marsh in 1770. Under the Tetney Enclosure Act of 1774[24] about 690 acres of the North and South Fittys were reclaimed on both sides of the canal. Parts of the sea bank for this were constructed of chalk, brought by barge from Hessle.[25] Finally in 1795 Anthony's Bank round the Wadhouse Enclosure in Humberston was completed.

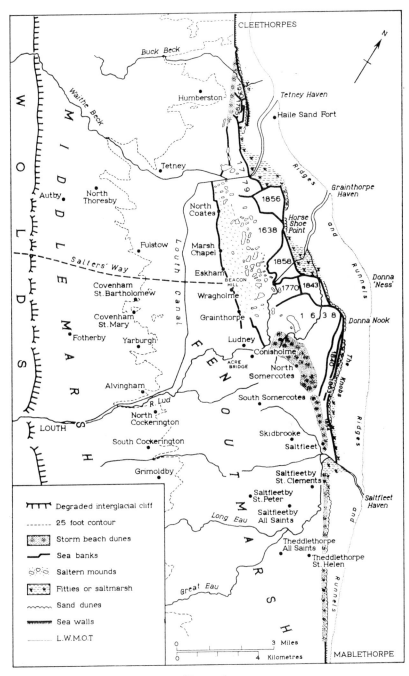

FIGURE 1
Coastal evolution in north–east Lincolnshire

The nineteenth century saw a series of reclamations which virtually produced the present coastline of headlands and bayment fitties. About 1840 the Donnanook Newmarsh, a two-and-a-quarter-mile strip of 300 acres, was taken in. In 1843 Henry Pye of Louth reclaimed 309 acres between Grainthorpe Haven and Stonebridge, the one-and-three-quarter-mile bank and sea sluice being constructed in four months.[26] In 1854 the Saltfleet New Enclosure of 250 acres was the first reclamation east of the Somercotes Warren in the six centuries since its formation. Jukes-Browne says that this was effected by 'fixing a line of fascines to arrest the sand which blows off the shore'[27] but it is likely that they were set in front of a clay bank. This reclamation effectively terminated the sea-bathing activities of the New Inn, Saltfleet, which was frequented by 'noblemen and other genteel persons' at the end of the eighteenth century.[28] It is situated on the Warren and formerly overlooked the beach. However, blowing sand was a problem and in 1822 some dunes in front were levelled and trees planted.[29] When the enclosure bank was constructed Saltfleet Haven must have been straightened and embanked and a new gowt (pointed sea doors) constructed for the Great Eau. These works resulted in rapid accretion in the shelter of the Haven, and a new dune line formed from Rimac House, Saltfleetby, to Oliver's Gap at Theddlethorpe, totally enclosing a strip salting which became brackish and now forms an important part of the Saltfleetby–Theddlethorpe Dunes National Nature Reserve.

North Coates Fitties of about 450 acres was reclaimed in 1856 and created the new headland of North Coates Point. The big fitty bayment at the head of which was Grainthorpe Haven was reclaimed in 1858 to produce the 446-acre Grainthorpe and Marsh Chapel Outmarsh enclosure.[30] Finally, about 1863, the 125-acre strip of the New East Marsh or Thimbleby's Enclosure was taken in.[31] Between 1883 and 1885 erosion of the boulder clay cliff at Cleethorpes was halted by the erection of the promenade; this was extended south to create the Kingsway in 1903–06, and to the outfall pumping station in 1912. In 1928–29 the Marine Embankment was extended south to join Anthony's Bank enclosing the 120 acres of Buck Beck Fitties.[32] In 1941 Grimsby Rural District Council reclaimed a small area between Anthony's Bank and the Humberston dunes.

### SEDIMENTS: SOURCE AND SUPPLY

There are vast quantities of sand and mud sediments on the north–east Lincolnshire coast and it is now generally accepted that beach material derived from the erosion of Holderness is the main source.[33] It would seem that some is also derived from offshore sources. Much of the present beach material may be fossil in the sense that it is glacial material from Holderness or offshore, including outwash sands and gravels, which has been resorted and redistributed by marine action. Some shingle consisting of glacially derived stones does occur sporadically southwards from Donna Nook, but not in a way to suggest a connection with the growth of Spurn. Nor does there seem to be any connection between the cyclical development of Spurn[34] and the periods of reclamation activity on the north–east Lincolnshire coast.

The tremendous thickness of deposits now forms a wide plateau-like beach at about 10 feet O.D. between North Coates Point and Theddlethorpe. There is 40 to 50 feet thickness of sand and silt, averaging 4,500 feet wide with a gradient of 1 in 2,750. Towards Cleethorpes and Mablethorpe the deposits decrease in width, height and thickness. The forebeach averages 1,200 feet in width with a gradient of 1 in 95; on this steep slope are ridges and runnels, the pattern of which is distorted by the outfalls of Tetney, Grainthorpe and Saltfleet Havens. The ridges have a seaward slope of about 1 in 33, variations in which can be shown to be related to sand grain size.[35]

Longshore drift will transport material along the Holderness coast to Spurn and A. H. W. Robinson has shown how the ebb/flood channel currents in the Humber estuary are responsible for transfer of material to the Lincolnshire side.[36] His calculations of residual currents, together with an analysis of tidal streams by the writer, clearly show an overall movement in that direction and would help to account for the movement of some material from offshore sources. This bears out the ideas put forward by Barnes and King.[37] The form of Clee Ness Sand, Haile Sand Flat and the Rosse Spit, as shown on Admiralty charts of 1890 and 1950, is also related to the ebb/flood tidal pattern.

Once emplaced on the foreshore, deposits would be subject to wave action. Aerial photographs of the beach taken at low tide show a distinct 'ness' north of Donna Nook. That longshore drift operates to the north–west of this is clearly shown by the westerly diversions of the outfalls of Grainthorpe and Tetney Havens. Until the early 1950s Tetney Haven reached low-water mark alongside the Haile Sand Fort and its boom. It changed course to flow through the boom, which was removed in 1966, and the outfall is now about a quarter of a mile north–west of the fort. South from Donna 'ness' the longshore drift is in that direction and is shown by the trend of channels from the shallow drainage basins on the plateau beach and the southerly diversion of the outfall of Saltfleet Haven.

From the thirteenth century there would be a plentiful supply of sand for the foreshore, and beach ridges would develop to maintain an equilibrium gradient on the beach.[38] This would probably result in a continuing shoreward movement of material which would constantly replenish the part of the foreshore where saltmakers collected their salty silt. It would also lead to the general heightening and thickening of material to its present form, although it is not clear when this stage was reached.

By the seventeenth century there would have been a zone of fitties or saltings up to a mile or more wide at North Coates and North Somercotes, and narrowing to north–west and south. Successive reclamations produced bayments occupied by Grainthorpe and Tetney Havens where sheltered conditions would induce deposition of mud. It may be that the reclamation limits of Donna Nook–Stonebridge and Horse Shoe Point, with very limited blown sand or salting accretion in front since the seventeenth century, indicate a decline of sediment supply over the last two centuries.

## SOME PRESENT-DAY FORESHORE FEATURES

Except where extensive beds of Marsh Samphire and clumps of Cord-grass (which have become more widespread in the last 15 years) occur on mud in the drainage basins of the main beach off Pye's Hall and Skidbrooke, the main vegetational development is at the back of the foreshore. At Humberston dune ridges which built up in front of

Anthony's Bank had reached their present seaward limit by about 1830. But, because of erosion by the sea and by human feet in the last 20 years, in 1962–64 a wire and slag sea wall was constructed. Subsequent scouring at the toe of this allowed slag and other rubble to fall out of the wire framework onto the beach. Erosion can be attributed to the shift in the outfall of Tetney Haven and to the increased holiday pressures on a short vulnerable stretch of dunes.[39] Between Pye's Hall and Donna Nook blown sand accumulated against the sea banks is now well colonised by Sea Buckthorn and the dunes have encroached round the old lifeboat house, abandoned about 40 years ago.

The large bayments of Tetney and Grainthorpe Fitties, of about 300 acres each, and south of Saltfleet Haven show the succession from the slobland state to mature marsh with Sea Lavender, Sea Aster, Sea Purslane and Sharp Couch-grass and an intricate creek drainage system. Their rate of growth outwards has been accelerated in the last 20 years by the appearance of Cord-grass as a direct result of extensive plantings on a four-mile stretch of the north Humber foreshore from Skeffling to Kilnsea between 1948 and 1954.[40] To repair the banks after the 1953 storm flood borrow pits were excavated in the saltmarsh and they rapidly went through the succession from slobland to mature marsh.

Between Thimbleby's Enclosure and Saltfleet Haven are the Knobs, a series of overlapping dune and salting systems which have developed over the last century. Each dune would appear to have been built on a high spring tide beach ridge or a minor storm beach. A further fringing salting is developing with Marsh Samphire and Seablite both here and at Saltfleetby, the outer edges of which have accumulated blown sand and are being colonised by Sea Couch-grass.

## CONCLUSION

The rise in sea level since Roman times led to the destruction of the offshore barrier of glacial drift islets but this has been compensated for by the deposition of vast quantities of sedimentary material. The rate of deposition has been greater than the rate of sinking, as is shown by the rate of outward growth of the coast together with the effective reclamation of saltmarshes. It has meant, however, that the lowest land is about four miles inland. The ings and fen are now about seven to nine feet O.D., compared with marshes reclaimed in the seventeenth century at 10 to 11 feet O.D., developing fitties at about 10 to 12 feet O.D. and the plateau beach at about 10 feet O.D. It would seem that the coastline is now basically stable with the rise of sea level being balanced by the rate of accretion.

## ACKNOWLEDGMENT

This paper is based on an unpublished M.Sc. thesis by the writer (University of Nottingham, 1956), for which research was carried out with the help of a grant from the Nature Conservancy.

NOTES

1 E. CHILDERS, *The riddle of the sands* (1903) (Penguin, 1952) 108.

2 H. H. SWINNERTON, The physical history of east Lincolnshire, *Trans. Lincs. Nats. Union* 9, 2 (1936) 100.

3 A. STRAW, The glacial sequence in Lincolnshire, *East Midland Geographer* 9 (1958) 29–40.

4 P. K. PARKINSON, A geographical study of the 22-foot shoreline in east Lincolnshire, *Unpublished final degree dissertation* (University of Liverpool, 1958).

5 H. H. SWINNERTON, Post-glacial deposits of the Lincolnshire coast, *Quart. Journ. Geol. Soc.* (1931) 360.

6 W. G. HOSKINS, *The making of the English landscape* (Hodder & Stoughton, London, 1955) 63.

7 D. M. WILLIAMSON, Some notes of the medieval manors of Fulstow, *Lincs. Architect. & Archaeol. Soc. Rep. & Papers* 4, 1 (1951) 42.

8 D. M. WILLIAMSON, *op. cit.,* 30.

9 Fulstow 26, North Thoresby and Autby 25, Tetney 13, Covenham 7, Grainthorpe 6, Fotherby and Thorganby 4, Little Grimsby 1.

10 A. E. B. OWEN, The early history of Saltfleet Haven, *Lincs. Architect. & Archaeol. Soc. Rep. & Papers* 5, 2 (1954) 87–100.

11 A. E. B. OWEN, Coastal erosion in east Lincolnshire, *Lincs. Historian* 9 (1952) 330.

12 C. REID, The geology of Holderness and the adjoining parts of Yorkshire and Lincolnshire, *Mem. Geol. Survey* (1885) 111.

13 *Rotuli Hundredorum* 13 (Edw. I) 276, 298, and 381.

14 Recent borings of shotholes for seismic work have confirmed the former outfall of the Withern Eau as a channel in the clays under the sand. Similar work also appears to have confirmed the former Wilgrip or Theddlethorpe Haven which existed into the eighteenth century: A. E. B. OWEN, Wilgrip Haven and Theddlethorpe, *Lincs. Historian* 2, 3 (1955–56) 37–41.

15 G. R. WALSHAW, An ancient Lincolnshire map, *Lincs. Mag.* 2, 7 (1935) 196–206.

16 Fitties: an old Norse word for outmarshes between the sea bank and the sea (G. R. WALSHAW, *op. cit.,* 198); salt pastures of the foreshore (A. E. KIRKBY, *Humberstone: the story of a village* (1953) 172).

17 E. H. RUDKIN and D. M. OWEN, The medieval salt industry in the Lindsey marshland, *Lincs. Architect. & Archaeol. Soc. Rep. & Papers* 8, new series (1960) 76–84.

18 *Holinshed's Chronicle* iv (1577) (1807 ed.) 255.

19 *Cf.* A. R. BRIDBURY, *England and the salt trade* (Oxford, 1955) 10–11.

20 Endymion Porter: D. TOWNSHEND, *The life and letters of Endymion Porter* (London, 1897) 161; G. HUXLEY, *Endymion Porter: the life of a courtier 1587–1649*, 211; G. G. WALKER, Mr. Endymion Porter and Porter's Marsh in North Somercotes, *Tales of a Lincolnshire antiquary* (Morton, Horncastle, 1949) 34.

21 P. SMITH, *The story of Claribel* (Lincoln, 1965) 30.

22 Lincs. Archives Office, Emeris Papers 29/1.

23 Lincs. Archives Office, Holywell Deeds 93.1.

24 14 Geo. III cap. 33; see also J. WILD, *A history of Tetney, Lincolnshire* (1901) 74.

25 Tetney Enclosure Award 1779; remains of part of bank exposed in 1953 borrow pit.

26 For a fuller account with specifications see: P. SMITH, *op. cit.,* 32.

27 A. J. JUKES-BROWNE, The geology of east Lincolnshire, *Mem. Geol. Survey* (1887) 112.

28 *Lincoln, Rutland and Stamford Mercury* (10th May 1799). The inn had a dining room to seat 100 people, bathing machines and a warm bath.

29 *Lincoln, Rutland and Stamford Mercury* (22nd March 1822).

30 Second Annual Enclosure Act 1855, confirmed by Grainthorpe and Marsh Chapel Outmarsh Enclosure Award 1858; 303 acres in Marsh Chapel and 142 acres in Grainthorpe (also known as Wragholme New Enclosure).

31 Unsubstantiated reclamation dates are based on notes by R. H. Adams, lately Engineer to the Louth Drainage Board.

32 F. BAKER, *The story of Cleethorpes* (Cleethorpes, 1953) 146–152.

³³ For fuller discussion see: T. SHEPPARD, *Lost towns of the Yorkshire coast* (Brown, London, 1912) 239–251; C. KIDSON, Movement of beach materials on the East Coast of England, *East Midland Geographer* 16 (1961) 6–7; A. H. W. ROBINSON, The inshore waters, sediment supply and coastal changes of part of Lincolnshire, *East Midland Geographer* 22 (1964) 316–318; and *ibid.,* The use of the sea bed drifter in coastal studies with particular reference to the Humber, *Zeitschrift für Geomorphologie* 7 (1968) 13–16.

³⁴ G. DE BOER, Spurn Point and its predecessors, *The Naturalist* (October–December 1963) 113–120; and *ibid.,* Spurn Head: its history and evolution, *Trans. Inst. Br. Geogr.* 34 (1964) 71–89.

³⁵ At Cleethorpes the median grain size is 0.185 millimetres on a slope of 1 in 55 and at Donna Nook the size is 0.22 millimetres on a slope of 1 in 32. A. H. W. ROBINSON, *op. cit.* (1968) 14–15, has shown that there is a general decrease in grain size between Donna Nook and Grimsby and links this with the transport of sediment towards the inner estuary where mud flats occur.

³⁶ A. H. W. ROBINSON, *op. cit.* (1964) 317; (1968) 12–13.

³⁷ F. A. BARNES and C. A. M. KING, The Lincolnshire coast and the 1953 storm flood, *Geography* 181 (1953) 157.

³⁸ C. A. M. KING and W. W. WILLIAMSON, The formation and movement of sand bars by wave action, *Geog. Journ.* 113 (1949) 83; and C. A. M. KING, *Beaches and coasts* (Arnold, London, 1959) 343–347.

³⁹ For full discussion see: D. N. ROBINSON, *Report on Humberston Fitties* (Lincolnshire Branch, Council for the Preservation of Rural England, December 1966).

⁴⁰ Undertaken by the then Hull and East Yorkshire River Board. At Buck Beck outfall Cord-grass has spread from a few clumps to an extensive meadow in the last 20 years.

# THE LOCATION OF THE BRITISH HOSIERY INDUSTRY SINCE THE MIDDLE OF THE NINETEENTH CENTURY

## D. M. SMITH

### INTRODUCTION

The hosiery industry, or the manufacture of knitted goods, is one of Britain's three major textile trades. National employment is at present about 128,000, with 76,000 of this in the East Midlands, compared with 155,000 in the woollen and worsted industry (110,000 in the West Riding) and roughly 150,000 in the spinning and weaving of cotton and man-made fibres (108,000 in the North–west).[1] Yet, with the exception of two papers,[2] the hosiery industry has been largely neglected in geographical literature, and its treatment in the text books is generally quite inadequate. This paper considers the development of the pattern of plant location as the factory system gradually replaced domestic production, from the middle of the nineteenth century onwards. The approach is largely descriptive, and the attempt to explain the process of change is confined to an informal interpretation within a framework of neo-classical location theory.

For more than 200 years the bulk of the British hosiery industry has been concentrated in the counties of Derbyshire, Leicestershire and Nottinghamshire. The industry's origin in Calverton, near Nottingham, and its subsequent growth in the East Midlands, under a domestic system of production, is well documented,[3] and only summary comments are necessary here. By the early nineteenth century the framework knitting industry was widespread throughout the area bounded roughly by Matlock, Mansfield and Southwell in the north and Hinckley and Lutterworth in the south. Much of the capacity was concentrated in Nottingham and Leicester and in the secondary centres of Derby, Mansfield, Sutton-in-Ashfield and Hinckley, but there were hardly any towns or villages of consequence without a few stocking frames. By the 1840s, when the domestic system reached its maximum extent, there were almost 50,000 machines in Britain, 90 per cent of them in the East Midlands, and the employment provided directly or indirectly must have exceeded 100,000.[4]

At the middle of the nineteenth century power-driven machinery was an isolated novelty in the hosiery industry. Steam-powered factories were operating successfully in Germany in the 1830s; the first in Britain was opened in Loughborough in 1839, and others soon followed in Leicester, Nottingham and Hinckley. At first the powered machines were capable of producing only the cheaper goods, but in 1864 William Cotton patented a machine on which finer work could be produced. This removed the last technical obstacle to the replacement of the domestic system by power-driven factories, but it was the beginning of the present century before the transition had been completed.

### PLANT LOCATION IN THE FACTORY HOSIERY INDUSTRY, 1864–1936

The reconstruction of early patterns of plant location is a difficult matter, because of the inadequacy of contemporary sources of data. The account which follows is based largely on information from *Kelly's*

*Directories,* whose listings of 'manufacturers' provide the only basis for detailed comparisons from year to year. But before proceeding it is necessary to make some important reservations about the reliability of this source. The focus of attention in this study is the location of hosiery factories, in the sense of buildings containing predominantly power-driven machinery, and the term manufacturer as used in the directories does not always refer to this kind of operation. During the early years of factory production the entrepreneurs of the domestic system, with their warehouses in the main cities, might be referred to as manufacturers, and this term could also be applied to operators of workshops with hand stocking-frames. This means that figures relating to the number of manufacturers will, in the early years, tend to overestimate the total number of power-driven factories and exaggerate the proportion in Nottingham and Leicester (the main warehousing centres under the domestic system). In addition, the directories make no distinction between different manu-facturers in terms of production, capacity, employment and so on. However, when these problems are taken into account the directories appear to provide a reasonably accurate indication of general location trends under the factory system, as confirmed by other documentary and statistical sources. The location of hosiery manufacturers at four selected dates is illustrated in Figure 1.

The erection of power-driven factories was at first confined to the larger towns. The immediate effect of the coming of the factory system was thus to increase the spatial concentration of production. Figure 1 shows that in 1864 the great majority of manufacturers were in Nottingham and Leicester, with half a dozen smaller towns accounting for practically all the rest. The two major cities contained about three-quarters of all manufacturers, and even if these figures included a substantial number who did not operate powered factories it represents a much higher degree of concentration of production than the 22 per cent of the capacity of the domestic industry that these cities contained in 1844. The outer edge of the hosiery-manufacturing region under the domestic system, as defined in 1844, emphasises the very considerable areas which the factory system had not reached.

This initial localisation of factory production was the result of basic changes in the cost structure of the industry when compared with domestic production. Under the domestic system the manufacture of hosiery was labour-intensive, and the high degree of dispersal of framework knitting was largely a response to the need to seek out cheap labour wherever it could be found, in conditions where capital equipment was fairly mobile. Under the factory system capital was substituted for labour, and the main organising centres under the domestic system, where the entrepreneurs already had their warehouses, must have seemed more secure as locations for major new investment than the country villages in which most of their domestic manufacturing capacity was located. Nottingham and Leicester also had good transport facilities, providing easy access to coal for the new factories as well as to raw materials. In addition these cities were the main centres for the finishing and marketing sections of the trade, and their banks and existing businesses made them the major regional sources of capital.

The concentration of factories in so few places created pressure on the local supply of labour. But reduced costs enabled the factory employers in the towns to offer relatively high wages in order to attract the workers

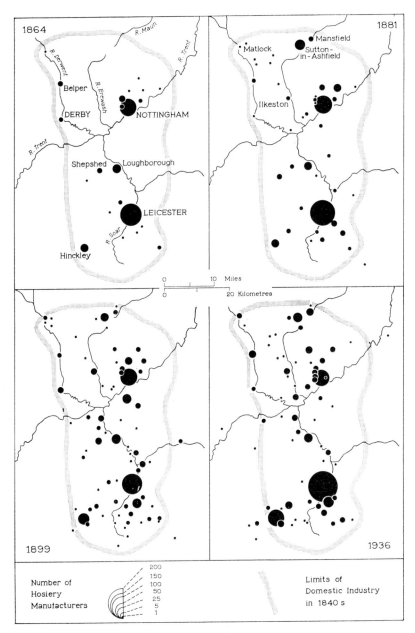

FIGURE 1

The location of hosiery manufacturers in the East Midlands, 1864–1936

The interpretation of these maps as indicative of changes in the location of the factory
hosiery industry is subject to the reservations made in the text

*Source: Kelly's Directories*

they needed: in 1860 one of the leading Nottingham manufacturers was paying an average of about 29s. a week for men and 17s. for women,[5] whereas earnings in the domestic industry were not half as much and in some cases not a third of this.[6]

By the beginning of the 1880s the distribution of the factory hosiery industry was still dominated by the two major cities, with Sutton-in-Ashfield, Hinckley and Loughborough as important secondary centres (Figure 1). But a significant change had taken place since 1864, with a considerable increase in the number of manufacturers recorded in the areas outside Nottingham and Leicester. Between 1864 and 1881 the proportion of all manufacturers accounted for by these two cities fell from 77 to 62 per cent, and the number in the rest of the three counties increased from 54 to 126.

During the 1880s this tendency for the dispersal of factory production gathered strength. In Nottingham and Leicester the development of other industries, in particular engineering, lace and footwear, was steadily increasing competition for labour, and wage-conscious trade unions were becoming active in the hosiery industry. In the country areas outside the two cities, however, and in particular in the villages where competition from the factories was destroying the domestic system, labour was unorganised, partially unemployed, and willing to accept wages well below union rates. Although country labour was somewhat less efficient than the city factory workers, wage rates might be between 30 and 50 per cent lower than those maintained in the towns by the unions, making possible a saving in manufacturing costs of quite 25 per cent.[7] Significant differences in labour costs could exist between places quite close together; for example, in 1888 it was reported that manufacturers would send work to Earl Shilton rather than Hinckley, four miles away, where labour was more expensive.[8] So spatial variations in labour costs became the critical factor in plant location, and more manufacturers went out into the villages looking for pockets of cheap labour, just as their counterparts under the domestic system had done during the eighteenth and early nineteenth centuries.

The effect of the dispersal of factory production during the last two decades of the nineteenth century is indicated in Figure 1. Between 1881 and 1899 the number of places recording hosiery manufacturers increased from 44 to 78, and the proportion of manufacturers in the two major cities dropped from 62 to 42 per cent. Although it is difficult to judge how far these figures accurately reflect the distribution of power-driven factories, it is clear that a fundamental change in comparative advantage had taken place as between 'core' (city) and 'peripheral' (county) locations.

The dispersal of factory production after the initial phase of concentration brought a tendency for the distribution of factories to resemble more closely the distribution pattern which prevailed under the domestic system. With only seven exceptions, all places with manufacturers (factories) in 1899 had had at least 60 stocking frames in 1844, and with only one exception all places with 350 or more frames had at least one manufacturer. The product-moment correlation coefficient between the number of stocking frames in 1844 and the number of manufacturers had reached 0.925 by 1899. Thus a domestic industry with 60 or more machines can almost be regarded as a necessary condition for the location of a hosiery factory during the second half of the nineteenth century, and 350 machines or more was virtually a necessary and sufficient condition for the establishment of at least one factory. This empirical generalisation is perfectly reasonable on *a priori* grounds, for the setting up of a factory required a certain minimum potential labour force, and in many cases the act of erecting a hosiery factory simply represented the manufacturer gathering together under one roof the people who worked for him under the domestic system. It is unfortunate that lack of information on factory employment or size of plant prevents a more rigorous exploration of the hypothesis that the local magnitude of the factory hosiery industry could be accurately predicted by the size of the original domestic industry.

The beginning of the present century is a convenient time at which to assess the overall impact of the transition from domestic to factory production on the location of the East Midlands hosiery industry. The relationship between the distribution of framework knitting at the middle of the nineteenth century and the extent to which the factory industry had spread across the region just prior to the First World War is illustrated in Figure 2. By 1912 all the framework knitting centres with 500 or more machines in 1844 had attracted manufacturers (i.e. factories), as had almost two-thirds of those with 100 to 500 machines. However, less than one in six of the places with one to 100 machines had recorded a manufacturer. The importance of participation in the hosiery industry under the domestic system as a pre-condition for the location of a factory is further emphasised by the fact that only 11 of the 104 places which had recorded a manufacturer by 1912 had had no stocking frames in 1844.

The distribution of symbols showing no manufacturer in Figure 2 suggests that certain areas were avoided by the factory industry despite their importance under the domestic system. This can be explained largely by the local development of other industries, which competed with hosiery for labour and, to a lesser extent, other factors of production. The Derbyshire coalfield, with its growing mining and metal industries, had developed few hosiery factories by the beginning of the present century, and Figure 2 shows a distinct concentration of places there with more than 100 stocking frames but no manufacturer. To the south the rise of the lace industry and its dispersal westwards from Nottingham appears to have kept hosiery factories out of most of the villages between Nottingham and Derby. There are a number of open symbols in the Leicestershire coalfield (Figure 2), and elsewhere in the county the failure of the factory system to develop to the extent which might have been expected can be explained by the growth of the footwear industry, which competed very actively for labour in some of the framework-knitting villages.

The maps in Figures 1 and 2 emphasise that very few factories were set up outside the traditional limits of the hosiery manufacturing district, as established under the domestic system. These limits appear to have acted as an important spatial constraint on the extent to which dispersal of factory production was possible. Evidence in support of this is provided in Figure 2, which shows that of the 40 places with manufacturers recorded at some date before 1912, but not in 1912 (which can generally be interpreted as factory closures), most occupied spatially marginal locations close to, or beyond the edge of, the traditional hosiery district.

By the First World War the transition from the domestic system to factory production had been virtually completed, and the subsequent location of the hosiery industry can be dealt with very briefly. There was a considerable increase in the number of manufacturers recorded, as the industry expanded to meet steadily increasing demand, and the proportion in Nottingham and Leicester indicates some reduction in the degree of dispersal since the end of the nineteenth century. However, the general pattern of plant location in the 1930s differed little from that observed in 1899 (Figure 1). Recent years have seen a few more firms leave the traditional hosiery district in search of female labour in the northern part of the Derbyshire–Nottinghamshire coalfield and in some of the market towns to the east, but the concentration of production in and around Nottingham and Leicester has continued. Even today the general form of the East Midlands hosiery manufacturing district is remarkably faithful to that imposed by the organisation of the domestic system in the late-eighteenth and early-nineteenth centuries.

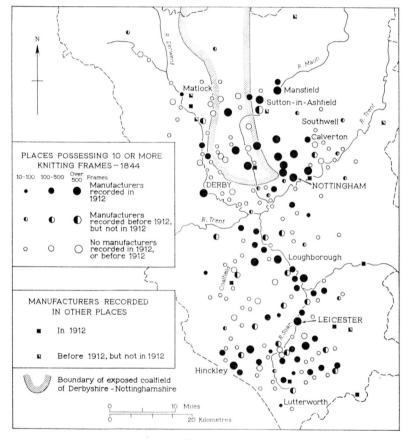

FIGURE 2

The relationship between the location of the domestic hosiery industry in 1844 and the development of the factory system up to 1912

*Sources:* The number of stocking frames in 1844 is based on: *Report of the commissioner appointed to enquire into the condition of the framework knitters, British Parliamentary Papers* XV (1845) Appendix, Part II; the presence of a factory is based on lists of hosiery manufacturers in *Kelly's Directories* (1864, 1876, 1881, 1891, 1899 and 1912)

## The Location of Hosiery Manufacturing at the National Level

In the 1840s, under the domestic system, 96 per cent of the capacity of the hosiery industry in England and Wales was in the East Midlands.[9] The development of the factory system did little to alter this regional concentration, and the census employment returns indicate very little change until 1891. This impression is supported by information from the returns of the Factory Inspectors relating to establishments liable to scrutiny under the Factory Acts: in 1890 only 13 of the 243 factories for which returns were made were outside the three counties, which contained 95 per cent of all factory employment.[10]

Since the early part of the present century, however, there has been a tendency for the East Midlands' share of the industry to be reduced, and the region now accounts for only about two-thirds of employment in England and Wales. The main factor in this national dispersal of production, as at the regional level, appears to have been labour costs. Between the wars the absence of national negotiating machinery for wage rates within the hosiery industry permitted the existence of large variations from place to place in labour costs;[11] in Lancashire wages in the hosiery trade are reported to have been two-thirds of what were paid in the East Midlands and in some cases only half, and this made it possible to undercut the East Midlands in some of the cheaper lines.[12] The presence of cheap mill buildings vacated by the cotton industry has helped to attract hosiery firms to the North–west, where employment is now almost 10,000. Availability of labour has also assisted the growth of the hosiery industry in some coastal towns. Expansion in and around London has raised employment in the South–east region to over 10,000, and in Scotland, which has had its own hosiery industry since well before the Industrial Revolution, employment has risen to more than 20,000.

## Towards an Explanatory Model

The student of industrial location aspires to the explanation of his observations in a rigorous scientific manner. Ideally, he would like to test his hypotheses by using location theory to generate a mathematical model capable of replicating his observations within acceptable margins of error. But in historical inquiry the quality of numerical data is seldom good enough to support this kind of approach. All that is possible in the present study is an informal development of the kind of model which, if it could be applied operationally, might well provide a basis for the explanation of the location of hosiery manufacturing since the middle of the nineteenth century.

Classical location theory, with its roots in the work of Alfred Weber, proposes that areal variations in the cost of inputs will give rise to an optimum location, which will be occupied by the profit-maximising entrepreneur. A modification of classical theory which is gradually gaining acceptance proposes that total cost and total revenue interact to produce spatial margins to profitability, within which firms can achieve viability in any location; inside the margin the precise pattern of plant location can be determined by random variables as well as by strictly economic factors.[13] This provides a convenient conceptual framework within which to interpret the location of the hosiery industry.

Under the domestic system labour costs favoured the dispersal of production, but the need to get materials from, and take the finished product to, the central warehouses imposed strict limits on how far away the industry could operate successfully.[14] The outer edge of the framework-knitting district shown on the maps in Figure 1 can be interpreted as the approximate position of the spatial margin at the middle of the nineteenth century. The introduction of the factory system was accompanied by a contraction of the margin, which for most firms was drawn tightly round the main towns until the 1870s. In Nottingham and Leicester various external economies acted as cost-reducing factors, which greatly outweighed any labour-cost advantages in the country areas. But during the last two decades of the century spatial labour-cost differentials became much more significant, while at the same time competition for factors of production and the general improvement of communications were lessening the cost advantages of a city location. The spatial margin was thus extended to include most of the former framework-knitting district, though in some areas the rise of other industries was a limiting factor. The approximate position of the margin at the beginning of the present century can be inferred from Figure 2. There have subsequently been occasional short-run contractions of the margin, for example during the first decade of this century, but the general historical tendency has been towards greater freedom of locational choice at both a regional and national level.

The general form adopted by the location pattern of the hosiery industry can thus be interpreted as a response to fluctuations in the position of the spatial margins to profitability, as determined by the geography of input costs. Within the margin the magnitude of the factory industry was partially determined by the size of the labour force inherited from the domestic industry, subject in some places to erosion from other activities, and partly by other economic factors such as transportation. But it is also important to recognise a random element in the selection of some villages for factories, and also in the timing and direction of the dispersal of the factory industry. For example, the early establishment of factories at some locations can probably be attributed to local enterprise, some firms and some places waited longer than others before going over to factory production, and some employers preferred to concentrate their capacity, while others spread theirs out.

The dispersal of factory production in the hosiery industry can in some respects be viewed as the diffusion of an innovation. Certain places at certain times were receptive to the idea, while others were not. Within the spatial limits imposed by the general geography of production costs, the probability of any place receiving a factory was a function of many variables, with the actual pattern of plant site selection subject to the operation of chance within this spatial probability framework. This discussion has thus arrived at a tentative model which combines variable-cost location theory with a stochastic model of the Monte Carlo type. It is unfortunate that the lack of suitable empirical data prevents the formal development and testing of this model in the hosiery industry.

## NOTES

1 Figures based on Department of Employment and Productivity estimates of insured employees for June 1968.

2 E. M. RAWSTRON, Some aspects of the location of hosiery and lace manufacture in Great Britain, *East Midland Geographer* 2, No. 9 (1958) 16–28; D. M. SMITH, The British hosiery industry at the middle of the nineteenth century: an historical study in economic geography, *Trans. Inst. Br. Geogr.* 32 (1963) 125–142.

3 For details, and references to the primary contemporary sources, see: F. A. WELLS, *The British hosiery trade* (Allen and Unwin, London, 1935); also D. M. SMITH, *The industrial archaeology of the East Midlands* (David & Charles, Newton Abbot, 1965) Chapter 2.

4 The geography of hosiery manufacturing at the height of the domestic system is described in some detail in: D. M. SMITH, *op. cit.* (1963).

5 *Report of the inspectors of factories for the half year ending on the 31st October 1860, British Parliamentary Papers* XXII (1861) 47.

6 *Report from the select committee on the stoppage of wages in the hosiery manufacture, British Parliamentary Papers* XIV (1854–55) 17; see also F. A. WELLS, *op. cit.* (1935) 148–149.

7 F. A. WELLS, *op. cit.* (1935) 195.

8 A. J. PICKERING, *The cradle and home of the hosiery trade 1640–1940* (Pickering, Hinckley, 1940) 114.

9 In 1844 the counties of Derbyshire, Leicestershire and Nottinghamshire contained 43,890 of the 45,612 stocking frames in England and Wales; in addition there were 2,605 in Scotland and 265 in Ireland (D. M. SMITH, *op. cit.* (1963) 126).

10 *Return of the number of factories authorised to be inspected under the Factories and Workshops Acts, British Parliamentary Papers* LXVII (1890).

11 *Board of Trade working party report: hosiery* (H.M.S.O., London, 1946) 100–101.

12 See: H. A. SILVERMAN, *Studies in industrial organisation* (Methuen, London, 1946) 11; and M. P. FOGARTY, *Prospects of the industrial areas of Great Britain* (Methuen, London, 1945) 303.

13 This concept was suggested in: E. M. RAWSTRON, Three principles of industrial location, *Trans. Inst. Br. Geogr.* 27 (1958) 135–142. It has been subsequently extended in: D. M. SMITH, A theoretical framework for geographical studies of industrial location, *Economic geography* 42 (1966) 95–113; and is featured in: H. W. RICHARDSON, *Regional economics* (Weidenfeld and Nicholson, London, 1969) 59–69.

14 There were also other local factors restricting dispersal in certain directions; see D. M. SMITH, *op. cit.* (1963) 136.

# THE EREWASH VALLEY INTERMEDIATE AREA

## J. M. SMITH

In September 1967 the government appointed Sir Joseph Hunt as chairman of a committee to investigate the situation in areas of the country where the rate of economic growth gave cause for concern. The committee's report concluded that no part of the East Midlands needed assistance.[1] Nevertheless, two so-called Intermediate Areas were subsequently designated by the government—the upper Erewash valley and the Worksop district (the latter to be considered as part of a Yorkshire Coalfield Intermediate Area). The designated Erewash Valley Intermediate Area (Figure 1) may be largely identified with that part of the exposed Derbyshire–Nottinghamshire coalfield lying south of the catchment of the River Rother. However, the upper Erewash in fact drains less than half the designated area, which also extends down the Doe Lea valley and includes the central part of the Amber valley and the headwaters of the Maun, Meden and Leen.

For a decade after nationalisation, in 1947, 25 collieries in the Erewash Valley Intermediate Area employed about 27,000 men to produce about 12 million tons annually,[2] usually at a profit of several shillings per ton.[3] (It may thus be argued that during this period the Erewash valley collieries were indirectly helping to delay closures in the uneconomic coalfields of the Development Areas.) Overproduction of coal in relation to a falling demand caused manpower reductions to begin in 1958, but up to 1965 New Langley was the only colliery to close. With so many collieries still at work, transfers of men to surviving collieries was no great problem. In 1965, when four collieries round Alfreton closed, the Derbyshire Branch of the National Union of Mineworkers brought together the local authorities situated between Ilkeston and Clay Cross and representatives of other bodies to form a *Colliery Closure Liaison Committee* to discuss common action to counter the effects of closures. This organisation was renamed the *Erewash Area Development Association* in 1969, its membership having expanded to include representatives of adjacent parts of Nottinghamshire.

### CONTROL OF INDUSTRY

The efforts of the Colliery Closures Liaison Committee were chiefly aimed at achieving a more liberal approach by the government departments controlling distribution of industry policy. About 1947 the Board of Trade had encouraged the establishment of light industries to employ females[4] and there had been little difficulty regarding the extension and rebuilding of existing factories, the largest of which were processing locally-produced minerals. On the other hand, the introduction of male-employing firms from other parts of Britain had been consistently opposed by the government. Moreover, during the period of prosperity in coal mining such firms had avoided the area because labour was scarce and most of the undeveloped land liable to subsidence. When the collieries closed, the number of enquiries from male-employing firms increased, but government policy remained unchanged because unemployment remained low and it was hoped that miners would move to the remaining collieries. Throughout the

80

period of closures the National Coal Board has sought to retain skilled workers in the industry and some have moved to homes nearer those collieries where production is expanding. The long-established outward movement of population from the area was thus accentuated by an outflow of displaced miners and their families. The prosperity of the newly-introduced light industries in which the miners' families were employed had by 1965 used up the immediately available female labour, and the loss of the miners accentuated the problems of female recruitment. The Board of Trade, therefore, began to oppose industrial building which would entail more female employment.

The strength of the government controls, as well as the level of industrial incentives in the Development Areas, was increased just as the economic crisis developed in the Erewash valley. In 1965 the East Midlands and other more prosperous parts of Britain became subject to a reduction in the maximum industrial floor space which could be erected without an Industrial Development Certificate. The limit was dropped from 5,000 to 1,000 square feet, and then raised to 3,000 square feet in 1966. Also in 1966 office development permits became necessary for office buildings in excess of 3,000 square feet, this figure being raised to 10,000 square feet in 1967. These additional controls necessitated an increase in the volume of applications handled by the Board of Trade and complaints of delays increased. Very few applications in the Erewash valley were in fact refused, though many were probably discouraged and others were granted after pressure by the local authorities.

DESIGNATION

The Hunt Committee received evidence from a large number of local authorities on the coalfields. The East Midlands Economic Planning Council and the Nottinghamshire and Derbyshire County Councils agreed that, within their respective areas, the Erewash valley was in greatest need of immediate assistance. The Committee considered that the prospects of the Nottinghamshire–Derbyshire coalfield were not sufficiently serious to justify coupling it with the Yorkshire coalfield, for which they recommended assistance, but suggested that the position should be closely watched as the mining run-down continued.[5] Had the Committee's recommendations been adopted, the area would have been even less likely to receive new industry than in the past, because the Yorkshire coalfield now due to receive assistance 20 miles to the north might well have attracted existing firms from the Erewash valley.

In announcing the designation of the Intermediate Areas on 25th June 1969 (the date from which most grants will operate) the government modified the Hunt Committee's recommendations (which, in any case, were not unanimous) regarding the benefits which would apply. No changes in the industrial development certificate or office development permit procedures were proposed, but the Intermediate Areas would get the same priority as Development Areas in the issue of these certificates. New industrial developments in the Intermediate Areas would qualify for 25 per cent building grants if sufficient new jobs were created. Training grants, help with the transfer of key workers, government-built factories and assistance with road-development schemes, on the same basis as in the Development Areas, were also promised. It was expected that the proposals would cost about £20 million annually, the money to be obtained by a

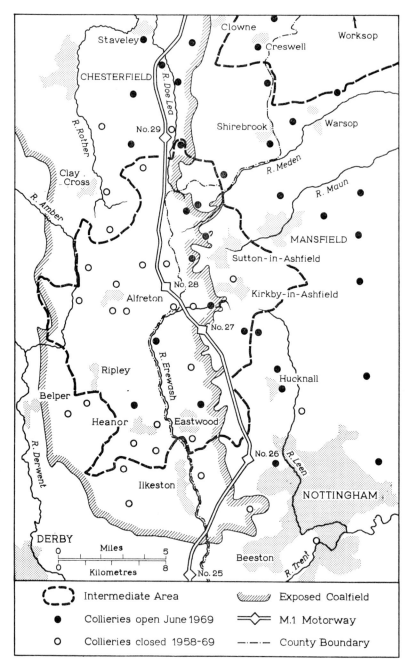

FIGURE 1

Intermediate Areas on the Nottinghamshire-Derbyshire coalfield

reduction in aid to Development Areas. The Development Areas, which have been receiving some £260 million[6] annually on incentives to industry alone, will clearly retain a substantial advantage, however. In addition to the specific proposals for the Intermediate Areas, the government proposed to increase, from 50 per cent to 75 per cent, the grant payable to local authorities in coalfield areas for losses sustained in reclaiming derelict land. The whole of the Nottinghamshire–Derbyshire Sub-region should benefit. The Local Employment Act to give legislative effect to the proposals was passed early in 1970.

### BOUNDARIES OF THE INTERMEDIATE AREA

In Figure 1 the limits of the designated Intermediate Area for the Erewash valley are shown in relation to county boundaries, the M.1 motorway, the exposed coalfield, and collieries, both active and closed. The area of 103 square miles is largely situated on the exposed coalfield but extends a short distance eastwards on to the concealed field. The M.1 motorway enters the area just north of junction 26 (A.610) at Nuthall and leaves it a little south of junction 29 (A.617) at Heath. Junction 28, at Pinxton, between Alfreton and Sutton-in-Ashfield on A.615, is of major importance to the area, being the point where the Derby–Sheffield trunk road, A.61, is linked to the M.1 by a dual carriageway opened in 1969. Junction 27, at Annesley on A.608, gives a useful link to Kirkby-in-Ashfield and Langley Mill.

The boundary excludes the Ilkeston and Belper areas, which contain parts of the exposed coalfield where five collieries were closed between 1960 and 1968. Inclusion of these areas would have brought the financial assistance as far as the suburbs of Nottingham and Derby. Although representations were made on behalf of Ilkeston, owing to the town's high degree of dependence on employment at Stanton Ironworks, the trends of employ-ment and unemployment showed such areas near Nottingham and Derby to be sharing in the prosperity of these larger neighbours. Two collieries (Clifton and Bestwood) in the Nottingham suburbs closed in 1967–68, but without noticeable effect on local unemployment.

To the north of the designated area there are 14 collieries still at work in Derbyshire, all but five of them on the exposed coalfield. Four collieries, all located in the short gap between the designated area and Clay Cross, closed between 1962 and 1968. The Derbyshire County Council, in its evidence to the Hunt Committee,[7] suggested that because unemployment had been high (average 4.1 per cent for seven years) in the Clay Cross area it should be included with the Erewash valley for priority treatment, while the whole of the rest of the coalfield in north–east Derbyshire should be given Intermediate Area status to enable prompt assistance to be given as further closures took place. The government did not accept that there was a case for designation at present, regarding the major towns of Chesterfield and Mansfield as sufficiently prosperous to sustain the local economy. Unemployment in the Chesterfield 'travel-to-work area' (the Employment Exchange Areas of Clay Cross, Eckington and Staveley, as well as Chesterfield itself) has been about three per cent in recent years. It seems probable that as collieries close unemployment will rise to a level where the government will be unable to resist local pressures to designate the whole Chesterfield area as Intermediate, thus linking together the designated areas of the Erewash Valley and the Yorkshire Coalfield.

The use of employment exchange areas to define the limits of areas eligible for assistance arises from the availability of employment and unemployment statistics, which enable monthly checks on variations in labour activity to be made. There will inevitably be complaints of unfair treatment from local authorities and industrial concerns just beyond the boundary. The Hunt Committee considered many similar cases in relation to the towns peripheral to the Development Areas. Round the Erewash Valley Intermediate Area the towns of Belper, Ilkeston, Mansfield, Chesterfield and Clay Cross may expect that some industries which might otherwise have taken sites will be attracted by the grants now to be available only a few miles away. Staveley, where the Urban District Council has provided industrial sites, is particularly badly placed between the two designated areas of the Erewash Valley and the Yorkshire Coalfield.

The boundary of the designated area follows County District and parish boundaries, except to the west of Ripley, where the boundary is that of the former civil parish, which disappeared when new ward boundaries were defined. The use of parish boundaries to delimit the area causes local problems. At Denby Hall, south of Ripley, and Holmewood, in the north–west, the boundary runs through colliery land where there are proposals for industrial development. In each case the colliery canteen and baths buildings, which are readily convertible to industrial use, lie a few yards outside the designated area. Nevertheless, the absence of building grants for extensions and other benefits has not discouraged firms from negotiating for these buildings since June 1969.

### POPULATION

The population changes for the various local government units since 1951 are summarised in Table I. Static or slightly declining population in the Derbyshire part of the Intermediate Area and in Sutton-in-Ashfield suggests a considerable outward movement of population, in view of the fact that they have a high rate of natural increase. Accurate figures for the 10 Rural District parishes are not available, and must be estimated by

TABLE I

Population of Erewash Valley Intermediate Area, 1951–68

|  | 1951 Census | 1961 Census | 1968 Estimate |
|---|---|---|---|
| Alfreton Urban District .. .. | 23,385 | 22,999 | 22,600 |
| Ripley Urban District (part) .. .. | 13,159 | 12,960 | 13,000 |
| Heanor Urban District .. .. | 24,406 | 23,870 | 24,390 |
| Ten parishes in Rural Districts .. .. | 30,078 | 30,562 | 30,680 |
| Sub-total, Derbyshire .. .. .. | 91,028 | 90,391 | 90,670 |
| Sutton-in-Ashfield Urban District .. | 40,518 | 40,441 | 40,740 |
| Kirkby-in-Ashfield Urban District .. | 20,133 | 21,686 | 22,440 |
| Eastwood Urban District .. .. | 9,894 | 10,607 | 11,450 |
| Five parishes of Basford Rural District .. | 17,289 | 18,154 | 20,159 |
| Sub-total, Nottinghamshire .. .. | 87,834 | 90,888 | 94,789 |
| TOTAL, Intermediate Area .. .. | 178,862 | 181,271 | 185,549 |

*Source of 1968 Estimates:* Registrar General's Mid-year Estimates, with calculations based on these for individual parishes, prepared by the County Planning Officers for Nottinghamshire and Derbyshire

reference to total change for the parent Rural Districts. The combined net movement of population from both Urban Districts and rural parishes must have been about 11,000 over the 17 years, 1951–68. On the other hand, the Nottinghamshire Urban Districts of Eastwood and Kirkby-in-Ashfield and the adjacent parishes of Basford Rural District recorded a marked increase of population, amounting to 6,733, or 16 per cent, in the 17 years. Net inward migration of about 2,500 persons is suggested by this increase. Eastwood is only eight miles from the centre of Nottingham and has proved popular as a residential area for workers in the city.

### INDUSTRIAL STRUCTURE

Table II shows statistically how rapid a change has taken place in the economy of the Erewash valley and also indicates how far there is to go before the elimination of coal mining is completed. One of the problems which must have faced the Hunt Committee's assessors was to obtain objective statistical data for areas such as this where the position changes month by month. Almost all the statistics quoted in the Hunt Committee's report relate to dates before the White Paper on Fuel Policy,[8] which led to an acceleration in colliery closures during 1968. In their report the Hunt Committee quoted 1966 statistics which indicated that 40 per cent of the males on the Nottinghamshire side of the Erewash valley were employed in coal mining, compared with about a quarter on the Derbyshire side.[9] In 1959 the figures were over half in both cases, while by about 1972 the Derbyshire figure may well be negligible and the Nottinghamshire one under a quarter.

The figures in Table II related to 1959 and 1968. By April 1969, the 11 surviving collieries employed about 13,000, compared with the 30,376 men in mining and quarrying in 1959 and 18,721 in 1968. Several of the collieries still at work were reducing their labour forces or had been officially described as 'in jeopardy'. During the period covered by the figures in Table II the Erewash valley mining industry declined rather less than the industry did nationally. The effect of the loss of basic male employment at this rate might have been expected to be catastrophic. The chief reasons why unemployment has been kept as low as four per cent have been the changes in movements to work and the ability of local manufacturing industries to employ very considerable additional numbers.

The movements to work were recorded in the spring of 1968,[10] by which time the labour force in the mines had been reduced by over 10,000 in a decade. It is, therefore, surprising to find that there was a net influx of miners into the area, amounting to 1,800, or 11 per cent of the total employed. This was attributable mainly to miners living in places to the south and west, where mining had ceased, but the Sutton-in-Ashfield area drew considerable numbers from the adjacent town of Mansfield. The movement of miners living in the Erewash valley to Nottinghamshire collieries further east was relatively small in scale, though the National Coal Board organised a fleet of small buses to make the journeys easy. It seems probable that after a short period of travelling the miners either left the industry or moved to houses near their new collieries.

The manufacturing industries in the Erewash valley are chiefly based on the iron industry, still represented by foundries and engineering works, and the hosiery industry, which has a very long history in this area. The increase in male employment in manufacturing was shared by these older industries and by a variety of others, often represented by a single dominant works or company, such as the metal-box company in the Sutton-in-Ashfield area and the timber-building concern at Langley Mill. Identification of firms new to the area, as opposed to those redeveloping within it, is difficult, owing to changes of ownership, but it appears that no more than 500 of the 6,035 additional male jobs in manufacturing in the 1959–68 period can be attributed to new concerns.

TABLE II

Changes in employment, 1959–68

Erewash Valley Intermediate Area

(Alfreton, Heanor and Sutton-in-Ashfield Employment Exchange Areas)

(A)  Numbers

| Industry group | 1959 Numbers | | 1968 Numbers | | 1959–68 Change | |
|---|---|---|---|---|---|---|
| | Males | Females | Males | Females | Males | Females |
| Agriculture and forestry | 489 | 62 | 289 | 38 | − 200 | − 24 |
| Mining and quarrying | 30,376 | 671 | 18,721 | 266 | − 11,655 | − 405 |
| Manufacturing .. | 10,249 | 9,377 | 16,284 | 13,552 | + 6,035 | + 4,175 |
| Services .. .. | 13,196 | 6,565 | 12,274 | 8,324 | − 922 | + 1,759 |
| Total insured employees | 54,310 | 16,675 | 47,568 | 22,180 | − 6,732 | + 5,495 |
| Of which unemployed | 970 | 350 | 1,820 | 190 | + 850 | − 160 |

(B)  Percentages

| Industry group | Erewash Valley | | Change | Great Britain | | Change |
|---|---|---|---|---|---|---|
| | 1959 | 1968 | 1959–68 | 1959 | 1968 | 1959–68 |
| Agriculture and forestry | 0.8 | 0.5 | −40.7 | 3.0 | 1.8 | −35.6 |
| Mining and quarrying | 43.8 | 27.2 | −38.9 | 3.9 | 2.2 | −41.5 |
| Manufacturing .. | 27.6 | 42.8 | +57.1 | 38.6 | 38.0 | + 3.6 |
| Services .. .. | 27.8 | 29.5 | + 4.2 | 54.6 | 58.0 | +11.5 |
| Males .. .. | 76.5 | 68.2 | −12.4 | 67.0 | 64.5 | + 0.5 |
| Females .. .. | 23.5 | 31.8 | +32.9 | 33.0 | 35.5 | +11.7 |
| Unemployed .. | 1.9 | 2.9 | +52.3 | 2.2 | 2.4 | +10.0 |

*Sources:* Department of Employment and Productivity, Employment Record II; and Employment and Productivity Gazette

*Note:* The above statistics include those registered as unemployed in the industry group in which they were last employed

In view of the complaints of labour shortage from existing firms, which led to stricter controls, it is surprising to find that female employment in factories grew by one-third between 1959 and 1968. Textiles, particularly hosiery, accounted for more than half the expansion, but the clothing industry recorded a higher proportionate increase. Part of this increase may, however, be attributable to more use of part-time workers. Comparison with national statistics shows that in 1959 the area was heavily deficient in female employment and despite rapid changes there was still a lack of balance in the male/female ratio in 1968. Female activity rates, particularly in the colliery villages, are still much lower than in the established textile towns, so that if suitable industries are attracted even more women may enter employment.

In the Erewash valley unemployment percentages remained low (generally below two per cent) until September 1968, when there was an increase to the present levels (Alfreton 6.6, Heanor 2.9 and Sutton-in-Ashfield 3.4 per cent). It is surprising that the loss of 3,200 male jobs in the Alfreton area in the nine months after September 1968 caused no greater increase. Of the 2,823 total unemployed in October 1969, 2,599 were adult males. There were more vacancies than unemployed in respect of women and juveniles.

### GROWTH POTENTIAL

Coal-mining activity has delayed the implementation of post-war plans for urban growth in the west Nottinghamshire and Alfreton areas put forward by the two County Councils. With the decline of mining there is now scope for diversification and growth. During 1969 both the East Midlands Economic Planning Council[11] and the Sub-Regional Planning Unit put forward strategies of expansion for the area between Alfreton and Mansfield. The Sub-Regional Study[12] has suggested an inward movement of 42,000 people and 30,000 jobs, mainly from Nottingham and Derby, between 1966 and 1986. The local authorities have bought land for industrial development and the two County Councils have jointly appointed an Industrial Development Officer to give publicity to their respective areas. In terms of accessibility it may be noted that the Erewash valley is nearer than any other area receiving government assistance to the prosperous South–east and Midlands. Within this new context the co-operation of local authorities, central government and nationalised and private industries can thus be expected to bring a rapid return to prosperity, as a prelude to the growth of employment and population envisaged in the Sub-Regional Study.

*Note:* In Statutory Instrument 308/70, relating to the Local Employment Act of 1970, the official title now given to the area is "Notts/Derby Coalfield Intermediate Area".

### ACKNOWLEDGMENT

The author wishes to thank the County Planning Officer for Derbyshire and the County Director of Planning for Nottinghamshire for their assistance in the preparation of this article.

### NOTES

1 *The Intermediate Areas: Report of a Committee under the Chairmanship of Sir Joseph Hunt,* Cmnd. 3998 (H.M.S.O., 1969).

2 *Colliery Yearbook and Coal Trades Directory,* various years.

3 K. C. EDWARDS, East Midlands coal production, *East Midland Geographer* 1, No. 6 (1956) 26–35.

4 W. F. LUTTRELL, *Factory location and industrial movement* (1962) Chs. 16 and 17.

5 *Hunt Report,* paras. 230–231, p. 68.

6 *Ibid.,* para. 98, p. 36.

7 DERBYSHIRE COUNTY COUNCIL, *Evidence to the Hunt Committee on the problems of the Intermediate Areas* (1968) 9.

8 *Fuel policy,* Cmnd. 3438 (H.M.S.O., 1967).

9 *Hunt Report,* para. 226, p. 67.

10 DERBYSHIRE COUNTY COUNCIL, *Miners' journey to work* (1968).

11 EAST MIDLANDS ECONOMIC PLANNING COUNCIL, *Opportunity in the East Midlands* (H.M.S.O., 1969) 11.

12 NOTTINGHAMSHIRE AND DERBYSHIRE SUB-REGIONAL PLANNING UNIT, *Nottinghamshire and Derbyshire sub-regional study* (1969) 108, Table 5.

# THE SPIRIT OF PLACE:
# D. H. LAWRENCE AND THE EAST MIDLANDS

L. SPOLTON

This contribution is a transparent attempt at reductionism. It aims to examine only a very small part of the work of D. H. Lawrence. To extract only one aspect and analyse it in isolation may be doing a disservice to the unity in which Lawrence so fervently believed. Nevertheless, this facet, small as it may appear when viewed against Lawrence's contribution as a whole, is not insignificant in its impact.

## DEVELOPMENT OF THE GEOGRAPHICAL APPROACH

*Geographical Feeling*

Kenneth Young, who has had the task of compressing an appreciation of Lawrence into the small compass of the *Writers and their work* series, writes:

> Re-reading them [his novels] today one is most forcibly struck by the page after page of magical description of nature, the sense of place, the atmosphere of the non-human world, whether it be a recreation . . . . . of the hills and dales of his native Nottinghamshire, the very air and breadth of Western Australia, or the brilliant, tortured earth of sun-baked New Mexico . . . . . Whatever his arrogances and erratic statements on other subjects . . . . . here Lawrence is the submissive instrument transmitting the purest essence of the external world.[1]

While one could take exception to the choice of the adjective 'magical' as having the wrong connotation for what is a marvellously acute observation of the environment and its subsequent portrayal in word pictures, the tone of this quotation echoes the feeling this article attempts to impart.

The spirit of place is not an original choice for a title. Richard Aldington used it, once as the title of a prose anthology of Lawrence's work, and, again, as a subsection of a series of Lawrence's essays. But he was only consciously echoing Lawrence, who uses the phrase more than once—most notably as the title of an essay which introduces *Studies in classic American literature*. Here he writes, introducing a tone of determinism which will be mentioned again later:

> But the spirit of place is a great reality. The Nile Valley produced not only the corn but the terrific religions of Egypt. China produces the Chinese and will go on doing so. The Chinese in San Francisco will in time cease to be Chinese.[2]

Lawrence is sometimes categorised as a regional novelist but again this is only half a truth. It is said he once expressed the wish to write a novel for every continent. Even in 1926, in *Return to Bestwood*, he could write:

> I came home to the Midlands for a few days at the end of September. Not that there is any home, for my parents are dead. But there are my sisters and the district one calls home, that mining district between Nottingham and Derby.[3]

Certainly the East Midlands was his 'home'; but he often felt more at home elsewhere. Wherever his wanderings took him geographically he used the landscape for the background of his writing. Schorer remarks:

> There is probably no other writer in literary history whose works responded so immediately to his geographical environment.[4]

So much so, in fact, that one critic supposes:

It would be easy to make the mistake of referring the development of Lawrence's ideas to his geographical migrations—to describe *Kangaroo* as inspired by Australia, *The Plumed Serpent* by Mexico and so forth. The fact is that it often worked the other way. Lawrence moves to a new country because he is developing new ideas, and needs a landscape to match them.[5]

But this can be disputed, for it pre-supposes a kind of geographical forecasting. What is certain is that many places quickly became like home to him. The essay *Flowery Tuscany*,[6] which, if it were not so much more, could be described as a phenological-ecological calendar, shows he knew the rhythm of the Tuscan seasons as well as those of his native Eastwood.

## Geographical Training

It would be comical to call Lawrence a geographer, yet he is in a class of his own at describing the essence of a place: at perceiving and recording areal differentiation. A reading of chapter four of *D. H. Lawrence: a personal record*,[7] entitled 'Literary formation', indicates the fatuousness of saying too much about his formal educational background. Nevertheless, his acquaintance with geography as a subject can be noted. At Nottingham High School his report lists eight subjects in Form One (1898) and several subjects in Form Five (1900), but geography is absent on both occasions. That he taught geography as a pupil teacher there can be little doubt. He brings a fragment of a lesson into *Mr. Noon* when Emmie visits her sister at the school house at Eakrast. Eakrast is a thin disguise for Eakring, where Lawrence visited a friend in August 1911 and wrote a typical card to Louie Burrows epitomising Eakring in a phrase:

It's such a quaint place Eakring . . . . . red houses among trees like apples in foliage. The school house is attached to the school.[8]

Referring to Eakrast, Lawrence writes:

The school and the school house were one building. In the front the long school-room faced the road: at the back, the house premises and garden looked to the fields and distant forest.

Emmie could hear Harold, on the other side of the wall, talking away at the scholars.

"Now then Salt what river comes next? Withan, [*sic*] Welland, Nen and Great Ouse—what comes after that?"

Emily guessed it was geography; therefore probably near the end of the afternoon.[9]

Obviously Lawrence was aware of capes-and-bays geography. In his teacher's certificate, taken at the College in Shakespeare Street, Nottingham, he obtained a distinction in geography. To Louise Burrows in October 1908 he wrote: 'I have distinctions in French, Botany, Maths and History and Geography: never anything in English—is it not a joke?'[10]

The teachers in training in the Department of Education followed courses in physical and local geography given by Dr. H. H. Swinnerton. Originally trained as a zoologist, he became lecturer in natural science in 1902, and, from 1910, Professor of Geology. In a letter Lawrence drafted in French, probably for Louie Burrows to send to a pen friend, he wrote:

Tous les samedis nous avons des assemblées du 'Students Associations.' Nous nous rencontrons à sept heures du soir . . . . . Demain il y a un 'Lecture on Prehistoric Man' par Dr. Swinnerton.[11]

In 1910 Dr. Swinnerton brought out the volume on Nottinghamshire in the *Cambridge County Geography* series. Though this was written to fit a country-wide pattern, it shows the emphasis in the geography of the time.

The chapters follow what would now be considered a routine geographical pattern, though sections on natural history; people—origin, race and population; history of the county; and antiquities would now be thought unusual. The Trent, Clifton Grove, the Hemlock Stone, the Bunter Sandstone outcrop, all figure there and were likely to be in the course. Nor would local geography stop at the county boundary. Extension into Derbyshire and Lincolnshire would include Crich and the Derwent Valley, the Lincoln Gap and the coast at Mablethorpe.

Lawrence continued his training with some attendance at in-service courses. In his first year of teaching at Croydon he wrote to Louie Burrows (March 1909):

> I am just going down town to a lecture by some pot or other on Arithmetic—
> I guess I shall be bored—we had a lecture on Geography last week by Dr.
> Herbertson—a very great gun from Oxford and he bored me excruciatingly.
> I liked Margaret von Wyss on Nature Study very much.[12]

The comment on Herbertson is not an example of Lawrence's harshness. O. G. S. Crawford, when a demonstrator under Herbertson in 1910–11, wrote of him, 'as a tutor he was excellent, but as a lecturer he was uninspiring at best, and at times far worse'.[13]

*Field Experiences*

Lawrence was fond of organising excursions. On Good Friday 1907 he wrote to Louie Burrows:

> Dear Louie,
> If this wonderful weather holds we shall have a delightful day on Monday ..... we will skip off for Alfreton. Thence we go across the Park and about four miles on to Wingfield. There I suppose we shall eat dinner and after a time proceed on to Crich ..... we shall leave Ambergate by the 7.45 ..... [14]

This excursion and a shorter walk to the Hemlock Stone form an important part of the chapter 'Lad and girl love' in *Sons and Lovers*. Twenty-five years later the Geology and Geography Department at University College, Nottingham, had an excursion map showing geological outcrops along the very route from Alfreton to Crich. Was it extant in Lawrence's time? These walks may have been made before in earlier years when it is said that Lawrence was not the prime mover, but fresh insights could have arisen from his training. Certainly he was always a keen walker. From Croydon he wrote on 18th September 1910: 'I go out all Saturday—walk 15 or 20 miles.'[15] Later he walked across the Alps several times. The 'geography through the soles of one's boots' cliché applied to Lawrence. Jessie Chambers tells how an outing with Lawrence was a memorable experience:

> ..... he persuaded mother to let us go on a day trip to Skegness ..... He knew all the land marks on the way ..... We had to rush to the carriage window to observe the graceful lines of Gedling Church spire rising sheer out of the valley. Further on there was Bottesford Church ..... and we tried to discern the outline of Belvoir Castle standing high on its ridge. At Boston we craned our necks to catch a glimpse of the famous Stump dominating the fens with its sombre dignity. But it was more than merely *seeing* these landmarks: it was a kind of immediate possession ..... [16]

*Geographical Thinking*

Lawrence was not teaching geography at the school in Davidson Road, Croydon, but did specialise in nature study and art apart from teaching general subjects. Examination of his letters during the Croydon years shows how progressive a teacher he was. Geography at the school was under the care of his friend McLeod, to whom he was to write some most vivid letters. Lawrence's geographical insight, as well as something of McLeod's teaching method, is well shown by a postcard he wrote to McLeod from Prestatyn, North Wales, in July 1911:

Very pretty place—face N.W. Gt. Orme a faint smudge crouching down; W., Snowdon; S.W., a big faint smudge . . . . . ; a three tone study: extremely geographic: reminds me of your plasticene relief map.

The hills jump up a mile from the sea—coast plain flat—shore sandy, blue with sea holly. The tide goes out far off—leaves streaks of water.[17]

In the interval between College and his first teaching post Lawrence was expressing thoughts which are quite remarkable from the point of view of environmental determinism. In a letter to Louie Burrows dated 2nd September 1908 he wrote:

We began to cut the corn on Monday. The crop is thin and wretched: the knife cottered and clogged vilely; it rained; I am sure Hell is a cold wet place; they invented the fiery business somewhere in Arabia, by the bright Sahara's sunny strand; my hell has a north–east wind and rain varying from drizzle to pelting sleet.[18]

Freeman, writing of geography in the early twentieth century, says: 'Environmental influence goes far beyond physical effects, and one of Miss Semple's most famous passages is on Hell, where the Jews expected to be permanently fried and the Eskimo permanently frozen.'[19] However, Miss Semple's work, *Influences of Geographical Environment,* was not published until 1911. The book is based on Ratzel's system of anthropogeography but there is no evidence that Lawrence had read Ratzel, a work written in very difficult German. Nevertheless, Lawrence was widely read in cognate areas. Jessie Chambers, in the chapter dealing with his reading, records:

The materialist philosophy came in full blast with T. H. Huxley's *Man's Place in Nature,* Darwin's *Origin of Species* and Haeckel's *Riddle of the Universe.* This rationalistic teaching impressed Lawrence deeply.[20]

Haeckel was the originator of the term 'ecology' in 1876, and defines it as 'the correlations between all organisms living together in one and the same locality and their adaptation to their surroundings.'[21] For Lawrence this idea applied to the human world. His first novel *The White Peacock* in two of its three main elements shows a close integration of Folk, Work and Place.

The four strands at the base of Lawrence's geographical awareness which this article has tried to document are some geographical training, a close personal observation of natural phenomena, knowledge from wide reading and a powerful insight and imagination. With this background in mind it is now appropriate to consider his writings on the East Midlands from a geographical viewpoint.

## THE GEOGRAPHICAL CONTENT

Five long novels are set wholly or largely in the area, as is one of the short novels. Two other novels contain some background. A number of short stories and some essays add interesting material.

### Rural beginnings

The first novel, *The White Peacock,* is set around Moorgreen Reservoir and integrates the Saxtons, a farming family, and the Tempests, a mine-owning family, both of which grow firmly out of the background with the

Beardsalls and their friends who have much more tenuous connections with the area and are much less real. The problem of farming light land over-run by rabbits is an important strand in the Saxton story. The actual mineworkers come into the novel only marginally. It deals mainly with a rather indeterminate class in society. Lawrence, at any rate later, was well aware of the barriers of Eastwood class. In *The Lost Girl* he explained the social structure:

> a vast sub-stratum of colliers, a thick sprinkling of tradespeople, . . . . . ; a higher layer of bank managers . . . . . and the managers of collieries: then the rich and sticky cherry of the local coal owner glistening over all.[22]

*The White Peacock* has been criticised for its unusual class structure and particularly for the artificiality of the occupationless Beardsalls. Sinzelle[23] has defended it against this accusation by referring to the material on the Lawrence circle in the years up to 1908, particularly the Jessie Chambers's memoir. This material shows a group of youngsters of working-class origin growing up as pupil-teachers with Lawrence, reading avidly and talking and discussing literature, art and poetry in a way not very dissimilar from that described in *The White Peacock*. With the growth of sociology it is common now to speak of modes of social ascent through education and to write of the problems of alienation from the working class as in *The Uses of Literacy*[24] or the work of Jackson and Marsden.[25] At a much earlier time than these works, Lawrence and his friends were striving to be different. *The White Peacock* idealises the process (for example, Mrs. Beardsall is called mater) but the germ of truth is there. This was a common factor of the social–human geography of west Nottinghamshire before the First World War.

The tale is set firmly in the march of the seasons described phenologically. Gadjusek,[26] in a paragraph of super-reduction, notes that 145 flowers, trees or shrubs are mentioned in the book. They are not mentioned; they are worked intimately into the round of the year in the Felley Mill valley to give a true regional description. A series of extracts could be chosen to set alongside the much later essay *Flowery Tuscany* as a contrast between that area and the Nottinghamshire valley. Lawrence began the story in his College days when his geographical horizons were limited. Felley Mill is a lovely area in its own right and Lawrence described it when close to his background. Later he became more critical. After less than a month in Croydon he wrote:

> Dear Lou,
>
> Now I've seen sweeter country than Quorn and Woodhouse . . . . . the sharp hills whose scarps are blazing with autumn, the round valleys where the vivid dregs of summer have collected . . . . .
>
> D.H.L.

Prosaically he added:

> I've come through Epsom to Dorking—am going on to Reigate.[27]

With longer experience in other regions his criticism increased. Notable in chapter six of *The White Peacock*, is an essay on September, a piece of fine writing. Lawrence was born in September and one can imagine in school he must have written on the topic of 'My favourite month'. This essay on September could well be a polishing of something written before. In it he extols the sun: 'only the clinging warmth of sunshine for a coat.' After many years in sunny lands Lawrence was back in Eastwood in September 1926, a year which had an excellent summer, and wrote: 'I cannot, cannot accept this thin luminous vaporousness which passes as a fine day in the land of my birth.'[28] To this extent *The White Peacock* gives an idealised picture, but the account is mainly an exact one.

*Urban realities*

Idealisation of the colliery area background is the criticism that has been levelled against *Sons and Lovers,* which deals with industry and urbanisation as well as the Felley fields and woods. Again Sinzelle has defended the accuracy of the portrayal by showing how the area has changed since Lawrence's time, 'when dirt was packed in the gob' and not turned up the pit to make a tip. Collieries were smaller and not excrescences on the countryside as the colliery along Engine Lane, which joins Eastwood to Moorgreen, is now.

*Sons and Lovers* was started in 1910. It began with an account of the development of Eastwood's urban pattern. When, in his essay *Nottingham and the Mining Country,* Lawrence returned to that theme after 20 years he only elaborated those first two pages; he did not alter his original approach. Only in the second part of the essay did he become critical. *Sons and Lovers* starts in *The White Peacock* country, includes the excursions to the Hemlock Stone and Crich already referred to with fine authentic detail, and soon extends to Nottingham and its region. Castle Rock is visited and, later, Wilford and Clifton. In the afternoon in Clifton Grove Lawrence is not too engrossed with the human action to forget the physical background. Erosion is made a necessary part of the episode. The Lincolnshire coast, especially Mablethorpe, is vividly described. Jessie Chambers, reading the manuscript in sections as it was written, believed it to be a true account and was shocked by Lawrence's later transpositions from reality to twist, as she regarded it, the facts. This again must have been helped by the authentic background. The walk from Felley Mill up the hill towards Annesley is a tiny example:

> They found at the top of the hill a hidden wild field, two sides of which were backed by the wood, the other sides by high loose hedges of hawthorns and elder-bushes . . . . . The field itself was coarse, and crowded with tall, big cowslips that had never been cut . . . . . One tiny space of light stood opposite at Crossleigh Bank Farm.[29]

This hidden field had still not altered after the Second World War, though now the M.1 motorway may have changed it. Throughout its length the novel has the complete stamp of topographical accuracy.

*The Rainbow,* begun in 1912, was finished in 1915. Much of the book was written while Lawrence was on the continent but its background is again west Nottinghamshire. In 1908, writing to Louie Burrows and criticising a short story she had written, Lawrence wrote: '. . . . . select some young fellow of your acquaintance as a type for a lover and think what he would probably do.' For *The Rainbow* and *Women in Love* (originally conceived as one novel, *The Sisters*) he selected the Burrows family, and used their house in Cossall to anchor the story. The details show Lawrence's vivid memory. In the introduction he shows the isolation of the Marsh Farm near Cossall alongside the river Erewash and the canal on the Nottinghamshire–Derbyshire border. Later the story moves to Church Cottage, Cossall, next to the 'old little church with its small spire on a square tower.' The Nottingham detail is also very clear and exact but, later in the story when the Brangwens move house to live in Willey Green (Moorgreen), which is given a grammar school, the background becomes more imaginative. Beldover also takes on an aspect more glamorous than the reality of Eastwood.

*Criticism of industrialism*

A vivid piece of writing on social geography in *The Rainbow* is the description of the new colliery village of Wiggiston. It had been a hamlet of 11 houses on the edge of heathy half-agricultural country:

Then the great seam of coal had been opened. In a year Wiggiston appeared, a great mass of pinkish rows of thin, unreal dwellings of five rooms each.[30]

Too long to quote in full, the whole description epitomises colliery villages of the period:

red brick confusion rapidly spreading, like a skin disease.

In the climax of his description,

there was no meeting place, no centre, no artery, no organic formation

can be heard the criticism of Eastwood in the final paragraphs of *Nottingham and the Mining Country* written 15 years later.

*Women in Love* starts in Willey Green and continually returns to *The White Peacock* region which is now glamorised excessively. Nethermere in *The White Peacock* is the reality whereas Willey Water in the chapter entitled 'Water-party' in *Women in Love* is some other romantic lake transformed from reality by a Venetian night's fantasy. Sometimes Lawrence catches the essence again, as in the description of Beldover (Eastwood) market in the chapter 'Coal dust', and in a flash in *Excurse,* where Ursula recognised to the right in a dip the form of Southwell Minster: ' "It looks like quartz crystals sticking up out of the dark hollow" said Birkin.' The chapter 'Industrial Magnate' is full of material useful in the social geography of colliery development but, generally, *Women in Love* is a different kind of novel which does not require an authentic background.

*The Lost Girl* tells of the class-structure in Eastwood and adds some material for the Hilltop area before the story moves away elsewhere. *Aaron's Rod* starts in Eastwood but remains there a very short time. *Lady Chatterley's Lover* is a return to the Nottinghamshire–Derbyshire border but the setting is further north, nearer to Chesterfield (Uthwaite) in the Shirebrook–Bolsover area. In the description of the journey by car through the industrial sprawl, Tevershall sounds remarkably like Eastwood: 'on a hilltop with the steep slope towards Derbyshire and the long slope towards Nottingham.'[31] But all the internal evidence situates Wragby further north. Lawrence knew the district well from his visits to the Dax family who lived in Shirebrook. In August 1911 he wrote from Shirebrook to Louie Burrows: 'Biked here—a Hell of a place—Mr. and Mrs. Dax very well.'[32] It could almost have been the original Wiggiston! In *Return to Bestwood* written in 1926 Lawrence describes how he went in his sister's motor-car to Hardwick:

Butterley, Alfreton, Tibshelf—what was once the Hardwick district is now the Notts.–Derby coal area. The country is the same but scarred and splashed all over with mines and mining settlements. Great houses loom from hill-brows, old villages are smothered in rows of miners' dwellings, Bolsover Castle rises from the mass of the colliery village of Bolsover—Böwser we called it, when I was a boy.[33]

Undoubtedly this was the area incorporated into *Lady Chatterley's Lover,* which was published in 1928. As another obvious response to geographical environment, Lawrence opposes the industrialisation in the valley to the park land on the Magnesian Limestone dip slope. Read in the expurgated edition, as this writer first read the story, this background becomes clearer, and the critical note more obvious: 'Ours is a tragic age . . . . . ; we are among the ruins.' The opening passage of the novel sets the scene.

SUMMARY

The short stories *The Shades of Spring, Daughters of the Vicar, The Sick Collier, The Odour of Chrysanthemums* and *Tickets Please* all add their quota of background. *Love Among the Haystacks* gives a wonderful picture of the fields leading down to Watnall from Greasley Church. But the five novels are of greatest importance. Together they trace the development of the area centred on Eastwood and extending to Ilkeston, Nottingham and Annesley through the first quarter of the twentieth century. In the 40 years since Lawrence's death changes have gone apace and, by 1969, the tips of Cossall which Lawrence once sketched framed with a rainbow[34] had been levelled, shaped, sown to grass and were being grazed by sheep. For an appreciation of the cultural landscape and social geography of the district there can be no better guide than Lawrence's writings: the beauty and the blight are both sensitively revealed.

ACKNOWLEDGMENT

Grateful acknowledgment is made to Laurence Pollinger Limited and the estate of the late Mrs. Frieda Lawrence for permission to quote extracts from *Lawrence in Love* (ed. J. T. Boulton) (University of Nottingham, 1968).

NOTES

[1] K. YOUNG, *D. H. Lawrence* (Longmans, Essex, 1969 edition) 4–5.
[2] D. H. LAWRENCE, *Studies in classic American literature* (Heinemann, London, 1924) 6.
[3] D. H. LAWRENCE, *Phoenix II* (Heinemann, London, 1968) 257.
[4] M. SCHORER, Lawrence and the spirit of place, *A D. H. Lawrence miscellany* (ed. H. T. Moore) (Heinemann, London, 1961) 282.
[5] G. HOUGH, *The Dark Sun* (Duckworth, London, 1956) 117.
[6] D. H. LAWRENCE, *Selected essays* (Penguin Books, 1950) 139–154.
[7] E.T. (Jessie Chambers), *D. H. Lawrence—a personal record* (Cass, London, 1935) 91–123.
[8] *Lawrence in love: letters to Louie Burrows* (ed. J. T. Boulton) (University of Nottingham, 1968) 127–128.
[9] D. H. LAWRENCE, *op. cit.* (1968) 170.
[10] J. T. BOULTON, *op. cit.*, 19.
[11] *Ibid.*, 174.
[12] *Ibid.*, 32.
[13] E. W. GILBERT, Andrew John Herbertson, *Geography* 229 (1965) 328.
[14] J. T. BOULTON, *op. cit.*, 5.
[15] *Ibid.*, 55.
[16] E.T. (Jessie Chambers), *op. cit.*, 38–39.
[17] *The letters of D. H. Lawrence* (ed. A. Huxley) (Heinemann, London, 1932) 9.
[18] J. T. BOULTON, *op. cit.*, 14.
[19] T. W. FREEMAN, *One hundred years of geography* (Duckworth, London, 1961) 79.
[20] E.T. (Jessie Chambers), *op. cit.* (1935) 112.
[21] T. W. FREEMAN, *op. cit.*, 174.
[22] D. H. LAWRENCE, *The Lost Girl* (1920) 1.

23 C. M. SINZELLE, *The geographical background of the early works of D. H. Lawrence* (Didier, Paris, 1964).

24 R. HOGGART, *The Uses of Literacy* (Chatto and Windus, London, 1957).

25 B. JACKSON and D. MARSDEN, *Education and the working class* (Routledge, London, 1962).

26 R. E. GAJDUSEK, A reading of 'The White Peacock', *A D. H. Lawrence miscellany* (ed. H. T. Moore) (Heinemann, London, 1961) 194.

27 J. T. BOULTON, *op. cit.,* 21–22.

28 D. H. LAWRENCE, *op. cit.* (1968) 258.

29 D. H. LAWRENCE, *Sons and Lovers* (Penguin Books, 1948) 290.

30 D. H. LAWRENCE, *The Rainbow* (Penguin Books, 1949) 345.

31 D. H. LAWRENCE, Nottingham and the mining country, *Selected essays* (Penguin Books, 1950) 115.

32 J. T. BOULTON, *op. cit.,* 128.

33 D. H. LAWRENCE, *op. cit.* (1968) 262.

34 See sketch in H. T. MOORE, *The Intelligent Heart* (Penguin Biography, 1960) 224.

# WIND-GAPS AND WATER-GAPS IN EASTERN ENGLAND

A. STRAW

INTRODUCTION

The Jurassic and Cretaceous cuestas of that part of England east of the vales of the Yorkshire Ouse and Trent comprise a series of asymmetrical ridges segmented by a number of irregularly-spaced gaps into discrete blocks of mainly limestone upland. The rocks of the cuestas and intervening vales alike were bent by Tertiary earth movements into broad folds, synclinal in the north, anticlinal in the south, pitching south–east. Relatively few minor folds and faults complicate the pattern, so that the rocks dip east or south–east at low angles, except in the north, where southerly dips prevail off the dome structures of the North York Moors.

The first serious consideration of the drainage pattern and the gaps was presented by W. M. Davis[1] in 1895, whose views were quickly extended by Buckman[2] and Cowper Reed.[3] These writers advanced what may be regarded as classic interpretations of drainage and cuesta development, but the distribution and character of the gaps and the inter-cuesta vales do not really conform to such simple models. These pioneers did, however, establish one general truth, namely that the history of the gaps is in essence the physiographic history of the whole of eastern England.

Early modifications to their views came from glacial geologists such as Harmer,[4] who ascribed the Lincoln and Ancaster gaps to erosion by overflow waters from ice-impounded lakes. In 1937, Swinnerton, whose long-standing interest in Lincolnshire had been expressed in a succession of papers, interpreted the county's gaps in terms of consequent river development following late Pliocene marine planation.[5] Versey,[6] however, working in Yorkshire, proposed a variation of Cowper Reed's theme, and later demonstrated that the Humber estuary coincided with a zone of tectonic disturbance.[7] In fact, structural control of several of the gaps has been suggested at one time or another, but is dismissed in this essay as of minor importance.

More recently, the possibility that marine planation was a critical factor in the development of both the hill summit surfaces of eastern England and the drainage pattern has received some support from work by Linton,[8] Clayton,[9] Straw,[10] and Lewin,[11] but, as a marine planation model in its simplest form is inadequate and unrealistic, some analysis and refinement is necessary, and it seems wise to proceed only from the following premises:

*(a)* the gaps have had different histories;
*(b)* they do not all necessarily date from a single period of consequent drainage development;
*(c)* drainage evolution has not followed a consistent sequence of events traditionally associated with cuesta development; and
*(d)* the only unassailable common attribute is that they breach escarpments of Jurassic or Cretaceous rocks.

In this short essay, a thorough description of all the gaps in turn is not possible, and a liberty is taken in presenting a retrospective view of the main events that have certainly modified them and perhaps even initiated

97

their development. Interested readers are invited to consult the relevant
Ordnance Survey maps, or better still to examine the features in the field.
Discussion, therefore, will devolve, perhaps more appropriately and
certainly more speculatively, on their evolution in space and time. The
Pleistocene terminology used is given in Table I.

TABLE I

Pleistocene terminology

| Epoch | Stage | Climatic episodes |
|---|---|---|
| Holocene | Flandrian | 'Post-glacial' |
| Pleistocene | Weichselian | Last Glaciation |
| | Ipswichian | Interglacial |
| | Saalian | Gipping (Penultimate) Glaciation |
| | Hoxnian | Interglacial |
| | Elsterian | Lowestoft (Ante-Penultimate) Glaciation |
| | Cromerian | Interglacial |

THE GLACIAL HISTORY OF THE GAPS

*Humber and Wash gaps*

Only the Humber and Wash gaps of the 10 under consideration (Figure
1) are penetrated by the sea, but their estuaries are of very different form
and occurrence. The Wash, the broader, lies across the Cretaceous rocks,
whilst the Humber transects the Jurassic as well, but both features have
extensive tracts of late Post-glacial alluvium along their flanks and at their
heads. Both gaps have had a long history, but, curiously, little of it can
be read from their morphology. The Humber, some four kilometres wide
within both the Chalk and the Oolites, is not flanked by terraces, and the
Chalk slopes bear the imprint only of late Pleistocene glaciation and
solifluction. The borders of the Wash are cliffed only at Hunstanton in
north–west Norfolk; elsewhere broad flats of saltmarsh and a few low
'Roman' banks separate it from a wide tract of reclaimed alluvium, and
the distance between the Lincolnshire and Norfolk Chalk is some 30
kilometres. Neither estuary has a strikingly over-deepened valley, though
Valentin has demonstrated a former more regular easterly course for the
Humber in pre-Weichselian times.[12] The regional significance of the gaps
lies in the fact that they attract most of the drainage of Yorkshire and the
East Midlands, and evidence points to there having been access to the
North Sea for Midland and Pennine waters across south and north Lincoln-
shire throughout the Pleistocene and perhaps much of late Tertiary time.

Both gaps were occupied by Weichsel ice (Figure 1), which at an early
stage impounded vast pro-glacial lakes in the Trent–Ouse vale and the Fen
basin, linked effectively through the Witham gap at Lincoln. Shoreline,
delta, and fluvial and glacifluvial terrace features confirm a maximum water
level at about 30 metres O.D. The disposition of the ice shows clearly that
the Humber and Wash gaps had acquired their present dimensions by the
onset of the Weichsel Glaciation, a fact which bears on their function as

major outlets for eastern drainage in Ipswichian times. The extreme width of the Wash gap may, however, be explained as a direct result of the Saale Glaciation, when North Sea ice streamed strongly through it to converge with central Lincolnshire ice in the Fen basin (Figure 1). By contrast, the Saale ice movement over most of Norfolk and the Lincolnshire Wolds was sluggish, which emphasizes the importance of the Wash gap as an enlarged ice-way through which the ice-sheet maintained sufficient momentum to reach into the south–western parts of East Anglia.

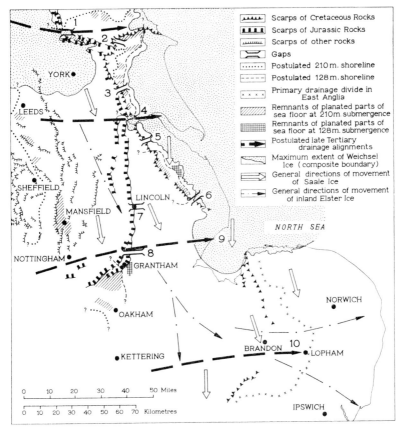

FIGURE 1

Some geomorphological and glacial features of eastern England
Wind- and water-gaps considered are:

| | | | |
|---|---|---|---|
| 1 | Coxwold–Gilling gap | 6 | Tetford gap |
| 2 | Winteringham gap | 7 | Lincoln gap |
| 3 | Market Weighton gap | 8 | Ancaster gap |
| 4 | Humber gap | 9 | Wash gap |
| 5 | Barnetby gap | 10 | Lopham gap |

*Coxwold–Gilling gap*

North of the Humber the east end of the Vale of Pickering was also plugged by Weichsel ice. Kendall's[13] classic interpretation concerning 'Lake Pickering' may now be judged too simple, for the glacial and

99

glacifluvial features around Scarborough and Filey record one or two major re-advances, and pro-glacial lakes existed at more than one dominant level and possibly at more than one distinct stage. At the western end of the Vale the Coxwold–Gilling gap through the Jurassic Howardian Hills had also reached its present width by the Weichsel Glaciation.

The modern outlet for the Vale of Pickering drainage, the Kirkham Abbey gorge, is a Weichsel feature in its entirety, and little more need here be said about it, except that current work suggests that its excavation was an early Weichsel event, possibly pre-dating the formation of both the York and Escrick moraines.

*Market Weighton and Wintringham gaps*

The Market Weighton gap across the southern Yorkshire Wolds provided temporary westward escape for Weichsel meltwaters which notched into a col at about 76 metres O.D. between the heads of what are now dry valleys.[14] The glacifluvially eroded section between the two dry valleys is short and no more than about 20 metres deep and 500 metres long. The col was part of a gap, other remnants of which form benches to the east, which in contrast to those already discussed was a dry high-level feature in the Ipswichian interglacial. One other broad high-level gap exists in the Yorkshire Wolds (Figure 1), some four kilometres south–east of Winteringham, with a col height of about 113 metres. It was not occupied by Weichsel ice and no meltwaters utilized it. The gap 'floor' is grossly dissected by dry-valleys, but remnants suggest a general level at 130 to 145 metres, at which height the gap was a mature feature over two kilometres wide through ground that rises well over 168 metres O.D. Some blown sand has been swept up into the head of the Winteringham valley and onto the col. Following Reed it can be regarded as a section of a former high-level westward extension of the Great Wold Valley, and is probably a feature of some antiquity.[15]

*Barnetby gap*

In the northern Lincolnshire Wolds, a breach some 13 kilometres south of the Humber transects the Chalk in an area of deceptively complex morphology and history. Much of the significance of this Barnetby gap pertains to its position west of a buried valley that Shillito called the Kirmington 'fiord'.[16] Shillito was impressed, as were later workers, by the form and alignment of this broad depression. Its floor descends to −73 metres beneath Immingham Dock and is at Ordnance Datum beneath Kirmington where there is about 30 metres of superficial deposits. The gap does not lie quite in line with the depression, and their proximity does not necessarily imply a causal relationship. Suggestions that both were produced by some stream from the west may be discarded on a number of grounds, and recent work points to the Kirmington depression as a glacial feature.[17] The gap carried some Weichsel meltwaters westward, for glacifluvial sands and gravels occupy its floor at 24 metres O.D. and fan out on the Kimmeridge Clay south of Brigg. Twidale claimed that Weichsel ice itself had entered the gap, producing its present morphology,[18] but the Weichsel limit is marked at Kirmington by weak terminal moraine and outwash features which flank the low residual mound of interglacial deposits. Glacial materials of Saale age are preserved on a Lower Kimmeridgian sandstone bench at 49 to 55 metres O.D. and on the spur which extends it westward on the north side of the gap.[19] Weichsel events modified the Barnetby gap relatively little, but its earlier history is more difficult to unravel. As the deposits on the bench and the Wrawby spur are relics of an outwash fan of chalky sands and gravels prograded from the east, it is implicit that a broad high-level gap existed here prior to the Saale Glaciation, during which most of Lincolnshire was overwhelmed by ice. The Kirmington interglacial deposits have a bearing on this problem, though their age is still undetermined in spite of recent attempts to apply palaeobotanical techniques.[20] The deposits are directly overlain by Weichsel till, and geomorphological evidence supports earlier views that an Ipswichian date is likely.[21] A Hoxnian correlation[22] for the deposits not only denies a Saale age for the Kirmington depression (probably the source of the Wrawby gravels) but creates great difficulty in accounting for the survival of these undisturbed unconsolidated sediments through the Saale Glaciation, when some 125 metres or more of strongly-flowing ice crossed the area, and surrounding tracts of Upper Chalk suffered considerable non-localized erosion.

*Lincoln and Ancaster gaps*

The Lincoln gap also participated in Weichsel events, for it was the sole link between pro-glacial 'Lake Humber' and 'Lake Fenland'. The Beeston terrace of the Trent passes through it,[23] but the rock floor is about −6 metres O.D.[24] The small dimensions of the Witham buried valley compared with that of the Humber can be taken as confirmation that the Trent was adding its waters to the Humber certainly by the end of the Ipswichian interglacial.

The Ancaster gap has no direct Weichsel glacial history. Floored only by Witham gravels of this date, its flanks carry blown sands and thin solifluction deposits. The rock floor was well above 'Lake Humber' level, but traces of a former higher floor at 55 to 67 metres O.D. carrying Saale till suggest, as at Barnetby, that a somewhat complex gap, this time transecting most of the Jurassic rocks, existed in pre-Saale times. Apart from the probability of some Saale glacial modification, the present gentle flanks owe much to Weichselian and Saalian cambering, a periglacially-induced phenomenon admirably displayed in the railway cutting east of Ancaster.

*Tetford and Lopham gaps*

The two remaining gaps both cross the Chalk. The south–eastern part of the Lincolnshire Wolds is severed from the remainder by the Tetford gap which was penetrated by a small lobe of Weichsel ice.[25] Meltwaters from the Wolds to the north later passed south–west through the gap into the valley of the River Lymn, and scored the Lower Cretaceous sandstone south of Tetford sufficiently to effect permanent diversion of the head of Calceby Beck to the Lymn. The breach in the Chalk again pre-dates the Weichsel Glaciation, but its existence in Saalian times is doubtful. The vale of the Lymn and its tributaries, like the Bain valley to the north,[26] was fluvially modified and somewhat widened in the Ipswichian interglacial, and the Tetford gap has every appearance of being produced by active scarp recession overtaking the branching head of a major backslope valley system. A similar event seems imminent with the Oxcombe valley to the north–west.

Near South Lopham, a few kilometres west of Diss in south Norfolk, the heads of the west-flowing Little Ouse and the east-flowing Waveney arise in a broad peaty tract occupying a shallow but distinct east–west depression. Overspill waters from 'Lake Fenland' coursed eastward toward lower ice-free areas in early Weichselian times, producing the slightly oversteepened character of the sides of this depression, and probably deposited valley-floor gravels along the upper Waveney which at present form a terrace with a surface slightly above the modern alluvium. This shallow depression is, however, merely the latest modification to a breach across the East Anglian Chalk that has an altogether longer history and greater significance. More readily appreciated on the map than in the field, it may be noted on Figure 1 that the main drainage divide curves east to cross the Lopham depression, and the subdued Chalk scarps of Norfolk and Suffolk tend to converge on the same point. Around Brandon the Breckland sands obscure a low-lying area of Chalk, the base of which is below Fen deposits west of Lakenheath. This latter circumstance, and the broad sag in the surface level of the East Anglian Chalk might be construed as evidence of local synclinal flexuring, but the relatively low level of the Chalk base on the Fen margin can equally well be ascribed to greater down-dip erosion of the Chalk than to the north or south–west, and a probable explanation for such erosion is not far to seek. Whereas ice in the Saale Glaciation moved in a generally north-to-south direction (Figure 1) over west Norfolk along the Cretaceous strike, eventually depositing sandy and chalky drifts in the Breckland region, in the preceding Elster Glaciation ice carried Jurassic Clay detritus from the southern Fen region east toward the North Sea. The distribution of Lowestoft Till[27] clearly confirms such a movement through the broad Lopham depression, whence the ice splayed out to reach the present coast between Scratby in the north and Aldeburgh in the south. Some scouring of the bedrock through the depression by Elster ice may fairly be surmised, accounting for localized eastward displacement of the base of the gently-inclined Chalk. A further observation is that the Elster ice most probably took advantage of an existing feature, which indicates a history for the depression extending back at least into the early Pleistocene.

The review so far has suggested that the gaps in East Anglia and Lincolnshire, except for that at Tetford, were present in some form in pre-Saale times. It is also difficult to consider the Yorkshire gaps as wholly Ipswichian features, and some pre-Saale history must be assumed. The course of the Elster Glaciation is singularly obscure in Yorkshire and Lincolnshire, but in east Norfolk, which was not overrun by Saale ice,[28] the erosional and transportational power of the Elster ice is fascinatingly displayed in the huge rafts of Chalk and non-glacial Pleistocene deposits incorporated in the cliffs near Cromer and Mundesley. It would not be stretching the imagination too far to assume that Elster ice had contributed to the excavation of the vales of York, lower Trent and Belvoir, and the central Lincolnshire and Fen basin, in a manner that may be more convincingly argued for the Saale ice. Yet, as the Elster ice moved generally along the strike, turning eastward only in East Anglia, it may be argued that, like the Saale ice, it was not responsible for initiating the gaps, and there is a case for considering all, except for the Tetford gap, as existing, no doubt in some shallower and narrower form, in pre-Elster time.

## THE PRE-GLACIAL HISTORY

If, as has been argued above, a high-level gap existed at most of the localities under consideration at the onset of the Elster Glaciation, it seems reasonable to assume that they had been formed by fluvial and mass-wasting processes. With gaps produced by the headward fusion of scarp and backslope valleys or by scarp recession encroaching onto backslope valley systems, a scarp-foot vale of some depth must already be in existence. On the other hand, gaps that are held to be remnants of high-level valleys produced by epigenetic streams demand, until river capture occurs, excavation at the same time and rate as the eventual scarp-foot vale. Confirmation of epigenesis of streams has been sought in the recognition of bevelled cuestas, but this is difficult when escarpment crests are rounded and undulating, and have been modified by glacial and periglacial processes. In eastern England, scarp crest bevels are of rather limited extent for these very reasons, but of course have great geomorphological significance when they occur. Superb examples remain near Ludford in the Lincolnshire Wolds, where the Red Chalk at the base of the Upper Cretaceous lies on the western edge of the summit flat, and near Harlaxton, south–west of Grantham, where the Lincolnshire Limestone has been trimmed off at 146 metres O.D. some distance behind the scarp brow and crest of Northampton Sands. What is impressive in the area east of a Leeds-Sheffield-Nottingham-Oakham-Kettering line, and has prompted a number of geologists and geomorphologists to examine the relation of planation to drainage development, is the general accordance at 137 to 198 metres O.D. of cuesta summits, excluding only the high plateau of the north–west Yorkshire Wolds, in areas where excessive glacial erosion did not occur. Discounting the Lincolnshire Limestone cuesta north of Grantham and the East Anglian Chalk which were strongly overrun by Elster and Saale ice (Figure 1), one may draw attention to the summit heights of the Lincolnshire Wolds, the southern and northern Yorkshire Wolds, the Howardians, and the Jurassic hills of Kesteven, Rutland and Northamptonshire. Westward, the highest ground on Triassic and Permian rocks, and the Coal Measure ridges around Mansfield lie accordant.

Acceptance of this general accordance as evidence of base-levelling does not require that the cuesta bevels or the gaps were initiated at one and the same time, for they are manifestly at rather different heights. The Humber and Barnetby gaps in north Lincolnshire were probably initiated by streams crossing an emergent 128 metres platform.[29] The marine transgression that produced it profoundly influenced the drainage development of the Lincolnshire Wolds, and may well be recorded in the Yorkshire Wolds as it is in south–west Lincolnshire. The development of the *present* Ancaster and Lincoln gaps, and possibly the Wash and Lopham gaps may also date from this phase.

There is, however, reason to infer trans-cuesta drainage in the Humber and Wash areas before this stage. The crestlines of the Chalk cuestas of Yorkshire and Lincolnshire decline gently toward both gaps, and the westward penetration of the 128 metres sea in north and south Lincolnshire, though partly controlled by tectonic movement in the Humber area,[30] was probably facilitated by existing breaches across the Cretaceous and perhaps the Jurassic cuestas. Evidence for such early egress of Pennine and Midland drainage to the North Sea derives from examination of the drainage development and planation of the whole area east of the Pennines. The general accordance at and below 200 metres, and Sissons's recognition of a 217 metres shoreline at his Bierley stage north of Sheffield argue for planation at this general level. But it would be grossly erroneous to postulate a plane surface over a west–east distance of some 90 kilometres, because the formation of such a marine abrasion platform adjusted to sediment transport would have required planation by a deepening and transgressing sea to commence in east Lincolnshire at no higher than 30 metres O.D. Alternatively and more reasonably, it can be suggested that the land area of eastern England had undergone a prolonged period of late-Tertiary denudation, and any transgressing sea towards the end of this era would have spread westward relatively quickly along low-lying areas. Some of the clay country west of the Yorkshire and Lincolnshire Wolds would, therefore, almost certainly have been flooded before the Lincolnshire Chalk was finally submerged. As the transgressing sea approached its maximum height, sufficiently deep water would have prevailed across the present vales of York and the Trent to allow wave attack on the Permian limestones and Coal Measure sandstones to cut the narrower abrasion platform which is partly preserved on these rocks between 168 and 210 metres. Thus no perfect marine plane can ever have existed east of the southern Pennines. The sea-floor would necessarily have been uneven, the deeper parts coinciding with pre-existing river valleys and the clay vales, and the shallower parts, planed by wave action, with the more upstanding rocks.

While it is acknowledged that a transgression to about 210 metres O.D. during the latest Tertiary is not substantiated by the preservation of marine sediments as in south–eastern England, the general summit accordance and evidence of regional drainage superimposition permit consideration of such an event at least as a working hypothesis. It is postulated, therefore, that a number of east-flowing streams came into existence during regression of the 210 metres sea, thereby constituting the general pattern of early Pleistocene drainage which was later modified by the 128 metres transgression and by repeated glaciation. But the initial pattern may not have been wholly new, and the larger streams might have revived even earlier alignments. There is evidence, admittedly slight, from the distribution of planation surface remnants above 137 metres O.D., that the late-Tertiary sea penetrated west of the Cretaceous and Jurassic rocks first in the areas of south and north Lincolnshire and the Vale of Pickering. This suggests that the transgressing sea took advantage of late-Tertiary valleys of the Trent, Humber and Ure (Figure 1), but the point has almost been reached where hypothesis becomes speculation.

There remains the question of the pre-Elster history of the Lopham gap. As the Wash gap and the Fen basin owe their present dimensions largely to excavation by Elster and particularly Saale ice, there is no compelling reason why the lower Great Ouse should always have followed a strike course to the Wash. The Great Ouse may well have crossed the Chalk somewhere in the vicinity of Thetford to reach the Crag estuaries of eastern East Anglia, and as it heads in areas beyond the supposed limit of the 210 metres sea, a gap across the East Anglian Chalk could have existed in this locality in Pliocene as well as Pleistocene times.

It has been claimed that the present morphology of the gaps owes much to middle- and late-Pleistocene events involving glacial, glacifluvial and periglacial activity. Certain of the gaps influenced the direction of movement and the erosive capability of the ice, functioning as ice-ways, and others participated in systems of meltwater drainage, but in almost all such instances, though modifications were effected, the ice and meltwaters took advantage of pre-existing features. The pre-glacial significance of the gaps lies in their location and spatial distribution, particularly in relation to relics of former drainage systems and planation surfaces. It must be stressed, therefore, that the present width, depth and appearance of the gaps contribute little to an assessment of Tertiary and early-Pleistocene events, and that the middle- and late-Pleistocene modifications to the gaps and also to the streams and remnants of the planation surfaces must be fully appreciated before a reasonably plausible explanation of the origin and early history of the gaps can be offered.

## NOTES

[1] W. M. DAVIS, The development of certain English rivers, *Geog. Journ.* 5 (1895) 127–146.

[2] S. S. BUCKMAN, The development of rivers, *Natural Science* 14 (1899) 273–290.

[3] F. COWPER REED, *Geological history of the rivers of east Yorkshire* (Clay, London, 1901).

[4] F. W. HARMER, On the origin of certain canon-like valleys associated with lake-like areas of depression, *Quart. Journ. Geol. Soc.* 63 (1907) 470–514.

[5] H. H. SWINNERTON, The problem of the Lincoln gap, *Trans. Lincs. Nat. Union* (1937) 145–153.

[6] H. C. VERSEY, The build of Yorkshire, *Naturalist* (1942) 27–37.

[7] *Idem*, The Humber gap, *Trans. Leeds Geol. Assoc.* 6 (1946) 26–30.

[8] D. L. LINTON, The landforms of Lincolnshire, *Geog.* 39 (1954) 67–78; and Geomorphology of the southern Pennines and parts of the eastern scarplands, *Field studies in the British Isles* (ed. J. A. Steers) (1964) 138–154.

[9] K. M. CLAYTON, The geomorphology of the area around Melton Mowbray, *East Midland Geographer* 2, no. 10 (1959) 3–8.

[10] A. STRAW, The erosion surfaces of east Lincolnshire, *Proc. Yorks. Geol. Soc.* 33 (1961a) 149–172; and The Quaternary evolution of the lower and middle Trent, *East Midland Geographer* 3, no. 20 (1963) 171–189.

[11] J. LEWIN, The Yorkshire Wolds: a study in geomorphology, *Occasional papers in Geography,* no. 11 (University of Hull, 1969).

[12] H. VALENTIN, Glazialmorphologische Untersuchungen in Ostengland, *Handbook of the Geography Institute* (Free University of Berlin, 1957).

[13] P. F. KENDALL, A system of glacier lakes in the Cleveland Hills, *Quart. Journ. Geol. Soc.* 58 (1902) 471–571.

[14] G. DE BOER, A system of glacier lakes in the Yorkshire Wolds, *Proc. Yorks. Geol. Soc.* 25 (1944) 223–233.

[15] F. COWPER REED, *op. cit.* (1901).

[16] C. F. B. SHILLITO, The Kirmington fiord, *Trans. Hull Geol. Soc.* 7 (1937) 125–127.

[17] D. L. LINTON, The forms of glacial erosion, *Trans. Inst. Br. Geogr.* 33 (1963) 1–28; and A. STRAW, An examination of surface and drainage in the Lincolnshire Wolds, with brief consideration of adjacent areas, *Unpublished Ph.D. thesis* (University of Sheffield, 1964) 140–143.

[18] C. R. TWIDALE, Glacial overflow channels in north Lincolnshire, *Trans. Inst. Br. Geogr.* 22 (1956) 47–54.

[19] P. E. KENT and R. CASEY, A Kimmeridgian sandstone in north Lincolnshire, *Proc. Geol. Soc. London,* no. 1606 (1963) 57–62.

[20] W. A. WATTS, Pollen spectra from the interglacial deposits at Kirmington, Lincolnshire, *Proc. Yorks. Geol. Soc.* 32 (1959) 145–151; and P. J. BOYLAN, The Pleistocene deposits of Kirmington, Lincolnshire, *Merc. Geol.* 1 (1966) 339–350.

[21] J. P. T. BURCHELL, Palaeolithic implements from Kirmington, Lincolnshire, and their relationship to the 100-foot raised beach of Late Pleistocene times, *Antiq. Journ.* 11 (1931) 262–272; and Some Pleistocene deposits at Kirmington and Crayford, *Geol. Mag.* 72 (1935) 327–331.

[22] W. A. WATTS, *op. cit.* (1959); and P. J. BOYLAN, *op. cit.* (1966).

[23] H. H. SWINNERTON, *op. cit.* (1937); and A. STRAW, *op. cit.* (1963).

[24] H. H. SWINNERTON, *op. cit.* (1937).

[25] A. STRAW, Drifts, meltwater channels and ice-margins in the Lincolnshire Wolds, *Trans. Inst. Br. Geogr.* 29 (1961b) 115–128.

[26] *Idem,* The development of the middle and lower Bain valley, east Lincolnshire, *Trans. Inst. Br. Geogr.* 40 (1966) 145–154.

[27] D. F. W. BADEN-POWELL, The Chalky boulder-clays of Norfolk and Suffolk, *Geol. Mag.* 85 (1948) 279–296.

[28] A. STRAW, A reassessment of the Chalky boulder-clay or Marly Drift of north Norfolk, *Zeit. für Geom.* 9 (1965) 209–221.

[29] A. STRAW, *op. cit.* (1961a).

[30] *Ibid.*

# TRAFFIC ON THE MIDLAND RAILWAY IN THE LATE NINETEENTH CENTURY

## B. J. TURTON

The bulk of the many published accounts of the growth of the British railway system have relied largely upon the minutes and reports of the nineteenth-century railway companies. The information contained in these and in related documents has formed the basis of detailed analyses of railway construction, commercial policy, legal activities, labour relations and many other social and economic aspects of what was indisputably Britain's leading 'growth industry' of the nineteenth century. From a geographical viewpoint the most serious omission from the existing literature is the analysis of traffic generation and distribution. It is unlikely that much can be done to remedy this deficiency since detailed traffic records for only a few railway companies have survived. The Midland Railway Company accounts of station passenger and goods receipts are among the few to have been preserved and present a valuable picture of the commercial fortunes of the company between 1872 and 1922.[1] The 1897 receipts, which form the basis of this examination of traffic in the East Midlands, illustrate the Midland system near the height of its prosperity in the region. A year later this position was to be strongly challenged with the completion of the Great Central Railway's lines from Lincoln, across the Nottinghamshire–Derbyshire coalfield, to Chesterfield, and from Kirkby-in-Ashfield southwards through Nottingham, Leicester and Rugby to London.

The Midland records relate only to the amounts of traffic received at, and despatched from, each station and depot and are, therefore, of most value in preparing a study of traffic generation. It is not possible to reconstruct the distribution of through traffic over the system using these records and it is essential also to recognise that certain East Midland towns were areas of competition between two or more railway undertakings. Thus the Midland statistics reflect the total industrial activity of a particular town only when no other railway offered alternative transport facilities. The detailed examination of the records is, therefore, preceded by a brief review of the Midland Railway's significance within the region in 1897 and the extent to which competing networks were eroding what in the mid-nineteenth century had been a Midland traffic preserve.[2]

Table I shows the type of information recorded in the station receipt books. Details of much of the traffic are concealed under the headings of 'carted' and 'not carted' goods, but the bulk of Midland freight in the East Midlands was derived from collieries, ironstone workings and limestone quarries and it is these freights which are analysed in more detail. Passenger traffic statistics do not distinguish between the suburban commuter and the longer-distance traveller, although the provision of 'workmen' trains and the introduction of season tickets had by 1897 already fostered a flourishing daily journey-to-work movement by rail around the major East Midland cities.

### THE MIDLAND SYSTEM IN 1897

The Midland Railway Company had been formed in 1844 by the amalgamation of the Midland Counties, Birmingham and Derby Junction, and North Midland Companies, involving lines from Derby and

Nottingham to Leicester and Rugby, from Hampton-in-Arden (near Birmingham) to Derby, and from Derby to Leeds respectively. This original system had by 1897 developed into a highly-successful national undertaking which, however, still emphasised its link with the East Midlands by retaining Derby as the Midland's engineering and administrative headquarters. The closing decade of the Victorian era thus saw the Midland Railway firmly entrenched in the region of its birth and operating prosperous extensions to London, Manchester and Carlisle (where traffic was exchanged for Scotland) and to the coast at Bristol and Heysham. It had maintained a monopoly over the Nottinghamshire–Derbyshire coalfield traffic until the opening of the Erewash and Leen valley branches of the Great Northern Railway (G.N.R.) in 1876 and 1882 respectively, but only the tenuous Great Northern branch from Grantham to Nottingham and Derby offered any challenge to the Midland company for the passenger and freight traffic of two of the leading regional centres. Other competition was faced mainly on the margins of the industrial core of the East Midlands: the G.N.R. operated lines into Newark, Lincoln and Stamford and the London and North Western Railway (L.N.W.R.) provided alternative facilities at Wellingborough, Market Harborough and Leicester. Many of the lines operated by these two companies were of branch status only, however, and the Midland trunk route passing through Chesterfield, Derby, Leicester, Kettering and Bedford still carried the bulk of traffic between the East Midlands, London and the north.

TABLE I

Sample headings from Midland Railway Company's station traffic and expenses records

| Number of passengers booked | Receipts (£s) | | |
|---|---|---|---|
| | Passenger | Parcels, horses, carriages, dogs | Total coaching receipts |
| | | | |

| Livestock, mineral and goods traffic | | | | | | Expenses of station (£s) |
|---|---|---|---|---|---|---|
| Livestock (trucks in and out) | Coal, coke, and limestone (in and out) (tons) | Carted in and out (tons) | Not carted in and out (tons) | Mineral class in and out (tons) | Trans-ships (tons) | |
| | | | | | | |

The 10 years preceding 1897 had also been a period of much new building for the Midland, with the opening of lines designed both to improve existing traffic arrangements and to tap newly-developing areas on the concealed coalfield. The Nottingham–Melton Mowbray and Manton–Glendon Junction railways were completed by 1880 to provide an alternative route between the Trent valley and Kettering and to link the Northamptonshire iron-ore deposits with the Derbyshire blast-furnace centres. New lines were built to serve the collieries between Pleasley, Bolsover, Staveley and Clowne and, on the borders of the region, the Edale trans-Pennine railway and the extension east of Melton (to link with the Midland and Great Northern Joint network in East Anglia) were both opened in 1893.

The Midland company rarely entered into joint working agreements with other undertakings in the East Midlands. The only noteworthy instance was the joint Midland–L.N.W.R. line linking Coalville and Moira, in the Leicestershire coalfield, with Nuneaton and even here the territory served was marginal to the Midland's network and the traffic derived from these lines remained negligible.

### FREIGHT TRAFFIC

The generation of freight traffic on the Midland system was dominated by the Nottinghamshire–Derbyshire coalfield, and the only other areas of any importance were the Leicestershire coalfield, the Northamptonshire ironstone field, and, to a much lesser extent, the Peak limestone district. The manufacturing industries of Nottingham, Leicester and Derby obviously generated large amounts of traffic for dispersal from the local Midland depots, but the available records give no details of this freight and, therefore, the most reliable index of industrial activity provided by the Midland statistics is the amount of coal despatched as industrial fuel from depots in Nottingham and other centres to local factories. Figure 1, therefore, illustrates the traffic handled by coal, coke and limestone concentration and distribution centres, with an inset of the principal iron-ore and other mineral centres on the Midland system.

In 1897 the leading freight depots, in terms of tonnage of coal-class traffic, were situated on the pioneer Erewash valley line of 1847, its 1862 extension northwards to Clay Cross, and on the former North Midland line from Clay Cross to Staveley and Eckington, close to the West Riding border. Stanton Gate depot handled over 900,000 tons of coal and limestone, the bulk of this being destined for the Stanton iron works. To this total may be added the 265,000 tons of iron ore sent north to Stanton Gate from the Jurassic deposits served by the Midland system near Kettering, Weldon and Wellingborough. The G.N.R. also had access to the Stanton blast furnaces *via* their Grantham–Derby branch but they were unable to offer the direct orefield-to-blast-furnace facilities that the Midland possessed and most of the G.N.R. traffic consisted of coal from the Pinxton collieries passing down the G.N.R. Erewash branch to Stanton.

Further north the Midland depot at Eckington and Renishaw dealt with 708,000 tons of coal-class traffic and 155,000 tons of other minerals, principally iron ore. The coal was collected from the Rother valley pits and the ironstone from Eckington itself, with supplementary supplies from Northamptonshire, and delivered to the Renishaw furnaces. Similar traffic was handled two miles to the south at Staveley Works station, adjacent to the Staveley blast furnaces: 659,000 tons of coal and limestone and 230,000 tons of iron ore were recorded here in 1897.[3] The two other Midland depots which each handled over 500,000 tons of coal were primarily coal concentration centres, located at Hasland and Westhouses. The latter depot was opened in 1881, north of Alfreton, and it was to

109

become the junction of the Pleasley and Teversall branch (opened in 1886 to serve both the exposed and concealed sections of the field). Most of the coal traffic at Westhouses originated from the Blackwell, Huthwaite and Hilcote collieries, which were also linked with the already-completed Great Central line between Staveley and Kirkby. The Westhouses depot formed the nucleus of one of the most prosperous sections of the Midland's coal network, as the neighbouring depots in the area between Clay Cross,

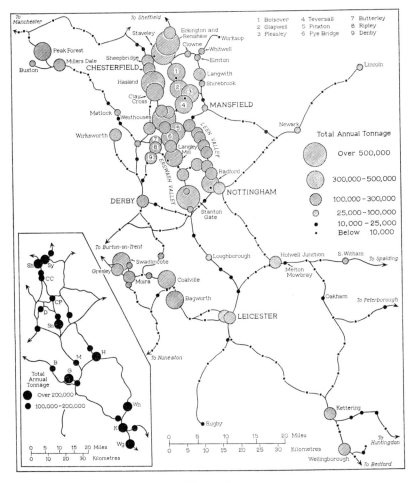

FIGURE 1

Coal, coke and limestone traffic at Midland Railway depots, 1897

INSET: Iron ore and other mineral traffic

| B | Bardon Hill | M | Mountsorrel |
|---|---|---|---|
| CC | Clay Cross | Sh | Sheepbridge |
| CP | Codnor Park | Sn | Stanton |
| D | Denby | Sy | Staveley |
| G | Glenfield | Wn | Weldon (Corby) |
| H | Holwell Junction | Wg | Wellingborough |
| K | Kettering | | |

Codnor Park and Sutton-in-Ashfield each handled over 100,000 tons. Hasland depot, between Clay Cross and Chesterfield on the former North Midland line, functioned in a similar way to Westhouses, receiving coal from the Rother valley pits at Grassmoor and near Wingerworth. Although this Hasland depot was close to the Wingerworth blast furnaces the latter received most of their iron ore from the Wingerworth depot (see inset to Figure 1).

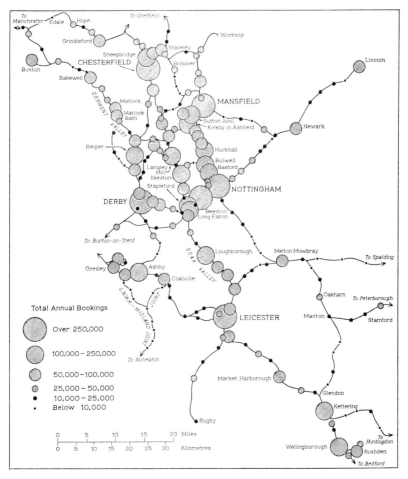

FIGURE 2
Passenger traffic at Midland Railway stations, 1897

Coal traffic from the concealed field began in 1859, with the opening of the Shireoaks pit, near Worksop, and during the period 1850–60 further shafts were sunk along the Leen valley, which carried the Midland branch to Mansfield. Thus by about 1860 the Midland was in the fortunate position of controlling the coal traffic from the exposed field, with its Erewash valley lines, and from the expanding concealed section *via* its Mansfield network. In 1897 most of the Leen valley coal depots were handling at least

111

100,000 tons of coal-class traffic and similar amounts were passing through the depots at Denby, Ripley and Butterley, on the Kilburn branch serving the Derbyshire section of the exposed field. In 1880 the Midland branch between Pleasley and Staveley Town was completed, tunnelling through the Magnesian Limestone scarp and serving the new mines opened at Glapwell and Bolsover in the Doe Lea valley. Production at these mines rose rapidly and by 1897 both pits were supplying over 300,000 tons of coal to the Midland network for distribution. It was the lucrative nature of the coal traffic in this section of the field which promoted the construction of the Manchester, Sheffield and Lincolnshire Railway's competing line from Lincoln *via* Bolsover to Chesterfield. Further east the development of mining on the border between the Magnesian Limestone and Bunter Sandstone outcrops was more limited and the Midland depots at Shirebrook, Elmton and Whitwell handled only between 34,000 and 63,000 tons of coal traffic. Ten years later, however, the traffic in coal at these three depots had risen to 322,000, 274,000 and 125,000 tons respectively.[4]

Coal output on the Leicestershire–south Derbyshire field was handled at Bagworth, Coalville, and Swadlincote (each over 300,000 tons), with secondary depots at Gresley and Moira (146,000 and 286,000 tons), The Midland exerted a monopoly over this traffic, apart from the isolated L.N.W.R. Coalville–Loughborough line and the jointly-operated Midland–L.N.W.R. lines running south to Nuneaton mentioned above.

Coal distribution to manufacturing areas away from the coalfields accounted for the bulk of coal movements in the remainder of the region. Nottingham, Derby and Leicester each handled between 200,000 and 260,000 tons in 1897, with Newark, Lincoln and Matlock as secondary distribution centres. The Jurassic iron-working industry received most of its coal from the Nottinghamshire field, the principal distributing centres being Melton (Holwell Junction with 125,000 tons), Wellingborough (150,000 tons) and Kettering (244,000 tons.) The latter town also received coal for the footwear industry.[5]

Although the tonnage of limestone traffic is grouped together with that of coal it is clear from Figure 1 that the large amounts of freight handled by the Midland depots at Wirksworth, Peak Forest, Millers Dale and Ambergate were obtained from Carboniferous Limestone quarries located on the system. Here again the Midland had acquired a near-monopoly with only limited competition from the L.N.W.R. Buxton branches.

The pattern of iron ore and other mineral traffic was dominated by the coalfield-based iron industry. Staveley, Sheepbridge and Stanton, already discussed in the context of coal supplies, were the largest centres, with smaller depots associated with the blast furnaces at Codnor Park, Denby, and Clay Cross.[6] Much of the ore handled at Wellingborough and Kettering was destined for the local furnaces, but the Weldon (Corby) depot was concerned only with shipping ore to other destinations, as smelting at Corby was not begun until after 1900. Although the mineral traffic on the Midland system was dominated by coal, iron ore and limestone, there were also a few localities producing other minerals. The Charnwood granite quarries despatched 144,000 tons of stone *via* the Midland depot at Mountsorrel, whilst the Pre-Cambrian grits and hornstones quarried at Bardon Hill yielded 192,000 tons.

The low level of industrial activity in rural Nottinghamshire and Leicestershire is reflected in the small amounts of freight generated on the lines east of the Trent and Soar valleys, although it must be remembered that, as with passenger traffic, certain of these lines frequently carried a heavy through traffic. Thus very little freight was handled by the inter-mediate depots on the Nottingham to Kettering line, although this railway conveyed a large part of the coal, coke and iron ore traffic between Derbyshire and Northamptonshire.

## PASSENGER TRAFFIC

The variation in the total numbers of passengers handled by the Midland stations was as great as that in freight traffic. Nottingham Midland, with 1,133,000 annual bookings, was the busiest centre, whilst some of the minor stations on the Lincoln branch and the Oakham–Glendon loop attracted fewer than 10,000 per year. Although the available statistics do not differentiate between long-distance and 'local' bookings it is clear from Figure 2 that much of the passenger traffic handled at certain stations was associated with a daily journey-to-work movement. On the Nottingham–Derby line, Beeston was outstanding as a suburban centre for Nottingham, and, to a lesser degree, Spondon, Borrowash and Draycott had become commuter stations for Derby. Heavy passenger traffic was also carried on the Leen valley route between Nottingham and Mansfield; annual bookings of over 100,000 were common on this line, but Lenton and Radford attracted fewer than 50,000 passengers. These latter stations were the nearest to Nottingham and it is probable that competition from the city's embryonic public road-transport system was responsible for the lower level of railway traffic. Both Radford and Basford were first linked with the city centre by tram in 1881 although the journey time of 70 minutes from Basford compared very unfavourably with the 20-minute rail timing.[7] An element of journey-to-work traffic was also responsible for many of the passenger bookings handled by stations in the Chesterfield–Staveley area and on the Soar valley line between Leicester and Loughborough.

The Midland Railway had pioneered the day-excursion train in the 1840s[8] and the tourist attractions of the Peak District were exploited by services on the Edale and Derwent valley lines. In 1897 traffic exceeded 50,000 passengers annually at Matlock (Bath and Town stations), Bakewell and Buxton and, further north, at Grindleford on the Edale line.

There was a marked contrast between the flourishing traffic on the lines serving the exposed coalfield south of Mansfield and that on the lines linking Mansfield with Worksop, Staveley, Clowne and Bolsover. Although the latter railways had been built to serve the newly-opened collieries of the concealed field, mining villages had yet to be established and passenger traffic in consequence was light. On the Pleasley–Staveley line, which traversed the Magnesian Limestone agricultural region, only Bolsover attracted over 25,000 passengers and the other stations (Palterton, Glapwell and Rowthorn) each dealt with fewer than 6,000.

South of Nottingham the three principal traffic-generating areas were Leicester, the Ashby–Moira–Gresley mining district and the manufacturing towns of the footwear and iron-working belt, principally Kettering, Wellingborough and Rushden. Leicester, with 689,000 bookings, was second to Nottingham as a passenger traffic centre on the Midland system in this region, although only two years were to elapse before the Great Central line was opened through both cities as a vigorous competitor for the long-distance traffic. In the eastern and southern agricultural areas of the East Midlands traffic was light, with an average of between 50,000 and 75,000 annual bookings in market towns such as Lincoln and Market Harborough, where there was very little or no opportunity for the generation of suburban traffic. The majority of intermediate stations and halts failed to attract above 20,000 passengers annually.

A study of passenger generation in this region certainly provides a useful guide to understanding the motives underlying Midland railway construction in the second half of the nineteenth century. Many of the lines built during this period were intended primarily as freight routes or as through passenger-traffic routes and the local passenger-generating potential was often a secondary consideration. This is clearly seen in the Coalville–Nuneaton area, where none of the stations of the joint Midland–L.N.W.R. lines (Nuneaton–Shackerstone–Coalville; Shackerstone–Moira) attracted more than 10,000 passengers annually and where several failed to attract even 2,000. Similarly, the Nottingham–Melton and Manton–Glendon Junction lines, already described as through routes, attracted very little local traffic. Only two stations (Melton and Weldon) recorded more than 10,000 bookings.

The provision of the Midland company's own route to London had repercussions on the fortunes of other parts of the system. The Leicester–Rugby line, opened in 1840 as part of the Midland Counties network, lost much of its original importance as a link in the through route from East Midland centres to London, *via* the L.N.W.R. main line, when the direct Midland Kettering–St. Pancras railway was completed. Traffic at the intermediate stations between Leicester and Rugby increased very slowly when the line was reduced to the status of a branch and it received a further blow with the opening of the Great Central line in 1899.

The Midland operated four branches in the east of the region. The Lincoln branch attracted a certain amount of suburban traffic from Nottingham as far east as Lowdham, but further down the valley few stations handled more than 15,000 passengers. Although the Midland company had been one of the first to provide Lincoln with railway services the bulk of long-distance traffic from the city travelled on the G.N.R., Manchester, Sheffield and Lincolnshire, and Great Eastern (G.E.R.)–G.N.R. Joint lines. Midland traffic, which amounted to 63,400 in 1897, was destined mainly for cross-country routes, although a London service was offered. The second branch was that from Wymondham, on the Melton–Kettering route, east to Little Bytham, whence the Midland and G.N.R. Joint Railway continued into East Anglia, providing in particular a useful cross-country holiday route to the Norfolk coastal resorts. Traffic was thus dominated by through services from the main industrial centres and none of the intermediate stations generated more than 7,000 bookings annually. The branch from Manton to Peterborough was opened in 1848 as part of the Leicester–Melton–Peterborough line and carried through traffic from the Midland system destined for exchange with the G.N.R. and G.E.R. networks at Peterborough. Local traffic at Stamford, Ketton and Luffenham was slightly higher than on the Lincoln or Bytham branches. South of Kettering the Midland branch to Huntingdon made a further connection with the G.N.R. and G.E.R. systems, but, as with the Peterborough line, local passenger traffic was light and only Thrapston, which was also served by the Nene valley branch of the L.N.W.R., attracted above 10,000 passengers.

114

CONCLUSION

The variations in traffic-generating potential illustrated in the maps of Midland freight and passenger station receipts underline the basic differences in the economies of the coalfield-industrial areas and of the primarily agricultural districts of the East Midlands. Coal and iron ore were the basis for the prosperity of many of the railway undertakings in the midlands and northern England and the success of the Midland Railway Company in developing a near-monopoly over the Nottinghamshire-Derbyshire coalfield is borne out by the heavy traffic handled by Midland depots in this region. The Midland records make it possible to reconstruct the relationships between local industrial activity and what was in the late nineteenth century the principal transport agency for the carriage of raw materials and manufactured goods.

NOTES

1 BRITISH TRANSPORT HISTORICAL RECORDS, Midland Railway traffic and expenses at stations (1872–1922), MID 4, Pieces 1–7.

2 Accounts of the rise of the Midland system in the East Midlands are provided in: C. E. STRETTON, *History of the Midland Railway* (1901); and H. ELLIS, *The Midland Railway* (1953).

3 For a detailed account of the iron industry, see: K. WARREN, The Derbyshire iron industry since 1780, *East Midland Geographer* 2, Part 8 (1961) 17–33.

4 BRITISH TRANSPORT HISTORICAL RECORDS, *op. cit.,* MID 4, Piece 6.

5 See: P. R. MOUNFIELD, The footwear industry of the East Midlands (III), *East Midland Geographer* 3 (1965) 445–448.

6 Clay Cross was also the site of the Midland company's locomotive coking plant. See: S. H. BEAVER, Coke manufacture in Great Britain, *Trans. Inst. Br. Geogr.* 17 (1951) 137.

7 R. MARSHALL, *A history of Nottingham City Transport* (1960) 5.

8 R. M. ROBBINS, *The Railway Age* (1962) 55–56.

PART TWO

Other Geographical Essays

# SETTLEMENT AND LANDSCAPE CHANGES IN A CAERNARVONSHIRE SLATE QUARRYING PARISH

## F. A. BARNES

### INTRODUCTION

The patterns of fields and buildings that characterise individual rural landscapes are products of complex sociological, technological and economic forces operating over long periods, and interacting with varying emphasis, usually within firm limits set by physical endowments. But these limits are not invariable, and the slate-quarrying belt of Snowdonia in north–west Wales provides good examples of landscapes that owe their individuality largely to one dominating circumstance—the growth of extractive industry—leading to the establishment of farm holdings in defiance of the harshness of the physical setting.

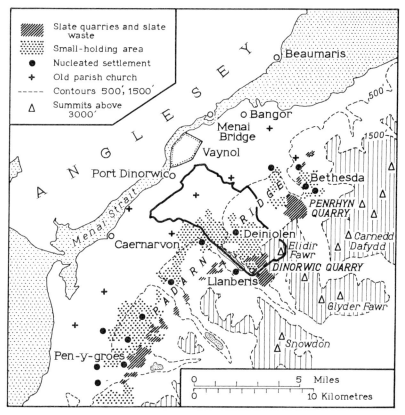

FIGURE 1
Location of Llanddeiniolen parish

119

In many respects Llanddeiniolen parish epitomises this area. It extends south–east from near the Menai Strait to the summit of Elidir Fawr (3,029 feet : 924 metres) (Figure 1), and thus it straddles the 'Caledonian' grain conferred by structure and emphasised by glaciation. It consists of a tract of marine-trimmed, drift-covered Plio–Pleistocene coastal platforms linked to a portion of steep mountain country by a transitional 'moorland fringe', associated particularly with the Padarn Ridge, which is formed of late Pre-Cambrian volcanics. In the upland zone where high-grade slate occurs in the intensely cleaved Cambrian rocks compressed against the ancient massif of Arfon and Anglesey, Llanddeiniolen includes a part of Dinorwic Quarry, probably the largest slate quarry in the world.

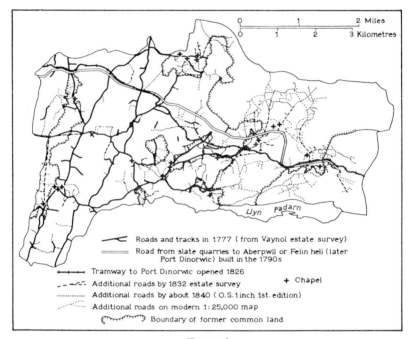

FIGURE 2
Roads and tracks in Llanddeiniolen

The broad distribution of settlement in the parish is indicated by the network of roads shown in Figure 2. An intricate pattern of tiny walled fields, with cottages set among them, forms a striking feature of south–east Llanddeiniolen. Until recently they made up smallholdings, mainly of three to 15 acres, and many of them on barren, bleak terrain at altitudes far above the normal upper limit of cultivation in western Wales. Some lines and clusters of cottages are found in the same area, with one larger village, Deiniolen. Most of this settlement is on land that was common waste or sheep walk two centuries ago. With some exceptions on former common, the farm and field pattern on the lowland shows a normal distinction between farm holding and house-and-garden. On the moorland fringe this distinction is often blurred by the essentially part-time character of the original smallholdings there, which were built upon and improved by quarrymen of almost exclusively Welsh rural origin and peasant tradition. This lowland–upland contrast in pattern of settlement and form of land holding has an underlying physical basis, but it derived directly from different histories of occupance and tenure.

## PRE-INDUSTRIAL EVOLUTION IN THE LOWLAND

The exposed hill country, with an average annual rainfall of more than 60 inches (1,500 millimetres), steep slopes, and mainly thin podzolic or wet gley soils, did not attract permanent settlement before the late eighteenth century. The lowland, by contrast, has a long history of agricultural use. It rises from 250 feet (75 metres) or below, in the rolling north–west, to 400 to 500 feet (120 to 150 metres) bordering the upland. Glacial interference with drainage and the rather level surface of the inner platform, where the annual rainfall reaches 50 inches (1,270 millimetres), has resulted in extensive tracts of peat and peaty gley soils (Figure 3); but the drift-covered slopes of the lowland characteristically carry well drained, slightly acid, moderately light brown earth soils of the Arvon series, which provided the traditional arable land for growing corn. The hill fort of Dinas Dinorwig (Pen-y-ddinas) and other remains of buildings (Figure 3) (often associated with traces of ancient fields or terraces)[1] indicate the presence of proto-historic agricultural and pastoral settlements in parts of lowland Llanddeiniolen, some of which probably persisted through the Tribal period (prior to 1282) and became bond communities subservient to the medieval princes of Gwynedd.

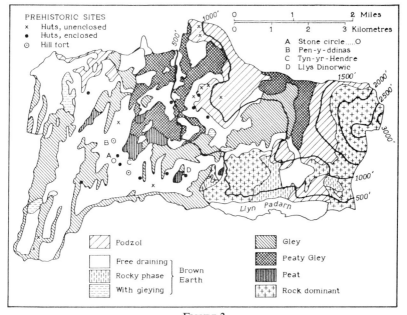

FIGURE 3
Soil types in Llanddeiniolen and ancient settlement sites

Llanddeiniolen parish was coincident with the 'manor or township' of Dinorwic[2] and the quasimanorial tenurial status of the medieval township was crucially significant for the whole of its subsequent development. In 1352, 70 years after the English conquest, Dinorwic was described as of the nature of *tir cyfrif* with bondmen holding 'two parts'.[3] By implication other land had been alienated, some before the conquest, to others, and though not held in tribal right it was later called freehold in the Crown. The arable *rhandiroedd* (sharelands) and associated meadow were shared equally *per capita* under the 'reckoned land' system by the decreasing bondmen.[4] The freeholdings were scattered in similar sharelands, but subject to inheritance by the rules of Welsh *gavelkind*. Both escheated to the Crown at the conquest as private estate of the Welsh prince, and subsequently they were granted separately for terms to some influential person who in turn leased holdings to tenants, respecting the rights of succession of 'ancient tenants'. The grantee, as lord of the manor, exercised jurisdiction over the common pasture and waste, in which both leaseholders and freeholders had grazing and other rights.

Henry Webb was granted the escheat lands of Dinorwic for 40 years in 1535,[5] but Thomas Wynn ap William (Thomas Williams), a scion of the powerful Cochwillan-Penrhyn family, inheriting episcopal lands, including Vaynol, in Bangor from his uncle in 1558,[6] got possession of Webb's patent, and in 1564 was granted 'the town of Dinorwic and tenements by Dinas Dinorwic' for 21 years, a grant converted to a 'lease for life in succession' to Thomas, William and Simon Williams in 1571.[7] The next 50 years saw a ruthless consolidation of the Vaynol interests in the parish, and an aggressive attack on the fragmentation and intermixing of holdings which had been perpetuated by freehold inheritance in *gavelkind* until its legal replacement by primogeniture, by Acts of 1539 and 1542, and its effective adoption over the period of the succeeding generation.[8] For example, in 1589 40 'ancient tenants' had been replaced by others, from whom Williams exacted £500 for their leases; and although some were reinstated after legal action in the 1590s, 10 still maintained in 1600 that William Williams (son of Thomas) 'now keeps 400 head of cattle on complainants' former holdings,' which can be identified. The next 20 years saw further complaints about the buying of claims and titles, followed by replacement of ancient tenants by others at sufferance of the farmer of the manor; freeholders persuaded to sell with promise of leases and then turned off their holdings; and ancient tenants persuaded to agree to exchanges.[9]

In 1596 'all that moiety of the township or manor of Dinorwic' containing 17 messuages was granted to John Panton for 21 years,[10] but in 1627 these additional holdings, presumed to be bond land alienated by the Conquest, were granted by letters patent to (now Sir) William Williams, and the Vaynol estate in the parish was virtually complete. It was hardly changed over the next 200 years.[11] It formed an irregular, but practically continuous, tract over which, despite bitter resistance from tenants, a major agrarian reorganisation had been effected; most isolated quillets eliminated, many enclosed fields formed; and, with the extinction of any remnants of bond hamlets, the homesteads were scattered on substantially consolidated holdings. But, throughout, the commons were jealously guarded against encroachment,[12] and the tenurial and agrarian changes were confined to territory already farmed in the thirteenth century. However, a number of freeholdings in the south–western part of the parish had been acquired by others, and, notably, from about 1550, by Hugh ap Rhys Wynn of Maesoglan in nearby Anglesey, or by his third son, Robert Wynn (ob. 1638), or his successors, to form the Glascoed estate (Figure 5), which passed to Rice Thomas of Coed Helen by marriage in 1717.[13]

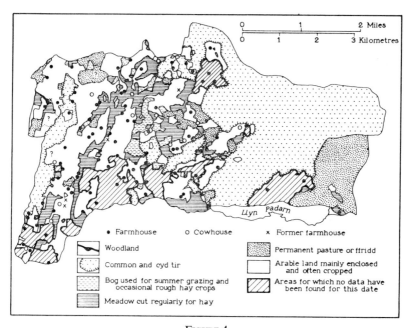

FIGURE 4

Land use and farmsteads in Llanddeiniolen in the 1770s
(Land use deduced from field names)

*Chief sources:* Vaynol Ms. 245 (1777); Lligwy Ms. 1409 (1773)

There followed a century-and-a-half of relative quiescence and slow population growth. A Vaynol rent roll of 1696 named 70 holdings in the parish with 59 tenants.[14] The names and rents show that with few exceptions these were the holdings mapped in a survey of the estate in 1777 [15] with very little internal re-allocation of land. This is not surprising, for a later Sir William Williams' activities in London left his estate after his death in 1696 entailed, burdened with annuities[16] and subject to exploitation[17] and stagnation[18] until the 1750s, when it passed to the Assheton-Smith family. It can be assumed confidently that the farm pattern of 1777 was substantially that of about 1625.

The field names of 1777 show the land use pattern of the time (Figure 4) to have been closely correlated with edaphic conditions (Figure 3) and the holdings (Figure 5) so constituted as to give to each a proportion of land of different qualities, an arrangement doubtless dating from the reorganisation of the sixteenth and early seventeenth centuries. Indeed, a land utilisation survey and field-by-field valuation of 1798[19] (not illustrated here) indicates that improvements projected in the middle eighteenth century[20] had done little to blur the sharp distinction between arable land, meadow, pasture and bog. But in 1810 Hyde Hall thought that the wretched appearance of agriculture in this 'wet, naked, black and ugly tract', with its low, inadequate fences, neglected drainage, and the nominally cultivated fields in a 'sore state of destitution', was due as much to the preoccupation of men and horses in carrying slates to the sea as to lack of tenant capital and poor methods.[21]

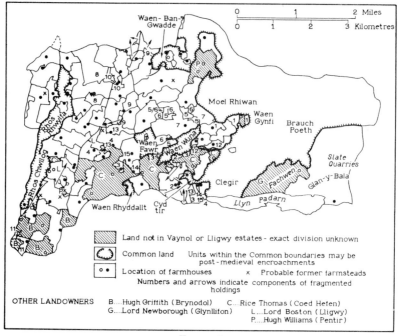

FIGURE 5

Pattern of holdings in Llanddeiniolen in 1777

*Chief sources:* Vaynol Ms. 245 (1777); Lligwy Ms. 1409 (1773); Porth-yr-Aur Ms. 13,230 (1810)

## EXPANSION ON THE COMMONS

Already by the 1770s population growth and the stirrings of the Industrial Revolution were focussing attention on the upland and the commons. As yet there were no nucleated settlements and, except for the winding Bangor to Caernarvon road, no roads other than local tracks, usually giving access to common grazings. In the 1760s or early 1770s the landlord of Vaynol, as lord of the manor, permitted some small enclosures for cottages on the peaty lowland commons in return for boon or harvest work at Vaynol, a curious example of quasi-medieval tenure.[22] The 'boon lands' were very restricted (Figure 6); but, as small-scale slate extraction developed, illegal encroachments on the mountain commons appeared. In the 1770s a few small one-man quarries on Glan-y-bala farm were laboriously sending slates by sledge, boat and cart to Caernarvon and Felin-heli (later Port Dinorwic), probably paying dues on tonnage. In 1788 Assheton-Smith of Vaynol let the largest quarry, then employing 30, for 21 years to two Caernarvon lawyers, and by 1790, on the mountain common, there were five cottages with illegal enclosures attached near Clwt-y-bont, and two further east near the quarries, as well as others on the lowland commons. Slate output grew rapidly after 1790, aided by a new road from the quarries to Felin-heli built by the landlord[23] (Figure 2), and unauthorised encroachments with cottages, and usually cowhouses, multiplied until by 1808 there were 14 near Clwt-y-bont, 10 near the quarries and two on Clegir, as well as nine on Waen wina, six on Rhos Chwilog and two on Waen fawr.[24]

124

By 1804 Thomas Assheton-Smith had decided to take over the promising slate industry himself when the lease ran out in 1809 for large-scale working on the model of the successful enterprise at Penrhyn, and was taking legal advice about dealing with squatters.[25] In 1808 he promoted an Enclosure Act for the parish which confirmed to their occupiers the ownership of the relatively few encroachments more than 20 years old, but confiscated the more numerous newer encroachments. This led to serious riots by quarrymen[26] but enclosure was eventually enforced, though most squatters had paid no rent by 1820,[27] and new quarries were opened by Assheton-Smith in 1810–11, and others in the boom of 1824–25, when a horse tramway to the improved Port Dinorwic was opened.

Squatting settlement on the commons of the neighbouring parishes continued unchecked as the slate industry rapidly grew, but in Llanddeiniolen, as in Llandegai with Penrhyn Quarry, there was a dominant landlord committed to large-scale industrial expansion to intervene. The Enclosure Act allotted most of the mountain common to Assheton-Smith[28] who recruited a quickly growing labour force with the aid of a controlled variant of the squatting process. Parcels of hillside, usually of three to 10 acres, were allocated to quarrymen to build upon and improve, at an initially low rent in consideration of their labour. Building materials were sometimes supplied, and progressively the smallholdings were subdivided by rough stone walls, often of mountain erratics cleared from the fields. Internal enclosure, like land improvement, was laborious and protracted; but by this building and improvement the capital value of high and difficult land was much increased.[29]

The allotted holdings, unlike the early encroachments of squatters, are characterised by a comparatively regular pattern of boundaries and fields. By the time of the second major estate survey, in 1832,[30] there were, on the Vaynol portion of the former mountain common, 20 houses on Clegir, 37 on Waen Gynfi and 34 near the quarries. Except for a cluster of 10 cottages near the quarries almost every house stood upon a smallholding. There were also 15 houses on Glan-y-bala, where the bigger quarries had opened, but as yet little or no smallholding settlement on Lord Newborough's Fachwen and its associated allotment of common. Only around 1850 was Fachwen subdivided, having been purchased by Vaynol in 1840.

But smallholding settlement had already reached above 1,000 feet at several points by 1832. Physical conditions influenced the choice of land for occupation, especially at a distance from the quarries, where proximity was not an over-riding advantage. The Arvon soils *(sols bruns acides)* were most commonly chosen by the early squatters. Afterwards, the planned development extended from the Clwt-y-bont encroachments upslope over the gley soils of the broad valley (Waen Gynfi) leading north–east to the col between Moel Rhiwen and Elidir, guided to some extent by two enclosure roads (Figures 2 and 6). The steepest slopes were avoided, and much of the rockier areas like Clegir remained rough, with small cottage holdings here and there. But eventually viable smallholdings extended onto barren podzols and wet, peaty land in country of high rainfall and frequent hill fog where any cultivation was very difficult; for to a countryman recruited for industrial labour, but without a guaranteed wage, a part-time holding that might support a cow, a pig, a few sheep and perhaps a patch of potatoes was much to be preferred to a rented cottage.

By 1848 the Llanddeiniolen quarries employed nearly 2,000 men, and those of Llanberis over 1,000. Even in 1831 over half the men of Llanddeiniolen were quarrymen,[31] and with the population of the parish increasing from 2,610 to 4,202 in the next 10 years, and to 4,894 by 1851, compared with the 1,039 of 1801,[32] the concentration of settlement in the moorland zone continued. As land suitable for smallholdings within reasonable distance of the quarries became fully occupied, other forms of settlement became more important. The building of cottages for sons or daughters led to subdivision of some of the original smallholdings, and a number of lowland farms in the nearby part of the parish were split into small units (Figure 6), a process begun early in the century;[33] but after the middle of the century cottages without land for farming attached were the predominant form of new settlement. They appeared in lines along roads, or in clusters, situated chiefly on former common land which had been allotted to minor landowners. Such land was interspersed with early encroachments which, together with the boon holdings, tended to form nuclei, especially where a Nonconformist chapel had been built. One of the first was probably Llanbabo, on the road from the quarries, a hamlet in existence by 1840 which has grown into Deiniolen.

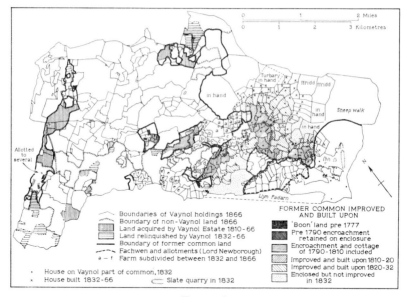

FIGURE 6

Progress of occupance on Vaynol estate land in Llanddeiniolen, 1777 to 1866

*Chief sources:* Vaynol estate surveys of 1777 (Vaynol Ms. 245), 1832 (Vaynol Ms. 255) and 1864–69; Porth-yr-Aur Mss. 13,005, 13,019, 13,020a, 13,030, 13,047, 13,055, 13,153a, 13,154, 13,211, 13,213, 13,223a, 13,225, 13,227, 13,228, 13,229, 13,230

### INDUSTRIAL DECLINE AND ITS CONSEQUENCES

By 1866,[34] and doubtless a decade earlier, smallholdings had reached their maximum extent in Llanddeiniolen, and ranged up to 1,400 feet (430 metres) O.D. After 1880 technical improvements in quarry working slowed the demand for more labour, and although the work force continued to grow until Dinorwic Quarry employed some 6,000 men at its zenith soon after 1900, the parish population declined from its peak of almost 7,000 to below 5,000 by 1921. The Vaynol smallholdings, improved by much new building in the later nineteenth century,[35] were carefully tended until after 1910, when the introduction of a minimum wage in the quarries initiated a decline of interest in farming them. The increasing competition from machine-made tiles led to a drastic reduction in slate quarry employment, and the rigours of the quarryman's life and the increasing attractions of urban living contributed to the drain of population between the wars. Part-time farming languished. Eventually holdings began to be abandoned, starting with the areas of high, poor land, and the reversion of the small fields to their natural rough state was very quick. Until 1939 the Vaynol estate was maintained in tolerable order only at great expense, but by the 1950s there was serious and widespread dereliction in the quarry district; the land in poor condition, drainage neglected, machinery impossible to use on the steep small fields, and the tenants apathetic and discontented.

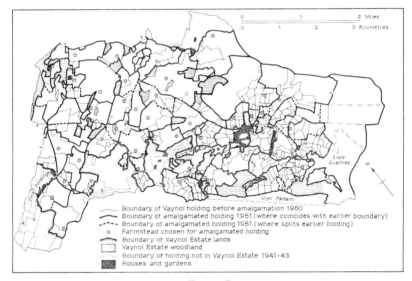

FIGURE 7

Amalgamation of holdings of the Vaynol estate in Llanddeiniolen, 1961

*Chief source:* Vaynol estate office maps

In 1957, on the appointment of a new agent at Vaynol, a drastic rationalisation of the estate was decided upon,[36] and there began a bold and vigorous effort to renovate the whole agricultural estate, the main part of which was in Llanddeiniolen. The most fundamental part of this operation was the amalgamation of small part-time holdings into viable full-time farms as shown in Figure 7. The chosen farmsteads were modernised and the remaining homesteads sold or leased to their occupiers. In late 1960 new full-time tenants were offered the reorganised farms under a new agreement, and the remaining 200, mostly full-time employees of the quarry, were given inducements to relinquish their land. The hope was that by the end of the decade the estate would have become a fully modernised group of profitable farms, yielding economic rents and making the best use of the natural potentialities of the land in the economic context of the 1960s.

For some years, therefore, the rural landscape of most of Llanddeiniolen has been in the process of another significant change, whereby a large part of what had become a rural slum on the moorland fringe—a relic, like most urban slums, of the Industrial Revolution—should be converted into a different and more productive farming landscape, albeit perhaps less productive in the upland district than it was a century ago. The eventual demographic consequences cannot yet be foreseen: but in view of the essentially part-time nature of the former smallholdings any substantial decline in population in the moorland zone will be attributable mainly to causes other than farm amalgamations, and the threat of final closure of Dinorwic Quarry will be one.[37] The most important development in the pattern of settlement may well be a further growth of the village of Deiniolen, with many of the scattered cottages becoming holiday houses. Much labour will be needed to remove unwanted field walls, and transform the field pattern into one more appropriate to the new scale of farming, so that the visual landscape will be transformed only gradually. The new farm pattern, discounting non-farm settlement, may well be not dissimilar to that which would have developed with enclosure had the slate quarrying phase not intervened.

The sale of the Vaynol agricultural estate in July 1967 to property companies which described themselves as 'temporary custodians' has initiated yet another phase of development, for though much open mountain land was subsequently acquired for the nation, most of the remaining farms were destined to be sold to their tenants. Although Vaynol's long domination has ended, the recent reorganisation was possible only because of the largely unified ownership, which had its origins in the inferior social class of the medieval communities that occupied Dinorwic township before the English conquest in the thirteenth century. In many nearby areas, with broadly similar physical attributes and social problems, any such reforming of the rural landscape would be severely hampered by a complex multiple ownership of land deriving from different tenurial histories.

ACKNOWLEDGMENT

Grateful acknowledgment is made of the generous interest and help of Sir Michael Duff (owner), Hon. D. R. M. Stuart (agent) and Mr. Alan Rickards (deputy agent) of the Vaynol estate.

## NOTES

[1] ROYAL COMMISSION ON ANCIENT MONUMENTS IN WALES AND MONMOUTHSHIRE, *Inventory of ancient monuments in Caernarvonshire* 2 (London, 1960), sites 1153, 1168–1192.

[2] D. ELLIS, Opinion, dated 18th January 1805. Ms. (no number) in Vaynol Estate Office. 'No boundaries by Reputation or otherwise can be affixed to this District of Dynorwick, but the Rights above mentioned have been exercised in through and over all the Wastes in the said parish of Llanddeiniolen, and hence it is urged that the Manor of Dynorwick is, at least, coextensive with that parish . . . . .' No Crown quit rents or Bishop's rents are known in the parish. See: Crown quit rents for Isgwyrfai in 1822, Porth-yr-Aur Ms. 14,105 (U.C.N. Wales); Extent of lands of the Bishop of Bangor (1335), Welsh Church Commission Ms. 1 (Nat. Lib. Wales); and Temporalities of Bangor, 22 Rich. II (1399), printed in *The Record of Caernarvon* (ed. H. Ellis) (Records Commission, London, 1838) 231.

3 Extent of Crown lands in Caernarvon in 1352, printed in *The Record of Caernarvon, op. cit.,* 21 (Harleian Ms. 696, fol. 14). Tenants of the third part failed to appear before the Surveyor; but later the tenant of 'Bolghdoyol' (probably the 'ffridd of Baladulyn' and later Glan-y-bala farm, attached to the lowland farm Rhiwen in 1696 and eventually the site of Dinorwic quarry) produced a charter granted by the Prince.

4 T. JONES PIERCE, Some tendencies in the agrarian history of Caernarvonshire in the later Middle Ages, *Trans. Caern. Hist. Soc.* 1 (1939) 18–27. Though Dinorwic was an exceptionally well populated bond township it was decaying in the fifteenth century, by the end of which villeinage was virtually extinct in Caernarvonshire, and the bond lands open to exploitation.

5 Exchequer Bills E/112/59/26/31 Eliz. (1589). See E. GWYNNE JONES, *Exchequer Proceedings (Equity) concerning Wales, Henry VIII–Elizabeth* (Cardiff, 1939).

6 J. E. GRIFFITH, *Pedigrees of Anglesey and Caernarvonshire families* (1914).

7 *Calendar of Patent Rolls Eliz. I (1563–66)* C 66/1018/1912 (14th December 1564). *Calendar of Patent Rolls Eliz. I (1569–72)* C 66/1080/2262 (14th February 1571). Exchequer Bills E/112/59/20/29 Eliz. (1587) (E. GWYNNE JONES (1939) *op. cit.*).

8 WILLIAM REES, *The Union of England and Wales* (Cardiff, 1938) 69–73. Reprinted from *Trans. Hon. Soc. Cymmrodorion* (1937).

9 Exchequer Bills: E/112/59/26/31 Eliz. I (1589), 59/40/36 Eliz. (1594), 59/43/36 Eliz., 59/66/42 Eliz. (1600), 59/70/n.d. (see E. GWYNNE JONES (1939) *op. cit.*); and E/112/147/133/13 Jac. I (1616), E/112/147/134/13 Jac. I (1616), E/112/147/163/17 Jac. I (1620) (see T. I. JEFFREYS JONES, Exchequer proceedings concerning Wales in Tempore James I, *Bull. Board. Celtic Studies: History and Law Series,* no. 15 (Cardiff, 1955)).

10 Exchequer Bills E/112/59/50/39 Eliz. (1597) (see E. GWYNNE JONES (1939) *op. cit.*).

11 The grants were periodically confirmed. See: Schedule of rents in Caernarvon, Anglesey and Merioneth, P.R.O., L.R. 2/271/22–26 Car. II (1681–85); P.R.O., L.R. 2/272/2 Jac. II–Wm. and Mary (1687–89). D. ELLIS (1805) *op. cit.,* notes confirmation by William III, and the Crown rents are recorded in eighteenth-century Vaynol papers.

12 For example: Exchequer Bills E/112/59/20/29 Eliz. (1587) and 59/21/31 Eliz. (1589) (see E. GWYNNE JONES (1939) *op. cit.*); and papers in Vaynol Estate Office relating to late eighteenth-century litigation.

13 Robert Wynn, his son Owen, and grandson Thomas (ob. 1687) all married heiresses (see J. E. GRIFFITH, *op. cit.*). The Glascoed lands are listed in marriage settlements of 1717 and 1778 (Coed Helen Ms. 3 and Mss. 38 and 39, Caernarvon Record Office).

14 'A Rent Roll of the estate of Sir Wm. Williams late of Vaynoll . . . . . as the same was lett in the yeare 1696 wn. Sr Wm. dyed.'; 'A rental of Sir Bouchier Wrey's estate . . . . at May 1708 [giving the tenants of 1708].'; both Mss. in Vaynol Estate Office. The rent roll for Llanddeiniolen totalled £431 10s. 8d., and most holdings also provided 'presents and services' or 'money in lieu thereof'; for example, 6s. 6d. for a wether sheep.

15 Survey of the Vaynol estate by William Williams of Llandegai and William Jones of Caerhun, Vaynol Estate Ms. 245, vol. 1. Excluding three cottage holdings on Waen Wina and 11 on Waen Fawr, and several cottages with gardens, there were 74 holdings. Since 1696 Rhiwen, Celyn and Coed Bolyn had been subdivided.

16 Details are given in: 'A particular of Vaynoll Estate with the incumbrances thereon, Ao. 1710', Ms. in Vaynol Estate Office. They are discussed in the Catalogue of Vaynol Estate Papers (1946, typescript).

17 For example, letters in Vaynol Estate Office of 20th June 1725 from Jno. Williams to Thomas Smith, and of 13th October 1728 from John Griffith, noting wholesale ruthless felling of timber.

18 This is clear from an interim report of a survey of 1756 for the takeover of the estate by Thomas Assheton-Smith (Vaynol Estate Office). Lines of improvement were proposed.

19 Valuations by J. Durnvile and Robert Lloyd, and by William Jones, Vaynol Estate Ms. 247 (1798). Durnvile's valuation ends with criticisms like those of 1756, of the low standard of husbandry, neglect of meadows, burning of dung for fuel, cutting of peat from meadows instead of commons, and excessive cultivation of gorse.

20 Interim report of survey of 1756, *op. cit.*

21 E. HYDE HALL, *A description of Caernarvonshire* (1809–11), Bangor Ms. 908 (U.C.N. Wales). See E. GWYNNE JONES, *Caern. Hist. Soc. Record Series,* no. 2 (1952).
22 D. ELLIS (1805) *op. cit.* The only manorial right exercised within memory of man was that 'Mr. Assheton-Smith and those who have claimed under the same title have from time of memory permitted and restrained the erection of cottages and inclosures upon all Wastes within the said parish' and that 'when such permission has been given it has ever been annexed with the condition of performing Boon or Harvest Work during a certain number of days upon the demesne lands held by the tenant of the Capital Mansion situate in the adjoining parish of Bangor.'
23 A letter of 1792 from Thomas Wright (agent) remarks 'Slate cannot possibly be brought down fast enough to answer the Demand. I have a scheme of making a new Road from the Quarries, which if you approve of when you see it may possibly be carried on and enable us better to supply the demand for slate.' Ms. in Vaynol Estate Office.
24 Persons who built houses on the commons of Llanddeiniolen. Porth-yr-Aur Mss. 13,005, 13,047 (1808) (U.C.N. Wales).
25 D. ELLIS (1805) *op. cit.*
26 The rioters and their localities are named in Porth-yr-Aur Mss. 13,030 (September 1809) and 13,033 (U.C.N. Wales).
27 Account of rent and arrears due from cottagers on Llanddeiniolen common to T. A. Smith, Porth-yr-Aur Ms. 13,154 (March 1820) (U.C.N. Wales). This Ms. distinguishes encroachments from inclosures.
28 Schedule of allotments, Llanddeiniolen, Porth-yr-Aur Mss. 13,213, 13,153a (U.C.N. Wales). See also Abstract of the Llanddeiniolen Award (25th March 1814) (Caernarvon Record Office).
29 Vaynol Estate Papers 107 to 180 (rentals dated between 1799 and 1841) and 245, 247 to 255, 258 (surveys and valuations 1777 to 1832) and the survey of 1864–69 (see note 34), Vaynol Estate Office.
30 R. LLOYD ELLIS (of Holyhead), Survey of the Vaynol Estate, 1832, *Vaynol Estate Papers,* 255–257.
31 Enumeration Abstract, Census of Great Britain 1831. Of 654 males of 20 years and over in Llanddeiniolen, 484 were non-agricultural labourers, and nearly all of these must have been slate workers. Some 99 families were supported chiefly by agriculture, and nearly 380 by the slate industry.
32 Enumeration Abstracts, Census of Great Britain for relevant years. Inhabited houses increased from 317 in 1821 to 510 in 1831, 863 in 1841 and 990 in 1851.
33 Land Tax Assessments for Llanddeiniolen, 1809, Porth-yr-Aur Ms. 13,020a (U.C.N. Wales).
34 Survey of the Vaynol Estate completed by 1869 in great detail by F. Jackson of Nottingham, Vaynol Estate Office.
35 Capt. Stewart's evidence to the Welsh Land Commission, 1893. See A. R. RICKARDS, Facing up to the sixties: Vaynol, Part I: The problem, *Journ. Chartered Land Agents' Soc.* 60 (4) (1961) 126–132. Between 1857 and 1892, with the slate industry booming, over £300,000 was spent on repairs and improvements on the Vaynol estate. Many smallholdings were provided with cowsheds and barns, and many farmhouses rebuilt.
36 D. R. M. STUART, Facing up to the sixties: Vaynol, Part II: The solution, *Journ. Chartered Land Agents' Soc.* 60 (5) (1961) 154–162.
37 *The Times* (17th November 1969).

# THE PROBLEM OF FIELD EVIDENCE IN GEOMORPHOLOGY

## K. M. CLAYTON

### INTRODUCTION

The subject matter of geomorphology is, in the words of Lester King, the form and development of the earth,[1] and, even if we wish to limit that broad definition, every geomorphologist is concerned with the surface forms of the whole globe. Two particular problems arise from this: the great complexity of the multivariate relationships with which geomorphologists are concerned, and the huge areal extent across which they operate.

In recent years the first of these problems has yielded somewhat to the power of the electronic computer, which is able to handle multivariate statistics. In addition, the quantity of data which the computer can handle makes it possible to use information from a wide area. As long as the data are available in a numerical form, or even in a present/absent form, generalisations can be tested against a large area, even against the whole of the earth's surface.

Geomorphology has no great reservoir of numerical data awaiting exploitation such as human geographers have in the published censuses. In one or two fields suitable information is available, notably in the river water and sediment discharge data collected in the United States. The existence of these recorded observations allowed the great step forward made in our understanding of fluvial geomorphology, summarised in Leopold, Wolman and Miller's *Fluvial Processes in Geomorphology*.[2] The statistical generalisations they make about the interrelationships between channel width and depth, mean stream velocity and discharge, are supported by a mass of observations and are demonstrably of wide application. Of course, just as the published censuses fail to answer some of the more detailed or localized problems that may concern the human geographer, the hydrological data has its limitations. Thus Schumm[3] attempted to use the published figures for alluvial streams to examine some of their features and was forced to the conclusion that the (understandable) location of gauging stations at relatively stable points on these channels distorted the information and limited its value.

For much of his data, the geomorphologist must turn to the field. He may visit it himself and use the data directly, or he may draw indirectly on the observations and records of others. If he relies on his own data he is assured of its quality (or, to put it a better way, knows its limitations!) but has to face the restriction of area that is imposed by the time (and money) available. Even if he mounts expeditions to distant lands, he must face the fact that he has seen but a fraction of the world and that his outlook will be coloured by the areas he has been able to see.

In practice all geomorphologists rely to a considerable extent upon the records and reports of others. Concepts are built up and rejected by comparison with descriptions of unvisited areas, supported by information included in maps or photographs. Currently very little of this information is available in numerical form, and it hardly seems conceivable that much of it can ever easily be summarised in this way. Instead it is usual to find a descriptive account, ostensibly factual, but in practice strongly selective and biased by the imposition of the theoretical concepts or practical aims of the field-worker involved. Selection is necessary or the field account would never be completed, the bias is often subconscious, but even where it is recognised I would not expect it to be completely suppressed. Complete objectivity is not a practicable achievement, for as Charles Darwin wrote a century ago:

> About thirty years ago there was much talk that geologists ought only to observe and not theorise; I well remember someone saying that at this rate a man might as well go into a gravel pit and count the pebbles and describe the colours.[4]

It seems to me that geomorphologists are far too sanguine about the chances of building up a body of objective knowledge that any one research worker may draw on. All the evidence I have seen suggests that the problems are serious and fundamental and need to be far more widely appreciated. If the rather pessimistic view put forward here seems too strong, it is rather that I am trying to show that the field data collected by others must be subject to very careful assessment. However, I feel that this may be an understatement and that it could be that much of this data is not merely worthless but is even dangerous and misleading. Maps and air photographs can do a good deal to convey field information without distortion, but inspection of the field evidence may be the only effective way of establishing the validity of an interpretation.

## OUR MODE OF PERCEPTION

The colouring of observation by theoretical understanding has received little attention. C. F. A. Pantin, in a most interesting essay on the contrast between what he called the restricted sciences (for example physics or chemistry) and the unrestricted sciences (for example biology or geology), refers to O. T. Jones's investigation of platforms in Wales:

> I found the conclusions fully comfortable with my own limited field of experience as an amateur geologist, and accepted them. I found it noteworthy that after learning of this work I immediately viewed various geological features that I encountered—for instance in South Devon and in parts of Brazil—with a different eye. It is not that I have the same perceptions as before and then apply Professor Jones's reasoning to them; it is as though my actual mode of perception has been changed by the historical experience of this argument.[5]

Pantin goes on to point out that this 'mode of perception' can easily lead to error. Agassiz gained an eye for the effects of glaciation in Switzerland, and applied it successfully in Scotland, demonstrating that almost every element of Scottish scenery bore witness to recent extensive glaciation. But he then went on to see evidence of glaciation in the Tijuca Hills behind Rio de Janeiro. In much the same way, ice-caps were postulated on some of the chalk cuestas of southern England on the evidence of a supposed local till (the Chiltern drift) or meltwater forms in the South Downs (the Devil's Dyke). Here the 'mode of perception' can now be rejected on the independent evidence Manley has established on the level of the Pleistocene snow-line in southern England—neither of these features was high enough, or wet enough, to sustain a local ice-cap.[6]

All too many geomorphologists have tended to push their current 'mode of perception' to the limits of the evidence and frequently well beyond the true area or features where their theoretical approach is wholly justified. Thus the remarkable scheme of de Geer, dating the retreat stages of the Scandinavian ice-sheet, was correlated on most slender evidence with varved deposits in other continents. Similarly, the sea-level height sequence that appeared to fit the river terraces of some of the rivers of Britain and France was extended to Morocco, Egypt, the East Indies, Australia and elsewhere. Fragments of evidence relating to morphological form, or the clay minerals present in ancient deposits, have been used to 'prove' that upland surfaces in central Europe evolved under a tropical climate and a savanna vegetation. The only corrective is when other geomorphologists with other 'modes of perception' view and report on the same field evidence.

## FIELD OBSERVATION

Insight into the complexities of the interpretation of field evidence comes from travel and in particular from taking part in field excursions with other geomorphologists. To go in the field with a group on an excursion at an international conference is to understand a little of the selection that operates when we view a landscape or a section in sediments. Few elements will engage the attention of everyone present, and there will be little agreement on which are the most significant features. Some stops will provide little of personal interest, yet others in the party cannot be prised away from some splendid detail which seems to them to be the key to the area! In the same way, it is enlightening to be taken (in Poland)[7] to an area of most interesting morainic ridges (Figure 1) and to be asked the direct question: 'You have seen a drumlin, are these drumlins?' They most certainly were not and it seemed curious that published accounts (and maps and photographs) of drumlins had not made this doubly clear. But it seems that nothing less than experience of a real drumlin can really settle this question: the object perceived in the field convinces in a way that the selection of data presented in a description or on a map can never do.

### The Missoula flood

A most convincing case of this is the Missoula flood (or floods), a catastrophic discharge of water released from Lake Missoula, Western Montana, when the ice-tongue dam failed. In the deeply incised valleys of the Columbia tributaries, such as the Clark Fork River, these discharges reached high speeds and produced such large fluvial forms that they proved exceedingly difficult to recognise as such. Further downstream, the floods broke out south from the Columbia river valley to flow across the loess-covered lava plateaus of eastern Washington to cut the Scablands (Figure 2). The scale of these floods is so great, and the features formed so remarkable and widespread, that there have always been many geomorphologists anxious to find a more credible explanation. W. M. Davis visited the Clark Fork River and described 'moraines' and 'ice-scoured slopes' as evidence of glaciation.[8] The valley is deep and trough-like, scoured free of most of its soil to a height of over 300 metres above the valley floor. Huge gravel benches lie across embayments in the valley side with their crests at 150 metres or more above the river. Pardee interpreted Eddy Narrows on the Clark Fork in terms of a catastrophic discharge of pro-glacial Lake Missoula.[9] He postulated a flow of water over 300 metres deep and with a wetted perimeter of 3,100 metres. For a time, the present valley functioned as a channel, and the gravel bars were massive point bars. Extrapolating from observations and relationships for much smaller channels, Pardee estimated a discharge of 10,950,000 cubic metres/second or 39.4 cubic kilometres/hour, with a mean velocity of 20 metres/second (70 kilometres/hour). These staggering figures are not easy to comprehend: the maximum discharge of the Amazon is only one per cent of the Missoula flood at Eddy Narrows. Despite the size of Lake Missoula (about 1,700 cubic kilometres above Eddy Narrows) it is clear that discharge at this rate could not have continued for more than a day or so.

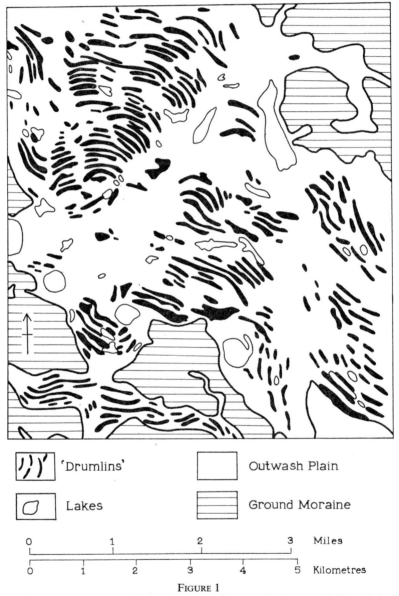

'Drumlins'   Outwash Plain

Lakes   Ground Moraine

| 0 | 1 | 2 | 3 | Miles |
|---|---|---|---|---|

| 0 | 1 | 2 | 3 | 4 | 5 | Kilometres |
|---|---|---|---|---|---|---|

FIGURE 1

Morainic ridges (crevasse fillings or cross-valley moraines) near Zbójno, Poland, described by Liberacki as 'drumlins'
The ridges are shown solid black. They lie in a low area and are surrounded by featureless till plateaus which are ruled. (After M. Liberacki,[7] Fig. 47.)

134

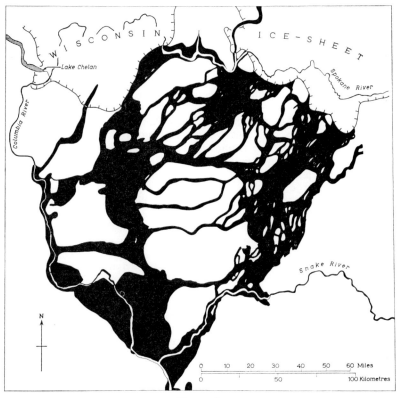

FIGURE 2
Channelled scabland of the Columbia Plateau, Washington, U.S.A.
The vast discharge from Glacial Lake Missoula occupied the whole area covered black

The perceptive work of Bretz (1923–32) established to his satisfaction that the ramifying network of valleys known as the Scablands were cut by a catastrophic flood.[10] Although Bretz was aware of Pardee's earlier work on Lake Missoula,[11] he interpreted the Scabland evidence independently and it was only in 1930 that he identified the sudden drainage of Lake Missoula as the agency. The field evidence left Bretz convinced that the 'valleys' of the Scablands were in fact abandoned channels, and further that they were not cut at different times but were somehow all occupied together by a discharge of water of remarkable volume. Very few were convinced by his papers, and his views were strongly opposed. Those who agreed that the channels were cut by water sought to show that it need not have occupied them all at the same time. Others sought alternative processes: glacial erosion, collapse of lava caves, rainwash and wind erosion of loess and so on. The invention of those unconvinced by the catastrophic flood hypothesis is remarkable, but their theories are incapable of explaining the field relationships. As Bretz and others showed, the only hypothesis capable of explaining all the field features is the catastrophic flood.[12] Yet after nearly 100 pages of close argument, of careful recapitulation of the field evidence, and of the newly-available aerial photographs and topographic maps of the area, one

senses that they feel the reader may still be unconvinced. They note that
A. C. Waters, well acquainted with the Scabland, wrote to the authors:

> the best thing you can do to convince your reader is to beg, cajole, even
> browbeat him into *really looking* at the region's topographic maps.[13]

And later:

> Before one commits himself as skeptical of the interpretation of the present
> study, he should examine the Benge, Haas, LaCrosse and Starbuck quadrangle
> maps. A topography probably without close approach to parallelism in his
> experience with maps or terrain is depicted on them.[14]

In the same way, any reader who finds Pardee's account of the giant
ripples below Wills' Creek Pass[15] unconvincing would surely be persuaded
by the field evidence. The ripples lie below a col in which the confined
waters were speeded up by the Venturi effect so that they tore out an
elongate closed lake basin, half a kilometre in length, from solid rock and
discharged over rock knobs, plucking them on their downstream face as
effectively as any roche moutonnée. It is the closest simulation of glacial
erosion I have ever seen, and convincing testimony of the volume and speed
of the discharge. In the case of the channelled Scablands and the Lake
Missoula flood(s) we may agree with Richmond and others that:

> Most of the workers *who have had an opportunity to study the features* described
> by Bretz and Pardee now accept the imaginative interpretation presented by
> Bretz nearly half a century ago.[16] [my italics]

*The Finger Lakes*

In 1960 I found myself in upstate New York, and reading Holmes's
account of the 'through' valleys of the glaciated Appalachian plateau south
of the Finger Lakes,[17] I found the evidence for the simultaneous occupation
and erosion by ice of the complex network of through valleys to be
unconvincing. Had not the same ice-sheet faithfully followed a series of
pre-glacial obsequent valleys further north to form the Finger Lakes? Yet
after only a few days' study *on the ground* I was prepared to concede the
explanation offered by Holmes, so that I was then led to examine the
Finger Lakes themselves more closely. Here I found that the accepted
account of their origin could not be sustained, and so I put forward the
view that they resulted from the modification of the entire landscape
(trough and interfluve alike) by an active ice-sheet with divergent
flow-lines. This view[18] has not been readily accepted from the written
account. Yet I could claim that careful study of the topographic maps, or
better still the field evidence, will demonstrate that the common view that
the lakes occupy deepened obsequent river valleys is untenable.

Geomorphology will make slow progress if the published report fails
as a means of communication. We can hardly expect much progress if the
spread of ideas is to depend on the field demonstration of the evidence.
It might seem that all that we need are more clearly presented papers and
a more ready acceptance of the evidence. The difficulty is that our caution
is well founded. Most papers present a very one-sided review of the evidence
and at times manage to distort it in a most disturbing way. It is not implied
that the distortion is deliberate, but a review of the controversy on tors,
or the case against pro-glacial lakes and overflow channels will show the
ways in which complex and extensive field evidence can be selectively
presented in effective support of a particular thesis. The championship of
pro-glacial lakes may in the first case have been extreme, but it seems
unfortunate if we can only reach the 'truth' through a number of violent
swings of the pendulum of geomorphological fashion.

## Morainic structures

One particular example of the interpretation of field evidence is the origin of contorted structures in glacial moraines. These are often termed *Stauchmoränen* or thrust moraines. A typical Canadian example is illustrated in Figure 3. In a series of papers, Krygowski has drawn attention to the fact that, in Poland, many of the terminal (or retreat) moraines show inclusions of Tertiary clays.[19] These clays generally outcrop at much lower levels, but within the moraines they seem to be carried up to perhaps 200 metres above their usual outcrop level. This has been quoted as evidence of glacial disturbance, the clay being sheared off and carried forward and upward by the ice movement.

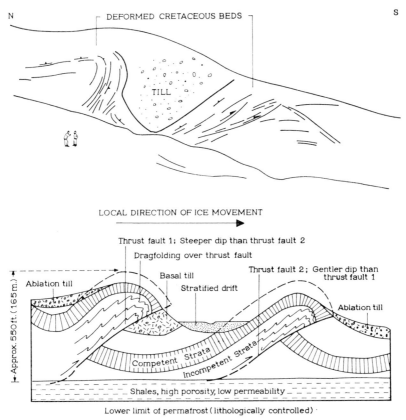

FIGURE 3

Ice-thrust structure in a moraine (after Kupsch,[20] Fig. 3)

Krygowski has developed an alternative theory, in which he regards the clay cores of the moraines as diapir-like intrusions forced up into the moraine. Indeed, much of the relief of the moraine ridge is thought to be the result of this upward movement of the Tertiary clays. The moraines are located across the southern margins of deep Tertiary basins, and it is held that ice loading on the thick clays initiated the squeezing-up of the beds, caused the foundation of a transverse ridge, and that this relief

137

feature was then transformed into a complex terminal moraine. Krygowski's theory may well explain the Polish cases he is concerned with, but it is unlikely to explain all the 'thrust' moraines that exist; glacial shear is a common phenomenon in any case. But if we now return to Kupsch's illustration,[20] aware of Krygowski's 'mode of perception', we can see that Kupsch has imposed his own mode of perception on the diagram. If, as in Figure 4, we remove the indications of shearing movement from the fault planes, the pattern that is left fits a diapir-like fold pattern at least as well, if not better, than the shear-failure pattern imposed by Kupsch. We clearly cannot go further without the photograph from which the diagram was drawn; more probably, as I have been arguing here, we cannot settle the matter without returning to the field evidence.

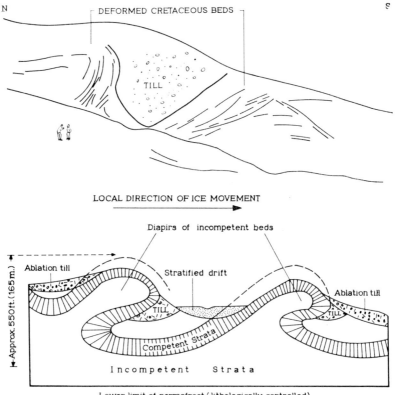

FIGURE 4

Alternative interpretation of Figure 3

The interpretive elements added by Kupsch to the sketch have been removed, while the lower diagram interprets the structure as the result of diapir-like intrusions, following Krygowski.[19] Even if the interpretation is unacceptable, the field evidence (above) is reported without an imposed interpretation

## CONCLUSION

Geomorphology is full of conflicting hypotheses; this is part of its intrinsic interest. But in attempting to distinguish between the relative merits of undercutting by wind, subsurface chemical weathering, or frost

*The problem of field evidence in geomorphology*

action, for some of the more spectacular tors at Brimham Rocks; or between the origin of the Dolly Ridge gullies, Schefferville, by solifluction ('vallons de gélivation' of Twidale)[21] or as sub-glacial meltwater chutes;[22] we are likely to be muddled by the conflict of evidence and views unless we can visit the site and select from the field evidence ourselves. This is so often true that it would seem we must accept it as a limitation on the speed with which we may advance our understanding. My own reading of the geomorphological literature suggests that it is a limitation that is generally overlooked, and in the case of the 'new' geomorphology seems to have been completely ignored. As Pantin wrote:

> The objects of study of geologists . . . . . are exceedingly varied. It is of course just this richness of their material which makes progress so much slower . . . . . than with the limited objects of study in the physical sciences.[23]

## NOTES

[1] L. C. KING, Geomorphology, *The encyclopedia of geomorphology* (ed. R. W. Fairbridge) (1968) 403–404.

[2] L. B. LEOPOLD, M. G. WOLMAN and J. P. MILLER, *Fluvial processes in geomorphology* (Freeman, San Francisco, 1964).

[3] S. A. SCHUMM, The shape of alluvial channels in relation to sediment type, *United States Geological Survey, Professional Paper* 352–B (1960) 17–30.

[4] C. DARWIN, *More letters of Charles Darwin* (eds. F. Darwin and A. C. Seward) 1 (1903) 195.

[5] C. F. A. PANTIN, *The relations between the sciences* (Cambridge University Press, 1968) 13.

[6] G. MANLEY, The range of variation of the British climate, *Geog. Jour.* 117 (1951) 43–68.

[7] M. LIBERACKI, Drumlins near Zbójno, *Guide-book of excursion from the Baltic to the Tatras, Part 1, North Poland* (ed. R. Galon) (INQUA, 1961) 115–117.

[8] W. M. DAVIS, Features of glacial origin in Montana and Idaho, *Annals Assoc. American Geographers* 10 (1921) 122–132.

[9] J. T. PARDEE, Unusual currents in Glacial Lake Missoula, Montana, *Bulletin Geological Soc. America* 53 (1942) 1959–1600.

[10] J. H. BRETZ, Channelled scablands of the Columbia Plateau, *Journal of Geology* 31 (1923) 617–649.

[11] J. T. PARDEE, The glacial Lake Missoula, Mont., *Journal of Geology* 18 (1910) 376–386.

[12] J. HARLEN BRETZ, H. T. U. SMITH and GEORGE E. NEFF, Channelled scabland of Washington: new data and interpretations, *Bulletin Geological Soc. America* 67 (1956) 957–1050.

[13] *Idem*, 960.

[14] *Idem*, 1045 (footnote).

[15] J. T. PARDEE, *op. cit.* (1942) 1584 and plate 3.

[16] G. M. RICHMOND and others, *INQUA, Guidebook for Field Conference E, Northern and Middle Rocky Mountains* (1965) 68.

[17] C. D. HOLMES, Glacial erosion in a dissected plateau, *American Journal of Science* 33 (1937) 217–232.

[18] K. M. CLAYTON, Glacial erosion in the Finger Lakes region (New York State, U.S.A.), *Zeitschrift für Geomorphologie* 9 (1965) 50–62.

[19] B. KRYGOWSKI, Some remarks about the age of the glacitectonic structures of western Poland and their diapir-like character, *Report VI International Congress on Quaternary, Warsaw, 1961* 3 (1963) 469–474.

[20] W. O. KUPSCH, Ice-thrust ridges in western Canada, *Journal of Geology* 70 (1962) 588.

[21] C. R. TWIDALE, Vallons de gélivation dans le centre du Labrador, *Revue Géomorph. dynamique* 7 (1956) 18–23.

[22] J. T. ANDREWS, 'Vallons de gélivation' in Central Labrador–Ungava, a reappraisal, *Canadian Geographer* 5 (1961) 1–9.

[23] C. F. A. PANTIN, *op. cit.* (1968) 17.

# THE RÔLE OF GEOGRAPHICAL ANALYSIS IN THE PLANNING PROCESS

## M. P. COLLINS

### INTRODUCTION

The planning profession has been bedevilled by demarcation disputes ever since 1911 when the Town Planning Committee of the Royal Institute of British Architects recommended that the architect should be solely responsible for planning decisions.[1] It was not until 1950, however, that the Schuster Report[2] suggested that the Town Planning Institute's basis of membership should be substantially broadened to accommodate those disciplines which make an essential contribution to planning. The geographer's case for active participation in the planning process was based upon a demonstrated ability to conduct surveys and present the results in an orderly manner.[3] Many were content to become collectors of field data and opt out of the decision-taking process on the grounds that geography was not a 'prescriptive' discipline. Others were less content with this subservient rôle.[4] This essay is not, however, concerned with an evaluation of the geographer's contribution to planning since this forms the subject of an accompanying contribution by A. G. Powell. Its main purpose is to examine some recent developments in the application of mathematical and statistical techniques to geographical analysis and assess their future rôle in the planning process.

### QUANTIFICATION

The *speculative* methodology of the social sciences is often criticized by those who seek universal solutions to human problems. Disciplines are commonly judged by their capacity to formulate general theory and this explains why the search for laws governing spatial relationships has been an essential feature of geographical study during the past 120 years.[5] Gottman argues that these spatial patterns have evolved with increasing rapidity and thus undermined the 'geographers' endeavours to find general principles in the distribution of these phenomena'.[6] It is just possible, however, that these phenomena do not conform to neat linear abstractions. Historians, for example, admit that there are occasions when it pays to '. . . . . relax the rules in favour of the phenomena'.[7] But few geographers would agree with this somewhat nihilistic view, judging from their increasing use of mathematical analogies.[8] This latter development certainly constitutes a further step towards the development of interpretative and predictive capability. The general availability of 'packaged' computer programs has enabled geographers to subject their observations to rigorous statistical analysis. It is now possible to discern meaningful relationships between a large number of disparate factors, and this detailed analysis of spatial correlation is gradually replacing the more descriptive scholarship of classical geographers. In this context it is important to distinguish between description (no matter how sophisticated) and any ultimate explanation of the observed phenomena. Some recent applications of multivariate analysis demonstrate this point very clearly.[9]

Factor analysis appeals to geographers because it provides a 'parsimonious description' of the essential information of the original set of variables.[10] The factor analysis model can be expressed succinctly as:

$$3ji = \sum_{p=1}^{m} a_{jp}F_{pi} + d_jU_{ji} \qquad \begin{array}{l} (i = 1, 2, 3 \ldots \ldots N) \\ (j = 1, 2, 3 \ldots \ldots n) \end{array}$$

where:

$3ji$ = the value of variable j for case i

$F_{pi}$ = the value of common factor p for case i

$a_{jp}F_{pi}$ = the contribution of each factor to the linear composite

$d_jU_{ji}$ = the remaining variance between the theoretical and observed values of 3ji

An important requirement of factor analysis is the existence of a linear relationship between every pair of variables and this may limit its usefulness as a tool for analysing socio-economic behaviour within a given spatial framework. A study of 157 British towns with a population of over 50,000 in 1951 confirmed that only a few of the selected variables were associated in a linear sense; for example, only 254 of the 1,653 correlation coefficients were greater than $\pm$ 0.500.[11] This explains, in part, why the four major components (social class, population change between 1931 and 1951, population change between 1951 and 1958, and overcrowding) accounted for only 60.4 per cent of the total variance. In circumstances such as this the application of cluster analysis[12] can assist in the definition of spatial units, or functional groupings, with a specified degree of homogeneity. But the geographical and planning significance of such units is limited by the highly derivative nature of their definition. Generally speaking, planners are more concerned with need for (and desirability of) spatial association than the precise measurement of its existence, and this may constitute a 'threshold' between geographical and planning analysis.

The application of statistical techniques to geographical analysis has been largely confined to examinations of an equilibrium or 'steady state'. A recent mammoth review of conceptual models in geography devoted only a few pages to time series analysis;[13] and this is very surprising, since it is virtually impossible to prove the existence of causality from static measurements of spatial correlation.[14] It is possible, however, to derive a testable form of causality from a time-ordered series of correlation coefficients. Several writers have suggested that time series analysis can be extended to spatial data[15] and this would seem to provide a powerful technique for trend *identification* (which is of primary interest to the geographer) and trend *prediction* (which is of primary interest to the planner). Some of the inherent statistical problems of spatial correlation still remain, namely the use of modifiable units, the non-linear nature of many socio-economic relationships, the phenomenon of autocorrelation, and the availability of time series data. But sufficient progress has already been made to demonstrate the advantages of spectral analysis[16] over such devices as the periodogram, moving averages, and auto-regression.

CONCEPTUAL MODELS

One of the most significant trends in contemporary geographical analysis is the development of conceptual models. Geographers have long recognized the need to bridge the ever-growing gap between our theoretical and empirical knowledge of geographical systems, and numerous models are now being developed to this end. The advantages of conceptual models are well documented and it suffices to note that they demonstrate complex relationships in a succinct manner, facilitate analysis and valid comparisons, and provide a testable form of hypothesis. On the debit side, however, it must be remembered that a mathematical model is, of necessity, 'an abstract idealisation of the problem, and approximations and simplifying assumptions generally are required if the model is to be tractable.'[17] In other words, the model may not constitute a valid, or useful, representation of the problem (or system) under investigation. One measure of a model's usefulness is its ability to establish the consequences of alternative policies in sufficient detail to narrow down the range of possible solutions. Ideally the model should select one optimal solution. But this would seem to be impossible, so far as planning is concerned, when one considers the multiplicity and importance of intangibles in plan evaluation. Attempts to assess the wider economic implications of road construction, for example, demonstrate this problem very clearly.[18] Generally speaking, the value of a road improvement reflects the monetary value that is accredited to induced traffic, and any savings due to accident reduction and economies in total journey time. This valuation is open to attack on the grounds that 'judgement plays such an important rôle in the estimation of benefit ratios that little significance can be attached to the precise numerical results obtained.'[19] The economic impact of these road improvements is also difficult to assess. Recent studies in the U.S.A. are criticized for their failure to distinguish between the net benefits to the community and the benefits to specific population groups; and for their failure to determine the net benefits which derive from induced changes in the nature and location of economic activity.[20] Similar criticisms are now being levelled at the Greater London Council's urban motorway proposals.[21]

The development of conceptual models is in danger of becoming an end in its own right. Social scientists are becoming increasingly pre-occupied with the identification, and partial explanation, of particular systems. In many cases, however, these explanations are based upon an arbitrary combination of variables (reflecting the availability of data) and an 'over-simplified' view of locational behaviour.[22] Deviations from the theoretical norm are treated as minor irritants while the more *mundane* problems of relating the model to its 'real-world' context are usually ignored. This reluctance to demonstrate the practical applications of many conceptual models explains why they play such a minor rôle in the statutory planning process. The framework within which the modelled system operates needs to be defined in a more comprehensive manner to enable the model to demonstrate its full potential. Operations research provides one possible approach to this problem and it also demonstrates the rank status of models in the decision-making process (Figure 1).

It must be recognized that the approach outlined in Figure 1 has already over-simplified the complexity of most planning problems. The identification and simulation of a particular urban system, for example, constitutes a major task in its own right and yet it is only the first step towards the identification of existing problems and the formulation/ evaluation of alternative solutions. One review of the Penn-Jersey, Pittsburg and San Francisco models concluded that they cost much more than was originally estimated, took far longer to complete than was expected, and were rarely used for the purposes which inspired their development.[23] A variety of modelling techniques have been applied to locational aspects of urban structure with only a limited degree of success.[24]

142

In most cases these models have explained locational behaviour in rather general terms, for example the minimization of trip-journey time (or cost), the gravitational attraction of existing related activities, and saturation levels of aggregation. It is often argued that the aim of urban land use models is to simulate the market processes which determine the use of land. This reliance upon the market mechanism is open to attack on several grounds:[25]

*(a)* that the basic assumptions which underpin the theories of rational choice and perfect competition are highly questionable;

*(b)* that the classical view of supply and demand relationship is not a valid picture of the real world;

*(c)* that urban systems encompass a variety of interrelated 'market situations' which operate over varying time and spatial scales, with subtly differentiated commodities, major inequalities in the bargaining position of some land uses and many individuals, and manifest imperfections in the dissemination of market information; and

*(d)* that local planning authorities often operate within a political framework which attaches more importance to the social implications of particular land-use policies, for example the London County Council's refusal to sanction residential densities in excess of 200 persons per acre.

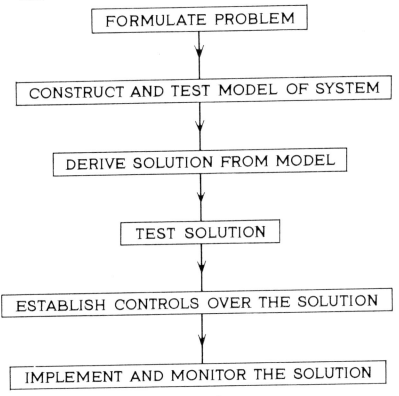

FIGURE 1

A typical operations research flow chart

There can be little doubt, however, that the supply and demand relationship plays a crucial rôle in determining city centre land values and rent levels. The introduction of additional planning controls over office development in Greater London resulted in spectacular increases in the rental value of existing office buildings. Rents in central London have risen on average from 45 shillings per square foot in 1964 to 90 shillings in 1969, with an estimated peak of £14 per square foot for the projected Sun Alliance building near the Bank of England.[26] At present there seems to be no end to the prospect of larger profits and it is estimated that the redevelopment of a six-acre site adjacent to the Stock Exchange will create an asset worth £225 million.[27] It is hardly surprising, therefore, that the search for potential office sites within central London has been intensified during the past few years. A number of factors determine the suitability of land for office development, for example its location, current land-use zoning, and the age, condition, aggregate floor space and existing use rights of the present buildings. The interaction of these factors over space and time often explains the geographical location of particular developments.

TABLE I

Persons employed in the London conurbation

|  | *1951* | *1961* | *1966* |
|---|---|---|---|
| *Persons employed in* |  |  |  |
| Central area .. | 1,251,791 | 1,441,600 | 1,283,590 |
| Remainder of conurbation | 3,113,549 | 3,059,610 | 2,927,840 |
| TOTAL | 4,365,340 | 4,501,210 | 4,211,430 |
| *Persons resident in the outer metropolitan area and employed within the London conurbation* |  |  |  |
| Central area .. | 123,980 | 197,650 | 185,570 |
| Remainder of conurbation | 118,550 | 204,210 | 209,900 |
| TOTAL | 242,530 | 401,860 | 395,470 |

TABLE II

Office space in London

| *Office floor space within central London (1)* | | *Outstanding planning permission for offices in Greater London (1)* | | *Office development permits for Greater London (2)* | | |
|---|---|---|---|---|---|---|
| | *millions of square feet* | | *millions of square feet* | | *No. of permits* | *Floor space* |
| 1948 | 77.5 | March 1966 | 16.8 | 1965 | 94 | 1.0 |
| 1957 | 152.6 | March 1967 | 12.4 | 1966 | 211 | 1.3 |
| 1962 | 174.5 | March 1968 | 11.7 | 1967 | 256 | 2.7 |
| 1966 | 178.6 | | | 1968 | 296 | 4.1 |
| | | | | 1969 | 188 | 4.2 |

*Sources:* (1) G.L.D.P. Report of Studies    (2) *The Economist* (8th November 1969)

Recent attempts to explain the changing distribution of specified land uses in central London have relied solely upon indices of accessibility, association, centrality and development potential. These growth allocation models of land development failed to explain the changing distribution of commercial, industrial and residential land uses, and this suggests that more attention must be paid to the political and statutory planning framework within which the market process operates. Recent events within the Greater London region indicate that the institutional constraints may prove to be a more critical determinant of land values than any short-term imbalance between the supply of, and demand for, office accommodation. Even the inflated price of office accommodation is difficult to explain in terms of simple supply and demand relationships when one examines the current trends with regard to central area employment, the provision of new offices and the issue of office development permits (Tables I and II).

*Retail distribution*

The advent of central place theory has greatly strengthened the methodology of urban geography by providing a 'plausible' explanation of urban hierarchies and the 'pattern through which wholesale, retail, service and administrative functions, plus market orientated manufacturing are provided to urban communities.'[28] Few local planning authorities within the United Kingdom have utilized central place theory to formulate their policies for controlling the growth of neighbouring town centres. For many years they relied upon universal standards such as those advocated in the Final Report of the New Towns' Committee, namely one shop per 100 to 150 persons. The need for a more precise method of determining the appropriate amount of retail floor space became evident in the early 1960s when the Ministry of Housing and Local Government encouraged private developers to participate in the redevelopment of existing town centres. The development companies sought re-assurance about the economic viability of these town centre schemes before investing their money, and consultants were employed to predict future levels of turnover for individual towns. In most cases the calculations were based upon predicted changes in the resident population, disposable income, and the accessibility and attractions of rival centres. These figures were then translated into retail floor space and sub-divided into lettable shop units. Since population and income constituted the main variables in all these assessments one might have expected some measure of comparability with regard to the final predictions. This was not the case, however, due to considerable variations in the relative weight that was given to the main variables; that is the final recommendation reflected the *initial* choice of consultant rather than the *objective* facts.[29] The serious nature of these problems was finally recognized by the Ministry in 1966. Circular 50/66 noted that work was progressing on several hundred town centre redevelopment schemes which *varied* considerably in their

> realism, soundness and prospects of implementation. Moreover proposals of individual towns are prepared in isolation and often take little account of proposals being put forward by neighbouring authorities. In total the proposed provision of facilities in town centre schemes up and down the country greatly exceeds the need and possibility of execution. Over-optimistic redevelopment schemes which fail to be carried out result only in blight.

The Ministry of Housing and Local Government is largely to blame for this chaotic situation since it is best placed to develop a satisfactory method for assessing future shopping needs, and solely responsible for ensuring that the plans of neighbouring authorities are mutually consistent. It was not until 1967 that the Ministry prepared a paper on the estimation of retail floor space requirements[30] but the suggested methodology (which

145

relies upon a modification of Reilley's Law) ignored the recent development of retail models[31] and mirrored the current practices of planning consultants.

*Shopping models*

Although a considerable number of models have been developed to assist in the task of retail floor space prediction, it is interesting to note that they differ only in points of detail. The gravity model would seem to be the most popular method of explaining consumer behaviour and it suffices to note the general argument which is that the percentage of retail expenditure attracted from zone (i) to a service centre in zone (j) reflects the total disposable income in zone (i), the size and composition of the service centre in zone (j), the distance between the zones, and the existence of competition from neighbouring centres:

$$S_{ij} = C_i \left( \frac{\frac{F_j}{(d_{ij})^\alpha}}{\sum_{j=1}^{n} \frac{F_j}{(d_{ij})^\alpha}} \right)$$

where $S_{ij}$ = the retail expenditure which originates in zone i and is spent in zone j

$C_i$ = the total retail expenditure generated by zone i

$F_j$ = the size and composition of the shopping centre in zone j

$d_{ij}$ = the distance between zones i and j

$\alpha$ = an exponent which reflects the frictional impact of distance upon different shopping trips

This type of model can provide an accurate simulation of the present pattern of retail expenditure, even in a complex metropolitan situation where there is more interaction between neighbouring shopping centres. Having demonstrated the model's ability to simulate the situation which prevails at a given point in time, its operators claim that it

> can then be used to predict the future sizes of the same shopping centres under alternative sets of assumptions. Thus, the flexibility of the model makes possible the measurement and assessment of the effect on other centres of raising one centre to a particular pre-planned level, or of introducing an entirely new centre into the present pattern of facilities in the area in question.[32]

There are still a number of procedural difficulties which have to be overcome in order to predict the future regional status and floor space needs of a particular shopping centre:

*(a)* the frictional effect of distance is decreasing in importance as a primary determinant of consumer behaviour;

*(b)* the attractiveness of rival centres is no longer a linear function of the number and range of shops; and

*(c)* the relationship between increased turnover and retail floor space has still to be defined.

Even if one accepts the basic proposition that there is an optimum relationship between population, disposable income and retail floor space there is no reason to suppose that it automatically operates in favour of the consumer. Developers are concerned primarily with the maximization of profit and the minimization of any risk which may accompany the over-provision of retail floor space. The comprehensive redevelopment of an existing shopping centre inevitably requires the provision of profitable and unprofitable elements and there is usually a loss on the cost of making land available for development. An examination of six shopping schemes in 1963 led the Ministry of Housing and Local Government to conclude that profitability is not 'the essential criterion for redevelopment schemes of this kind.'[33] The local planning authority has to arbitrate between the conflicting demands of the developer, existing small traders and essential civic uses as well as satisfying the more general needs of shoppers. In certain cases the proposed development may have a particularly harmful effect upon neighbouring centres, especially if it involves the construction of an 'out-town' shopping centre. When faced with such a proposal at Haydock Park the Minister decided that its success could only be achieved at the expense of several neighbouring Lancashire towns with 'severe problems of urban obsolescence.' Similar arguments were paraded recently at the public inquiry into the proposed construction of 814,000 square feet of shopping floor space at the Brent Cross junction of the North Circular (A 406) and Hendon Way (A 41). Once again this demonstrates the importance of clearly defining the framework within which the planning decision is taken.

## CONCLUSION

This brief review of recent developments in geographical analysis has tried to demonstrate that related planning problems cannot always be solved by '..... the mere selection of some logically consistent methodology.'[34] While geographers explain the spatial patterning of central place functions in terms of *a priori* models, which only partially represent the implicit theory, the planners seek to maximize communal welfare without undermining the economic forces which gave rise to the observed patterns. In other words, the establishment of casual relationships is only the first step towards the preparation and evaluation of alternative strategies in as much as it helps to reduce uncertainty in the decision which has to be made. In an imperfect world the ultimate decision will always involve a high degree of value judgment, for the planners are nearly always plagued by insufficient time, inadequate data and no agreed scale of communal values.

## NOTES

[1] TOWN PLANNING COMMITTEE R.I.B.A., Suggestions to promoters of planning schemes, *Jour. R.I.B.A.,* 3rd series, 18, 62–68.

[2] *Report of the committee on qualifications of planners,* Cmd 8509 (H.M.S.O., 1950).

[3] T. W. FREEMAN, *Geography and planning* (Hutchinson University Library, London, 1956).

[4] R. H. BEST, *Jour. Town Planning Inst.* 44 (July–August 1958) 223.

[5] R. J. CHORLEY and P. HAGGETT, *Frontiers in geographical teaching* (Methuen and Co. Ltd., London, 1965) 3–6.

[6] J. GOTTMANN, *The renewal of the geographic environment* (Clarendon Press, Oxford, 1969) 5.

[7] H. R. TREVOR-ROPER, *The past and the present: history and sociology,* 1968 Oration (London School of Economics and Political Science, 1969) 5.

[8] P. HAGGETT, *Locational analysis in human geography* (Edward Arnold, London, 1965).

[9] J. H. DUNNING, The City of London, *Town Planning Review* 40, no. 3 (1969) 219–223.
N. A. SPENCE, A multifactor uniform regionalisation of British counties on the basis of employment data for 1961, *Reg. Studies,* no. 2 (1968) 87–104.

[10] H. H. HARMAN, *Modern factor analysis* (University of Chicago Press, 1968) 4.

[11] C. A. MOSER and W. SCOTT, *British towns: a statistical study of their social and economic differences* (Oliver and Boyd, Edinburgh, 1961) 61.

[12] W. S. PETERS, Cluster analysis in urban geography, *Social Forces* 37 (1958) 38–44.

[13] *Integrated models in geography* (eds. R. J. Chorley and P. Haggett) (Methuen & Co., London, 1969) 555–559.

[14] C. W. J. GRANGER and M. HATAMAKA, *Spectral analysis of economic time series* (Princeton University Press, 1965) chapter 7.

[15] M. S. BARTLETT, *An introduction to stochastic processes* (Cambridge University Press, 1955) 188.
P. WHITTLE, *Prediction and regulation* (English Universities Press, 1963) 63.
M. B. PRIESTLEY, The analysis of two-dimensional stationary processes with discontinuous spectra, *Biometrika* 51 (1964) 195–217.

[16] C. W. J. GRANGER and H. REES, Spectral analysis of the term structure of interest rates, *Review of Econ. Studies* 35 (1968) 67–76.

[17] F. S. HILLIER and G. J. LIEBERMAN, *Introduction to operations research* (Holden-Day Inc., London, 1968) 15.

[18] T. M. COBURN, M. E. BEESLEY and D. J. REYNOLDS, London–Birmingham motorway, *Road Research Technical Paper No. 46* (1960).
E. VICTOR MORGAN, *Economic and financial aspects of road improvements* (Roads Campaign Council, 1966) chapter 5.

[19] A. SMITHIES, *The budgeting process in the U.S.A.* (Committee for Economic Development Research Study, McGraw-Hill, New York, 1955) 344.

[20] M. MOHRING and N. HARWITZ, *Highway benefits: an analytical framework* (Northwestern University Press, 1962) 132–133.

[21] J. M. THOMSON, *Motorways in London* (Gerald Duckworth and Co. Ltd., London, 1969) 70–71.

[22] A. J. SCOTT, Spatial equilibrium of the central city, *Jour. of Reg. Science* 9, no. 1 (1969) 29–45.

[23] *Operations research for public systems* (ed. P. M. Morse) (M.I.T. Press, London, 1967) 50–51.

[24] A. G. WILSON et al., New directions in strategic transportation planning, *Centre for Environmental Studies Working Paper CES WP 36* (1969) 61.

[25] I. S. LOWRY, A short course in model design, *Jour. American Inst. Planners* (May 1965) 158–165.

[26] *The Economist* (8th November 1969) 59.

[27] *The Times* (4th July 1969). Four buildings worth £225 million on an island in the city.

[28] B. J. BERRY, Theories of urban location, *Association of American Geographers Resource Paper No. 1* (Washington D.C., 1968) 16.

[29] H. R. COLE, Shopping assessments at Haydock and elsewhere: a review, *Urban Studies* 3, no. 2 (June 1966) 147–156.

[30] *A method of estimating retail floor space requirements in small and medium sized towns outside the conurbations* (Ministry of Housing and Local Government, 1967).

[31] S. EILON, R. P. R. TILLEY and T. R. FOWKES, Analysis of a gravity demand model, *Regional Studies* 3, no. 2 (September 1969) 115–122.
M. F. DACEY, *A model for the areal pattern of retail and service establishments within an urban area* (Department of Geography, North Western University, 1966).
T. R. LAKSHMANAN and W. G. HANSEN, *A market potential model and its application to a regional planning problem* (Highway Research Board, Washington D.C., 1965).
D. L. HUFF, Defining and estimating a trade area, *Journal of Marketing* 28 (July 1964) 34–38.
*Ibid.,* A probabilistic analysis of shopping centre trade areas, *Land Economics* 39 (1963) 81–90.

[32] T. RHODES and R. WHITAKER, Forecasting shopping demand, *Journal of the Town Planning Institute* (May 1967) 188–192.

[33] Town centres: cost and control of redevelopment, *Planning Bulletin No. 3* (H.M.S.O., 1963) 17, table 3.

[34] D. HARVEY, *Explanation in geography* (Edward Arnold, London, 1969) 482.

# THE SOVIET FAR EASTERN FISHING
# INDUSTRY: A GEOGRAPHICAL ASSESSMENT

The Soviet Union is the third largest catcher of fish, including whales, in the world after Peru and Japan. One-third of the Soviet catch comes from the Far East fisheries which are important earners of foreign currency through their exports of canned crab and salmon to the West and raw fish to nearby Japan. In terms of *direct* employment the industry occupies 160,000 fishermen, as well as large numbers of processing workers and seasonal labourers, and it generates about one-quarter of the gross value of industrial output of the Far Eastern economy.[1] From the viewpoint of a regional balance of trade it is the Far East's exports of fish (and timber), including inter-regional exports to large European Russian markets, which help to pay for its imports of essential grains, meat and fruit and manufactured producer and consumer goods.

In the current Five Year Plan (1966–70) it is expected that the Far Eastern gross fish catch, including whales, will grow from under two million metric tons (1965) to almost three million tons (1970 Plan), an increase of 50 per cent. On a U.S.S.R. basis the Plan will lift *per capita* supplies of fish by around three-fifths to 20 kilograms.[2] But there are several factors retarding the real growth of the industry, the most significant of which is a belated recognition of the need for improved quality rather than a greater quantity of fish. In the Far East the partial exhaustion of some fish resources, the lag in the provision of processing, port and handling facilities, the introduction of a new system of bonuses for catches of first-grade fish, together with a system of profit accounting *(khozraschot)* all point to more selective fishing and the likelihood of plan under-fulfilment by at least one-fifth.

## THE FISHING GROUNDS

In 1913 the Far East fisheries caught little more than one-tenth of the Russian commercial catch; the Caspian Sea was the most important fishing ground with over three-fifths of the catch.[3] Fifty years later the share of the Caspian grounds had dwindled to less than eight per cent, whereas the Pacific Ocean grounds had become the second most important in the U.S.S.R. with 34 per cent of the total catch. Salinity and silting in the Caspian, Aral and Azov seas will hasten their decline. In the other 'inland' seas (the Baltic and the Black Sea) small boats will find it increasingly difficult to compete against the large ocean-going ships of the Pacific and the Atlantic. It is the Atlantic grounds with their 42 per cent share of the catch and their relative proximity to European Russian markets which present a long-term threat to the Far Eastern fisheries.[4] The latter, however, is the base not only for ships operating in the north Pacific but also for vessels ranging southwards into the Indian, south Pacific and Antarctic waters.

Because of a lack of reliable data from Soviet sources this paper is limited to a discussion of the activities of *Dal'ryba* (Far East Fishing Organization) in the north–west and north–east Pacific fishing grounds. Those grounds include the Japan Sea, the Sea of Okhotsk and the Bering Sea and they extend some 3,000 miles from Peter the Great Bay (near Vladivostok) to Sakhalin and Kamchatka, along the Aleutian islands to Bristol Bay in

149

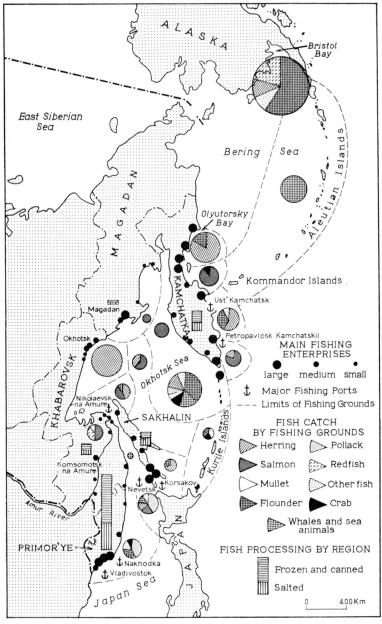

FIGURE 1

Fishing grounds and fish catch: Soviet Far East

Alaska (Figure 1). Through the possession of southern Sakhalin and the Kurile islands since 1945, the Sea of Okhotsk in particular has become virtually an inland sea for *Dal'ryba*. The discharge of the Amur river into this sea provides a substantial source of fish foods and the eastward chain of the Kurile islands, with their shallow intervening straits, limits the inflow of cold deep-sea water from the Oyashio current and so helps fish breeding.[5]

There are considerable hazards for boats operating in these grounds. In the winter there is a firm cover of ice all along the coast from the Tatar Straits as early as December; by February the entire northern half of the Okhotsk Sea is blanketed in blocks of ice which often form a continuous cover until broken up by a storm.[6] The sea is not free of ice until mid-June, and ice persists in the northern bays until July. In the northern Bering Sea navigation is usually possible from the end of May until mid-October. In summer, though, cloud prevails and dense fogs are frequent in May, June and July. Storms are particularly numerous in spring and autumn and are especially severe in the Okhotsk Sea off the west coast of southern Kamchatka. But it is the hazards of the winter that limit the main fishing season, when 75 per cent of the catch is taken, to the second and third quarters of the year.

THE FISH CATCH AND FISH SPECIES

The initial progress of the industry was slow. Until the late 1920s development was largely in the hands of the Japanese. Under the terms of the Russo-Japanese Fishing Convention of 1907, Japanese fishermen had the same rights as Russians to fish in the Okhotsk Sea. After the Revolution the Soviets found that, because of the shortage of local labour, they still needed Japanese help for seasonal work. In 1928 53 per cent of seasonal workers in the Far Eastern fishing industry were Japanese, but by 1933 the U.S.S.R. announced that it required no more Japanese labourers. The Second Five Year Plan (1933–37) provided for more canneries (which increased from two in 1913 to 42 in 1938), cold-storage plants, port facilities and the creation of a large State-owned trawler fleet.

The Far East catch grew rapidly from less than 162,000 tons in 1928 to over 405,000 tons in 1937. In 1936 the Japanese still leased almost 400 fishing lots in Soviet waters but during the Second World War the leases were suspended and afterwards they were annulled. By 1955 the catch had risen to over 647,000 tons and Soviet fishing activities in the area were assisted further by the signing in 1956 of the Soviet Japanese Fishing Agreement which declared the Okhotsk Sea a restricted area and set strict quotas for Japanese salmon fishing in the north–west Pacific.[7]

But the most spectacular expansion in the catch was in the Seven Year Plan (1959–65) when it rose by 134 per cent to 1.98 million tons and compared with an average Soviet growth rate of 97 per cent. If, however, we take the output of *edible* foodstuffs only the rate of growth becomes 56 per cent whereas the U.S.S.R. average was 60 per cent. Indeed, between 1964 and 1967 the catch of edible fish in the Far East actually *fell* by 38,700 tons as a result of fishermen's attempts to fulfil planned quotas which were set too high and without any regard to quality differentials, particularly for first-grade edible fish.[8] The average proportion of inedible fish landed in the U.S.S.R. is 16 per cent of the catch but the norm for the Far East is over 20 per cent.[9] Most of the inedible fish is reduced to fertilizer or meal but agriculture is not very strongly developed in the Far East and so inedible products are hauled long distances at high cost across Siberia to be used on European Russian farms. The limited assortment of fish landed (herring, flounder and cod) has also presented *Dal'ryba* with marketing problems.[10]

151

TABLE I

Far East fish catch by departments of *Dal'ryba*
(thousand metric tons)

| Department | 1940 | | 1950 | | 1955 | | 1960 | | 1965 | |
|---|---|---|---|---|---|---|---|---|---|---|
| | Quantity | Per cent | Quantity | Per cent | Quantity | Per cent | Quantity | Per cent | Quantity | Per cent |
| Primor'ye .. | 150.2 | 46.7 | 147.7 | 30.5 | 228.3 | 36.0 | 364.1 | 42.3 | 1023.7 | 51.7 |
| Kamchatka | 88.9 | 27.6 | 98.4 | 20.3 | 222.9 | 35.1 | 253.8 | 29.5 | 418.1 | 21.1 |
| Sakhalin | 18.9 | 5.9 | 151.1* | 31.2 | 129.1 | 20.3 | 168.4 | 19.6 | 370.2 | 18.7 |
| Khabarovsk | 49.5 | 15.4 | 71.1 | 14.7 | 33.0 | 5.2 | 53.9 | 6.2 | 107.9 | 5.4 |
| Magadan Trust | 14.3 | 4.4 | 15.6 | 3.3 | 21.5 | 3.4 | 20.8 | 2.4 | 61.7 | 3.1 |
| Far East | 321.8 | 100.0 | 483.9 | 100.0 | 634.8† | 100.0 | 861.0 | 100.0 | 1981.6 | 100.0 |
| As percentage of U.S.S.R. | 22.9 | | 27.6 | | 23.2 | | 24.3 | | 34.3 | |

*In 1945 the southern part of Sakhalin was re-possessed by the U.S.S.R. from Japan

†Other sources put this figure at 647.4 (24.6 per cent of U.S.S.R.)

*Sources*: N. P. SYSOEV, *Razmeshchenie Rybnoi Promyshlennosti* (Moscow, 1967) 62; and *Narodnoe Khozyaistvo S.S.S.R. v 1965 g*, 138–139

Thus, after the gross live-weight catch has been reduced to usable fish products and after the inedible proportion of that has been deducted, the net proportion of the catch used for human consumption is about 35 per cent. In 1966 only 711,400 tons of fish were used for food out of a gross live-weight catch for the Far East of 2,056,000 tons.[11] As a result of these disturbing trends in the fish catch a high-level conference was held at Vladivostok in 1968; a new method of incentive payment was proposed in which fishermen's earnings will now depend on the catch of edible fish. Wages are expected to rise by one-quarter over the old quota system.[12] Catches of inedible fish, no matter how large, will not attract incentive payments.

The relative importance of the regional departments of *Dal'ryba* as contributors to the fish catch is shown in Table I. In the 10 years ended 1965 the Primor'ye fisheries increased their share of the catch, mainly at the expense of Kamchatka,[13] due to the concentration of the ocean-going fleet at the large ports of Vladivostok and Nakhodka in the southern Primor'ye. These ports have good rail links for the movement of fish across Siberia to markets in European Russia, while in Kamchatka there is a shortage of port and repair facilities, and the fish unloaded there has to be backhauled, after processing, and reloaded onto 'mainland' railway terminals for marketing. The ocean-going capabilities of the Primor'ye fleet also enable it to range further and provide a more regular supply of fish.

Most of the fish caught by the Magadan and Khabarovsk departments is coastal or river (salmon) but only 30 per cent of Primor'ye fish is so caught. Much of the coastal fishing is organized by collective fisheries which are particularly active in the spring and summer and at other times of the year engage in seasonal work (forestry or trapping). Overall, though, State-owned fisheries account for 70 to 75 per cent of the catch and the share of collectives is declining because of the diminishing productivity of some coastal fishing grounds and because most of them cannot afford large sea-going vessels.[14] Some collectives rent vessels from State fishing enterprises and deliver the catch to be processed at State *rybokombinats* (factories); other collectives do their own processing because of the shortage of seasonal labour for the factories.

The fish varieties caught in the Far East are mainly herring (32 per cent), flounder (29 per cent) and Pacific cod (15 per cent) including large quantities of Alaska pollack; Pacific salmon comprises about 10 per cent of the catch.[15] The balance of around 14 per cent is whales, crab, sardines, redfish and mullet. Basically not more than 20 types of fish are caught in Far Eastern waters, whereas Japanese fishermen in the same waters utilise more than 100 species for food; sea products such as octopus, cuttlefish and oysters are not popular in the U.S.S.R. and, so far, Soviet catches of tuna, sea perch, bream, mackerel and anchovy are small.

Before the Revolution salmon (red, silver and king) comprised 89 per cent of all fish caught here but by 1957 the proportion was less than 19 per cent. In an effort to conserve supplies quota restraints have been imposed;[16] in the lower Amur the Gorbusha, or Humpback, salmon now only appears at intervals of two years because of intensive fishing in the past.[17] King crabs are important in the waters around Kamchatka but in recent years the southern Kuriles (Kunashir and Shikotan) have increased their catch. Marine mammals such as seals, walrus and whales (sperm, fin and blue) are hunted in the Bering Sea and on the Kommandor islands on a restricted basis.

TABLE II

Far East fish catch by species and by fishing grounds, 1962

(thousand metric tons)

| Fish species | Bering Sea | Olyutor Bay* | North Kuriles West Kamchatka | Okhotsk–Magadan | Primor'ye | Sakhalin | East Kamchatka | Amur | South Kuriles | Total |
|---|---|---|---|---|---|---|---|---|---|---|
| Herring | 24.5 | 164.0 | 2.9 | 117.2 | 0.9 | 11.0 | — | — | — | 320.5 |
| Mullet | — | — | — | — | — | — | — | — | 44.8 | 44.8 |
| Large chastik† | 61.9 | — | — | — | 6.6 | neg. | — | 5.5 | 0.1 | 74.1 |
| (Large redfish) | 61.7 | — | — | — | 1.0 | — | — | — | — | 62.7 |
| Small chastik† | — | — | 3.5 | 0.1 | 7.4 | 9.9 | 1.7 | 4.9 | — | 27.5 |
| Pacific cod | — | — | 2.7 | — | 0.6 | 0.8 | 5.3 | — | — | 9.4 |
| Wachna cod | — | — | 15.7 | 0.4 | 1.4 | 3.8 | 4.7 | 0.1 | — | 26.1 |
| Alaska pollack‡ | — | — | — | — | 79.4 | 14.6 | 3.2 | — | — | 97.2 |
| Flounder | 142.8 | 0.1 | 48.8 | — | 5.6 | 7.4 | 14.3 | — | — | 219.0 |
| (Flounder paltus) | 1.0 | 0.1 | 0.2 | — | — | — | 0.6 | — | — | 1.9 |
| Other fish§ | 10.7 | — | 13.0 | 14.5 | 2.1 | 7.7 | 14.5 | 12.8 | — | 75.3 |
| Shrimps | 0.25 | — | — | — | — | — | — | 0.02 | — | 0.27 |

*North-east Kamchatka  †Mainly redfish species, the rest is predominantly mackerel and common bream
‡A variety of Pacific cod  §Includes sardines, sturgeon, halibut and some salmon
*Source:* A. N. IVANIS, *Rybnaya Promyshlennost' Dal'nego Vostoka* (Vladivostok, 1963) 47–48; note—excludes marine mammals and crabs

Data given by Ivanis for the fish catch by species and fishing grounds are shown in Table II.[18] Herring is caught mainly in the Olyutorsky Bay off north–east Kamchatka and in the Okhotsk Sea; around Hokkaido and the Kuriles the catch has been severely depleted and in 1969, for the first time, fishing was restricted. Pacific cod is becoming more important, especially Alaska pollack caught in the Japan Sea. The Bering Sea is the main fishing ground for flounder, redfish and mackerel; mullet is caught off the south Kuriles. The map shows that the Bristol Bay of Alaska has become the most important single fishing ground for the Far Eastern fleet, especially for flounder.

## FISHING FLEET AND PORT FACILITIES

*Dal'ryba's* headquarters in Vladivostok controls the entire Far Eastern fishing fleet and shore-based processing facilities. In 1966 there were 5,320 vessels in the fleet, of which some 3,200 were self-propelled; capital investment was 4,444 million roubles.[19] Four whaling fleets, 'Aleut', 'Vladivostok', 'Sovetskaya Rossiya' and 'Dal'nii Vostok', operate out of the Far East, two in the waters of the Kuriles, Kommandors and Aleutian islands, and two in Antarctic waters. Excluding whalers, medium sized trawlers (S.R.T.R.'s and S.R.T.'s) are the most important component of the fleet; but the emphasis now is on commissioning large refrigerated vessels and floating factory ships (Table III).[20] Not only are larger ships more efficient in their scale of operations but they also enable *Dal'ryba* to range much further for new fishing grounds in the Pacific. Large vessels can be geared more closely to the supply requirements of shore-based *rybokombinats* processing 20,000 to 30,000 tons of fish a year.[21]

TABLE III
Fishing vessels used by *Dal'ryba*, 1962*

| Designation | Share of 1962 catch,† tons | Description of vessel |
| --- | --- | --- |
| B.M.R.T. .. | 43,300 | Large refrigerated trawler; engine capacity 2,000 h.p. |
| S.R.T.R. .. | 119,500 | Medium-sized trawler with cooling hold; engines 400 to 540 h.p. |
| S.R.T. .. | 203,600 | Medium-sized trawler; length 30 to 35 metres; engines 300 to 400 h.p. |
| S.O., R.S. .. | 103,900 | RS = fishing seiner; and<br>SO = ocean-going seiner;<br>both same length and power as S.R.T.s |
| Others .. | 111,600 | Small coastal boats, including M.R.S.–80s |

*F. V. D'YAKONOV et al., Dal'nii Vostok, ekonomiko–geograficheskaya kharakteristika (Ak. Nauk SSSR. Moscow, 1966) 132.
†Total catch of State-owned fleet 581,900 tons; almost 93 per cent of the fleet is State-owned.

Floating canneries are an integral part of the fleet and until 1965 the Far East was the only Soviet territorial fishing ground where these ships operated. Three-fifths of all canned fish processed aboard Soviet floating canneries comes from the Far East—especially crab and salmon.[22] Floating canneries help to take the pressure off shore-based *rybokombinats* at the peak of the season.

Table III indicates that the smaller vessels of the fishing seiner class will be important for some considerable time, but already by 1964 the large refrigerated trawlers were leading the catch with 218,950 tons, or an average haul of 9,100 tons per ship, compared with less than 2,000 tons for the seiner class.

Port facilities for this quickly growing fleet are inadequate. Improvements to Vladivostok, Nakhodka and Vanino are planned for 1966–70 but the volume of landings will probably have risen by about a quarter. The strain on unloading facilities is so great that at Nakhodka over 40,000 ship hours are lost annually owing to delays; this is equivalent to five ships being out of operation permanently. Labour is so short that fishing vessel crews take part in the loading and unloading operations; Poliakov, Chief of the Far Eastern trawler fleet, claims that in 1967 his medium trawlers spent an average of 42 per cent of the calendar year in repair, mainly because 700 skilled workmen left their jobs in the shipyards, commonly because of the shortage of housing.[23] Despite these problems, it is expected that large fishing vessels, including factory ships of the 'Vostok' class,[24] will be based increasingly on Vladivostok/Nakhodka and not at the only other deep-sea port facility, Petropavlovsk–Kamchatskii, where the costs of operating and repair are much higher.[25] In 1964 the gross registered deep-sea tonnage at Vladivostok/Nakhodka was 188,503 tons (compared with 25,051 tons at Petropavlovsk); only Murmansk had more deep-sea fishing tonnage.

## Labour Problems

In the U.S.S.R. there is a surplus of labour in European Russia and a chronic shortage in the Far East and Siberia, especially in labour intensive industries such as fishing. Attracting settlers to the Far East is not easy: it is almost 6,000 miles from the densely populated regions of European Russia, the climate is severe, the cost of living is high, the supply of essential commodities is frequently disrupted away from the main cities, and the availability of housing, educational and welfare facilities is poor. Living conditions are particularly backward in the north–east and 40 per cent of the migrant workers there leave within one year of arrival. In the food processing industry of Kamchatka, which is dominated by fish processing, the turnover of workers in 1965 was 105 per cent.[26] This was due partly to the fact that until recently workers in light industry did not receive the special regional wage allowance applying to workers in heavy and extractive industries. Since January 1968 regional wage incentives have applied to all workers and are particularly favourable in hardship areas equalized to the Far North, including the central parts of the Far East.[27]

Seasonal workers are assigned to the Far East fisheries by the State and in 1964 19,200 such workers, including students, were sent there; transportation costs alone were over 6.7 million roubles. The time lost by each worker travelling to and from the fisheries and European Russia is almost one month. They work mainly in the coastal canneries where their efficiency is 30 per cent less than that normally attained by a permanent worker. If these seasonal workers were gainfully employed in their regular jobs in European Russia they would produce an additional 40 to 50 million roubles worth of goods.[28]

## COSTS AND PROFITABILITY

For a long time the Far Eastern fishing industry operated at a loss: in 1955 the deficit was 118 million roubles. But for the four years ended 1967 it made a profit of 333 million roubles.[29] Part of this changed situation is due to greater efficiency of operations through the use of B.M.R.T.s. The most important factor, however, has been the introduction of a more realistic pricing policy under the new economic reforms. Profit accountability, as a percentage of capital invested, has forced *Dal'ryba* into more selective fishing activities aimed at catching marketable fish by offering higher prices and discouraging catches of fish in weak demand by setting lower prices. Anomalies still exist though and complaints have been voiced about inflexible prices in relationship to changing market conditions. The fish for which demand is growing sometimes make a loss: thus the production cost for one ton of frozen cod is 390 roubles but its selling price is only 270 roubles.[30] On the other hand, frozen Pacific herring, for which demand is falling, costs 190 roubles but sells for 580 roubles. The transfer to a *khozraschot* basis is not proceeding as smoothly as might be expected. However, *Dal'ryba* as a whole did not complete the transfer until July 1968 and it *has* tried to encourage a move away from inferior products (such as strong salted herring) to higher quality products (medium and mild salted herring).[31] Also, it has adjusted the price paid for inedible fish, for fish meal, to less than one-third of the edible price to discourage spoiling.

Yet there are strange discrepancies between the relative profitability of *Dal'ryba* and some of its subordinate regional departments. In 1967, for instance, almost all of the chilled fish delivered at sea by the Kamchatka department's S.R.T. vessels to the refrigerator ships of *Vostokrybkholodflot* (a branch of *Dal'ryba*) were sold at a loss.[32] The alternative, of freezing the fish on shore at Kamchatka and double loading it back to a Primor'ye port and thence onto a railhead, adds 59 roubles a ton to costs and so offsets Kamchatka's relatively cheap catching costs. Similarly, the Sakhalin department is making a loss of four to five million roubles a year because the price obtained from *Dal'ryba* for Alaska pollack does not cover costs. *Dal'ryba* has fixed low purchasing prices for live pollack delivered to it but after processing made a large profit of 6.43 million roubles in 1967.[33]

Another serious problem is the sharp increase in production costs because of mounting delays incurred in unloading fish either at the ports or onto processing ships on the high seas. In the first three-quarters of 1968 the Sakhalin fishing vessels lost 1,633 ship-days because of such delays and so forewent catches of 23,000 tons of fish valued at four million roubles.[34] In 1967 the Kamchatka department lost 370 ship-days due to delays in transferring fish from its trawlers to *Dal'ryba's* processing ships.[35] With delays the quality of fish deteriorates rapidly, especially in the summer months; sometimes it is fit only for meal. Delays have been largely responsible for a 58 per cent rise in the costs of fish caught by large trawlers between 1958 and 1964; further rises will result from the new wage incentives now operating.[36]

## MARKETING

Of the edible fish landed in the Far East about 54 per cent was frozen for marketing in 1965 compared with 34 per cent in 1958. Live, fresh or chilled fish are not very important because of the long distance (upwards

157

of 6,000 rail miles) to the main urban consuming centres in European Russia. Salted herrings and other salted fish are still important commodities on the Soviet market although in the Far East they have declined from 56 per cent of the edible catch in 1958 to 33 per cent in 1965.[37] This trend is to the advantage of the Far East because the local shortage of salt has involved buying about 200,000 tons a year, at a cost of some seven million roubles, from Eastern Siberia and the Urals, some of which is shipped *via* the Black Sea. Smoked or dried fish is not very common either, being a mere 7,960 tons in 1965.

The most rapidly growing marketing outlet is for canned fish. This has been stimulated not only by rising domestic demand but also because of strong export sales for canned crab and salmon. In 1913 there were only two canneries; by 1940 production was 46.9 million cans, from 42 canneries, which accounted for 40 per cent of the entire Soviet canned fish output.[38] At this time the Far East's distance from major markets was a strong factor in favour of canning. Between 1950 and 1960 output rose from 63.7 to 146.7 million cans, but the Far East's share of U.S.S.R. production declined as other fishing areas in European Russia received modern canneries. In the mid-1950s the efficiency of the industry was assisted by the amalgamation or closing down of many small factories in the Far East to obtain economies of scale. By 1965 production had reached almost 244 million cans or 26 per cent of total Soviet output, two-fifths of the 85,300 tons of fish being canned in oil. Half of this came from floating canneries. Only the western canneries of *Zapryba* (the Atlantic-based organization) are more important because of their proximity to markets in European Russia, Eastern and Western Europe.

The utilization of canning capacity in the Far East is 64 per cent compared with the Soviet average of 72 per cent. It is usual to have some unused capacity because of the seasonal nature of fishing and irregularities in supplies due to bad weather. But in the Far East use rates should be higher because of the greater mobility of floating canneries; on the other hand, there are no alternative (agricultural) products available for off-peak canning. In 1965 the unused capacity in the Far East was equivalent to 135 million cans, which if fully utilized would have added another 14 per cent to Soviet production.[39]

One of the marketing problems is the full utilization of available cool-stores capacity in the Far East which results partly from a lag in building new stores, partly from delays in obtaining freight cars to dispatch fish on the over-worked Trans-Siberian railway and partly from the large quantity of fish remaining unsold in store because of inadequate demand for particular types of fish.[40] Retail outlets in the Centre have problems selling the fish supplied to them by *Dal'ryba*: in the first quarter of the year, for example, 80 per cent of the fish supplied from the Far East is flounder. Fish are still being caught irrespective of the level of demand just to fulfil some arbitrary directive from *Gosplan* (State Planning Committee) in Moscow. Potentially valuable earners of foreign exchange, such as Alaska pollack or hake, are virtually ignored, whereas fish in domestic demand, such as herring or salmon roe, are still being processed in an inferior way so that their quality deteriorates. In the retail shops so-called fresh frozen fish is often displayed in un-appetizing 20-kilogram cartons containing a great variety of scarcely distinguishable species.[41] Herring is delivered in 200-kilogram barrels and, in a typical village or suburban shop, a large part of it will go rotten quickly once it is opened. Filleting of fish for sale is scarcely known in the Far East because of the shortage of labour there. Most of the fish exported to Japan is sold whole, including heads.

## OUTLOOK

The prospect is for the Far Eastern fishing industry to continue its rôle as an important supplier of fish to an estimated 55 to 60 million Soviet citizens and as the source for at least one-third of Soviet fish and fish products exports. The disadvantage of distance from the main consuming centres in the U.S.S.R. will be offset increasingly by sales of fish to nearby Japan. But *Dal'ryba* will have to pay closer attention to quality controls for edible fish and also to the need for supplying an improved variety of fish currently in demand both within the Soviet Union and overseas. Moreover, in the next Five Year Plan (1971–75) more capital investment will have to be earmarked for the Far Eastern fisheries if the acute shortages of port facilities and labour are to be overcome.

## ACKNOWLEDGMENTS

The writer wishes to thank Professor Leon Vstovsky, Director of the Laboratory of Export–Import Specialization, Khabarovsk Complex Research Institute, Siberian Branch, U.S.S.R. Academy of Sciences, for providing useful Soviet research materials.

## NOTES

1 F. V. D'YAKONOV *et al., Dal'nii Vostok, ekonomiko-geograficheskaya kharakteristika* (Ak. Nauk S.S.S.R., Moscow, 1966) 126; fishing, forestry and mining are included under the term 'industry' in the U.S.S.R. (see p. 129 for source of Fig. 1).

2 *Pishchevaya Promyshlennost' S.S.S.R.* (ed. V. P. Zotov) (Moscow, 1967) 188.

3 *Ibid.,* 159.

4 E. I. FUTTER and V. S. IVANOV, *Ekonomika Flota Rybnoi Promyshlennosti S.S.S.R.* (Moscow, 1966) 6–7.

5 E. THIEL, *The Soviet Far East—a survey of its physical and economic geography* (Methuen and Co. Ltd., London, 1957) 101.

6 *Ibid.,* 103; at Nikolaevsk the mouth of the Amur is covered with solid ice for an average of 184 days a year; even the 'ice-free' port of Vladivostok has to be kept open by ice-breakers for three months of the year.

7 V. CONOLLY, *Beyond the Urals* (Oxford University Press, London, 1967) 309.

8 *Ekonomicheskaya Gazeta,* no. 8 (February 1968).

9 (ed. V. P. ZOTOV), *op. cit.,* 176; see also N. P. SYSOEV, *Razmeshchenie Rybnoi Promyshlennosti* (Moscow, 1967) *passim,* for a discussion of the loss from gross live weight to usable net weight and the share of edible fish.

10 In December 1967 the Far Eastern fishing industry had 77,300 tons of fish unsold in its cool stores, *Ekonomicheskaya Gazeta, op. cit.*

11 I. P. MAL'TSEV, *Ekonomicheskoe Stimulirovanie v Rybnoi Promyshlennosti v Novykh Usloviiakh Planirovaniya* (Moscow, 1968) 10.

12 *Ekonomicheskaya Gazeta, op. cit.*

13 In Kamchatka the fishing industry still employs 53 per cent of the industrial workforce directly; a further nine per cent work in the timber industry, nine-tenths of the output of which is used in the fishing industry; also much of the employment in mechanical repairs (11 per cent of the workforce) is occupied in the repair of fishing boats. Along the entire Far Eastern coastline from Nikolaevsk na Amure to Magadan, and again around the Kamchatka peninsula to Anadyr' in Chukotka, fishing provides the only source of livelihood and the only reason for settlement beyond fur hunting and some reindeer farming (F. V. D'YAKONOV, Ekonomiko–Geograficheskie Osobennosti i Problemy Kamchatskoi Oblasti, *Sibirskii Geograficheskii Sbornik,* no. 5 (Ak. Nauk S.S.S.R., Leningrad, 1967) 13).

[14] N. P. SYSOEV, *op. cit.*, 69; the number of fishing collectives in the Far East has fallen from 148 in 1960 to 82 in 1965; over half of them are located in the lower Amur below Komsomol'sk for seasonal salmon fishing; the eastern coast of Kamchatka is also very important.

[15] F. V. D'YAKONOV *et al., op. cit.*, 132.

[16] About 90 million salmon roe are bred each year on the island of Iturup in the Kuriles as a conservation measure.

[17] E. THIEL, *op. cit.*, 161.

[18] A. N. IVANIS, *Rybnaya Promyshlennost' Dal'nego Vostoka* (Glavnoe Upravlenie Rybnoi Promyshlennosti Dal'nego Vostoka, Tsentralnoe Buro Tekhnicheskoi Informatsii Glavdal'vostokrybproma, Vladivostok, 1963) *passim.*

[19] Z. I. FUTTER and V. S. IVANOV, *op. cit.*, 128–129; depreciation is calculated at 8.6 per cent per year but rises to 12.3 per cent in Magadan because of higher repair and maintenance costs.

[20] F. V. D'YAKONOV *et al., op. cit.*, 132.

[21] A typical modern *rybokombinat* has cool stores and a cannery and makes fish meal, oil and vitamins. There are 35 *rybokombinats* in the Far East.

[22] N. P. SYSOEV, *op. cit.*, 85; 75 per cent of the canned crab is exported.

[23] *Ekonomicheskaya Gazeta*, no. 8 (February 1968).

[24] The 'Vostok' class factory ships displace 43,000 tons and can process 300 tons of fish a day; construction started in February 1965.

[25] O. KRIVORUCHKO, *Planovoe Khozyaistvo*, no. 8 (1967); running costs for a B.M.R.T. based at Vladivostok are 500,000 roubles a year less than for such a ship based on Petropavlovsk.

[26] *Problemy Ekonomicheskoi Effektivnosti Razmeshcheniya Sotsialisticheskogo Proizvodstva v S.S.S.R.* (ed. Ya. G. Feigin) (Ak. Nauk S.S.S.R., Moscow, 1968) 114–115.

[27] *Pravda* (27th September 1967).

[28] N. P. SYSOEV, *op. cit.*, 20.

[29] A. A. ISHKOV (Minister for Fisheries), *Ekonomicheskaya Gazeta*, no. 50 (December 1967).

[30] I. P. MAL'TSEV, *op. cit.*, 61.

[31] In Sakhalin strong salted herring incurs a loss of 240 roubles a ton whereas medium and mild salted herring brings a profit of 300 to 400 roubles.

[32] *Ekonomicheskaya Gazeta*, no. 2 (1968).

[33] *Ekonomicheskaya Gazeta*, no. 7 (1969); it made 8.75 million roubles profit in the first half of 1968 whereas the Sakhalin department incurred extra interest charges alone (for overdue credit from *Gosbank* because of delays by *Dal'ryba* in paying for fish delivered to it) of 450,000 roubles in 1967.

[34] *Ibid.*

[35] *Ekonomicheskaya Gazeta*, no. 9 (1969).

[36] Wages account for 30 to 35 per cent of total ship running costs; the wage increases will fall heavily on the smaller, relatively labour-intensive trawlers.

[37] (ed. V. P. Zotov), *op. cit.*, 170.

[38] N. P. SYSOEV, *op. cit.*, 86; one conventional can equals 350 grams net weight.

[39] *Ibid.*, 85–86.

[40] *Ibid.*, 77–78; utilization of cool-stores capacity is 99.5 per cent for *Dal'ryba* but only 78 per cent in the U.S.S.R. as a whole.

[41] *Ekonomicheskaya Gazeta*, no. 50 (December 1967).

# THE URBAN CONCEPT IN RELATION TO INTER-TROPICAL AFRICA: A RE-APPRAISAL

## J. O. N. EZE

### INTRODUCTION

Literature dealing with the evolution and growth of towns and cities throughout the world provides the necessary empirical information enabling the theory of the urban concept to be defined. In particular, available literature in urban studies shows that a great deal is known about town development in Europe and regions of European settlement; yet, although in the past decade there has been a growing number of publications on cities in non-Western areas, there is still a great gap in our knowledge of the urban process in such areas, especially in inter-tropical Africa. The similarity between the pattern of world urbanization and that of the distribution of available literature on the subject is striking. Table I shows that Europe and the European-influenced regions of Oceania and North America have the highest percentage of urban population in the world both for towns of 20,000 inhabitants and over, and for large centres of 100,000 and over. These are the regions where both intensive and extensive urban studies have been carried out. The table also reveals the youthful stage in the progress of urbanization in the developing countries of Africa, Asia and Latin America, where urbanization is weak and the majority of the urban population is concentrated in a few large cities.

TABLE I

Percentage of the urban population of the world by regions, c. 1950

| Regions | Percentage of total population living in towns/cities | | Percentage of urban population living in towns/cities |
| --- | --- | --- | --- |
| | of 20,000 and over | of 100,000 and over | of 100,000 and over |
| World .. .. .. | 21 | 13 | 62 |
| Oceania .. .. .. | 47 | 41 | 87 |
| North America (U.S.A. and Canada) .. .. | 42 | 29 | 69 |
| Europe (excluding U.S.S.R.) | 35 | 21 | 60 |
| U.S.S.R. .. .. | 31 | 18 | 58 |
| South America .. .. | 26 | 18 | 69 |
| Central America .. .. | 21 | 12 | 57 |
| Asia .. .. .. | 13 | 8 | 63 |
| Africa .. .. .. | 9 | 5 | 51 |

*Source:* J. BEAUJEU-GARNIER and G. CHABOT, *Urban Geography* (1967) 19.

In the absence of fuller information on the origin of towns in the developing countries, our knowledge of urban origins and development is anything but precise. Much of the literature is based in part on legend, myth, and speculation, in part on archaeology and only to a small extent on the known facts concerning certain towns that have emerged during the period of recorded history.[1] Consequently there is a tendency to think of settlement geography generally and urbanization in particular in terms of

161

the experience and related hypotheses of the economically developed countries. Thus Oram conceives an African town as a settlement having 'a built-up shopping and business area with a network of streets'[2] but land-use zonation was by no means practised as such in the indigenous (pre-colonial) cities of inter-tropical Africa. As Turner[3] observed in the case of India, the concept of the C.B.D. is irrelevant to the understanding of such cities as it can scarcely be said to exist except in a few colonial centres, notably the sea-ports.

It should be observed at this point that, although a high degree of urbanization is a marked characteristic of 'developed' countries, urban growth as expressed by both the number of towns and cities and the number of people living in them is by no means a phenomena character-istic only of such countries. Table II shows that, of the 1,334 agglomerations in the world about 1960 with 100,000 or more inhabitants, nearly a third are in Asia and nearly a quarter in Europe. Africa and Australia with 6.4 per cent and 0.8 per cent respectively have the smallest number of large agglomerations. The table also reveals that 47.2 per cent, or nearly half the total agglomerations, are found in the developing countries of Asia, African and Latin America, compared with 41.8 per cent in Europe, North America and Australia.[4]

TABLE II

Localisation by continents of agglomerations of over 100,000 inhabitants (1960)

| *Continental area* | *Number of agglomerations* | *Percentage of total* |
|---|---|---|
| Australia  ..         .. | 11 | 0.8 |
| Africa  ..         .. | 84 | 6.4 |
| U.S.S.R.  ..        .. | 148 | 11.0 |
| America  ..        .. | 323 | 24.4 |
| *(a)* Canada          .. | 110 } | 16.2 |
| *(b)* U.S.A. ..        .. | 107 } | |
| Europe  ..         .. | 327 | 24.8 |
| *(a)* U.K.  ..        .. | 45 } | 7.2 |
| *(b)* West Germany  .. | 51 } | |
| Asia  ..          .. | 442 | 32.6 |
| *(a)* India  ..        .. | 97 | 7.2 |
| *(b)* China  ..        .. | 102 | 7.8 |
| *(c)* Japan  ..        .. | 115 | 8.8 |

*Source: United Nations Demographic Year Book* (1960)

## THE APPLICATION OF WESTERN-DERIVED CONCEPTS

In the sense that theories are generalizations which have to be tested in individual cases and often modified and rebuilt, the present Western-based concepts of urbanization are invaluable for workers in non-Western areas. As Haggett[5] has observed, we are only just emerging from a half-century of cautious fact-gathering, a marked feature of which has been an unwillingness to risk launching new hypotheses. During this period, geographers working in non-Western areas have had the opportunity to test existing theories based on Western experience. One classic example of an area where such studies have yielded fruitful results is Japan. According to Ginsburg,[6] the publications of Japanese scholars display

> a commendable familiarity with basic concepts concerning urban functional organisation, the dynamics of urban morphological change, centrality and accessibility, cultural inertia and other influences on the urbanisation process,

and ecological relationships that in the United States tend to be of greater interest to sociologists than to geographers. While arguing for more comparative and cross-cultural studies, they refer back frequently to questions of the cultural relativity of the urbanisation process. Out of their work are coming some stimulating applications of Western-derived concepts and techniques and possibly some important modifications, as well as confirmation of theories concerning the functions, structure, and patterns of cities and urban systems.

In contrast to the contribution made by Japanese geographers, similar studies of cities and urbanization in inter-tropical Africa by some pioneer Western scholars showed little appreciation of the significance of cultural, political and economic forces in urban development. Hence indigenous towns have often been referred to as 'villages', as in Uganda;[7] 'urban villages' in Yorubaland[8] and 'village-groups' in Eastern Nigeria.[9] Though the classic works of scholars like Miner,[10] Bascom[11] and Mabogunje,[12] to name only a few, have led to the recognition of medieval urbanization in parts of West Africa, there is still the tendency to associate indigenous urban development exclusively with highly centralized political systems and to regard the process of urbanization in vast areas of the continent as colonial in origin. Thus Dresch[13] declared that all the towns of Congo–Kinshasa were founded by Belgium, and Prothero[14] that 'urbanisation was completely alien to (Eastern) Nigeria before the establishment of British Administration.' As has been shown elsewhere,[15] towns and cities existed in Eastern Nigeria well before the colonial period. Prothero's failure to identify them was probably due to the problem of perception and the rôle of pre-conceived ideas in geography.

### POPULATION AS AN URBAN INDEX

In highly industrialized countries, it has often been observed that at certain population levels, urban functions are well represented in the settlement pattern. Thus Osborne[16] observed that, in much of Great Britain, civil parishes with a population of 2,500 or more in either 1951 or 1961, have developed urban functions and that in terms of occupations, agricultural employment has become negligible or even disappeared completely. While population represents at least a fair index of urbanization in many such Western countries, it is a most unreliable index in inter-tropical Africa. The use of this index by a number of European and American scholars represents an aspect of the wholesale application of Western-derived concepts in non-Western areas. Trewartha and Zelinsky,[17] by classifying centres with 5,000 or more inhabitants as urban, were neglecting the different historical, social, political and economic circumstances in the development of these centres. Similarly, Bascom[18], in his brief comparison of urbanization in Yorubaland and the Eastern Region of Nigeria as in 1952, classified as cities all centres with 5,000 or more inhabitants, and hence calculated a series of unrealistic and abnormally high percentages of urbanization for the two areas and their Provinces. Thus 53.5 per cent of the population of Yorubaland was regarded as urban, as against 32.1 per cent for the Eastern Region. At the Provincial level, he found that 69.1 per cent of the population of the former Onitsha Province (in Iboland) lived in cities, a proportion only exceeded by that of Ibadan Province (in Yorubaland) with a figure of 69.5 per cent. The indigenous centre of Enugu-Ezike, near Nsukka in Eastern Nigiera, with a population of over 61,000 in 1952, could scarcely be classified as urban in the functional sense of the term, but Bascom would

163

regard much smaller settlements as cities! His totally misleading picture of the proliferation of urban centres in Southern Nigeria, in 1952, was perhaps only exceeded by that of Talbot[19] who, also using a solely statistical index, namely a population of 2,000 inhabitants and over, calculated the urban population of Southern Nigeria in 1921 to be 69 per cent and then was surprised that such 'a purely agricultural country' should have an urban population nearly up to the proportion (78 per cent) of that then obtaining in England and Wales. It is significant that Talbot, instead of modifying his concept of an urban centre in the light of the country's socio-economic and political conditions, with which he was very familiar, proceeded to justify the high proportion of urban population in most unconvincing terms, inferring that

> as civilisation developed, the gregariousness and desire for a social life also increased among the negroes, who are very sociable and fond of dancing, etc., which they find most enjoyable in large numbers.

Buchanan and Pugh,[20] while showing an understanding of the nature of indigenous towns in Nigeria, could not adapt certain urban aspects of their Western scholarship to local, historical and cultural conditions. While recognizing that some indigenous towns are often predominantly agricultural in function and 'lack the basic services and functions which constitute the criteria of an urban area in the West,' they would not regard the trading town of Otuocha-Aguleri (1952 population 6,303) as an urban centre, despite its predominantly urban characteristics (predominance of trading and other non-agricultural activities, a heterogeneous population of Hausas, Yorubas, Nupes, Ibos, Ibibios, Ijaws, etc.). While they were prepared to dismiss such settlements as 'scarcely more than five-figure clusters of population with little functional significance,' they were willing to use the arbitrary statistical figure of 10,000 or more inhabitants as an appropriate index of urbanization, apparently because, a few years earlier, the European Statistical Conference in Prague[21] recommended that compact groups of 10,000 or more inhabitants can automatically be classed as urban.

In a recent study of the size and growth of urban population in Africa, the United Nations Economic Commission for that continent adopted the following definition of urban places so as 'to preserve uniformity' with definitions primarily based on the experience of the industrial countries of the West:

*(a)* urban population—population in towns with 20,000 and more inhabitants;

*(b)* city population—population in cities of 100,000 and more inhabitants; and

*(c)* big-city population—population in 'big cities' with 500,000 or more inhabitants.[22]

Here it must be emphasized that the United Nations figure of 20,000 is as arbitrary in the context of inter-tropical Africa as that of 1,000 used by Harvey for Sierra Leone. The justification for the use of 'a threshold figure of 1,000 [was] because settlements above this number include both large villages and well developed towns'![23] Whereas Harvey, using the 1963 census figures, identified 160 urban places in Sierra Leone, the recent United Nations definition would exclude all but two centres—Bo (26,613) and Freetown (127,917), since none of the others has over 20,000 inhabitants. Similarly, of Kenya's 34 urban centres (1962 census) only four

164

would qualify as such according to the United Nations definition. In Eastern Nigeria, such stranded indigenous centres as Okposi (21,771 in 1952) would apparently qualify for urban status while the urban growth centres of the colonial politico-economic system like Ahoada (4,191) and Nbawsi (5,607) would not.

While it is recognized that cities, rather than being completely unlike, bear close resemblances to each other in both form and function, there are nevertheless important differences resulting from differing forces of urbanization, changes in economic and political development, traditional social outlook and value systems. The problem facing scholars working in developing countries, especially in inter-tropical Africa, is to recognize the importance of these forces in the evolution of growth centres and stranded (or defunct) centres.[24]

## The Rôle of Definitions with Particular Reference to Nigeria

One of the greatest obstacles to our understanding of cities in inter-tropical Africa may be traced to the tendency for many scholars to regard official definitions as dogmas which can neither be modified nor rejected. This expediency of regarding as scientific things which are true only by definition has in the past led to the acceptance of arbitrary and often erroneous definitions which seek to distinguish rural and urban settlements for statistical or census purposes. Too often we have allowed our search for generalities to blur our conception of individual cases. While accepting the desirability of a universal definition, it must be stressed that the concept of a town varies with both the historical and geographical setting and that, within a particular area, micro-cultural and politico-economic differences influence the development of city systems as well as the morphological and functional patterns of members of a system. It is, therefore, no longer surprising that the city has for so long defied a universal definition which is acceptable to all. The city, a product of numerous varying elements, is too rich and varied to be explained by static definitions. A universal definition, which must above all be flexible and dynamic, will become nearer as we achieve uniformity among the factors that give birth to cities.

We have nevertheless made a number of advances in the past decade or so. Though we think of most cities as being densely populated, we now accept that this need not be universally true.[25] Though many cities, particularly in Western Europe and North America, are 'engaged primarily in non-agricultural occupations,'[26] we are now prepared to accept that, in a socialist economy, a city may be 'a residential centre bound up almost exclusively with agriculture.'[27] Thus, though we like to think of towns as exclusively urban settlements, we have conceded that not all towns are predominantly urban in function. Similarly, we have also come to accept that not all urban settlements are classified as towns even though their size and form may justify such a classification, for, in the final analysis, a town is what the State is prepared to call a town.[28] In England, for example, where the distinction between town and country is in real terms very artificial, many urban centres peripheral to the large cities and conurbations are still classified as villages. Because we are now better informed on the influence of cultural differences and value systems on systems of cities over time and place we are able to appreciate why every country should have its own definition of towns. In fact, multi-national countries like the U.S.S.R. already have one definition for each of the component nations,[29] reflecting the variety of cultural, historical, geographical and economic conditions in the country.

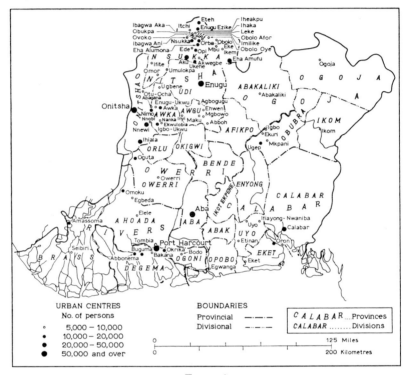

FIGURE 1
The census towns of Eastern Nigeria, 1952

While some definitions may not lead us far in understanding the nature of towns and cities, others may positively mislead our understanding of them. This is the case in Nigeria, where towns are officially defined as 'centres forming compact groups, each with a population of not less than 5,000.'[30] The definition gave no indication as to what constitutes compactness or as to how it was measured. However, compactness, as a measure of housing density, is a very unsatisfactory index of urban status because it is influenced by tradition, military and administrative necessity, physical and economic scarcity of land, etc., and unlike population density does not change at the same rate as function. The result is that settlement forms indicative of earlier urban functions persist long after their functions have changed and within them rural functions take place in a seemingly urban environment. This is particularly true of the 'stranded' members of a system of cities which has undergone successive rapid changes in response to changing politico-economic organization. It is not difficult to see that the Nigerian definition contains little (if any) element of urban status, for neither an arbitrary figure of 5,000 nor a vaguely conceived notion of compactness tells us much about urban–rural differences in such an extensive multi-national country formerly under a colonial administration. The map of urban centres for the Eastern Region (Figure 1) which depicts

166

Nsukka Division, to the north, as highly urbanized, and an extensive central area, including the whole of Afikpo, Okigwi, Orlu, Bende, Enyong, Ikot-Ekpene and Abak Divisions,[31] as completely rural, shows beyond doubt that, as far as the Region is concerned, the 1952 census definition and its application are highly misleading.

The 1931 Census Report provides the necessary background for an understanding of this definition, for it states that the definition of a town was adopted from that of the Indian census, namely, 'every continuous collection of houses which the Census Officer may decide to treat as a town for Census purposes.'[32] The same census gives a clue as to how the arbitrary number of 5,000 was arrived at. Meek, the then Anthropological Officer for Southern Nigeria, though unsuccessful in his attempt to persuade the census authorities to use a figure of 5,000 in 1931, nevertheless convinced them that the

> criterion of urban population as composed of persons living in towns of 5,000 inhabitants and over, gives a truer picture of the segregation into urban and rural habitat.[33]

It is, however, satisfying to note that the census authorities fully realized that

> more exact definitions of a town would have to take account of economic considerations, for example, of market facilities, or of the proportion of persons engaged in trade, manufacture or the professions, as compared to those occupied in agriculture

but this approach was rejected on the ground that 'such a definition would require ad hoc investigations for each area far beyond the scope of a "vital" census.'[34]

It is to be expected that a definition in which so much was left at the discretion of so many Administrative Officers with questionable relevant training and limited experience will lend itself to numerous interpretations which will vary not only from Region to Region but also from District to District. The criterion of compactness, as Mitchell[35] observed, ruled out a large number of settlements in the Eastern and Northern Regions, while that of size ruled out a large number of small 'growth centres' of the colonial politico-economic system which generally had a population of over 2,000 but less than the 5,000 required by the census officers. A detailed study of the distribution of Nigerian census towns reveals a concentration in the former Onitsha Province, with 50 of the 79 'towns' enumerated, while in Owerri Province only three towns (Aba, Owerri and Oguta) were recorded. Of the 30 settlements with over 5,000 inhabitants in Nsukka Division, only two, Edem (6,551) and Nibo (5,377), were excluded from the census list, but in the adjacent Udi Division none of the 27 settlements with between 5,000 and 29,000 inhabitants was included even though they were as compact as those of Nsukka Division. In Owerri Province, such important towns as Umuahia (12,259), Okigwe (6,807), Uzuakoli (9,507), Nbawsi (5,607), Omoba (5,140) and Ogwe (5,358) were excluded from the census list for no apparent reason. Also excluded were a number of indigenous market towns and service centres similar to those included in Nsukka, Awgu, Awka and Onitsha Divisions. These include Ndizuogu (13,459), Nguru (18,398), Mbieri (20,979) and Uli (16,112). According to Mitchell[36] these indigenous towns differ from Yoruba towns of their size only in their morphology—in the presence of much compound land and oil palm trees between their quarters, and in the absence of a strong central authority, i.e. a divine kinship of 'Oba'. The inconsistency in the interpretation of the 1952 census definition is further manifested by the exclusion of such important centres as Ikot-Ekpene (18,070), Okopedi-Itu (12,425), Atani (6,280), Agbani (6,050), Arochukwu (6,342), Igrita (5,601) and Nomeh (5,309), all of which satisfied the census requirements. It is not, therefore, surprising that the Western Region, where the definition was more consistently applied, was recorded as having an urban population of 3,045,000 (47.9 per cent), whereas in the Eastern Region only 1,130,000 (14 per cent) was recorded as urban. One wonders whether the very low figure returned for Northern Nigeria may not be attributed to similar inconsistencies! Perhaps the most disturbing aspect of the problem is that of the many scholars who have studied various aspects of urban settlements and urbanization in Nigeria, with reference to the 1952 census, few have questioned the census definition and its application and none has wondered why such major towns as Umuahia and Ikot-Ekpene were excluded.

There were in 1952 many small centres in the Eastern Region which were favourably located as foci of spatial integration and were highly generative of economic growth in the context of the then colonial economy. They had attracted large numbers of immigrant population from various parts of the country and although few of them had up to 5,000 inhabitants many had a population of between 2,000 and 5,000 people. They were primarily either commercial centres handling the products of the import–export trade as well as those of the internal exchange economy, for example Azumini (4,344), Imo-Obigbo (4,933), Ogrugu (3,672), Omerum (2,938), Ediba (2,725) and Owerrinta (2,088), or the principal administrative centres of the colonial government, which also functioned as market towns, each with educational, medical and postal facilities, for example Ahoada (4,191), Abak (3,470) and Orlu (3,861). In view of the heterogeneous and predominantly non-agricultural character of their population and the fact that, in size, they were well above the average for many tropical countries,[37] it was most unrealistic to have denied them urban status, more so when it is recalled that Nigerian towns were then completely pre-industrial and were mostly centres of commerce and administration in an otherwise predominantly agricultural environment. They were definitely more urban in character than many 'stranded' indigenous towns (for example some of Morgan's 'grassland towns') which were listed in the census reports as urban centres.

CONCLUSION

It is evident from the above observations that the 1952 census definition and statistics for Nigeria—the latest available for the country—do not give a true picture of the nature and pattern of urbanization in the Eastern Region. This reinforces the view held by Mitchell[38] that a classification that holds good for one Region may not necessarily be applicable to either of the other Regions. In general it illustrates that inter-tropical Africa is by no means a homogeneous area and that there is still the need to relate census definitions to sub-regional differences in historical, cultural and politico-economic factors.

NOTES

[1] P. M. HAUSER, Urbanisation: an overview, *The study of urbanisation* (eds. P. M. Hauser and L. F. Schnore) (John Wiley & Sons, London, 1965) 1.

[2] N. ORAM, *Towns in Africa* (Oxford University Press, London, 1965) 1.

[3] *India's urban future* (ed. R. Turner) (University of California Press, Berkeley and Los Angeles, 1962) 67.

*The urban concept in relation to inter-tropical Africa: a re-appraisal*

4 These figures are based on the *United Nations Demographic Year Book* (1960) and
it is important to draw attention to the limitations of the statistics. These are based
on figures supplied by individual countries, and in inter-tropical Africa many of
them were based on estimates and censuses of questionable reliability. Even where
census figures are available and fairly reliable, they are not always comparable as
to date and definition.

5 P. HAGGETT, *Locational analysis in human geography* (Edward Arnold, London,
1965) 277–278.

6 N. S. GINSBURG, Urban geography and non-Western areas, in (eds.) Hauser and
Schnore, *op. cit.,* 327.

7 K. M. TROWELL and K. P. WACHSMANN, *Tribal crafts of Uganda* (Oxford University
Press, London, 1953).

8 K. M. BUCHANAN and J. C. PUGH, *Land and people in Nigeria* (University of London
Press, London, 1955) 63.

9 G. I. JONES, Ibo land tenure, *Africa* XIX, no. 4 (1949) 310.

10 H. MINER, *The primitive city of Timbuctoo* (Princeton University Press, Princeton,
1953).

11 W. BASCOM, Urbanisation among the Yoruba, *American Journal of Sociology* 60,
no. 5 (1955) 446–454; and Urbanism as a traditional African pattern, *Sociological
Review* 7 (1959) 29–43.

12 A. L. MABOGUNJE, *Yoruba towns* (Ibadan University Press, Ibadan, 1962); and
*Urbanisation in Nigeria* (University of London Press, London, 1968).

13 J. DRESCH, Villes Congolaises: étude de géographie urbaine et sociale, *Le Revue de
Géographie Humaine et d'Ethnologie* 1 (1948) 3.

14 R. M. PROTHERO, The population of Eastern Nigeria, *Scottish Geog. Mag.* 71,
no. 3 (1955) 168.

15 J. O. N. EZE, The towns of Biafra: a study of changes in an urban system in response
to changes in politico-economic organisation, *Unpublished Ph.D. thesis* (University
of Nottingham, 1969).

16 R. H. OSBORNE, *Atlas of population change in the East Midland counties, 1951–
1961* (Department of Geography, University of Nottingham, 1966) 7–9.

17 G. T. TREWARTHA and W. ZELINSKY, Population patterns in tropical Africa, *Ann.
Assoc American Geographers* 44 (1954) 144.

18 W. BASCOM (1959) *op. cit.,* 21–33.

19 P. A. TALBOT, *Peoples of Southern Nigeria* IV (1926) 13.

20 K. M. BUCHANAN and J. C. PUGH, *op. cit.,* 63.

21 UNITED NATIONS, *Etudes Démographiques* (New York, 1949).

22 UNITED NATIONS ECONOMIC COMMISSION FOR AFRICA, Size and growth of urban
population in Africa, *The city in newly developing countries: readings on urbanism
and urbanisation* (ed. G. Breese) (1969) 129–130.

23 M. E. HARVEY, Town size, *Sierra Leone in maps* (ed. J. I. Clarke) (University of
London Press, 1966) 48.

24 For details of the concept of 'growth' and 'stranded' centres, see J. O. N. EZE, *op.
cit.,* 223–297.

25 E. JONES, *Towns and cities* (Oxford University Press, London, 1966) 4.

26 R. E. DICKINSON, *City, region and regionalism* (London, 1947) 25.

27 See P. GEORGE, *Précis de géographie urbaine* (Paris, 1961); and A. L. MABOGUNJE,
*Yoruba towns* (Ibadan University Press, Ibadan, 1962).

28 E. JONES (1966) *op. cit.,* 4.

29 P. GEORGE, *op. cit.*

30 NIGERIA, EASTERN REGION, *Population census of the Eastern Region of Nigeria 1953*
(Census Superintendent, Lagos, *c.* 1955) 20.

31 The administrative Divisions and Provinces were those in existence in 1952–53.

32 NIGERIA, *Census of Nigeria 1931* I (Crown Agents, London, 1932) 11.

33 NIGERIA (1932) *op. cit.,* 12.

34 NIGERIA (1932) *op. cit.,* 11.

35 N. C. MITCHELL, The Nigerian town: distribution and definition, *University College
(Dept. of Geography) Ibadan, Research Notes No. 7* (1955) 1–13.

36 N. C. MITCHELL, *op. cit.,* 11.

37 See J. O. N. EZE, *op. cit.,* 63.

38 N. C. MITCHELL, *op. cit.,* 6.

# SEQUENT OCCUPANCE IN THE NORTHERN KING COUNTRY, NORTH ISLAND, NEW ZEALAND

J. W. FOX

## INTRODUCTION

It is now more than 40 years since Derwent Whittlesey[1] published his ideas on sequent occupance and made two significant points: first, that human occupance of an area carries within itself the seed of its own transformation; and, secondly, that an appreciation of change is essential in chorological studies. The first of these observations has provided the basis for many an academic argument, and is still well known. The second has been neglected, being one of those tenets which geographers hold to be generally obvious yet tend never to demonstrate in the particular. This dereliction is perhaps most noticeable when chorological studies are directed towards regional geography—a matter of interest to Whittlesey in later years—and for this reason, among others, much regional geography has become stereotyped and arid.

Today, when the notion of the geographic region is scorned by many, when process is regarded as the essential element in any geographical exegesis, it may be useful to look again at Whittlesey, and to remember such mentors as K. C. Edwards who, in the '30s, following the tradition of Vidal de la Blache, insisted that students who pretended to geographical wisdom should at least understand its historical components.

Much has been written on the relationships between geography and history. Suffice to say that these disciplines represent, respectively and in a broad sense, the chorological and chronological viewpoints of reality, and are concerned with the same phenomena; and that historical geography may be interpreted as the geography of past periods. Sequent occupance, therefore, is part of historical geography—that part which lays emphasis on man's contribution to the distinctiveness of places at different periods—and is studied in order to appreciate, in Whittlesey's words, 'the genetics of each stage in terms of its predecessor.' He thus postulates a form of process applicable to chorology, so raising the latter above mere chorography; and in a final analysis this may be regarded as the contribution of sequent occupance to the evaluation of the nature of the geographic region.

The present purpose is to demonstrate these ideas with respect to the Northern King Country in the North Island of New Zealand, to indicate how sequent occupance as a 'vertical' association of phenomena in terms of time has its counterpart in the 'horizontal' association in terms of area, and that in toto the stages of occupance and the areas they distinguish are essential components of a geographic region.

## THE NORTHERN KING COUNTRY

Southwards from the Puniu River, a tributary of the Waipa, to a line joining approximately Urenui on the Taranaki coast and Mount Ruapehu, between the sea and the elevated mass of the Volcanic Plateau, extends a land which has no counterpart in New Zealand (Figure 1). It was into this country that the Maori king and his supporters retreated after defeat in the Maori wars of the 1860s, to remain inviolate until the early 1880s. Whilst in the South Island the golden ages of wool and metal and grain heralded expanding economies and spreading settlement, whilst in the North Island the forests were cleared and grasses sown and towns were built, the King Country remained apart, for no pakeha dared set foot across its boundaries.[2] Most of those who had lived there and in its vicinity, mainly missionaries, had been forced to leave, and their work was destroyed. The King Country was indeed the domain of the Maori for almost 20 years.

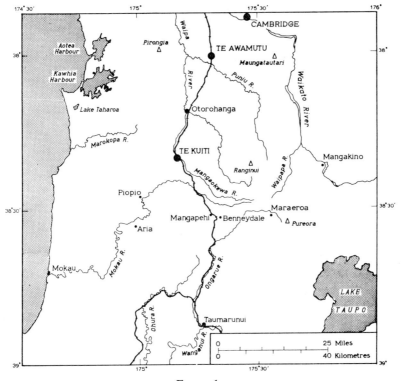

FIGURE 1
Localities in the Northern King Country

It was not until 1883 that this isolation was broken when the *mana* of the Maori king, a Waikato, waned as his supporters quarrelled increasingly with the Ngatimaniapoto, their hosts, and as pressure was brought to bear to allow the railway to be built that would eventually link Auckland with Wellington. In that year the first surveyors began work, to be followed by timber-getters and miners, and, later, railway construction gangs. Permanent settlement came slowly, for land was not available except through the Crown,[3] and as late as 1892 'not an acre of King Country land had passed into white farmers' hands'.[4] Only at the turn of the century, and in the decade before the First World War, did the pakeha begin to establish his farms; only after that war did development really get under way; and only after the Second World War did real prosperity come to the

171

King Country as a whole, especially to its northern part. There, in the present-day counties of Otorohanga and Waitomo, from the Aotea Harbour to Pureora Mountain, from the mouth of the Mokau to the headwaters of the Puniu River, is a region where the events of history are discernible in the lineaments of its geography, where the Maori and his land and the pakeha and his technology, each in their impact upon the other, have created something that is unique.

In 1966 the Northern King Country, an area of 1,320,000 acres, carried more than three-and-three-quarter million stock units. Yet only 51 per cent of the two counties was in grass, and 53 per cent improved, so that carrying capacity was 545 stock units per 100 acres, which was twice the figure obtaining in the early years of the century. The growth of 60 years is remarkable (Figure 2A). In the same year the population numbered 22,634, one-quarter of whom were Maoris, figures which show a decline from the previous census of 1961. These figures also serve to underline the fact that the acreage of improved land *per capita* of rural population has shown a steady increase since the Second World War,[5] though only now approximating the proportions characteristic of the decade 1916 to 1925 (Figure 2B). Where once it was a question of a large rural population on a pioneer fringe, it is today a matter of technological efficiency on well-established farmlands. Moreover, despite the decrease in the total population of the Northern King Country, that of the two towns, Te Kuiti and Otorohanga, has grown steadily until recently, especially the Maori component.

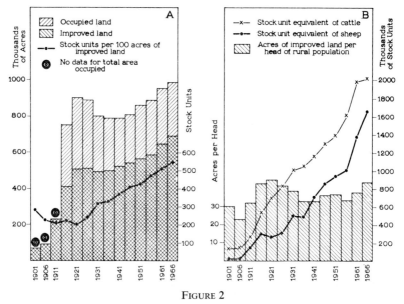

FIGURE 2

Agricultural statistics for the Northern King Country, 1901–66

Change, then, in place and time, has always characterized this part of the North Island of New Zealand. Whereas today the movement is one of consolidation and retreat from rural areas, it was from the present foci of Te Kuiti and Otorohanga that penetration once occurred. Rudimentary cultivation by both Maori and pakeha, exploitative economies, extensive stock raising, intensive sheep rearing, and dairy farming, each succeeded the other as farmland was won from bush and scrub, each provided the genesis of the next, until stability was achieved in terms of existing technology and economic circumstances. Occasionally retreat occurred, but in general the pattern was one of advance (Figures 2A and 2B), each stage of occupance leaving behind relics which have persisted to this day. From the intensive dairy-farming country of the Otorohanga lowlands to the newly-developed lands of Ranginui, from the streets and lights of Te Kuiti to the roughness of the timber-millers' camp at Maraeroa or the loneliness of the Maori *whare* at Taharoa the successive phases are evident. Their elements constitute the complex of features that distinguish the Northern King Country as a geographic region.

*Maori occupance: to 1892*

To the Maori this land of the Ngatimaniapoto was important in that it lay athwart the main route between Tamaki and Taranaki that followed the Waikato and Waipa Rivers to the Mokau and the sea. Food was readily obtainable on the journey (fern roots, eels and birds) and the alluvial lands could be cultivated for *kumara*. The rocky ignimbrite outcrops provided sites for many a *pa*, refuges for the Ngatimaniapoto when inter-tribal warfare swept from north to south, and the open fernland was dotted by *kainga,* occupied when conditions were peaceful.

This subsistence pattern changed slightly with the advent of missionaries in 1834, through to about 1846. The period from 1845 to 1860 has been called the 'Golden Age before the War' when settlements became numerous and the Maori grew fruit, wheat and other crops, not only for their own use but also for the Auckland market and even export to the Californian goldfields. The characteristics of Maori occupance were intensified, not changed, by this grafting of European technology upon Polynesian practices. Population shifts did not occur to any degree, except perhaps the abandonment of *pa* and concentration on the *kainga* along the traditional routeways; the digging-stick gave way in part to the plough; and cows and sheep were depastured for the first time. But all was destroyed in the war in the Waikato.

For some time vestiges remained. The Kingites at the height of their influence maintained the gardens and the stock, and initiated new ventures under the guidance of pakeha who had remained within the King Country because of marriage to Maori women. However, by the early 1880s, tumbled buildings, patches of English grasses, and cattle run wild were all that was left of the former stage of occupance. The cultural frontier had retreated to the political line of demarcation along the Puniu River, and the question of the Maori and his land became both perennial and cardinal in the King Country.

Today the problem remains, but the subsistence occupance of the Maori has practically disappeared. Only on the confines of the Northern King Country is it to be discerned, such as in small concentrations like that at Taharoa remotely situated on the coast south of Kawhia Harbour, where, in 1966, there were 64 Maoris and no Europeans; or at the timber-milling camps in the south–eastern interior, where Maoris still remain in the majority. Yet none of these are subsistence farmers in the true sense, and even at Taharoa isolation may soon be rudely destroyed as an exploitative economy supervenes, for the ironsands of this coast are raw material for New Zealand's infant iron and steel industries.

*Pioneer settlement: to 1921*

The opening-up of the King Country by the Ngatimaniapoto chiefs was not followed by any rush of pakeha settlement. Negotiations by the government through the Maori Land Court for the purchase of Maori land were slow, except for the area needed immediately for railway construction. It was not until 1893 that the first selections were taken up, and at the census of 1906 only 600 pakeha inhabited this former Maori territory.[6]

However, before the farmers came the exploiters. Mining never has been significant in the Northern King Country, although coal has been won since 1886—first along the Mokau River, and later in the south–eastern interior. No metallic ores brought rushes to the area, and today only a few thousand tons of coal are dug annually from small opencast pits where the seams are exposed at the base of the Tertiary rocks which constitute the Te Kuiti syncline above the greywacke undermass. Yet at Benneydale, the site of the state mine responsible for more than 70 per cent of the total Northern King Country production between 1886 and 1962, a township remains as evidence of planned advance into the remote hill country.[7]

The milling of timber presents another facet, namely that of steady advance south–eastwards from the kahikatea stands in the marshy valleys near Otorohanga, first cut over in 1890, to the ordered exploitation of Pureora today. Apart from the kahikatea, podocarp-deciduous forest, mainly rimu and tawa, occupied the higher greywacke country to the east and west and provided barriers to both Maori movement and pakeha settlement. However, the building of the railway from Te Kuiti towards Taumarunui provided means of access, and piecemeal logging gave way to ordered development with the establishment of sawmills at Mangapehi in 1904 and 1912. Bush tramways and bullock roads for many years thereafter served as routes towards the interior, and as the loggers moved on pioneer farmers came in their wake. Today the felled timber from Pureora is hauled still to the Mangapehi mills past newly-established farmland and the derelict mine at Benneydale, but on what is now a main highway linking Mangakino and Te Kuiti.

But the newly-established farms on the agricultural frontier of the present bear no resemblance to the pioneer farms of the turn of the century. The first settlers walked in, or travelled by boat along the Mokau, along the old Maori routeways. They drove their stock before them and packed the grass-seed on their backs, and, having arrived, set about clearing the forest with fire and axe. They sought the forest as 'strong' country in preference to the scrub or fern, in contradistinction to the Maori who avoided it whenever possible except for brief bird-snaring expeditions, and soon clearings with English grasses among stumps and blackened skeletons of trees pocked the landscape.

During the 20 years before the First World War progress was slow. Land remained difficult to acquire, either freehold or leasehold, roads were difficult to build, and it was not until 1908 that the Main Trunk Railway was completed. Subsistence economies prevailed, for stock and dairy produce could not be readily transported, and although legislation in 1909 rendered easier the leasing of Maori land and led to undue speculation and overcapitalization, 'this was truly a pioneer period . . . . . the logical

174

completion of that earlier period of settlement so rudely interrupted by the Maori wars.'[8]

War was to interrupt yet again. In 1914 many farmers in the Northern King Country left their properties to the care of wives or relatives, or merely quit, and the shift of the agricultural frontier was checked just as mounting prosperity promised its advance. For the next four to six years high prices meant consolidation, even though husbandry suffered, and by 1921 the area occupied reached proportions not reached again until the late 1950s (Figure 2A). The acreage of improved land per head of rural population in fact reached its apogee (Figure 2B). But in 1921 wool prices fell, and those for butterfat a year later. Most faced ruin, many walked off their land, and the Northern King Country with its legacy of Maori land problems, poor communications, overcapitalization and land deterioration became notorious among the farming districts of New Zealand.

Today echoes of that notoriety remain, but pioneer development by a man and his family is a thing of the past. The small farm in the bush exists no longer, though many a tumbled house and ancient orchard stand as reminders of an occupance on which later prosperity was built.

*Farm consolidation: to 1945*

During the next ten years consolidation characterized the economic activities of this part of the North Island. The exploitation of timber was abandoned by small mills operating on the forest fringes and became concentrated in large concerns like those of Mangapehi. Coal mining showed diminishing returns, and only the quarrying of limestone, mainly for agricultural purposes, showed an increase as farmers began to concentrate their resources. The area occupied was reduced, but the proportion of improved land expanded, and numbers of stock, especially cattle, climbed steadily. Stock units per acre of improved land mounted (Figure 2A). More attention was paid to the fern and scrub of the lowlands, the marginal farms of the uplands were abandoned to regenerating forest, and as swamps were drained and shelterbelts established, the more intensive stages of agricultural occupance began to dominate in the lowlands of the Waipa and its tributaries. Where once the mission stations had stood, where once the Maori had cultivated his plots, and where the timber-getter had passed and, later, the first pakeha farmers, the small paddocks of the fat-lamb producer and dairy farmer now figured prominently. Store sheep and cattle occupied the hill farms, but did not thrive, for the fertility of the bush-burn country was exhausted and 'bush-sickness' on lighter soils had appeared. Noxious weeds, ragwort in particular, were rife, and hill farmers fought an endless battle against forest regeneration where rainfall was of the order of 60 inches a year.

With the recession of 1931 the reputation of the Northern King Country was rendered even worse. The reward for perseverance, even for good management, was an income below subsistence level, and added debt. Not only sheepmen, but also dairy farmers, abandoned the struggle, leaving the mortgagees to handle things as best they might. Some yielded to the inevitable, many more attempted to give up leases on Maori land taken out in the boom of 21 years before, but the Maori could achieve even less with his land, and so it remained with the pakeha—to become a bone of contention another 21 years later when again the leases fell in.

The time had arrived for the government to intervene. To arrest the retreat from farming various expedients were adopted, among them a Small Farms Scheme which presaged a return to quasi-pioneer settlement. Eventually this was absorbed into a general programme of land development by the government as conditions improved, so setting the pattern which persists to this day. For those who struggled on, a return to dairying with its monthly cream cheque became almost a necessity, and sheep numbers fell (Figure 2B).

However, by this time roads had been improved as the internal combustion engine made its universal impact, and, more important, technology and research were providing solutions to farming problems. The use of phosphatic fertilizers as topdressing for pastures became general, replacing what had been lost when the induced fertility from bush-burns was exhausted. Carrying capacities increased (Figure 2A). Moreover, it came to be realized that bush-sickness in stock was a matter of trace-element deficiency, and cobaltized superphosphate was to provide a solution to farming problems on the remoter hill country where light soils derived from ash-showers predominated.

By the outbreak of the Second World War prosperity in the Northern King Country had been re-established, only again to be checked as the young men left for military service. But on this occasion an older generation was able to maintain what had been won, and, indeed, improve upon it despite shortages of labour, fencing wire, machinery and fertilizers. Land development by the government, however, did suffer and the new-style pioneer fringe remained static. Only with the advent of peace could the next stage of occupance evolve from what had gone before.

### *Economic take-off: to 1966*

In 1946 the Northern King Country was carrying four stock units to the acre of improved land—four sheep, or one breeding ewe plus dry sheep and cattle. Recovery from war shortages was relatively slow at first, but the fillip of high wool prices in 1951 promoted an ever-increasing expansion in the area both occupied and improved, and in the number and quality of stock. New techniques appeared based on aircraft for spreading fertilizer and larger tractors and discs for bringing-in the steeper country. In 1947 a larger area of grass was sown on virgin country than ever before, or since, and in 1951–52 settlement of ex-servicemen on farms reached its maximum. Many of these farms were parts of holdings abandoned 15 to 20 years before, now rehabilitated by the government, and as the years progressed new farms were won from the bush as large-scale development proceeded. No longer was the pioneer pitted alone against the forest and the scrub. Established grassland, ring fences, a house and minimum stocking were his on which to improve, the roads were built and schools and cultural amenities were no more distant than the bus or car could carry him. Thus, today, on the margins of the Volcanic Plateau and western hill country, men and machines, cobaltized superphosphate and technical know-how have carried the agricultural frontier to the limits of the Northern King Country, passing on the way the abandoned timber-milling settlements. Beyond, in Pureora, the last major stands of rimu and matai are being logged and replaced, in part, by *Pinus radiata* in a planned silvicultural economy.

Yet one problem in particular persisted throughout this period of expansion, as it did in previous periods to differing degrees. From about

176

1948 onwards the question of Maori leaseholds became acute. The growing prosperity, coupled with an awakening sense of distinctiveness among Maoris and a greater assurance of their own capabilities, meant that the owners were anxious to secure the return of their properties. Deterioration of Maori land, either as the result of intentional pakeha neglect or of Maori inability to combat the difficulties of multiple ownership, emphasized again the notoriety of the Northern King Country, and led eventually to government intervention. Various Acts of Parliament, especially that of 1953, resolved the immediate problem of leaseholds and put pressure on the Maori to utilize properly his weed-infested, badly-used land. Development of Maori land was instituted along lines similar to those adopted for Crown land, and eventually new farms, better roads and a new order came to mark the progress of Maori settlement in areas once remote, abandoned or, even, forgotten. Nevertheless, little change occurred at Taharoa on the coast, and on lands in the south–eastern interior. Only now do they command attention as they are opened up to exploitative economies.

Today the Northern King Country approaches optimum land utilization under present economic conditions. Expansion will continue as the frontiers advance and as full use is made of areas not yet fully or properly farmed. Significantly this expansion will occur not in the area of most intensive production, that is to say the dairying country around Otorohanga, nor on the 'pioneer' fringe where development of virgin land is almost complete, but in the areas of fat-lamb and beef production, namely the undulating lowlands and easy hill country with 40 to 60 inches of rain. The area given over to dairy farming, despite a steadily increasing number of cows in milk, is decreasing, and at Otorohanga is found the last remaining dairy factory in the Northern King Country.

Better roads and better transport have resulted in the decline and, often, the disappearance of the small service centre, the one-teacher school, and the local dairy factory. More and more the population concentrates on the two towns of the area, Te Kuiti and Otorohanga, and, indeed, Hamilton and Auckland to the north. Between 1961 and 1966 the total population of the Northern King Country declined by 3.2 per cent, the urban proportion showing a slight increase. Both pakeha and Maori are involved. The intercensal growth of 14.6 per cent in Te Kuiti and of 19.5 per cent in Otorohanga of the Maori urban component underlines the significance of the retreat from the countryside. By returning to communities established along the traditional routeway, the Maori demonstrates again the permanence of the threads of the past woven into the fabric of the present. Another stage of occupance supervenes, and sets a pattern for the future.

PROCESS AND PATTERN

The geographic character of the Northern King Country is distinctive. In no other part of the North Island, or in New Zealand as a whole, are the processes of sequent occupance so clearly defined in present-day landscapes. The rudimentary economy of the Maori has all but disappeared, but vestiges remain; the missionary era and early pakeha influence is marked in a few sites of settlement; exploitative economies persist, but are now no longer wasteful nor far-ranging; pioneer farming in its modern guise marks the agricultural frontier; extensive sheep and cattle rearing amid logs and stumps is a feature of the more remote hill country; fat lambs and beef and dairying on easier terrain reflect an increasing intensification of land use which culminates in urban patterns and functions. And overall persists the problems of the Maori and his land.

From Otorohanga to Pureora and Mokau these elements of sequent occupance are discernible. They constitute the unique complex of a geographic region which may be defined as the Northern King Country.

## NOTES

[1] D. WHITTLESEY, Sequent occupance, *Annals Assoc. Amer. Geogrs.* 19 (1929) 162–165.

[2] The word 'pakeha' (stranger) is used in New Zealand popular parlance to distinguish those who are not 'Maori' (native).

[3] As part of the agreement to open up the King Country, the Crown had assumed pre-emptive rights to land in order to avoid a repetition of the Waikato and Taranaki conflicts of the '40s and '60s.

[4] J. COWAN, *Settlers and pioneers* (Wellington, 1940) 79.

[5] A fall in the period 1951–55 is attributable to the number of new farms established as part of the scheme to rehabilitate ex-servicemen.

[6] There were approximately 2,000 Maoris. This was the last census in which they constituted a majority.

[7] The mine was operated by the state from 1940 onwards. It is interesting to note that Benneydale (named after the then Minister of Mines) is the only non-Maori place-name of significance in the Northern King Country.

[8] J. B. CONDLIFFE, *New Zealand in the making* (London, 1959) 231.

# TOWARDS A BETTER UNDERSTANDING
# OF SHOPPING PATTERNS

## B. J. GARNER

### INTRODUCTION

Perhaps as a result of the renewed interest in central place theory, an impressive amount of research effort in geography has in recent years been devoted to studies of the so-called 'journey-to-shop'. Although much of the recent work has been placed within a quantitative framework this has not added significantly to our understanding of the topic. Rather, it has generally resulted in a more precise description of patterns and of the relationships involved. This suggests that the benefits of our quantitative revolution have not been fully realised. The reason for this could be that, despite the more rigorous methods, we are still lacking more sophisticated concepts, and particularly those relevant for a deeper understanding of spatial behaviour. Fortunately this has not gone unnoticed and there is a growing literature suggesting what form these needed concepts should take, and from where they might perhaps be taken.[1] Within this context, the objective of this essay is to look at some of the implications of the trend towards a more behavioural approach in geography as they pertain to studies of the ways in which buyers are paired with sellers within the urban area to give rise to shopping patterns. Previous studies will be very generally reviewed with a view to isolating the deficiencies in our present understanding of the problem, and some directions for future research will be suggested which may eventually lead to a better understanding of this aspect of spatial interaction.

### PREVIOUS STUDIES

A review of the extant literature dealing with shopping patterns suggests a classification of studies on the basis of their nature and purpose into three fairly broad, but nevertheless distinct, groups. The first group, which is perhaps the most impressive in volume, comprises studies that are largely descriptive in content. Here the emphasis is typically on variation in the distances consumers travel to shop and how this is related to such things as, for example, socio-economic characteristics of the shopper, mode of travel, type of trip undertaken, the kind of goods sought, and so on.[2] The relationships between variables may or may not be quantified, and if they are it is usually in a simple way. Most of the studies are cross-sectional in approach and so far we have learned very little about the way the patterns change over time. The results of these empirical studies are extremely valuable however, since they are often suggestive of more specific hypotheses for subsequent research.

The second and third categories differ from the first not so much by what is studied as in the ways study is undertaken. Thus, although works included in the second group may contain an important descriptive component, this is normally only by way of background to the explicit testing of hypotheses about shopping behaviour. They are explicitly placed in a quantitative framework and rely almost exclusively on the method of statistical inference. There is also a tendency for these studies to be concerned with specific concepts, such as, for example, the range of a good, trip utility,

179

and so on.[3] The third category includes studies in which the goal is to develop models of shopping behaviour. In terms of Lowry's distinction between descriptive, predictive, and planning models, most of the effort to date has been directed at formulating descriptive models.[4] The rather limited objective of these is to replicate the relevant features of existing shopping patterns. Despite their essential simplicity, they are of important scientific value because they

> reveal much about the structure of the urban environment, reducing the apparent complexity of the observed world to the coherent and rigorous language of mathematical relationships.[5]

Another important feature of most of the shopping models developed so far is that they operate at a fairly high level of data aggregation and thus attempt to replicate mass behaviour. One justification for this is that it offers more immediate rewards in the planning context, and it is not, therefore, surprising to find that the most active development of these models is in the hands of practising planners today rather than geographers.

*Shopping models*

A number of different strategies have been adopted within the broad framework of the descriptive modelling of shopping patterns. An obvious distinction is that between conceptual models on the one hand and operational models on the other. In models of the first kind emphasis is on identifying relevant variables and specifying the way they are inter-related to give rise to regularities in shopping behaviour.[6] The operational models take some of the observed regularities as a starting point and attempt to reproduce them using mathematical equations. A basic difference within this category is that between deterministic and probability formulations. The deterministic models are based, for the most part, on the use of multiple regression analysis, and attempt to 'explain' the variation in distances travelled to shop as a function of a wide range of spatial, social, and economic variables.[7] Increasingly, however, models of shopping behaviour are placed in a probability framework. An early attempt was that by Nystuen to simulate multiple-purpose shopping trips using Monte Carlo methods,[8] an approach which, incidentally, might be worthwhile exploring further in the future. More recent attempts have generated models of spatial interaction based on modifications of the intervening-opportunities approach and the methods of entropy maximisation from information theory.[9] In a slightly different context, there has been some experimentation with the use of specific probability distributions, and particularly the Poisson distribution, as a highly generalised basis for describing consumer shopping behaviour.[10]

*The gravitationalist approach*

Despite these recent developments, most operational models of shopping behaviour are still direct descendants of the gravity model introduced by Reilly over three decades ago.[11] They differ from the original formulation in three important respects:

*(a)* movement for all kinds of goods is considered;

*(b)* they describe interaction between a continuous distribution of population and shopping opportunities; and

*(c)* to incorporate this *many-centre* interaction and the element of consumer choice it implies, the dependant variable is, initially at least, specified as a probability.

Following the presentation by Huff,[12] the probability of a given shopping centre being selected by the shopper from the available alternatives is:

$$P_j = \frac{U_j}{\sum\limits_j U_j}$$

in which $U_j$ is the *utility* associated with the jth centre.[13]

The concept of *place utility,* an extremely important one for the study of spatial behaviour,[14] has traditionally proved difficult to handle empirically. In shopping models it is simply defined as a ratio of the *attractiveness* ($A_j$) of a given shopping centre to the *distance* ($d_{ij}$) separating it from the consumer residing at place i. As developed by Lakshmanan and Hansen[15] the probability of a consumer resident at place i patronising centre j is given as:

$$P_{ij} = \frac{A_{ij}^{\alpha}/d_{ij}^{\beta}}{\sum\limits_{j=1}^{n} A_{ij}^{\alpha}/d_{ij}^{\beta}}$$

Operation of the model necessitates a division of the urban area into a number of residence zones. When the probabilities are related to the population of the zones, the model states that the expected flow between place i and centre j is:

*(a)* directly proportional to the attractiveness of the centre;

*(b)* inversely proportional to some function of distance; and

*(c)* inversely proportional to the total competitive attractiveness of all the other shopping centres included in the model.[16]

For its application, the parameters in the equation must be estimated and the variables indexed. The first problem is essentially technical but is critical for the successful operation of the model, the effectiveness of which is largely conditioned by the specific values given to the exponent of distance. The second problem is largely definitional, and concerns ways of quantifying the rather elusive concept of attractiveness. Normally this is defined as the size of centre and is indexed by such measures as total floorspace, retail sales, or the number of functions and establishments present. Although there are conceptual problems in handling the distance variable, the use of air-line distance or driving time seems to give satisfactory results.

The success of the model is normally measured by the correlation between observed and expected flows, and despite the model's simplicity its application in a number of planning studies has been highly successful by this standard.[17] Nevertheless, there may often be large discrepancies between observed and expected flows and modifications of the model to improve its performance are continually being suggested. Thus, for example, Huff has suggested that the model be disaggregated by class of good to take account of the observation that consumers are prepared to travel greater distances for more specialised commodities.[18] More recently, Parry Lewis and Trail have introduced the notion of competition between *claimants* at shopping centres, and have suggested a modification of the distance variable to incorporate this into the model.[19] It is not difficult to think of many other ways of making the model more realistic.

## The Need for a more Behavioural Approach

Despite the attractiveness of these highly aggregated approaches to modelling shopping patterns, particularly for planners, it is obvious that they contribute only marginally to our understanding of consumer spatial behaviour. They contribute practically nothing to the development of the theories we so badly need. Taking stock of what has been accomplished through the various approaches to the study of shopping patterns to date, it seems that there is a realistic need for us to tread new paths in the future if we are to capitalise on what we already know to gain deeper insights into this and other aspects of spatial interaction. This, initially at least, may involve study at a more elemental scale but it will most certainly involve a more precise specification of postulates about spatial behaviour.[20]

Human geographers have always made assumptions of some kind about human behaviour. The problem is, as Harvey has demonstrated, that these assumptions have been for the most part only implicit in geographical analysis rather than explicitly formulated.[21] This has certainly been the case in our studies of shopping patterns. This is not to deny that in the past geographers have been unaware of the need to incorporate behavioural postulates into their work. Traditionally we have relied on economics, and to a lesser extent sociology, for these; and these fields have had a lasting and enduring influence on geographical research. Increasingly, however, it is to the powerful behavioural postulates in psychology that geographers are turning. This is giving rise to a definite shift in the orientation of certain research, and a more explicit behavioural approach is emerging. There can be little doubt that this will be of lasting significance to the subject.[22]

In this so-called behavioural approach, the specific emphasis is upon various 'social and psychological mechanisms which have explicit spatial correlates and/or spatial structural implications'.[23] The relevance of this shift should be self-evident, for in order to understand and explain spatial patterns, it is imperative that we consider the antecedent decisions and behaviours which underly them. Behavioural postulates are relevant in human geography, then, for the development of theory.[24] The need to turn to other social sciences for them stems in large part from the shortcomings of existing postulates, especially some of those from economics. In particular, the notions of a rational 'economic man' leave much to be desired, and the normative theory which it gives rise to is so obviously inconsistent with much overt behaviour in the real world. Wolpert thus states, of farmers in Sweden,

> that the concept of the spatial satisficer appears more descriptively accurate of the behavioural patterns of the sample population than the normative concept of economic man. The individual is adaptively or intendedly rational rather than omnisciently rational.[25]

That this kind of thinking is relevant for the study of shopping patterns is well illustrated by the shortcomings of using marginal analysis from classical economic theory as the rationale for consumer behaviour in central place theory. The result is a theory which specifies that the consumer *rationally* balances travel costs with the selling price of a given good, to result in rather simplistic patterns of behaviour in which flows are hierarchic and the consumer always travels to the closest centre for the satisfaction of a given want. There is ample empirical evidence suggesting that consumers do not behave in this way.[26]

## SOME NEW CONSIDERATIONS

Although it is clear that a more behavioural approach is both relevant and needed in studying shopping patterns, it is difficult to know where to start and what to include. This is largely because we have not yet adequately sorted through the potentially rewarding source of behavioural postulates in other disciplines, nor ascertained their usefulness in the spatial context. For some, a logical starting point may be to understand more about the way in which consumers *in fact* make decisions. The analytic models developed by psychologists regarding goal objectives, drives, motivations, and the stimuli lying behind decision-making are obviously essential in this context.[27] Whether this is beyond the scope of geographical enquiry is debatable, but there is no doubt that we should at least be more familiar with such concepts and the consequences of them if we are to give more than lip-service to a behavioural approach.

Whatever the importance of the mechanisms underlying individual decision-making, one thing is already very clear: individuals make decisions within the framework of their *perceptions*, or images, of physical space. Lee suggests that these are formalised by the individual in the form of *schemata*, and he further suggests that the concept of the schema will be one of the most helpful in studying human behaviour in space.[28] The images can thus be thought of as variables intervening between the individual and the environment, and as an extremely pervasive influence on behaviour. The important thing is that the individual's images or schemata 'are related to, but by no means coincident with, the physical reality that lies outside us'.[29] Hence what constitutes the retail structure of the urban area as we know it from our geographical inventories may often only have a very general significance for the individual shopper.

He does not know all about the alternative opportunities available at a given instant in time, and all that he is cognitive of may not be relevant for his particular pattern of behaviour. This is because

> there is a certain difference between the images which [we] have of physical objects in space and time and the *valuations* which [we] put on these objects.[30]

The images of fact are what constitute the consumer's imperfect knowledge of the retail structure. The behavioural space within which shopping patterns are developed however, relates to the images of value, since these are what underlie differences in the relative attractiveness of the various parts of the retail structure for the shopper. It is presumably *via* these value images that consumers express preferences for one shopping centre over another or the goods of one retailer over those of another. Obviously, knowledge of the individual's value system is fundamental to a proper understanding of the way in which such preferences are developed. That marked preferences are important in affecting behaviour is self-evident and this is undoubtedly another important reason for the observation that consumers often appear to travel much further than they need to in order to satisfy their wants—even for convenience items.[31] A possible implication from this is, contrary to the gravitationalist's belief, that utility in shopping behaviour may be much less dependent on distance within the urban area than we have hitherto supposed—at least for shoppers with well-developed space preferences.[32]

There can be no doubt that distance does exert powerful influences on behaviour, and in this regard the principle of least effort has served us well in the past as a general framework for the study of many aspects of spatial interaction. However, there is also no doubt that physical distance, and the time-cost transformations to which we subject it, cannot give us all the answers. Subjective distance, the individual's movement imagery, and the rôle these play in structuring space for the individual, must obviously be considered as well if we are to obtain a better understanding of shopping patterns.

*The strategy for research*

The view taken here, then, is that a potentially fruitful way in which a better understanding of shopping patterns may be obtained is by studying the images consumers have of the urban retail structure and the way these relate to their behaviour spaces. The case for such a cognitive-behavioural approach to the study of spatial interaction in geography has been elegantly argued elsewhere.[33] As it pertains to the study of consumer behaviour, there would appear to be, initially at least, four broad problem areas for future research.

The first of these is the fundamental one of specifying the nature of the images consumers have of the urban retail structure. As a working hypothesis it seems reasonable to adopt the view that the individual's images of space, and what that space contains, are not completely idiosyncratic and unpredictable. Although there must obviously be a proportion of 'unique image', the scanty evidence to date suggests that a certain proportion of the images are *common* to groups of individuals,[34] and it is with this common part of the spatial image that we must first concern ourselves. The problem is essentially one of measurement, and its reduction will necessitate familiarity with different kinds of quantitative techniques from those which have traditionally been included in our tool kits. Of particular importance in this respect are the general methods of attitude scaling in psychology, and the application of some of these in geographical studies has already yielded promising results.[35]

The remaining areas for future research are contingent upon the first. Once the common part of the images can be isolated and the details specified, then two sets of relationships are worthy of investigation. The first of these concerns the relationships between the consumers and the images they hold. Here the emphasis would be on the socio-psychological characteristics of the consumer, and it is in this respect that direct considerations of such things as the value system, motivation, and goal objects will probably be needed. The wealth of empirical findings linking shopping patterns with general socio-economic characteristics will also be relevant in this context.

The second set of relationships is that between the images and the nature of the urban retail structure. Here attention would focus on the aspects of retail structure that are filtered out as significant for the schemata; on the images of fact. What does the consumer understand as the retail structure? Although we have little, if any, knowledge of this as it pertains to the retail context, the results of investigations of perception within the broader urban environment suggest that individuals are highly selective and that the images are quite fragmentary. Vast areas of the physical space are left untouched and, indeed, are unknown as far as the individual is concerned. Moreover, the elements comprising the images tend to hang together topologically, indicating that perhaps the emphasis on distance and the Euclidian framework it involves may not be the most appropriate for a deeper understanding of spatial behaviour.[36] Similarly, the images of value must be considered and the important factors underlying preference structures must be isolated.

The remaining area in the research strategy proposed here is perhaps the most significant in view of the cross-sectional nature of most of our studies of shopping patterns to date. It concerns the question of how the images arise, how they are shaped by experience, and how stable they are through time. There is a continuous input of sensory information from the physical environment as a result of our everyday experiences with it. These impressions are not, however, allotted an equal-sized pigeon-hole and stored *ad infinitum* or until such time as they might be needed:

> Many are rejected at once because they don't fit in with what is there or because they don't contribute anything new. The rest make their mark and impress.[37]

It is also probably true that, unless there is some steady reinforcement of the images, parts of them tend to fade away and ultimately disappear.

New elements appear in the retail structure, old and familiar elements are forever disappearing, and the images are subject to continual modification as a result of exploration of the urban retail structure and the learning process. Consumers at any given moment in time will be in different stages of the learning process and this is probably reflected in their particular shopping patterns. The application of learning theories from psychology can, as Golledge has demonstrated, contribute much to our understanding of the way in which shopping patterns develop and change, and further experimentation with these is to be encouraged among geographers.[38]

The implications of the cognitive-behavioural approach to traditional geographical problems are far reaching. There is no doubt that as a general framework it will aid us immensely in the search for lawfulness and regularity underlying shopping patterns, besides many other kinds of spatial interaction, and will be of fundamental importance in constructing theories about spatial behaviour from which future patterns may be at least statistically predictable. It will, however, take a very long time for us to reach this level of sophistication, but in working towards this goal we can get considerable moral support from the psychologist himself, for he realises, none better, 'that behaviour is fantastically complex, but he declines to deduce from this that it is magical'.[39]

## NOTES

[1] See in particular: D. HARVEY, Behavioural postulates and the construction of theory in human geography, *Seminar Paper Series* 6 (Department of Geography, Bristol University, 1967).

[2] For example: G. A. NADER, Socio-economic status and consumer behaviour, *Urban Studies* 6 (1969) 235–245; and P. J. AMBROSE, An analysis of intra-urban shopping patterns, *Town Planning Review* 38 (1968) 327–334.

[3] W. A. V. CLARK, Consumer travel patterns and the concept of range, *Annals Assoc. Amer. Geographers* 58 (1968) 386–396; and D. F. MARBLE and S. R. BOWLBY, Shopping alternatives and recurrent travel patterns, in Geographic studies of urban transportation and network analysis (ed. F. Horton), *Studies in Geography Northwestern University* 16, (Northwestern University, Evanston, Illinois, 1968) 42–75.

[4] I. S. LOWRY, A short course in model design, *Jour. of the Amer. Inst. of Planners* 31 (1965) 158–166.

[5] *Op. cit.,* 159.

[6] Examples are: W. J. BAUMOL and E. A. IDE, Variety in retailing, *Management Science* 3 (1956) 93–101; and D. L. HUFF, A topographical model of consumer space preferences, *Papers and Proc. Reg. Sci. Assoc.* 7 (1960) 159–173.

[7] See: B. J. L. BERRY, H. G. BARNUM, and R. J. TENNANT, Retail location and consumer behaviour, *Papers and Proc. Reg. Sci. Assoc.* 9 (1962) 65–106.

[8] J. D. NYSTUEN, A theory and simulation of intra-urban travel, in Quantitative geography, Part I (eds. W. L. Garrison and D. F. Marble), *Studies in Geography Northwestern University* 13, (Northwestern University, Evanston, Illinois, 1967) 54–83.

[9] B. HARRIS, A note on the probability of interaction at a distance, *Jour. of Reg. Sci.* 5 (1964) 31–35; and A. WILSON, Notes on some concepts in social physics, *Working Paper* 4 (Centre for Environmental Studies, London, 1968). For a general review of the main types of shopping models, see: M. CORDEY HAYES, Retail location models, *Working Paper* 16 (Centre for Environmental Studies, London, 1968).

[10] L. CURRY, The geography of service centres within towns: the elements of an operational approach, *Proc. of the I.G.U. Symposium in Urban Geography, Lund* (ed. K. Norborg) (1960) 31–53.

[11] W. J. REILLY, *Laws of retail gravitation* (Knickerboker Press, New York, 1931).

[12] D. L. HUFF, *Determination of intra-urban retail trade areas* (Real Estate Research Program, University of California, Los Angeles, 1962).

[13] In this formulation a closed system of centres is assumed. This is not essential, however, and a good example of the application of the model in an 'unclosed' system is that by: J. BLACK, Some retail sales models, *Paper for the Urban Studies Conference* (1966).

[14] A good discussion of this is given in: J. WOLPERT, Behavioural aspects of the decision to migrate, *Papers and Proc. Reg. Sci. Assoc.* 15 (1965) 159–169.

[15] T. R. LAKSHMANAN and W. G. HANSEN, A retail market potential model, *Jour. of the Amer. Inst. of Planners* 31 (1965) 134–143.

[16] The model can also be used to predict total sales at a given shopping centre, and total sales by residents of a particular zone, by suitable manipulation of the equation.

[17] See: G. W. COWLEY, *Shopping report* (County Planning Department, Bedford, 1967); and T. RHODES and R. WHITAKER, Forecasting shopping demand, *Jour. of the Town Planning Inst.* 53 (1967) 188–192.

[18] D. L. HUFF, A probabilistic analysis of shopping centre trade areas, *Land Economics* 39 (1963) 81–90.

[19] J. PARRY LEWIS and A. L. TRAIL, The assessment of shopping potential and the demand for shops, *Town Planning Rev.* 38 (1968) 317–326.

[20] D. HARVEY, *op. cit.*

[21] D. HARVEY, *op. cit.*, 1.

[22] For examples of this approach, see: Behavioural problems in geography: a symposium (eds. K. R. Cox and R. G. Golledge), *Studies in Geography, Northwestern University* 17, (Northwestern University, Evanston, Illinois, 1969).

[23] *Ibid.*, 3.

[24] D. HARVEY, *op. cit.*

[25] J. WOLPERT, The decision process in a spatial context, *Annals of the Assoc. of Amer. Geographers* 54 (1964) 558.

[26] See for example: W. A. V. CLARK, *op. cit.*; and R. L. JOHNSTON and P. J. RIMMER, A note on consumer behaviour in an urban hierarchy, *Jour. of Reg. Sci.* 7 (1967) 161–166.

[27] J. D. EYLES, On the concept of motivation in geography, *Discussion Paper* 14 (Department of Geography, L.S.E., 1968).

[28] T. R. LEE, Psychology and living space, *Trans. of the Bartlett Soc.* 2–3 (1965) 9–36.

[29] *Ibid.*, 25.

[30] K. E. BOULDING, *The image* (University of Michigan Press, Ann Arbor, 1956) 11.

[31] W. A. V. CLARK, *op. cit.*

[32] For discussion of this in a broader context, see: M. M. WEBBER, Culture, territoriality, and the elastic mile, *Papers and Proc. Reg. Sci. Ass.* 13 (1964) 59–69.

[33] See particularly: D. HARVEY, Conceptual and measurement problems in the cognitive-behavioural approach to location theory, in K. R. Cox and R. G. Golledge (eds.), *op. cit.*, 35–68.

[34] P. R. GOULD, On mental maps, *Discussion paper* 9 (Mich. Inter-Univ. Community of Math. Geographers, 1966). Also in this context, see: R. DOWNS, Approaches to, and problems in, the measurement of geographic space perception, *Seminar Paper Series* 9 (Department of Geography, Bristol University, 1967).

[35] See, for example, the use of the semantic differential in: B. J. GARNER, The analysis of qualitative data in urban geography: the example of shop quality, *Techniques in urban geography* (I.B.G. Study Group in Urban Geography, 1968) 16–30.

[36] K. LYNCH, *The image of the city* (M.I.T. Press, Cambridge, Mass., 1960).

[37] T. R. LEE, *op. cit.*, 23.

[38] R. G. GOLLEDGE, The geographical relevance of some learning theories, in K. R. Cox and R. G. Golledge (eds.), *op. cit.*, 101–145.

[39] T. R. LEE, *op. cit.*, 12.

# TRANSPORT AND ECONOMIC GROWTH IN DEVELOPING COUNTRIES: THE CASE OF EAST AFRICA

B. S. HOYLE

## INTRODUCTION

The emergence of a viable and efficient system of modern transportation is clearly an essential element in the growing infrastructure upon which the expanding economies of the less developed countries must be based. Many analyses of transport problems in such countries emphasize the specific problems associated with road, rail or sea transport media, and frequently confine discussion either to the economics of transportation or to the geographical disposition of the facilities available. Relatively few studies attempt to view the economic geography of transport networks within an area as a whole, or to examine the nature of the relationship between transport provision and economic growth. These two aspects of transport geography are of vital significance in the less developed countries, especially in view of the need to achieve maximum economies within the development process. East Africa provides an example of an area where rail, road, sea and air transport systems are all reasonably well developed but lack close integration, and where existing networks are currently subject to considerable changes and are, therefore, objects of political and economic attention. This paper attempts to set railway and port systems serving East Africa within the broader context of ideas relating transport development with economic growth.

## VIEWPOINTS ON THE RÔLE OF TRANSPORT IN LESS DEVELOPED COUNTRIES

In recent United Nations studies transport has been described as 'the formative power of economic growth and the differentiating process',[1] and attention has been directed to the fact that

> transport difficulties have considerably retarded the exploitation of natural resources, industrialization, expansion of trade, . . . . . and in some cases the achievement of national unity.[2]

Whilst these statements are certainly valid in general terms, as many examples illustrate, the interlinkages between the dual processes of economic growth and transport development will bear closer examination. On a world basis Berry has provided a useful general analysis of the relationship between road and rail transport network densities and the general level of economic development in a range of countries; the results suggest that some less developed countries have placed undue reliance upon selected transport media and that balanced transport development has not paralleled overall economic growth.[3] The transport/development relationship is clearly dependent upon the specific type or range of transport media involved in a given area, upon the type of economy the transport facilities are required to serve, and upon the level of economic development at which transport media are introduced. So many variables are involved that, beyond a certain point, comparisons become relatively valueless, but theoretically there exists for a given area at a given stage of development an *optimum transport capacity* yielding efficient service without the dangers of over-capitalization.

A distinction should be made in this context between two basic phases in the evolution of modern transport systems in less developed countries. The first phase, which may be termed *initial transport provision*, involves the construction of major rail arteries, modern roads and port facilities, and relates frequently to the earlier years of the colonial period. An outline system is thus established which permits economic growth up to a certain point, beyond which its shortcomings begin to restrict economic development. A second phase, which may be described as *transport elaboration* and which frequently refers to the later years of colonial dependence and to a period of political independence, involves the extension of the basic system including improvements in its efficiency, which permits a higher level of economic development. The two phases are contrasted in their economic impact in the sense that the first phase obviously permits (and is likely at least initially to stimulate) economic growth, whilst the second phase is generally merely permissive in economic terms and is not the direct stimulant to development that many politicians and some economists have thought likely. Transport is the key to modern economic growth in the less developed countries in the sense that it is a *sine qua non*; but transport elaboration in an already partially developed economic system does not necessarily encourage any further growth, and indeed is unlikely to do so unless further positive steps are taken to maximize the utility of the facilities provided by encouraging the geographical coincidence of development projects from several economic sectors.

## THE GROWTH OF RAIL NETWORKS

In the less developed countries the decision to build a major rail artery belongs generally to the phase of initial transport provision and is frequently of greater long-term significance than any other transport development. Such a railway tends to control the overall pattern of a country's expanding transport network and thereby to influence profoundly the pattern of its economic geography for a considerable length of time; this is especially important in those less developed countries which depend largely upon a single rail artery penetrating inland from a major port. Less significance is generally attached to roads, branch railways and minor ports, since although these may individually represent considerable capital investment the basic transport system of an area is not significantly disrupted if a decision to elaborate in a particular locality proves wrong and has to be reversed. Only when road/rail competition over long distances becomes intensive and a major railway loses its economic predominance, as in Ivory Coast and Sierra Leone, does the close association between an arterial railway and the economic geography of an area begin to disintegrate.

The geographical analysis of the changes involved in such situations constitutes an interesting area of research. Related studies have been undertaken, for example, within the Transport Research Programme of the Brookings Institution.[4] In East Africa the impact of recent rail extensions in Uganda has been analysed by O'Connor[5] but no overall survey of the East African railway system in economic terms has yet been made. East Africa is now provided with a railway system unified both physically and administratively, linking the three countries of Uganda, Kenya and Tanzania.[6] The system is based upon two rail arteries, respectively linking Mombasa with the Lake Victoria basin and Uganda, and Dar es Salaam with Lakes Victoria and Tanganyika (Figure 1). The elaboration of the system has been outlined elsewhere,[7] and is discussed here in the context of a comparative model framework.

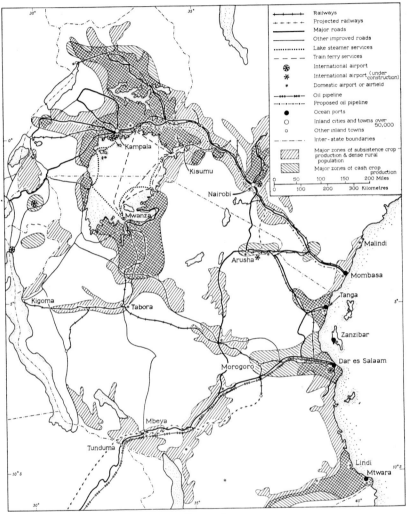

FIGURE 1
East Africa: some aspects of transport and economic activity

## A Model of East African Transport Development

In a well-known paper, Taafe, Morrill and Gould discussed the evolution of transport patterns in less developed countries and proposed a model for the analysis of such patterns.[8] Based originally upon studies in Ghana and Nigeria, the model has wide applicability.[9] Figure 2 represents an application of this model to the East African case.

The first stage of the model represents conditions over a period from the first to the early nineteenth century. The diagram shows a scatter of small coastal ports, largely isolated from one another and linked more

189

firmly with the maritime trading circulations of the Indian Ocean than with those parts of the interior from which slaves, ivory and other goods were regularly extracted. Although few ports or routes significant in medieval times continued to grow in later periods, the transport pattern shown in stage *(a)* underlines the historical precedents of modern systems. Stage *(b)* represents the zenith of the period of Arab trading activity based upon the island emporium of Zanzibar, from the outports of which trade routes radiated inland as far as western Uganda and Tanzania and indeed well beyond the confines of present-day East Africa. The concentration of transport routes upon Zanzibar at this time reflected the predominant role of the port in the economic and political life of the entire area, and involved a sharp decline in the fortunes and number of mainland trade centres.[10]

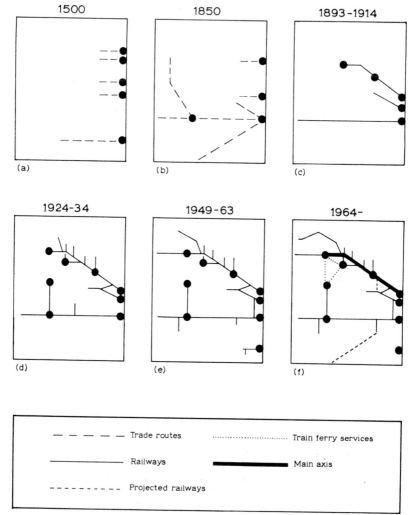

FIGURE 2

East Africa: an application of the Taafe–Morrill–Gould model of transport network development

The central Tanzanian transport axis initiated by the Zanzibar–Tabora slave route is re-emphasised in stage *(c)* by the Dar es Salaam–Kigoma railway, paralleled in Kenya by the Mombasa–Kisumu line. These two rail arteries, together with the less successful Tanga–Moshi line, have subsequently influenced profoundly the pattern of transport development and economic expansion in East Africa, particularly in the spheres of mineral exploitation, cash crop production, and rural and urban settlement. Since all three lines were initially based upon political rather than economic motivations, it is interesting to speculate upon the likely present-day patterns of East African economic geography had the railways been differently located.

Stages *(a)* to *(c)* of the model thus represent the broad phase identified earlier as initial transport provision, with particular emphasis on stage *(c)*. Stages *(d)* to *(f)* indicate successive eras in the broad phase identified as transport elaboration, and the routes represented are mainly rail transport routes since roads are often either parallel or locally tributary to railways, and since railways in East Africa still carry a majority of long-distance bulk consignments. Stage *(d)* saw the elaboration of the three original railways by branch- and feeder-lines designed to serve areas of increasing settlement and cash crop production, and by important extensions to Arusha, Mwanza and Kampala. Stage *(e)* is marked by the brief appearance of a railway serving the hinterland of the then newly-established deep-water port of Mtwara, by the interlinkage of the Tanga and central Tanzanian lines in the coastal zone, and by the two major extensions of the rail network to the west and north of Uganda respectively.

These developments had varying economic relevance. The Mtwara line, designed to evacuate anticipated groundnut harvests from southern Tanzania, failed in this objective (and was lifted in 1963) partly because the new port merely supplemented rather than replaced the lighterage port of Lindi to the north, with its road-feeder system.[11] The principal advantage of the Mnyusi–Ruvu link is that rolling stock may be moved as required between the Kenya–Uganda and central Tanzanian sections of the system, and substantial economies result from this in view of the complementary seasonal pattern of much of the cash crop freight which is handled. The Uganda extensions, built respectively to transport copper from the west and cotton from the north, do not yet appear to have attracted a significant volume of other traffic, and together provide the main body of contemporary evidence from East Africa that transport elaboration within an established economic system is not likely to accelerate development unless further steps are taken to utilise more fully the facilities provided.[12] The final stage of the model indicates the intensification of surface transport along the Kampala–Nairobi–Mombasa axis (now obviously well-established as 'main street, East Africa'),[13] reflects the introduction of train-ferry services on Lake Victoria, and shows the contemporary transport extensions towards Zambia from the central Tanzanian axis.[14] This southern branch of the East African transport network is rapidly becoming a major international axis in its own right, and is already identified by an oil pipeline and a major road in course of improvement; the decision to construct a Tan-zam railway based on Chinese surveys and loans was taken in November 1969. These developments are clearly related not only to the Zambian situation but also to specific agricultural development schemes[15] and potential coal and iron ore developments in southern Tanzania.

191

Proposals for the construction of a 600 MW hydro-electric power station in southern Tanzania were also announced in 1969.

Thus a close relationship between the broad pattern of East Africa's transport system and many other aspects of the geography and economy of the area. In the pre-railway stages East African trade was channelled into limited arteries linked with the Indian Ocean maritime transport system; other movements were mainly local in origin and destination. Nevertheless, these early stages provided established modes of access to and movement within the East African interior and this influenced the alignments of the pioneer railways. These in turn, with their later elaborations, are part of the infrastructure upon which the modern economy is based. In geographical terms, the specific location of the various nodes and links in the transport network (particularly the rail network) has very strongly influenced the location and economic growth of those areas that are heavily involved in the cash economy (Figure 1). The transport of East Africa's bulk agricultural products (notably coffee, cotton, sisal and tea) and the export of minerals such as copper and soda ash are very largely dependent upon rail facilities. Whilst it is true that road feeder lines are important in cash crop producing areas, and that road/rail competition for transport to the ports is intensifying, the rail arteries have in a sense controlled the location of such areas. Areas of East Africa without reasonable access to rail transport but with considerable economic potential (for example parts of southern Tanzania) have been relatively slow to develop and have not generally emerged as economic core areas either during the colonial period or subsequently. In the context of the distinction made earlier between initial transport provision and transport elaboration it does not follow that contemporary transport improvements will encourage the emergence of new economic foci, but the historical relationship between transport media and patterns of economic growth is very clear.

## The Critical Rôle of the Seaport[16]

A very high proportion of the external trade of the less developed countries passes through their seaports (in Africa only six per cent is overland trade)[17] so that a seaport is particularly well-placed to act either as a growth pole or as a restrictive influence upon economic development. The provision of port facilities can thus be regarded, throughout the underdeveloped world, as an essential pre-condition for modern economic growth; in a less developed country ports assume a critical role in the development process, and the stage of economic development attained is to a considerable degree a measure of the capacity and degree of sophistication of the port facilities available. The less developed countries are today attempting to establish or renew their port systems in the context of rapid changes in the technology of maritime transport, exemplified by the increasing use of containers and the increasing size of bulk carriers; thus they have the opportunity to incorporate these changes at an early stage in the process of port growth, and to ignore this opportunity would merely serve to widen the gap between the richer and the poorer countries.

### East African seaports

These problems may be illustrated by the East African seaport group, which comprises five terminals handling ocean-going vessels together with a number of minor coastal ports.[18] Mombasa is predominant; in 1968 it handled 68 per cent of the total traffic of the mainland seaports.[19] Dar es Salaam is the chief port for Tanzania, and the ports of Tanga, Zanzibar and Mtwara are relatively minor. Together, the five ports handled 14.2 million tons of shipping and 8.1 million tons of cargo in 1968.[20] The port group forms a dynamic hierarchy, which has experienced successive eras of concentration and diffusion of activity along the coast, and now shows a very marked emphasis upon the port of Mombasa as a centre of *sustained port dominance*.[21] Although the modern ports vary widely in terms of equipment and the volume of cargo handled, there is a fundamental similarity in their pattern of development which may be expressed by means of the *Anyport* model.[22] From its original function as a shelter for Arab sailing dhows trading around the Indian Ocean, *Anyport* in East Africa has successively developed primitive jetties which were replaced by lighterage quays, superseded in turn by deep-water quays to which are now added the specialised facilities for bulk oil and grain cargoes.

## Problems of congestion and cargo-handling techniques

Two main problems affect the further development of the East African seaport group, and both are closely related to the technological, political and economic factors which have influenced the emergence of the port group in its physical and historical setting. The first, which has been discussed elsewhere, is that of equating available facilities with actual and estimated traffic demands, together with a range of related questions involving congestion in the ports, the seasonal nature of traffic flows, the application of capital resources and the effects of delays upon economic development.[23] The basic question is that of acquiring and applying capital resources at the right time and in the most profitable manner. At both Mombasa and Dar es Salaam extensions to the available deep-water quayage are in progress, stimulated at Dar es Salaam by increasing Zambian traffic.[24] The second is the problem of the adaptation of East African ports to modern techniques of cargo handling, including the increasing unitisation of cargo and the use of containers, the elaboration of specialised cargo-handling facilities, and the physical amelioration of the harbours in order to allow the entry of large bulk-carriers.

The less developed countries have been faced in recent years with the need to consider to what extent it is in their interests to participate in the 'container revolution' in transport technology. World trends towards the increasing unitisation of cargo movements, stimulated by the need to increase efficiency and reduce costs, have not left ports in the less developed countries unaffected since all ports serve the same world fleet of shipping and must provide at least a minimum range of similar facilities in order to attract traffic. Today the pattern of inland transport in East Africa is characterised by minimal unitisation, and although pallets have been extensively used in the ports for almost 20 years there is little sign as yet of the more widespread use of pallets or containers. Part of the reason for this situation is the relatively small volume and the very varied nature of East African trade, dominated by bulk agricultural exports and imports of consumer goods; anxieties have also been expressed about the reduced labour requirements which unitised systems would involve in the context of East Africa's chronic unemployment problems. A large proportion of East African exports are already efficiently handled in bulk and relatively few benefits would accrue from further unitisation; but containerised import cargoes receive a 20 per cent rebate on port charges, and National

Trading Corporations may encourage the unitisation of imports by establishing wholesale distribution centres inland.[25]

Existing deep-water berths in East Africa are suitable for the handling of some forms of unitised cargo although problems are likely to arise from the shortage of transit space near the quays. It may be argued that the use of containers might effectively reduce congestion at Mombasa and Dar es Salaam without necessarily involving any further immediate increases in berth accommodation, and in this respect whilst new methods complicate the forward planning of port development they nevertheless improve considerably the long-term prospects of the deep-water terminals. Prospects for the three smaller East African terminals are less assured, however, since, although Mtwara may secure a share in Zambian traffic[26] and benefit from the growing emphasis on southern Tanzanian development, the possibilities for expansion at the lighterage ports of Tanga and Zanzibar are limited and their traffic seems likely to suffer a continued relative decline as the very uneven distribution of East African maritime trade between the five seaports becomes increasingly marked.[27]

With these considerations in mind, it would seem to be in East Africa's interests to develop an intermediate technology rather than to attempt to establish a complete container programme which the area cannot afford and which is in any case inappropriate in the present stage of development. The basis of successful container operations in advanced economies is the relatively high-value two-way flow of manufactured goods in quantity. This is not yet relevant to the East African traffic situation, but palletisation can improve efficiency considerably without the radical changes and heavy capital expenditure which containerisation would involve. The application of methods of unitisation must be based on local circumstances, and in East Africa these indicate that a modest capital outlay on cargo palletisation and pre-slinging equipment will be worthwhile but that the construction of specialised container berths (at an estimated cost of £2 million to £3.5 million each) is not yet an economic proposition. Nevertheless, the port authorities must clearly watch their investment programme with great care so that facilities developed for use by conventional ships can be converted for use by specialised container vessels at a later date with minimum disruption and expense.[28]

### CONCLUSION

Hance has emphasised 'the great power of improved transport to quicken the economic pulse of a region',[29] and it is clear that all transport media are vital factors in the economic growth of the less developed countries. In most such countries transport systems have developed without any overall plan, and frequently the construction of a road or a railway has been a political issue rather than an economic matter. Today the shortcomings of transport systems so haphazardly developed are everywhere apparent, but the developmental role of transport is more complex and more sensitive than has commonly been stated. Transport media are permissive rather than stimulative in themselves, but potentially they may effect widespread economic transformation in association with other development schemes. In the case of East Africa, as in many other less developed areas, 'the goal should be integrated development'.[30] If the railways and ports are to continue to facilitate and not to discourage economic expansion, a continuing need exists for heavy expenditure on the improvement and adaptation of existing facilities, and for the integration of transport planning within the East African Economic and Social Community.[31]

## NOTES

[1] F. VOIGT, *The importance of the transport system for economic development processes* (United Nations Economic Commission for Africa, Addis Ababa (E/CN. 14/CAP/3G), 1967).

[2] *Transport development* (United Nations Economic and Social Council, New York (E/4304), 1967). See also: *Transport problems in relation to economic development in East Africa* (United Nations Economic Commission for Africa, Addis Ababa, 1962).

[3] B. J. L. BERRY, An inductive approach to the regionalization of economic development, *Research Paper 62* (Department of Geography, University of Chicago, 1960).

[4] *Transport investment and economic development* (ed. G. Fromm) (Brookings Institution, Washington D.C., 1965); and *The impact of highway investment on development* (ed. G. W. Wilson) (Brookings Institution, Washington D.C., 1966).

[5] A. M. O'CONNOR, *Railways and development in Uganda* (Oxford University Press, Nairobi, 1965).

[6] Administrative unification was provided by the East African Railways and Harbours Administration in 1948; all sections of the system were physically linked by 1963.

[7] B. S. HOYLE, Recent changes in the pattern of East African railways, *Tijd. Econ. Soc. Geog.* 54 (1963) 237–242.

[8] E. J. TAAFE, R. L. MORRILL, and P. R. GOULD, Transport expansion in under-developed countries: a comparative analysis, *Geog. Rev.* 53 (1963) 503–529.

[9] A Malaysian case study is provided by: M. I. WARD, Progress in transport geography, *Trends in geography* (eds. R. U. Cooke and J. H. Johnson) (Pergamon, London, 1969).

[10] A more detailed discussion of pre-twentieth-century transport is contained in: B. S. HOYLE, Early port development in East Africa: an illustration of the concept of changing port hierarchies, *Tijd. Econ. Soc. Geog.* 58 (1967) 94–102.

[11] This point is elaborated in: A. M. O'CONNOR, New railway construction and the pattern of economic development in East Africa, *Trans. Inst. Brit. Geog.* 36 (1965) 21–30.

[12] A. M. O'CONNOR, *Railways and development in Uganda*.

[13] The construction of an oil pipeline from Mombasa *via* Nairobi to Kampala is under consideration in the context of East African inter-state discussions on transport problems.

[14] I. L. GRIFFITHS, Zambia's links with East Africa, *E. Afr. Geog. Rev.* 6 (1968) 87–89. A Tanzania–Zambia railway authority was constituted in October 1968.

[15] On agriculture in this area see: R. JATZOLD, *The Kilombero valley* (Weltforum Verlag, for Ifo Institute for Economic Research, Munich, 1967).

[16] The general discussion in the first part of this section is based upon a more extended treatment in: *Seaports and development in tropical Africa* (eds. B. S. Hoyle and D. Hilling) (Macmillan, London, 1970).

[17] *A survey of economic conditions in Africa* (United Nations Economic Commission for Africa, Addis Ababa (E/CN.14/397), 1967).

[18] B. S. HOYLE, *The seaports of East Africa* (East African Publishing House, Nairobi, 1967).

[19] EAST AFRICAN RAILWAYS AND HARBOUR ADMINISTRATION, *Annual report for the year ending 31st December 1968* (Nairobi, 1969) 66.

[20] *Idem.* These figures represent a record level of traffic flow through the port group as a whole, in spite of the problems arising from the continued closure of the Suez Canal.

[21] A useful discussion of Nigerian seaports in this context is: B. OGUNDANA, Patterns and problems of seaport evolution in Nigeria, in Hoyle and Hilling (eds.), *op. cit.* 167–182.

22 'Anyport' is a hypothetical port which represents the common experience of the port group as a whole. B. S. HOYLE, East African seaports: an application of the concept of 'Anyport', *Trans. Inst. Brit. Geog.* 44 (1968) 163–183.

23 B. S. HOYLE, *The seaports of East Africa, op. cit.*

24 Four additional deep-water berths (nos. 16–19) are under construction at Mombasa, and at Dar es Salaam three new deep-water berths (nos. 4–6) are due to be brought into service in 1970.

25 The first containerised cargoes despatched from U.K. to an inland East African destination arrived in July 1968 and were handled by East African Containers Ltd. (a subsidiary of the Express Transport Company).

26 Zambian copper exports reached Mtwara by road (*via* Tunduma) from September 1967, but ceased in late 1968 due to poor road conditions.

27 In 1968 Mombasa and Dar es Salaam together handled 94.8 per cent of the total cargo traffic of the four mainland seaports (East African Railways and Harbours, *loc. cit.*).

28 Three of the deep-water berths currently under construction at Mombasa (see note 24) are designed to facilitate adaptation as container berths.

29 W. A. HANCE, *African economic development* (Praeger, New York, 1967) 117.

30 *Ibid.,* 118.

31 In 1969 the governments of Kenya, Tanzania and Uganda commissioned an East African Transport Study to provide 'recommendations . . . . . to co-ordinate the use and development of the various modes of surface transport . . . . .' (cited in East African Railways and Harbours Administration, *op. cit.,* 4), and also secured an £11.4 million loan from the World Bank for improvements in bulk cargo handling facilities at Mombasa and Dar es Salaam.

# THE CHANGING FACE OF CANTERBURY, NEW ZEALAND[1]

## W. B. JOHNSTON

Canterbury was to be a Wakefield settlement, churchy, Anglican, selective. Here was to be established a 'vertical cross-section' of English society, excluding the lowest stratum, of course. However, the ideal colony of Wakefield's 'gorgeous fancy'—as *The Times* put it—was doomed even before the first four ships embedded their anchors in the fine silt of Lyttelton Harbour. For one thing, New Zealand had in effect been for over 30 years the colony of a convict settlement, namely Sydney. Early European enterprise in Canterbury, as in New Zealand generally, is substantially the tale of an Australian frontier, that is to say born of poverty and hatred but giving birth to wealth and hope. And out of the serious crisis in the Australian pastoral industry in the late 1830s came squatters, or would-be squatters, to the South Island, as well as to the North. Almost every ship crossing the Tasman Sea brought land-hungry passengers from New South Wales—the shagroons as they were called.

And so, in the end, the Pilgrim Fathers turned out to be not strictly middle class only but mixed with foreign blood, rather less than royal blue, and little different from other colonists of the time. Yet to this day there are attempts to resurrect and exemplify the Utopian ideals of the original Canterbury Association, notably in an aristocratic crust to Canterbury society. You may see it at the Christchurch Club if you are privileged to be invited, you can savour it still in some high country homes, and of course it thrives in the organs of Empire, notably the Royal Overseas League and Royal Commonwealth Society.

### POLYNESIAN MEN

Man came late to New Zealand in comparison with the rest of the world. As Duff[2] has shown, the first reasonably developed moa-hunter occupance was about 950 A.D. and as far as we know these eastern Polynesian people did not practise agriculture. However, the archaeological evidence strongly supports their rôle as hunters of the moa and users of fire in their economy. Whether or not the moa-hunter killed the last moa, it is likely, as Murphy has said, that this is 'one of the few known cases in which aboriginal man seems to have harried an animal to extinction.'[3] Whether climatic change or cultural interference was the prime determinant of the extensive forest destruction during the Polynesian era, there is little doubt as to the occurrence of several large and numerous small fires, beginning about 1,000 years ago.[4]

It is not yet clear what relationship existed between the moa-hunters and the classic Maori culture of the late eighteenth century, but in any case the Maori culture of the eighteenth century was significantly different from that of their Polynesian prototypes. While it is likely that most of the moa-hunters lived in the South Island, this island clearly supported few Maoris on the eve of the arrival of the European and it may well be true that the number was even fewer than that supported by the moa-hunting economy. The Maori population of New Zealand in 1750 was about a quarter of a million, with perhaps 10,000 in the South Island, of which three or four thousand may have lived in Canterbury.

## EUROPEAN INNOVATIONS

Although Abel Tasman sighted the west coast of the South Island in 1642—and named it New Zealand—the land of Canterbury was first sighted by Europeans only in 1770 during Cook's circumnavigation of the South Island. For the next 60 years the only apparent contact was from rare visits of flax traders, although elsewhere in the South Island and more so in the North Island, sealers, whalers and traders had been rapidly exploiting the resources of sea and littoral. But by the 1830s Banks Peninsula had become an important whaling base, the first shore station being erected in 1837 at Peraki, where storehouses, dwellings and a try-works were established with the assistance of Maori labour. By this time Banks Peninsula had a European population of nearly 100, and shore whaling had made Banks Peninsula the site of early European settlement and experiment.

Near at hand a farming venture on the Canterbury Plains, alongside Riccarton bush, was short-lived, but long enough to put at least 30 acres under the plough before a Maori fire, set alight on the banks of Lake Ellesmere, finally destroyed the farm as it swept 20 miles across the plain. On grassy spurs near the entrance to Akaroa harbour the first cattle station in Canterbury, indeed in the South Island, was established in 1839 with a herd of 30 or 40 shorthorn cattle. From the French whaling element developed an attempt to establish a permanent French colony at Akaroa. The French colony was restricted by events to Akaroa harbour, and was very much a local subsistence agricultural venture but, as the Canterbury poet, Basil Dowling, pens it:

> History camped here awhile, and left behind
> A Whiff of Europe in its stamped-out embers.
>
> *(Akaroa)*

However, the impact of early European contacts was not limited to the land and coastal waters. New tools, new weapons and new diseases wrought havoc among the local Maori population and the devastation was completed by invasions of North Island tribes, always militant but now musket-carrying; some 800 local Maoris were massacred by their North Island cousins at Kaiapohia in 1832. When the first detailed census of the Maori in Canterbury was made in 1848–49, there were only four or five hundred living, and 300 of these were on and about Banks Peninsula.

## EUROPEAN OCCUPANCE

In many ways Canterbury was ready for settlement after 1840. As Thomas was to report in 1849, there was a large area of open grassland, an accessible sheltered harbour, absence of Maori population, accessible if small patches of timber and the accumulated experience of the Deans brothers, who had been successfully farming the plains near Riccarton bush for six years.[5] The arrival of the first four ships in 1850 saw the founding of the Canterbury settlement, and the Pilgrim Fathers were able to conquer the country without force or danger. Allen Curnow, an ex-Canterbury poet, puts it neatly in his satire entitled *Not in narrow seas* when he says:

> Not leap of capture theirs
> But as who safely dares
> Seizing without sword
> Front garden and backyard.

With the Canterbury pioneers, whom Wakefield described as 'not merely a nice, but a choice society of English people', their leader, John Robert Godley (whose statue stands haughtily in Cathedral Square in Christchurch) hoped to found a colony he saw as English, Anglo-Catholic, conservative and agricultural. But by the time yeoman farmers began to seek their farms on the plains, the Nelson hill country to the north was filling with squatters who were indoctrinated by sheep grazing and high-living Australian instincts and who, with a large sheep population, began to covet the tussock grasslands of Canterbury. Even the Deans brothers, hitherto agriculturalists, had started to run sheep on the inner plains. The era of the pastoralist had arrived and the race for land was on.

The land of Canterbury was quickly taken up in the middle of the nineteenth century, mainly in the form of extensive pastoral leases of several thousands of acres, reaching 100,000 acres on the Glenmark run in North Canterbury and the Levels run in South Canterbury. By 1860 runholders had penetrated the High Country along valleys of the main rivers, moving forward from foothills to inland valleys and basins and to the very margins of snow and ice of the alpine high country. However, within the 'Canterbury Block', as the plains land available to the Canterbury Association became known, some districts were selected and surveyed at the beginning of European occupation as farming settlements to be based on cropping. Here yeoman farming was attempted on the English model, based on small areas of cleared forest or drained swamp. Through the later decades of the nineteenth century, the extension of small farms, ranging from 20 to several hundred acres in size, continued to make inroads on leasehold runs of the plains and downlands.[6]

However, runholders generally had pre-emptive rights to purchase leased land, depending on the type and value of improvements; for example, so many acres for the homestead, for each shepherd's hut, for each chain of fencing. Consequently they purchased strategic areas such as watering places, bush land, and valley bottoms. Another device to maintain command of large areas was 'grid-ironing', whereby land was purchased so as to leave alternate isolated blocks of just under 20 acres, as any sections under 20 acres had to be sold by auction and hence the runholder became aware of anyone seeking to buy part of his run. These practices undoubtedly led to a spotty distribution of freehold and leasehold land, often in small blocks, and during succeeding decades the sequence of purchases of these blocks accentuated fragmentation of farm land.

In brief and in such a manner, the land of Canterbury has been subdivided for farming. Only in the high country has the huge pastoral run persisted and here the size of individual runs has tended to increase by amalgamation. With a notable absence of significant mineral resources Canterbury has depended on the use of the soil but the establishment of modern farming has taxed the ingenuity of man, even on the Canterbury plains, which must have seemed to the early settlers to be the easiest land to occupy.

## Working the High Country

The tussock grassland community that covered much of the Canterbury plains and high country was not easy to occupy or use. Dense clumps of thorny matagouri scrub, appropriately known as Wild Irishman, and, nearer the hills, thick and large Spaniards made it difficult if not at times impossible to get sheep onto unburnt country or to find grazing when they got there. Thus the first thing that the pastoralist did was to fire the country and this practice persisted unchecked through nearly a century of occupation of the high country. It is no wonder that another Canterbury poet, Jessie Mackay, entitled a poem *Spring fires* and records:

> The running rings of fire on the Canterbury hills,
>   Running, ringing, dying at the border of the snow.
> Mad, young, seeking as a young thing wills,
>   The ever, ever-living, ever-buried Long Ago.

And she talks of:

> The quiet bloom of haze on the Canterbury Hills!
> The scent of burning tussocks on the Canterbury Hills!

To deliberate and accidental burning must be attributed much of the progressive deterioration of the tussock cover that had provided an intravegetational climate for more succulent herbage. But a century of sheep trampling has accentuated the disturbance of the ecological balance; persistent grazing and overgrazing of a depleted vegetation cover by both sheep and, until recent years, by rabbits has assisted fire in exposing soil to extreme climatic conditions. Accelerated soil erosion has brought unsought fame to the Canterbury high country. Nor must we forget the rôle of man in introducing game animals, such as deer, chamois and thar which rapidly multiplied to become major pests in the mountain core where man is now busy slaughtering as many of the animals as can be stalked in the back country or killed for profit by rifle teams operating from helicopters even in the most isolated valleys.

The economic return on man's interference in the high country cannot be assessed solely or even primarily in terms of the value of wool clips because the region has an ever-increasing rôle in relation to hydro-electricity, flood control, water supply and recreation, in which tourism ranks very high. To meet these new demands restrictions have had to be placed on man's misuse and use of the land. Yet only in co-operation with high-country pastoralists themselves can conservation measures be successful. This does not require, as some would claim, either the complete withdrawal of pastoral activities or a decrease in production from the area; rather it requires the wise application of accumulated knowledge in conjunction with the result of current scientific investigations.

### CLEARING LOWLAND FORESTS

The Nothofagus or beech forest that was associated with the tussock community of the high country was not milled for timber nor was it deliberately cleared for farm land; it retreated under the impact of fire and grazing animals.[7] In contrast the mixed podocarp forest on Banks Peninsula and of the plains and foothills was subjected to a deliberate policy of milling and clearing. The most extensive of these forests was on Banks Peninsula but it was ravaged early in European occupance. Working from numerous bayheads of the Peninsula, sawmillers cut out valuable timber trees and by 1880 substantial inroads had been made on the more accessible areas. By 1900 the ruthless onslaught was complete, the miller being increasingly aided by a series of accidental and, in some cases, deliberate fires. In the warm ashes and among the cut-over areas and charred stumps, English grasses were surface sown, responding rapidly to the enhanced fertility of bush burns. In this new pasture community, cocksfoot became the outstanding grass, the seed being in high demand after 1880 in the establishment of pastures on the bush-cleared areas of the developing North Island.

Today the Peninsula has no large remnant of forest; the former timber cover has been reduced to a spotty distribution of tiny clumps of trees and second growth. With the processes of forest clearing, establishment of new pastures and introduction of sheep and cattle, Banks Peninsula is a bit of Canterbury not unlike former bushlands of the North Island.[8]

The concentration of milling and pit sawing on the forests of the Peninsula and foothills was the result of their tremendous significance for settlers of an area where millable timber in accessible places was in very short supply for building homes, barns, stockyards and railways. Nevertheless, the record of destructive fires is abundant witness to man's indiscriminate actions in destroying a scarce resource, and inspired the lament *By the River Ashley* of Mary Ursula Bethell, another Canterbury poet:

> Too late we hear, too late the undertones
> Of lamentations in all the natural songs—
> What have you done with my mountains?
> What have you done with my forests?
> What have you done to your rivers?
> Too late.

Many of the smaller settlements of Canterbury originated as saw-milling centres—for instance, Oxford, Rangiora, Waimate, Woodbury—and in several cases they reached their greatest populations at the peak of the saw-milling era. But now they generally have only village- or smalltown-level functions in the central place hierarchy.[9] With the destruction of accessible supplies of indigenous forest, Canterbury became seriously deficient in timber. From the early days of settlement the planting of exotic trees for shade and shelter was actively pursued but it was not until the turn of the century that the State embarked on an active programme of exotic forestry. Competition among alternative land uses has restricted the two large exotic plantations of Balmoral and Eyrewell to unsuitable, shallow, gravelly areas where wind-throw is serious and where heavy frosts, droughts, low humidities, and high winds, with a consequent risk of fire damage, add to the hazards of forestry in Canterbury. Insufficiency, instability and impermanence are characteristics of the exotic forests of Canterbury.

### Grass to Grass

In 1858 less than 7,500 acres in Canterbury were under the plough, but within 25 years half a million acres were being cropped for wheat, oats and barley. The '70s and '80s were decades of bonanza wheat cropping under the impetus of food demands of the goldfields population and a developing Australian market. After 1870, plains and downlands were differentiated from the tussock grasslands of the high country by a new mode of occupance. Wheat became the key crop of the small farmer but even more striking were the great wheat fields of the large estates. The tussock sod was turned under by the plough and the soil was put into wheat year after year, resulting in a rapid mining of soil, declining yields and damage to soil structure. The amount of precious top soil that was blown out to sea off the newly-exposed wheat fields during the two decades cannot be estimated, but the prevailing, boisterous north–west winds wrought great havoc on soil unturned and broken down by man, horse, plough, wheat and sheep. Since then the planting of shelter belts and hedgerows, both composed of introduced plant species, has done much to reduce subsequent soil loss by lowering the effectiveness of wind erosion; and even on bare stoney expanses of braided riverbeds adventitious invasions of gorse and broom have not only covered the surface but also captured flood silt.

The fundamental change, however, has been man's realisation of the robber economy that he had established and the new techniques and skills that he developed and used to establish a new, balanced and conservative agriculture. The introduction of refrigeration opened large overseas markets to frozen meat, stimulating the development of a mixed agricultural economy in which livestock fattening, rotational pastures and cash and fodder crops are basic elements. Crop rotation, topdressing with lime and artificial fertilizers, improvement of grasses, introduction of clovers and lucerne have produced a new appearance to plains and downlands. The dominant land use element is once again that of grassland but now one in which exotic species are everywhere dominant in place of indigenous tussock grassland.

### WATER MORE OR LESS

An integral part of the agricultural revolution was subdivision of large estates into the current pattern of farm holdings and in this process man faced a new problem in the need to bring water to dry plains which often lie several hundred feet above the deeply entrenched beds of the large rivers. The lack of surface water was first made manifest in the division of the plains into pastoral runs when each run was given a river frontage and the area adjacent to water became ewe and hogget country while Merino wethers were put out for up to 12 months on waterless land of the high interfluves. To bring water to the surface of the high plains, the technique of the water race, initially developed on goldfields, was widely introduced. Tapping the rivers as they emerge from the hills, water was brought by gravity along narrow, shallow channels, initially to quench the thirst of horses during the great plough-up of the wheat era, and later of sheep and cattle that now feed on exotic pastures and fodder crops that replaced the bonanza wheat fields. Many rural homes and some small settlements still draw domestic water from the races, as do fire-fighting services.

Towards the close of last century the bringing of water to the plains began to take on a new significance as some Canterbury farmers commenced pasture irrigation. The diversion of water from the Rangitata into Rakaia river has been a dual-purpose scheme for irrigation and hydro-electric power generation. Other schemes have been single-purpose irrigation projects largely as an insurance against drought and to maintain pasture growth on light land. Irrigation has, however, had its problems. A few years ago some South Canterbury farmers complained that seepage from the Levels irrigation scheme had reduced thousands of acres of fertile land to a swampy and unproductive state. The opportunity for satire was too good to miss for 'Whim Wham', whose topical verse attracts all readers of Saturday's Christchurch paper, *The Press*. Under the title *Hydroponics* he wrote:

> Here to fetch water, monstrous Pipes are laid
> By Engineers, the Plumbers of the Plains;
> There, by excessive Watering dismayed,
> Go Farmers angrily demanding Drains.

## The changing face of Canterbury, New Zealand

> Who Knows? Perhaps our hapless Heirs may find
> (A hundred years or so from now, may be)
> The Canterbury Plains, all undermined,
> Subsiding soggily into the Sea!

Whereas in some areas of Canterbury there is too little water, in others there is too much, and this is particularly true of the heavy lands of the coastal plains where extensive swamps have been drained and converted into some of the most valuable and productive farm land of Canterbury. Removal of surplus water and local lowering of water tables were early and important activities of European settlement in the neighbourhood of Christchurch. The transformation of the swamps of Coldstream-Longbeach of mid-Canterbury into high-production farms is an epic story that is paralleled in other areas.

### MAN—THE ECOLOGIC DOMINANT

It is in the nature of man to alter things and in so doing to transform himself. The process is never-ending. One outstanding example in Canterbury is the way in which soil fertility under a mixed farming economy has been greatly improved. Reaction against the bonanza wheat farmer of the '80s led to a black-listing of wheat but now it is being shown that the enhanced fertility of the soil is so high that mixed farming can benefit by more regular and widespread use of wheat in the crop rotation. Increasing intensification of farming and the turning of attention to features hitherto regarded as minor, have produced remarkable advances in the provision of critical trace elements in the soil. The application of insecticides to control pests in crops and pasture has increased production but their use must be tempered with wisdom if the meat product is not to be tainted and rejected by discerning overseas markets.

Over much of Canterbury man has become the ecologic dominant. The changing face of Canterbury is, however, a function of the quantities as well as the qualities of the human groups that have occupied the area. The third of a million people who now live in Canterbury represent the greatest number ever supported in the region. With a density of nearly 25 per square mile, this is well above the average density for the South Island as a whole. But this population is markedly uneven in its distribution over the land. In the high country few people live although many at one time or another are visitors; and even large parts of the plains and downlands are 'empty' of people. More and more people are living and working in a small number of places—in Christchurch, Timaru, Ashburton, Rangiora, and Kaiapoi. The rural areas have shown no significant increase, and on Banks Peninsula there has been general stagnation and decline. Christchurch has proved the main magnet, with over 80 per cent of the regional increase in population in the last half-century. With a quarter of a million people in Christchurch, two-thirds of Canterbury's total population is in one metropolitan centre and there is no reason, local or national, to predict any trend other than a reinforcement of this metropolitan dominance.

In mid-twentieth-century Canterbury, many areas have acquired a new value, that is to say an amenity value, which is less a measure of physical quality of land than an index of relative accessibility to dollar-happy urban clusters. The growing shanty settlements along the sweeping sand-dune belt north of Christchurch pose new questions of sand stabilisation, sewage disposal, water supply and aesthetic order. How long will it be before all this country is filled up with weekend batches of Christchurchites? And what is this human pressure doing in the way of upsetting environmental systems? No-one knows and, still more important, no-one yet really seems to care.

This, then, is something of the changing face of Canterbury. To Charles Brasch, Canterbury's most notable poet, it was, in the 1930s, *The Silent Land*, where the intimacy of the land we inhabit had still to be learnt, or as he put it:

> The plains are nameless and the cities cry for meaning,
> The improved heart still seeks a vein of speech.
> Besides the sprawling rivers, in the stunted township,
> By the pine windbreak where the hot wind bleeds.

Forty years on, the plains of Canterbury are no longer nameless and the cities no longer cry for meaning.

## NOTES

[1] The physical geography of Canterbury is described in: JANE M. SOONS, Canterbury landscapes: a study in contrasts, *N.Z. Geogr.* 24 (1968) 115–132.

[2] R. DUFF, *The moahunter period of Maori culture* (Wellington, 1956).

[3] R. C. MURPHY, Man and nature in New Zealand, *N.Z. Geogr.* 8 (1952) 4.

[4] B. P. J. MOLLOY, C. J. BURROWS, J. E. COX, J. A. JOHNSTON, and P. WARDLE, Distribution of subfossil forest remains, Eastern South Island, New Zealand, *N.Z. Journ. Botany* 1 (1963) 68–77.

[5] C. R. STRAUBEL, A site for Canterbury, *A history of Canterbury* (eds. J. Hight and C. R. Straubel) 1 (1957) 113–132.

[6] R. G. CANT, The agricultural frontier in miniature: a microstudy on the Canterbury Plains, 1850–75, *N.Z. Geogr.* 24 (1968) 155–167.

[7] C. J. BURROWS, Recent changes in vegetation of the Cass area of Canterbury, *N.Z. Geogr.* 16 (1960) 57–70.

[8] W. B. JOHNSTON, Pioneering the bushland of lowland Taranaki, *N.Z. Geogr.* 17 (1961) 1–18.

[9] L. J. KING, The functional role of small towns in Canterbury, *Proc. Third N.Z. Geography Conf.* (1961) 139–149.

# AN EVALUATION OF CENSUS DATA FOR SHOWING CHANGES IN INDUSTRIAL LOCATION: FOOTWEAR MANUFACTURE IN BRITAIN

## P. R. MOUNFIELD

In 1968, 200.8 million pairs of footwear, of all types, were manufactured in the United Kingdom[1] and in 1965 the two federations of British footwear manufacturers[2] could claim a total membership of 482 firms, employing over 85,000 workers.[3] From a domestic craft, practised with simple tools by individual shoemakers in nearly every town and village, footwear production has evolved into a modern factory industry of considerable magnitude and some sophistication. The transition from attic and workshop to factory took place later in footwear than in some other long-established British industries[4] but, when it did occur, the change was accompanied by marked shifts in the location of the industry, particularly important being the emergence of distinct concentrations of manufacturing plants in certain parts of the country in place of the formerly widely-scattered handicraft producer.

This short paper has a threefold objective. First, it describes the geographical distribution of the footwear industry at the present day. Secondly, by using the occupation data contained in the published tables of the census,[5] an attempt is made to discern the formative phases through which the distribution pattern may have passed since 1841, the first year for which the census reports provide tables suitable for the purpose. No attempt is made to explain either the modern distribution pattern or the phases through which it has passed, but the reliance on the census data is deliberate and is designed to fulfil a third, major, objective, i.e. to discuss the extent to which these data constitute an adequate time series for portraying long-term changes in the location of manufacturing industry.

### THE LOCATION OF THE MODERN FOOTWEAR INDUSTRY

The Industry Tables of the 1961 Census, published in 1966, contain the most recent set of census figures treating industrial occupations and thus might be regarded as an obvious source for cartographic representation of employment in the modern footwear industry. However, the smallest areas for which industrial employment data are provided in these tables are Standard Regions and official conurbations. Separate analyses for Administrative Counties, County Boroughs and other towns with more than 50,000 inhabitants are given in the Occupation and Industry County Tables, but information is not provided for smaller towns. Moreover, 1961 was the first time that the census relied on a sample rather than on complete coverage for many of the questions dealing with economic matters. A 10 per cent sample was used and the tables include data that are subject to sampling error and error due to bias. The present distribution of the industry is thus more suitably portrayed by alternative data provided by the two federations of footwear manufacturers. Not all footwear firms belong to these organizations but, as far as can be judged, those that do

205

not are shared fairly equally between the producing districts. Nevertheless, the data from the manufacturers' federations, on output, employment, and numbers of firms, are likely to understate the real values.

The pattern is dominated by five major concentrations of production, which together account for 93 per cent of the volume of output from federated firms. The five are as follows:

*(a)* A very large concentration of manufacturing capacity in the *East Midlands,* especially in *Northamptonshire* and *Leicestershire.* In 1965, the 43,000 employees of the 293 member firms in these two counties provided 66 million pairs of footwear, or 44 per cent of the total of 153 million pairs produced in the United Kingdom by federated firms.[6]

*(b)* *Lancashire,* with 38 firms in 1965, accounted for 19 per cent (30.7 million pairs) of the total. Some 10,000 people were engaged in the industry in Lancashire, mainly in Rossendale, in the three towns of Haslingden, Rawtenstall and Bacup.[7]

*(c)* *Bristol, Kingswood* and *Street* There were only eight federated firms in this cluster in 1965 but they included some of the largest and fastest-growing concerns in the country and employed a labour force of over 11,000. This was the only one of the five major concentrations to show an increase in the labour force between 1955 and 1965 (+ 4,240) accompanied over the same period by a substantial increase in the volume of output, from 7.2 to 20.9 million pairs, the latter figure amounting to 13.6 per cent of the total volume of output from federated firms in the year.

*(d)* *London,* including Chesham and East Tilbury, with 36 firms, a labour force of 4,800 and an output of 15.7 million pairs, or 10 per cent of the total.

*(e)* *Norwich*, with 22 firms, a labour force of 7,600 and an output of 8.5 million pairs (5.6 per cent of the total).

In addition to the five major concentrations, there were three others of less importance individually but which together accounted for nearly five per cent of the total output. These were:

*(f)* *Leeds,* with eight firms, an output of three million pairs and a labour force of 1,050.

*(g)* *Stafford* and *Stone,* with four firms, an output of 2.5 million pairs and a combined labour force of 2,360. Stafford is the headquarters and main seat of manufacturing operations for the large 'Lotus' group, which now has a virtual monopoly of the industry in the two towns.[8]

*(h)* *Kendal,* with a labour force of 1,200 and an output equivalent to 1.5 per cent of the United Kingdom total. Kendal, like Stafford, is the home of one of the biggest shoe-manufacturing concerns in the country, the firm of Somervell Bros. ('K' Shoes) Ltd.

If due allowance is made for firms outside the manufacturers' federations, the major and minor centres listed above accounted for 78 per cent of the total volume of all manufacturers' sales in the United Kingdom in 1965, and 83 per cent of the industry's labour force. The balance of output was made up by various types of footwear manufactured by a number of widely-scattered plants at places such as Cockermouth (Cumberland), Heckmondwike (Yorkshire), Eyam and Stoney Middleton (Derbyshire), Mansfield (Nottinghamshire), Chesham (Buckinghamshire),

Kilmarnock (Ayrshire, Scotland), and Bridgend (Glamorgan). In addition, rubber and canvas footwear was produced by some of the big rubber companies.

## THE EVOLUTION OF THE DISTRIBUTION PATTERN

*The data*

A series of maps has been constructed from the census data in an attempt to identify what may have been crucial phases in the creation of the modern map of footwear manufacture. A census was not taken in 1941 but, with this exception, the requisite data are available at 10-yearly intervals from 1841 onwards and maps have been constructed accordingly. To save space, only seven of the maps are reproduced here (Figures 1a to 1g), but the discussion that follows is based upon all of them.

Both the maps and the data on which they are based suffer from certain defects. In the first place, the distributions revealed by the maps clearly would have achieved a finer texture and greater reliability if a unit smaller in area and of more uniform population size than the county could have been used. The Registration Districts might have served this purpose but they disappear from the Census Reports after 1911. Indeed, although the compilers of successive Census reports have for the most part left a record of boundary changes between one enumeration and another, considerable care has to be taken when census statistics relating to different years are compared. Even the counties have not remained constant. At the present time, England and Wales are split into 58 Administrative Counties, 83 County Boroughs and the area of the Greater London Council. The Administrative Counties, with their territorially associated County Boroughs, came into existence in the late 1880s; they were preceded in the Census Reports by the Ancient Counties and also, from 1851 to 1921, by the Registration Counties (aggregations of Registration Districts, usually co-terminous with Poor Law Unions). The Administrative County, including any associated County Borough(s), is more or less identical with the Ancient County in many cases, but the correspondence between the Ancient County and the Registration County was only very approximate.

Secondly, although at every census the total population figures refer to people of all ages, there are frequently minimum age limits for the industrial occupation categories and these differ from one census to the next. For each census from 1841 to 1881, shoemakers of all ages are included; from 1891 to 1911 the statistics refer to shoemakers over 10 years of age; for 1921, 12 years and over; for 1931, 14 years and over; and, for 1951, 15 years of age and over. This could be an important element of variation in the data, but its effect is mitigated to some extent by the fact that most full-time shoemakers would be over these ages at the dates stated owing to Factory Act legislation and the progressive raising of the school-leaving age.[9]

In view of these variations, measurement of the employment in footwear against total industrial employment, instead of against the total population of a county, would have been an advantage. This is made difficult by the fact that the early census reports do not categorize the various types of manufacturing activity in a manner that facilitates comparison with more recent census data. For example, the 1851 and 1861 censuses specify a separate category of 'shoemakers' wives' not mentioned in previous or subsequent years. P. G. Hall has argued that inclusion of this category artificially inflates the figures for 1851 and 1861,[10] but outworkers frequently used the whole family to undertake work and this alone would seem to justify their inclusion. Similarly, in the early census reports, clog and patten makers are separately distinguished, whereas in later reports their numbers are included with the total shoemaking labour force, in such a way that it is impossible to treat them separately.

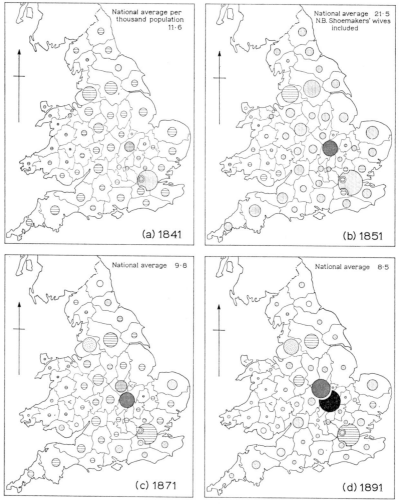

FIGURE 1

Employment in the footwear industry of England and Wales, 1841 to 1951, by counties

*Note:* Ancient Counties to 1891, thereafter Administrative Counties (with associated County Boroughs)

1841   Shoemakers' wives not specified; patten and clog makers excluded
1851   Shoemakers' wives included, patten and clog makers excluded
1871   Shoemakers' wives, patten and clog makers excluded
1891   Shoemakers aged 10 years and over, patten and clog makers included
1911   Shoemakers aged 10 years and over
1931   Shoemakers and slipper makers aged 14 years and over
1951   Shoemakers aged 15 years and over, minimum list heading 148 only (i.e. excluding repairers)

Data from Census of Population, England and Wales

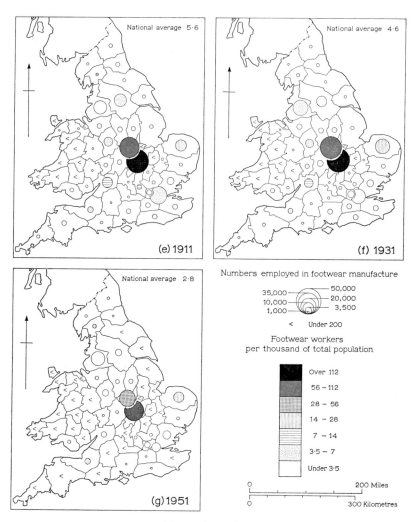

FIGURE 1—*continued*

For the industrial geographer, the Industry Tables of the 1951 census are perhaps the most useful ever to have been issued by the General Register Office, mainly because of the manner in which the statistics are organized and presented. Even so, the 1931 and 1951 maps are not strictly comparable. In 1951 the data for the Industry Tables were enumerated on a basis of place-of-work but, in 1931, according to place-of-residence. The discrepancy gives the impression that places with industrial estates, such as Bridgend, experienced an unduly high increase in workers between the two censuses. Also, in 1931 the data were classified on the basis of occupation type, whereas in 1951 all persons, including administrative, technical, clerical and ancillary staffs employed in an industrial establishment, were included in the employment figures for the industry to which they belonged, irrespective of their type of job. Finally, although they do not seriously affect the footwear employment figures, some changes were made in the content of the industrial groups used in the Industry Tables of the two censuses. Whilst it is possible to equate most of the 1931 and 1951 groups, there are some instances when this is not quite such a straightforward task as it might seem at first sight.

Additional difficulties arise in any attempt to establish a data time series for geographical areas smaller than the county. It is frequently impossible, for example, to obtain from the census reports a complete chronological range of data of broadly comparable nature for even the largest of the towns where the footwear industry is now concentrated. Figures are provided in the 1841, 1851 and 1861 reports for all the main towns involved in the industry, but not for smaller places such as Street, Rushden, Bacup and Kingswood. In 1871, figures relating to industrial occupations are provided for people of all ages at county level, but only persons of 20 years of age or over are given for towns such as Norwich, Northampton, Bristol and Stafford. In the 1881 and 1891 reports no occupation data are provided for towns with a population of less than 50,000, thus excluding places like Stafford and Kendal. The figures in the census from 1841 to 1871 refer to 'principal towns', while in 1881 and 1891 they are given for Urban Sanitary Districts. Moreover, the area included within the town limits under either definition does not always coincide with the administrative areas of more recent census years. At a very detailed local level, invaluable information on occupations and demographic structure can be culled from the manuscript schedules of the 1841, 1851 and 1861 censuses, housed at the Public Records Office, but the 'hundred years rule' means that comparable data for later census years cannot be made available to the researcher.

*Examination of the maps*

The shortcomings of the census data are such that even simple maps, such as those represented by Figure 1a to 1g, have to be interpreted with care. The maps obviously are not useful for examining detailed locational shifts, but it is possible to draw from them some information concerning broad changes. Also, something is known of the origins and growth of the regional concentrations of footwear manufacture in England and Wales from sources other than the census.[11] It is possible, for example, to date with fair accuracy the beginning of wholesale footwear production, as distinct from bespoke work, in each of the existing concentrations.

For want of anything better, population has to be regarded as a convenient proxy for the market, with the assumption that the volume of demand for footwear is directly a function of population numbers. In this respect, the 1841 and 1851 maps show some important features. At these dates there was still a fairly close coincidence between population distribution and the distribution of shoemaking. This impression is confirmed by Thorold Rogers when he states: '. . . . . until the second half of the nineteenth century almost all boots and shoes were made by individual cobblers who formed part of the social structure of every village.'[12] There were, however, some interesting exceptions to the generally close tie with population. The industry was evidently of more than local importance in London and Northamptonshire. There were 28,500 shoemakers in London in 1841 and the ratio of shoemakers per thousand of total population stood at 15.2, second only to Northamptonshire. Although the number of shoemakers in Northamptonshire was much lower

(7,021), the number per thousand of population was 35.2, considerably higher than the figure of 13.4 for England and Wales as a whole. There was no sign of any concentration of the industry in Leicestershire. Neither is there much indication in the maps of any above-average scale of production in any of the other counties where concentrations of the industry exist today. Thus, the fact that counties are used as the geographic area does seem to disguise local variations in the pattern, for it is known that wholesale footwear production had begun by 1760 in Stafford and by 1792 in Norwich.

There was obviously a considerable alteration in the geographical distribution of the industry between 1851 and 1911. By the latter date, Northamptonshire and Leicestershire had achieved a dominant position and within both counties the footwear industry by this time had come to employ a considerably larger proportion of the population than in any other county containing a concentration of production. Somerset was one such county, where, in 1833, James Clark had begun the wholesale manufacture of slippers in his brother's fellmongering concern at Street. Another was Westmorland, where, in 1842, Robert Miller Somervell had started his business in Kendal. Gloucestershire was a third, the Derham brothers having commenced manufacturing in Bristol in 1845. Thomas Crick had started to make riveted footwear in Leicester in the late 1840s, and by 1876 J. W. Rothwell and Samuel McLerie were making slippers out of ends of felt in two old textile mills at Waterfoot, in Rossendale. By the 1880s the factory manufacture of boots, shoes or slippers was firmly established at all of these places. The 1891, 1901 and 1911 maps reflect these developments fairly clearly. Figure 1e shows that the industry had become of some significance in Norfolk and Gloucestershire, although both counties had fewer people employed in footwear than either London, Lancashire or the West Riding of Yorkshire. The maps indicate the existence of the industry in Staffordshire, Westmorland and Somerset, and the rapid rise of the industry in Leicestershire is also apparent. The impression is conveyed that, by 1911, footwear employment in most other parts of the country had declined to a state of insignificance. From the late 1850s onwards a variety of machinery was being introduced to the industry and Table I shows that increasing regional specialization was accompanied by a movement of the labour force into factories, coupled with a decline in the numbers of those employed in workshops.

TABLE I

The movement from workshop to factory in the footwear industry

| | Numbers employed in factories | | | Numbers employed in workshops | | |
|---|---|---|---|---|---|---|
| *Year* | *Males* | *Females* | *Total* | *Males* | *Females* | *Total* |
| 1889 .. | 35,103 | 13,934 | 49,037 | n.d. | n.d. | n.d. |
| 1895 .. | 59,844 | 23,727 | 85,571 | 27,144 | 10,391 | 37,535 |
| 1905 .. | 71,022 | 31,467 | 102,489 | 15,528 | 6,175 | 21,703 |

*Source:* BOARD OF TRADE, *Inquiry into earnings and hours of labour* (1906)

On comparing Figures 1e and 1f it is evident that some further modification of the modern distribution pattern took place between 1911 and 1931, although the scale of change was much less than in the period from 1851 to 1911. Northamptonshire and Leicestershire retained their leading position. In employment terms, Lancashire moved into third place instead of London and the proportion of Lancashire's population employed in the industry also increased. Norfolk was in fourth place by 1931, with London fifth. Gloucestershire and Staffordshire remained approximately the same in 1931 as in 1911 but employment in the industry in the West Riding fell over the 20-year period.

Comparison of the 1931 and 1951 maps is to some extent misleading because of the different manner in which the Industry Tables of the two censuses were compiled. There is no question that the general decline in employment that is indicated did take place, but it was not on quite such a drastic scale as the two maps imply. The decline in the labour force was accompanied by steadily increasing productivity per employee and by a decrease in the number of factories in operation in each of the concentrations except Lancashire. There was a significant increase in the number of footwear-manufacturing employees in Essex, due mainly to the arrival of the Bata company at East Tilbury in the inter-war period.

CONCLUSION

By using simple cartographic techniques this paper has outlined some of the broad locational changes that have occurred in the location of the footwear industry over the past century. If the investigation were to proceed further, to attempt an explanation of these changes, what useful guidelines for further analysis would be provided by these maps? The answer to this question seems to fall into three parts:

*(a)* A broadly similar locational pattern of footwear production has existed in England and Wales since the time of the 1911 Census. Because the overall pattern has shown only a small degree of change since then, it becomes apparent that any investigation of causes must be concerned, first and foremost, with the locational forces in operation and contributing towards the formation of the pattern before 1911. A rigorous examination of the factors involved in the evolution of the pattern before 1911 would seem to constitute an integral part of the explanation of the industry's present-day distribution. For most of the country it might seem unnecessary to go back much further than the middle of the nineteenth century. However, there are two areas, Northamptonshire and London, where the maps indicate that this would not be sufficient and, moreover, the coarse statistical mesh which results from using counties has the effect of smoothing out the existence of early local developments in Norwich and Stafford.

*(b)* The second major point is hardly less important than the first. In any investigation having pretensions to accuracy, it would clearly be necessary to discover and evaluate the nature of the conditions that have enabled the pattern to retain its general outline since 1911.

*(c)* Although the pattern has remained similar in its broad outlines, the situation in 1951 was not completely identical to that existing in 1911 and there have been variations in the relative importance of the individual centres of production. For example, Lancashire has strengthened its position since 1911, whilst that of Leeds has decreased. Such changes as these call for explanation because they have contributed to the relative importance of the concentrations of the industry at the present time.

Perhaps a general conclusion can be drawn that, despite defects in the data on which they are based, the maps do provide useful guidance both to the nature of past locational trends in the footwear industry and to the manner in which these should be investigated further. However, this does not necessarily mean that similar treatment of other industries would produce equally profitable results. Furthermore, it could well be argued that a more sharply defined insight into the process of locational change in the footwear industry may have resulted from more sophisticated manipulation of the census data: perhaps through using Dunn's 'shift-and-share' technique,[13] or by applying methods of economic base analysis through Mattila and Thompson's index of surplus workers,[14] or, indeed, by employing one or more of the standard location quotients or indices of concentration. In principle, with good data, all or any of these could have proved better analytical tools than those applied here. In fact, the data on which Figures 1a to 1g are based are currently being reworked in a number of ways but, from the results that have been obtained to date, it seems likely that the main result of such manipulation will merely be to produce an impression of greater accuracy and sophistication which, because of basic flaws in the statistics, is often spurious. If this proves to be the final conclusion, it must be regarded as a rather sad reflection on the usefulness to geographers of the industrial employment data that have been included in the census reports for nearly one-and-a-half centuries.

L. M. Feery and others have pointed out that the compilers of successive census reports have endeavoured to give guidance on matters affecting the comparability of statistics on the same subject with those previously published.[15] However, this guidance has been restricted mainly to the differences between any one census and that immediately preceding it. Disheartening problems arise for the researcher when comparing the occupation statistics in the census reports over a long period, and the difficulties stem not just from one source. They arise from changes in the form in which the information is obtained; from changes in definition; from changes in classification; and from changes in the boundaries of the areas to which the data relate. It is natural, perhaps, that much of the pressure for census reform that has come from geographers[16] has concentrated on the last of these issues. There now seems to be a good chance that grid squares will be used as the basic unit for data collection in future censuses. If this happens, a major discontinuity in the census data will result, but also there will be, for the first time in Britain, a system of census data collection that is independent of changes in the boundaries of administrative areas. The fact remains, however, that in establishing a data time-series that is useful for tracing changes in the location of industry, an equally important problem is posed by the alterations that have taken place over the years in the classification of occupations. These often make it impossible to compare earlier and later figures in the census relating to large sections of the occupied population.

### NOTES

[1] BRITISH FOOTWEAR MANUFACTURERS FEDERATION, *Footwear industry statistical review* (1969) 2. This production figure refers to manufacturers' sales during 1968.

[2] The British Footwear Manufacturers Federation, 72 Dean Street, London, and the Lancashire Footwear Manufacturers Association, Farholme Lane, Stacksteads, Bacup, Lancashire. After many years of independent existence the Lancashire Association joined the Federation in 1966.

[3] The total insured labour force in the footwear industry in Great Britain in 1965 was 102,320. This figure includes all operatives, administrative, technical and clerical staff, warehouse employees, packers, despatch workers, road transport drivers, labourers and canteen staff. It does not include those employed in footwear retailing.

[4] R. LAWTON, Historical geography: the Industrial Revolution, *The British Isles: a systematic geography* (eds. J. Wreford Watson and J. B. Sissons) (1964) 225–227.

[5] The first Census of population was taken in 1801. By the Population Act of 1840, responsibility for taking the Census was given to the General Register Office, where it has since rested. The 1841 Census was the first to provide detailed tables of occupation data.

[6] For a detailed treatment of this concentration see: P. R. MOUNFIELD, The footwear industry of the East Midlands, *East Midland Geographer* 3 (1964) 293–306; 3 (1965) 394–413; 3 (1965) 434–453; 4 (1966) 8–23; 4 (1967) 154–175.

[7] For an illuminating account of the early days of the industry in Lancashire see: P. CRONKSHAW, The development of the shoe and slipper industries in Rossendale: an industrial romance, *Trans. Lancs. and Cheshire Antiquarian Soc.* 60 (1948) 28 *et seq.*

[8] P. R. MOUNFIELD, The shoe industry in Staffordshire 1767 to 1951, *North Staffs. Journal of Field Studies* 5 (1965) 74–80.

[9] After Forster's Act of 1870, which made available sufficient elementary schools for the purpose, school boards were permitted to frame by-laws making school attendance compulsory up to the age of 12, unless exemption was obtained by reaching a certain standard of educational proficiency at an earlier age. In 1881, Mundella made the framing of such by-laws compulsory up to the age of 13, and in 1900 the age was raised to 14. Under Fisher's Act of 1918 the local education authority was allowed to insist on school attendance up to 15. Local authorities were thus permitted or compelled to raise the compulsory school leaving age, but in addition the government also fixed a minimum age for employment below which no exemptions were allowed. Under Lord Sandon's Act of 1876 this was any age between 10 and 14 at which a child could satisfy the inspectors that it had attained a certain standard of efficiency. The lower age limit was raised to 11 in 1893, then to 12 in 1899, except for agriculture. In 1918, Fisher's Act made 14 the minimum legal age for employment for more than an hour or two a day, thus establishing a uniform national minimum where previously there had been considerable diversity between localities.

[10] P. G. HALL, The east London footwear industry: an industrial quarter in decline, *East London Papers* 5 (1962) 4.

[11] Particularly from business histories and individual firms' records; also from directories, contemporary accounts, newspaper archives and other library material.

[12] THOROLD ROGERS, *Six centuries of work and wages* (1890) 46.

[13] E. S. DUNN, A statistical and analytical technique for regional analysis, *Papers and Proceedings of the Regional Science Association* 6 (1960) 97–112.

[14] J. M. MATTILA and W. R. THOMPSON, The measurement of the economic base, *Land Economics* 31 (1955) 215–228.

[15] L. M. FEERY, M. S. STRICKLAND and I. HUTCHINSON, *Census Reports of Great Britain 1801–1931*, Interdepartmental committee on social and economic research, Guide to official sources no. 2 (H.M.S.O., 1951). This is essential reading for anyone wishing to use the census data, as is: B. BENJAMIN, *The population census*, Review No. 7 (Social Science Research Council, 1970).

[16] Particularly from the Population Studies Group of the Institute of British Geographers.

# AFRICAN PREHISTORY AND GEOGRAPHICAL DETERMINISM

## M. POSNANSKY

As a discipline, only Geography endeavours to maintain . . . . . an awareness of the intricate relationships between man and his environment.[1]

One of the principal attractions of prehistory is the opportunity it affords for studying the interplay of social aspirations and environing nature over long periods of time . . . . . The relationship between Man and external nature . . . . . is a dynamic one.[2]

### INTRODUCTION

Geographical determinism as a philosophical concept has undergone many vicissitudes since its heyday more than 50 years ago in the writings of Semple and Huntington. It has been discredited and rejected by Hartshorne[3] of the American school of geographers as too constrictive, modified by the theory of possibilism of Vidal de la Blanche[4] and of probabilism by Spate[5] but still it has adherents. Eyre and Jones[6] in viewing *Geography as human ecology* feel that it is the geographer's contribution to learning to relate the natural to the human environment. Martin[7] in 'The necessity for determinism' sees a place for geographical determinism in the fact that geography has claims to be scientific and as such must formulate laws, one of which concerns the basic hypothesis of the influence of the geographical environment. He would further maintain that as geographers are concerned with the geographical environment, however widely or narrowly construed, it is their particular business to examine geographical determinants rather than others. The geographical determinism of Semple and Huntington was discarded, not because the fact that the natural environment can affect human activity was not recognized, but largely because its proponents overstated their case and in detail their case could be refuted. In their broad scope they ignored the closer analysis of 'areal variations' that Hartshorne considered the chief concern of the geographer. The prehistorian dealing with the un-documented cultural development of mankind from his earliest origins has similarly concerned himself with geographical determinants. Many prominent geographers have realized the importance of the prehistoric dimension in geography, well summed up by E. Estyn Evans, who wrote:

To approach an understanding of regional variety we need to know all we can about the history—and prehistory—of human occupance, for man's choice of action at the point in time is restricted by actions previously taken.[8]

Crawford,[9] Fox[10] and others stressed the importance of the geographical environment in British prehistory. It might be said that, like their colleagues in geography, the prehistorians overstretched themselves. The obvious traces of neolithic and bronze age settlement on the lighter chalk and gravel soils of southern England distracted them from finding the less obvious, but nevertheless real, traces of settlement on clay lands and flood plains. But, nevertheless, they conditioned later generations of prehistorians who became as aware of the importance of the geographical aspects of their subject as of the chronological or behavioural. Gordon Childe, for nearly 30 years after the publication of his *Danube in prehistory*,[11] interpreted archaeological data from a materialist viewpoint, which in such classic works as *Man makes himself*[12] can clearly be seen as a modified form of

215

geographical determinism. Scholars as long ago as Herodotus had observed that 'Egypt is the gift of the Nile', Childe's achievement was to describe the mechanism by which natural influences were brought to bear on the history of Egyptian civilization. The mechanism was seen by him as the processes involved in what he described as the agricultural and urban revolutions. Childe, largely due to the unevenness of evidence from the rest of Africa, underrated the influences of the African hinterland on the Nile Valley. His materialist approach dealt with the interrelationships that exist between environment and man, particularly in the way that the politically centralized, unified, imperial state of Egypt owed its origin to the human need to co-operate to control the Nile floods, and the material necessity to quarry and build in stone to overcome the deficiencies of an alluvial environment. Since such pioneer studies, prehistory has expanded and it is the purpose of this paper to explore the control that environment has exercised on the cultural development of Africa.

## THE MYTH OF AFRICAN PLUVIALS

In the study of the Stone Age there have been differences of opinion between those who feel that climate was an important determinant and those who feel that its influence has been overstated. In its extreme form a series of four Pluvials and four inter-Pluvials was postulated based on evidence assembled from 1919 by E. J. Wayland in Uganda[13] and by L. S. B. Leakey in Kenya from 1926. Geological sections were interpreted with climatic inferences, 'dated' by specific types of stone tools, and correlations were freely made across thousands of miles with the same Pluvials quoted for western and southern Africa as for east Africa. The evidence was often of the slenderest kind. Archaeologists ran riot with geomorphological data often gathered in the most subjective way. Downcutting and gravels were normally interpreted as indicating pluvials without reference to other factors of stream history. Sequences of terraces, such as those of the Vaal or Kagera, were related to fluctuations of sea or lake level; lacustrine deposits were seen invariably as evidence of wetter conditions; reddening of surfaces as evidence of drier conditions, and the fossil remains of past faunas were assigned to woodland, aquatic or desertic habitats. In recent years there has been a realization, well expressed in key articles by Flint,[14] Hay,[15] Temple,[16] Bishop,[17] Partridge and Brink,[18] that there was no foundation for the pluvial edifice. Former east African lakes could be explained by reference to the tectonic activity of the Rift Valley in which grid faulting would create lake basins and later faulting would facilitate their drainage. Crustal warping in western Uganda and the downcutting of the Nile outflow at Ripon falls were demonstrated as playing a major role in the history of Lake Victoria and the formation of the Kagera river sediments. Ecological studies of present-day African faunas reveal that many species have a greater climatic tolerance than had hitherto been supposed, whilst many of the terrace and other river features can be related to non-climatically induced river rejuvenations and to the normal processes of cutting, fill, braiding and hill wash.

## ENVIRONMENT AND CHANGES IN STONE AGE TECHNOLOGY

The archaeologist is as a result presently constrained to interpret his stratigraphic sections in purely local terms. If pollens are present, as at Kalambo,[19] a vegetational history can be established with climatic inferences but otherwise caution prevails. Though the strict regimen of pluvials has gone, cultural explanations based on climatic change survive. A notable advocate is Professor J. D. Clark[20] who interprets changes in tool kit from the Acheulian (up to 50,000 B.C.) to the Sangoan (50,000 to 30,000 B.C.) industrial complexes as being due to vegetational changes and states that 'environment was . . . . . the most important single factor influencing cultural and biological evolution'. He sees the decrease in relative numbers of large cutting tools like hand-axes and cleavers and their replacement by small informal scraping, gouging and cutting tools and heavier pounding, abrading and chopping tools—like picks, core-axes and spheroids—as indicating an increase in woodland. The tool forms are certainly those which can be used to shape wood, pound roots or sharpen sticks into lances, but can we be sure that a change in the environment is a key factor? I would prefer to see man's growing adaptability, environmentally conditioned perhaps, as being the key determinant. By around 60,000 to 50,000 B.C. new tool-making techniques had been evolved which allowed smaller tools to be made, fire had become a tool to use at will for keeping warm and perhaps for cooking inedible roots and processing gums, insects and vegetable matter into mastics, poisons and medicine. Man was thus able to cope with environments hitherto hostile either because of their inclement climate or thick vegetation. The new technology had evolved slowly and man in the central African Stone Age was heir to the tool-making traditions, not only of his own ancestors, but of those of the different foraging groups with which he came into contact. In a similar fashion he was able to adapt his expanding tool kit to provide points for lances in the more open bush terrain. It was mankind's growing adaptability, exhibited in his cultural evolution, that ultimately enabled one species of man to inhabit a large part of the world.

Though one may vary the emphasis, the influence of environment was fundamental in Stone Age times. It has been argued that the break-up of the Miocene forest cover necessitated the bipedal locomotion of the primate ancestors of man. The protein deficiencies of a grassland habitat for non-cud-chewing primates was undoubtedly a factor in leading to scavenging and hunting. The necessity to drink governed human distributions. It is possible to multiply the examples which illustrate the environmental determinants of the Stone Age and even of the origins of the first farming societies, due in no small measure to the presence of suitable agricultural staples. The prehistorian, however, also deals with more evolved societies for which the nature of the determinants and the mechanism by which they affect human development are harder to adduce. This has, of course, long been recognized, as Sorokin clearly realized in 1928 when he wrote:

> the more complex are the forms of civilization, the less noticeable, the less definite and the less tangible is the correlation between geographical conditions and Social Phenomena.[21]

A good example of differing attitudes to the environmental determinant is presented by the various interpretations given to the rôle of the Sahara in African prehistory.

## THE RÔLE OF THE SAHARA IN AFRICAN PREHISTORY

For long the Sahara was regarded as the essential geographical divide between northern and southern Africa which only sprang into importance with the camel caravans of the Arabs carrying the Guinea gold used by the Islamic world and Europe to buy the exotic luxuries of the Orient. As research has expanded into the desert in the last 40 years, it has been appreciated that the Sahara has a vital prehistory of its own which affected that of the Nile Valley and west Africa. Thousands of rock-paintings and engravings have been found in the Hoggar, Tassili, Tibesti and other high rocky areas of the central Sahara, testifying to rich hunting cultures followed by no less abundant pastoral societies. Ground stone tools, querns, stone-hut circles and hearths indicate agricultural societies in the now-arid Tibesti. For a time the actions of man, in destroying the vestigial vegetation, introducing the goat and cultivating thin and easily eroded soils, were seen as the cause of the form of the present Sahara, but now ample evidence is being revealed from the Chad basin, Tibesti and the Nile Valley[22] to indicate that the desiccation was due to natural causes. The main period of the drop in level of a once-large Lake Chad seems to have occurred 4,000 to 2,500 B.C. Research in Nubia[23] suggests, however, that since 2,000 B.C. the climate has not significantly altered. Hobler and Hester,[24] from surveys in the Libyan desert, have suggested that a wet phase may have begun as early as, or earlier than, 6,000 B.C. and they have reconstructed (Figure 1) the Saharan isohyets for the period, which indicate the high plateaux of the Sahara as receiving an annual rainfall of up to 200 millimetres. They have also described in some detail the Libyan complex of industries, dating to around 6,000 B.C., largely situated around playa depressions which presumably in the past were moist or held water. Stones and retouched implements resembling sickle blades suggest the possibility of incipient agriculture.

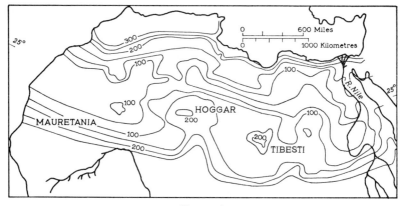

FIGURE 1
Suggested isohyets (mm.) for the Sahara around B.C. 6500–5000
*After* Hobler and Hester (1969)

It is apparent that in an area like the Sahara small climatic changes can drastically affect settlement history and it is to such marginal zones that the determinist concepts apply with force. It is not inconceivable that there were some agricultural origins in the Sahara itself. Mori[25] has described pastoral societies dating from 5,800 B.C. but the sparsity of the present-day flora precludes the possibility of determining what wild cereals may have been grown. The results of the desiccation were varied. Some Saharan Stone Age groups moved into the Nile Valley, as is attested by the lithic material of the Nile Valley predynastic 'neolithic' cultures. Other groups must have

218

moved into the moister, higher interior mountainous zones. For some time there was close contact with the Nile valley, where amazonite and other Saharan semi-precious stones were used for beads and pendants. Dotted wavy-line impressed wares have been found in an area stretching from Khartoum to the Hoggar, whilst bone harpoons of a fairly similar form occur wherever a little fishing or fowling was possible. The pastoral scenes cease within the fourth millenium B.C. and it is apparent that the pastoralists themselves moved. Lhote[26] and others who have studied the Tassili paintings suggest that the pastoralists moved to the south, which seems plausible as in the Sudanic savannah belt, which still supports pastoralists, the earliest 'neolithic' dates to the fourth millenium B.C. in Niger and Mali and is characterized by impressed wares not all that dissimilar to those of the Khartoum neolithic. The splitting-up of the Congo–Khordofanian language family of Greenberg,[27] with the Khordofanian groups now minute and isolated in the Nuba hills, and the Niger–Congo groups spread over most of sub-Saharan Africa, probably dates from this period. Populations expanded with the coming of agriculture and groups spread along the Sudanic belt and to the fringes of the west African forest. Climatic change was crucial to the peopling of west Africa but so also was the spread of agricultural techniques. Later in west Africa it was the location of exploitable ores, of copper in Mauretania and of gold in the Upper Senegal and the Guinea forest regions of present-day Ghana, that were to influence the course of cultural development. It was probably because of the routes that existed across the Sahara until at least 2,000 B.C., and into the plateaux areas until much later, that the first north African metal workers had access to the western Sudan, where dry stone enclosures of people cultivating grains[28] have been found in Mauretania dating to the second millennium B.C. as well as copper arrowheads with affinities to those of Bronze Age Morocco and southern Spain.[29]

## DISPERSION IN NORTH–EAST AFRICA

Though an irrefutable case can be made for the influence of environment in the dispersion of agricultural practices to west Africa and the beginnings of trade across the Sahara there are other areas where at times geographical determinants have been cited but where the evidence is far from conclusive. An example that can be discussed is the area comprising the Middle Nile, Ethiopia and the Horn of Africa. In this area between A.D. 1200 and 1600 a sequence of events took place which altered the history of eastern Africa. In the thirteenth century, from the Khartoum area and north of the confluence of the Nile and Atbara, there existed three Christian Nubian kingdoms which had been established after the arrival of Christianity in the sixth century. Their Christianity was distinguished by fine hagiographical art well displayed in the frescoes of the Faras basilica. To the east the medieval Christian kingdom of Ethiopia flourished in isolation and it is to this period that the famous rock-cut churches of Lalibela are assigned. The southern Sudan appears to have been quiescent whilst only in the Horn of Africa, where Somali pastoralists were expanding, was the imminence of later change apparent. By the middle of the sixteenth century the Christian kingdoms of Nubia had completely collapsed, the last one, Alwa, falling in 1504, and the forces of Islam had expanded into the middle Nile valley; from the Bahr-el-Ghazal, the Nilotic-speaking Lwoo peoples had dispersed into northern Uganda, bringing to an abrupt end the

Bacwezi state of western Uganda; the medieval kingdom of Ethiopia had fallen to the newly introduced Ottoman firearms of Mohammed Gran and only a shadow of the former state survived through intervention of Christopher de Gama and a small group of Portuguese. To the south and east of Ethiopia and into Ethiopia itself had expanded Galla pastoralists, who themselves were to ravage parts of the east African coast in the seventeenth century. A question that is often not asked is why did all this happen?

Historians are concerned with describing what happened in the past. Explanations have often been provided for different parts of the dramatic series of events described above. Quite often the individual explanations cancel each other out. The Lwoo expanded because other Nilotic peoples expanded from the east,[30] but why did the latter expand? Attempts have been made to explain the historical developments in terms of power politics. The Christian kingdoms of Nubia supported the Fatimid dynasty in Egypt against the Seljuk Turks; on the collapse of the Fatimids the Ayyubids decided that their effective control should extend into Nubia. In the Red Sea area the Muslim states of Eritrea, like Adal, needed to expand inland to more fertile areas for both trade and pasturage. In the Chad area the expanding state of Bornu was exerting pressures against lesser sultanates to the east. The Christian kingdoms of Nubia formed a block between Muslim Egypt and the states of the western Sudan.[31] Trade and pilgrims from the western Sudan had to cross the Sahara, a journey which even at the peak of the camel caravan trade involved at least 100 days of gruelling march, payments to the Tuareg, and often heavy losses in men, camels and merchandise. In the long term it was in the interests of trade and of Islam that Nubia and Ethiopia should fall. Their fall was not sudden. The power and territorial confines of the Christian kingdoms were slowly eroded away, Arabic infiltrated an area where Greek was previously written, cultural isolation led to cultural stagnation and economic collapse. In Ethiopia the Galla had been expanding for at least 100 years before the fall of the medieval kingdom. The disintegration of a previously relatively stable area must have had an effect on the areas to the south of Nubia and west of Ethiopia. Elsewhere,[32] I have speculated that a series of ripples of disturbance in the form of refugees, movements of whole societies from marginal areas, and raids by dispossessed or unrestricted pastoralist leaders, affected the southern Sudan and led first to the Madi expansion and later to the Lwoo movements.

Other explanations of a more geographical nature can, however, be postulated. Peoples move for various reasons—because of a desire for land, a need by young leaders to carve out new states, attack from outside or sheer population growth in which sons leave the parental home and move to adjacent marginal areas. Most movements are slow and the result of many tiny movements spread over a considerable number of years, often centuries. The expansion of the Lwoo was, however, rather more sudden, particularly in its effect on Uganda. Climate can be blamed in two ways for the movement. The region of the Bahr-el-Ghazal is relatively marginal in agricultural productivity. It is good pastoral country in the higher area, though away from the river and to the west the land becomes drier with rainfalls well below 30 inches (750 millimetres) per annum. With a more favourable climate cattle populations and probably human populations would increase and the tendency would be to expand. Expansion could not be towards the north, which is drier and from where peoples were moving consequent upon the fall of the Nubian kingdoms, nor to the west, which is also drier, whilst to the east the swamps of the Sudd are not conducive to pastoralism and the related Nuer and Dinka peoples were firmly in occupation. A tradition of generations of cattle keeping, combined with the inability to move in any other direction, meant that expansion could only be to south *via* the savannah grasslands (Figure 2), which finally led them to northern Uganda. Conversely, if the climate deteriorated there would also have been a need to expand from marginal pastoral areas and in addition there would have been pressures from groups expanding for identical reasons from the north and west. There is certainly well-attested evidence[33] from the northern hemisphere for a climatic deterioration in the fourteenth century, though as yet its effect on Africa has not been demonstrated. The incidence of somewhat drier conditions would definitely have had significant results in the marginal areas under discussion.

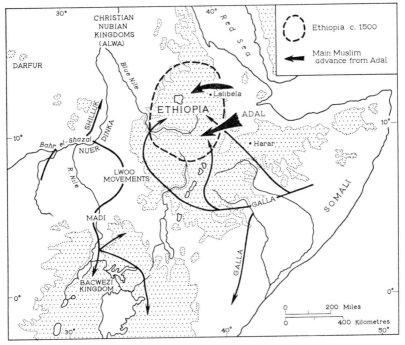

FIGURE 2

North–east Africa in the late fifteenth century A.D., showing Nilotic (Lwoo), Galla and Muslim movements

Galla movements after J. D. Fage, *Atlas of African History* (1963)

It can thus be seen that in considering this north–eastern sector of Africa the nature of the environment controlled the directions that movements would take—the Lwoo to the south and the Galla into Ethiopia and to the south–east. Climatic change may have induced the major movements of both groups. But the picture is more complicated and cannot be clarified without looking at events in the Red Sea, an area to some extent affected by events in the wider world of the Indian Ocean, and in Cairo and Bornu.

221

In addition, the study of the oral traditions of Nilotic- and Cushitic-speaking peoples[34] is indicating many highly pertinent factors of local politics which influenced local movements. The smaller the area studied the more important seem the personal factors and it is only when one takes an overall view of the political geography that the background environment factors assume significance.

## CONCLUSION

Do the two examples that we have cursorily reviewed allow us to draw any conclusions as to the validity of geographical determinism? On the face of it the desiccation of the Sahara played a very important rôle in the prehistory of Africa, whereas in the north–east of Africa either climatic amelioration or deterioration may have had remarkably similar effects. It has to be borne in mind, however, that in the first example the period of time involved was considerable, perhaps two or three millennia, whereas in the second we were dealing with at most two to three centuries and a far smaller area. Moreover, detailed information is known about the movement of the peoples of north–east Africa in the second millennium A.D. as compared with the movements of far fewer people in and around the Sahara 5,000 years before. A further factor of importance is that the societies involved in the second example were mostly more highly evolved socially, culturally, economically and politically. It would appear that in such complex societies many other determinants are at work. It might be concluded that the opponents of geographical determinism were correct. That as soon as a small enough area is studied and sufficient details of its history are known then the geographical determinants become unimportant and are perhaps only marginally affected by the possibilities open to the society under consideration. Advocates of determinism, however, could reply that if a sufficient time scale and geographical area are considered, then the influence of environment will be seen to be quite considerable and it is for this reason perhaps that so many African prehistorians have shown determinist tendencies. It is evident that whatever the emphasis that is placed on the environmental aspects of the study of man it is necessary to have a realization of the environmental background of former human populations. Nearer the present day the environment played a slighter rôle and the main determinants are to be seen in the fields of economics, politics, group and individual psychology, and sociology, but nevertheless because we cannot immediately see the rôle that environment played we should not dismiss it even for the history of fairly modern, complex social groups. Often the rôle of environment can only be seen when looking at comparative history and seeing the inter-relationships that existed between contiguous societies. It is for appreciating the subtle environmental effects that the geographer is partly trained and can contribute most readily in any dialogue with the historians. In this sense I would maintain that African prehistory can demonstrate the need for a geographical determinist approach, though in so concluding I would not advocate a return to the provocative and sweeping theories of Huntington, but rather an inevitable acceptance of Martin's[35] philosophical conclusion that mind and matter do influence each other and that environment in some small part does influence man at all stages of his development.

## NOTES

1 H. ASCHMANN, quoted in *Geography as human ecology* (eds. S. R. Eyre and G. R. Jones) (Edward Arnold, London, 1966) 1.

2 G. CLARK, *Prehistoric Europe: the economic basis* (Methuen, London, 1952) 7.

3 R. HARTSHORNE, *Perspective on the nature of geography* (Murray, London, 1960).

4 P. VIDAL DE LA BLACHE, *Principles of human geography* (Constable, London, 1926).

5 O. H. K. SPATE, Toynbee and Huntington: a study of determinism, *Geog. Jour.* 118 (1952) 402–428.

6 Eyre and Jones (eds.), *op. cit.*, 6.

7 A. F. MARTIN, The necessity for determinism: a metaphysical problem confronting geographers, *Trans. Inst. Br. Geog.* 17 (1951) 1–11.

8 E. ESTYN EVANS, quoted in Eyre and Jones (eds.), *op. cit.*, 24.

9 O. G. S. CRAWFORD, Prehistoric geography, *Geog. Rev.* (1922) 257–263.

10 C. FOX, *The personality of Britain* (National Museum, Cardiff, 1932).

11 V. G. CHILDE, *The Danube in prehistory* (Oxford University Press, London, 1929).

12 *Idem, Man makes himself* (Watts, London, 1936).

13 E. J. WAYLAND, Rifts, rivers, rains and early man in Uganda, *Journ. Roy. Anth. Inst.* 64 (1934) 333–352.

14 R. F. FLINT, Pleistocene climates in Eastern and Southern Africa, *Bull. Geol. Soc. America* 70 (1959) 343–374.

15 R. L. HAY, Revised stratigraphy of Olduvai Gorge, *Background to evolution in Africa* (eds. W. W. Bishop and J. D. Clark) (Chicago, 1967) 221–224.

16 P. TEMPLE, E. J. Wayland and the geomorphology of Uganda, *Uganda Journal* 31 (1967) 13–13.

17 W. W. BISHOP, Annotated lexicon of quaternary stratigraphical nomenclature in East Africa, in Bishop and Clark (eds.), *op. cit.*, 375–380.

18 T. C. PARTRIDGE and A. B. A. BRINK, Gravels and terraces of the Lower Vaal River Basin, *South Afr. Geog. Journ.* 49 (1967) 21–38.

19 J. D. CLARK, *Kalambo Falls prehistoric site* 1 (University Press, Cambridge, 1969).

20 *Idem*, The influence of environment in inducing culture change at the Kalambo Falls prehistoric site, *S. Afr. Archaeol. Bull.* 19 (1964) 97.

21 P. SOROKIN, *Contemporary sociological theories* (Harper, New York, 1928) 105.

22 J. ZIEGERT, Zur Pleistozän–Gliederung in Nordafrika, *Africa Spectrum* 3 (1967) 5–24; and Pleistocene climatic changes and human industries in the Central Sahara, *Actes du Colloque International d'Archéologie Africaine* (ed. J. P. Lebeuf) (Paris, 1970, forthcoming).

23 L. P. KIRWAN, The land of Abu Simbel, *Geog. Journ.* 129 (1963) 261.

24 P. M. HOBLER and J. HESTER, Prehistory and environment in the Libyan Desert, *S. Afr. Archaeol. Bull.* 23 (1969) 120–130.

25 F. MORI, The absolute chronology of Saharan prehistoric rock art, *Simposio Internacional de Arte Rupestro* (Instituto de Prehistoria y Arqueologia, Barcelona, 1968) 291–294.

26 H. LHOTE, *The search for the Tassili frescoes* (Hutchinson, London, 1959).

27 J. H. GREENBERG, *Languages of Africa* (Mouton, The Hague, 1963).

28 P. J. MUNSON, Recent archaeological research in the Dhar Tichitt region of South-Central Mauretania, *The West African Arch. Newsletter* 10 (1968) 6–13.

29 R. MAUNY, Essai sur l'histoire des métaux en Afrique Occidentale, *Bull. Inst. Franc. Afr. Noir.* 16 (1952) 545–593.

30 D. W. COHEN, The River–Lake Nilotes from the fifteenth to the nineteenth century, *Zamani, a survey of East African history* (eds. B. A. Ogot and J. A. Kieran) (E.A.P.H. and Longmans, Nairobi, 1968) 149.

31 P. L. and M. SHINNIE, New light on medieval Nubia, *Journ. Afr. Hist.* 6 (1965) 263–273.

32 M. POSNANSKY, East Africa and the Nile Valley in early times, *The Sudan in history* (ed. Y. F. Hasan) (1970, forthcoming).

33 W. G. EAST, *The geography behind history* (Nelson, London, 1938) 62.

34 C. EHRET, Cushites and the Highland and Plains Nilotes, in Ogot and Kieran (eds.), *op. cit.*, 158–176.

35 A. F. MARTIN, *op. cit.*, 8.

# THE GEOGRAPHER IN REGIONAL PLANNING

A. G. POWELL

## INTRODUCTION

This essay is written from the point of view of an applied geographer employed by central government in regional planning and gives a personal interpretation of developments.[1] If within it the thread of geography appears to become tenuous or lost in the changing canvas of evolving processes, then this is a true reflection of the place of geography in real life, for it is more a discipline of thought than a subject of study.

## THE BEGINNINGS OF APPLIED GEOGRAPHY

The application of geography grew alongside its recognition as an academic discipline. Stamp's Land Utilisation Survey[2] was the first major breakthrough of geography into the practical field. Fawcett, studying urban growth in relation to motor transport, defined the British conurbations.[3] The Barlow Commission noted many contributions from geographers in the essentially geographical investigation of the Distribution of the Industrial Population.[4] Stamp became vice-chairman of the complementary Scott Commission on Land Utilisation in Rural Areas;[5] but, these apart, pre-war geography remained on an academic plane.

The First World War began a process of change from imperial Britain towards European Britain. The Second World War accelerated technologies from transportation to nuclear power and focussed attention on the problems of redeveloping a country possessing limited natural resources but abundant intellectual wealth. In 1943 a group of geographers was called into the new Ministry of Town and Country Planning to study the problems likely to face post-war Britain. This original band of geographer–planners included K. C. Edwards as the Ministry's Research Officer in the 'North Midlands' region. With a small group of other social scientists he and his colleagues formed the Research Class working alongside a Planning Class of architects, engineers and surveyors.

In these early years, their emphasis was properly on 'research'. They surveyed their regions and analysed their problems. In Edwards' case interdepartmental co-operation spread readily from the University, for F. A. Wells, then Reader in Economics, filled the complementary rôle of Research Officer in the Board of Trade. In the many exercises in industrial relocation, Edwards and Wells among others were instrumental in beginning the industrial revolution of environment on the Lincolnshire Humber Bank for new chemical industries requiring abundant water and effluent disposal facilities. Again, the two Research Officers foresaw the problems arising from colliery closures in the Derbyshire coalfield. Always interested in the decline of the original coal-measure ironstone industries between Stanton and Dronfield, and with Clay Cross providing a stark indicator of the future, Edwards became absorbed in the problems of this corner of the region. In collaboration with Wells, he produced *A survey of the Chesterfield region*.[6] He could scarcely foresee that within 25 years the coalfield would be receiving government aid as a 'grey area' in the national economic landscape. Having established himself and the Ministry as partners with the local authorities and laid firm foundations upon which

224

others could build, Edwards gradually withdrew from the government planning field as the birth of the University of Nottingham and his Chair of Geography approached. His wartime experience awakened a deep interest in the application of geography to regional planning which has blossomed in his students and culminated in his membership of the East Midlands Economic Planning Council and his recent C.B.E. for services to it. He finally handed over to the present writer in 1947 and has remained an invaluable friend, adviser (and critic) ever since.

This recapitulation of early geographer-participation in planning is justified by the contribution of the man in whose honour this volume is produced, by the methods which he and his colleagues established, and by its reflection of social, economic and environmental planning as a team effort from the beginning.

### THE GEOGRAPHER IN POST-WAR PLANNING

The post-war years have seen geographers using their discipline as applied geographers in professional planning teams. Their basic training was the traditional scientific approach of survey, analysis, selection of significant elements and their synthesis into an understanding of the causal relationships of given problems, and especially to inter-relationship in spatial terms. This was an insufficient base for planning, which called for the additional dimension of forecasting. Even now this additional requirement is not readily grasped. Professional planning becomes meaningful only when it solves existing problems by foreseeing and directing future trends. Too often, planners tend to start with a desired objective and assume that work and people will follow. One function of the geographer is to correct such thought; to emphasize the significance of past trends and the power of underlying forces. The planning process only becomes realistic when it calculates the extent and speed with which existing trends can be bent towards more desirable patterns. No geographer would claim this as his sole field, nor would his economist and sociologist colleagues. These are comprehensive problems to which each discipline contributes within expert teams.

For several years after the war Research Officers were building up operational capital by continuing the work of their predecessors through intensified regional surveys. F. H. W. Green developed his national spheres of influence study based on public transport.[7] Regional studies were made of work, shopping, educational and recreational movements to reveal the pattern of overlapping spheres of influence in a hierarchy of settlements bounded by transition zones. The North Midlands pioneered journey-to-work surveys for the whole region on a parish basis.[8] W. I. Carruthers developed the thesis of a hierarchy of urban centres and their hinterlands both nationally and in the complexity of Greater London.[9]

The North Midlands offered an excellent field for study of mineral problems, after-treatment and land conservation. Research planners secured the filling of gravel pits with powdered fuel ash from new power stations, first at Castle Donington and Hemington and later at Drakelow Park and elsewhere. At Nottingham itself, unsuccessful attempts were made to plan between Beeston and the Wilford power station by working gravel and tipping ash in a narrow belt moving westwards and thereafter providing the industry and recreation which the local plans proposed.

The South Derbyshire coalfield is a vignette of problems and potentialities. Over 150 feet of shallow coal seams, intercalated with fireclays, produce severe surface subsidence. Parts have sunk 30 feet during this century and the whole is shrouded in the fumes from the manufacture of salt-glazed drainpipes. A pleasant, stable environment exists a mile away where the Boothorpe Fault sharply limits the coalfield. Local officials combined with Ministries in the mid-40s to analyse this Swadlincote sub-regional problem. The radical answer was to rebuild the town beyond the Fault and open up mineral reserves previously sterilised by development. Ultimately, a complex alternative devised by Derbyshire County Council and the National Coal Board phased redevelopment with coal working so that new building took place where subsidence had largely ceased. Geographers played a full part in both plans.

The regions were left much to their own devices, though with regular interchanges of experience. Research Officers followed lines of research generated by the geographical environments in which they worked. East Anglia specialized on the problems of declining rural population and paved the way for later town expansion schemes. The North East studied the problems of declining coalfield communities and the encouragement of new growth at Newton Aycliffe, Peterlee and Tees-side. In the North West, R. T. White developed an understanding of the forces of decline in Lancashire and the potential offered by Cheshire and Merseyside and also began the studies (unpublished) of inter-regional natural change, migration and its characteristics, which have made him an expert on planning demography.

The geographer–planners of the 1945–55 decade promoted much capital knowledge dictated by the geography of the regions within which they worked. Under J. R. James in Whitehall, experiences were co-ordinated by the 'Northern Group' of regional officers under his command to form the geographical, economic and social foundations of a regional planning theory based on wide practical experience. But quantification and analysis of the *forces* of change are still too little understood and remain the main field for future geographic, social and economic contribution.

## THE PLANNING ACTS

New legislation institutionalized planning from 1944 onwards. The first task of civil servants is to administer and the planning staffs were occupied in advising new planning authorities on new plans, feeding in capital and knowledge in a mutually co-operative effort.

The 1947 Act required county plans on a one-inch scale and town plans on six-inch or larger scales. This promoted a division of responsibilities in which the Regional Planning Officers tended to be concerned with detailed urban problems while Research Officers were more concerned with the inter-urban activities and spatial relationships of regional planning. This division was never rigid; physical planners played their part in country planning, while research staffs were concerned with the demographic, industrial and community structure of towns. Nevertheless, the research planners tended to move into the *regional* planning field while the physical planners were concerned with *town* planning problems. In 1954, Planning and Research Officers were integrated into a single Planning Directorate within the Ministry; 'research' had now become a misnomer; Research Officers were socio-economic planners.

226

PLANNING DIALOGUE: THE 60S

The past decade has been vital in the history of planning. There was much to discuss. Twenty years of operative planning were widely questioned. Man could conquer space but the earth was characterized by worsening social relationships and growing urban problems. Initial rumblings gathered momentum into the great debate on the future of town and country; roads, noise, pollution and motorized recreation in conflict with the beauty, historic heritage and ecology of coast and countryside.

Much of the debate had its origins in the United States. The Americans developed techniques without adequate powers, while Britain practised without adequate techniques. The American city disintegrated as urban freeways promoted development regardless of declining centres occupied by immobile urban poor. Social conscience was awakened: sociologists took an increasing part in planning.

British planners rested on their laurels. The capital accumulated after the war became out of date. Britain remained the centre of all that was best in planning practice—but was adding little new. Government was preoccupied with the modernization of local administration. The first sub-regional conurbation planning authority was formed in Greater London. Elsewhere in England and Wales the 1958 Act proved too restrictive to create the sub-regional units required for local planning in a technological revolution.

Circumstances brought renewed government intervention at regional level. The South East, North West and West Midlands Studies followed the 'Hailsham' Report on the North East.[10] The comprehensive revival of regional planning in 1964 and the establishment of Regional Planning Councils was the logical conclusion. Yet it was significantly more. Problems posed were commonly economic; solutions propounded were essentially physical. The new councils were Economic Planning Councils and brought the first full-time economic expertise into regional planning. This was a marked advance but still not enough. Planning is for people and the sociologist still remained outside.

What of the geographer in this period? From 1961 to 1968 a geographer was Chief Planner in the Ministry. John James was heavily involved in the Regional Studies. He was concerned with macro-problems, and played his part in developing this to its legislative conclusion in the 1968 Town and Country Planning Act. He assisted in the creation of the Centre for Environmental Studies as a national focus of planning research. He supported a strong British contribution to international co-operation in planning in which Ministry geographers played a leading part. The present writer had been among the first of the questioners in a paper on London regional planning read to the British Association in 1959.[11]

Geography dons joined the Planning Councils and increasingly engaged in planning affairs. Peter Hall[12] gazed towards 'London 2000' and launched the basis for the radial strategy for the South East. Experience emphasized the need for more than broad generalizations. He developed planning computer work and is developing an Urban Systems Research Unit at Reading, to which, among other geography departments, practising geographer–planners look for practicable new techniques. This is properly a university function: practising planners preparing plans and involved in administration have little time to develop methodology. Much of the future

227

geographical contribution depends on university development of new predictive techniques. Peter Haggett[13] realistically foresees the need for 20 years of research before practical methods are perfected. At Cambridge, Haggett began his computer research on geographical distribution, D. E. Keeble[14] made important contributions to studies of industrial location, linkage and movement and R. E. Pahl[15] switched from social geography to become the first of the regional sociologists. Elsewhere others recognized that generalizations were no longer good enough; effective geographical contributions to planning depend on fully quantified studies if findings are to carry conviction.

## THE CURRENT SITUATION

Returning to the Government aspects of regional planning, five aspects are worthy of mention:

*(a)* The 1968 Act establishes a new hierarchy of plans. Sub-regional structure plans must fit logically within regional frameworks and be approved by Government. These are exercises in the time–space inter-relationships of employment, population, major shopping centres, leisure, etc., in the context of transport networks and physical environments. They call for a team effort in which the geographer has a clear rôle. Architects and others play their part in 'local plans' for the creation of new and restructuring of old communities and in the unobtrusive integration of new transport systems into existing fabrics.

*(b)* Regional frameworks are required into which the mosaic of structure plans logically fall to make a whole greater than the sum of its parts. In 1968, the Government, the Regional Planning Council and the local planning authorities of the South East, commissioned a framework plan as a basis for structure plans and Government investment. The resulting South East Joint Planning Team is the first inter-disciplinary team to operate:

(i) in a highly developed democratic society which has adequate powers of implementation; and

(ii) in perhaps the most complex region of that society.

It must test alternatives in economic and physical terms and recommend a preferred solution. It consists of 30 to 35 professional officers including 15 geographer–planners working with engineers, architects, industrial and transport economists and, for the first time in a regional plan, sociologists. It will make mistakes and learn from them. It is already clear that complex regional inter-relationships make economic, social and physical planning inseparable. Physical plans not based on understanding of economic and social forces cannot be viable. A sound regional plan will involve not only land, building and communications but the educational, technological and welfare services equally serving the people for whom it is produced.

*(c)* Absence of data at a sufficiently fine level for new regional models is a serious drawback. It will create even greater problems at the structure plan stage unless sample survey techniques are widely applied. Data on mobility of people and jobs; occupations; social class distribution; incomes; recreational needs; investment; and so on, are notoriously deficient. The most important single need for future planners is a regular social survey, rather than a census of

population, using sampling techniques with suitable co-ordinate referencing for the collection of data and computer mapping techniques to give advanced bases for analysis.

*(d)* Lack of data is a positive danger in view of the rapid development of computer methodology. Far-reaching assumptions are necessary to transpose available data into a suitable form for planning models. It is as important for all planners to recognize the limitations of computer input data as it is to understand the major forces operating in the real world. The computer is nearing perfection for the rapid examination of *facts*. It *predicts* only on the assumptions it is programmed to make. American experts summarize the situation in their phrase 'garbage in—garbage out'. They warn that acceptance of the dogma of electronic infallibility is changing this true interpretation to an unreasoning belief that 'garbage in' means '*gospel* out'. Here lies the real danger to planners. The computer produces an *apparent* 'best buy' from many variables which is likely to be adopted to produce 'the self-deceiving prophecy' which, once investment begins to flow in conformity with it, becomes 'the self-fulfilling prophecy'. Ultimate planning decisions are taken by men for men and, at least until the quality of planning data is vastly improved, value judgments must remain. Geographers must know and recognize the limitations of new tools.

*(e)* Planning a regional framework for 30 years ahead is a hazardous and possibly foolhardy process. Humility is a basic necessity. In retrospect, who in 1940 could have foreseen the conditions of 1970? The planner must be both visionary and realist. Plans must be sufficiently flexible to accommodate the constancy of change; yet total flexibility produces the non-plan. Once investment begins to flow into an infrastructure, it becomes difficult to change course. Again, understanding of the power of current forces is paramount; again, the geographer–planner has his part in inter-relating the expertise of his colleagues. In South East England, as in many areas, the most important single factor influencing any plan is what exists now. The historical geography of London's expansion must continue in some form. Recent metropolitan expansion has rippled beyond the Green Belt into the Outer Metropolitan region and onwards into the East Midlands. The outward ripple will inevitably continue, if only because the cost of reversal is too astronomic to contemplate. Planning has been described as 'the art of the possible'. In the South East, the possible is a careful assessment of how far powerful current trends can be bent into more desirable patterns; taking into account the pressure of social desires, the feasibility of accelerating or decelerating economic influences and the new measures necessary to achieve them.

### CONCLUSIONS

A genuine or wilful lack of understanding by planners and others of geography, geographers and their contributions to the planning process still persists. The still prevalent misunderstanding of what modern geographers can do is a reflection of the youthful status of geography as a university discipline and of much bad school-teaching which lasted at least into the '50s. It taught the factual nonsense of 'cape and bay' geography without the vigorous breath of reality brought by the dawning understanding of how and why man lives as he does in a given environment. A true understanding of modern geography is not assisted by dissensions among geographers themselves and failure to accept geography as primarily a disciplined process of thought. Some planners draw the unacceptable distinction between the 'participators' in planning—the chartered planners, who do the real job, and the 'contributors'—the geographers, sociologists, economists and others who merely shovel in the facts!

The true elements of the modern geographer's contribution are four-fold:

*(a)* His basic study of the inter-relationship of man and his environment, developing from the simplest studies to the effects of increasing control over environment and the repercussions of an increasingly man-made environment upon man himself, reaching a climax in the complex inter-relationships of sophisticated urban–technological societies. There is not a cut-off point at which geographical study must cease. The predominantly man-made environment of 'megalopolis' is as much a part of geographical study as the simple relationship of eskimo to ice and seals. Advanced geographical studies imply increasingly detailed attention to the micro-urban geography which leads to an understanding of the potentiality, processes, viability and costs of change and their repercussions on human activity. The geographer is basically at least as well equipped as any other in the fundamental processes of regional planning. The Planning Advisory Group, the 1968 Act and the report on the reorganisation of Local Government all recognize the inter-action of town and country as vital and that plans must be based on city-regions over much of urbanized Britain.[16]

*(b)* 'Spatial inter-relationship' is a central feature of geographical discipline, but is it meaningful outside geographical circles? It implies studies of:

  (i) how and why man lives, works, plays and moves and the consequences of the resulting patterns of land use and movements upon each other and back upon man;

  (ii) the inter-action of resources and the consequences of their development in, for example, landscape and mineral workings; water supply, flooding and drainage; landscape, transport and countryside recreation; and so forth; and

  (iii) the causal relationships and consequences of growth and decay of resources, technology and man's ingenuity.

Together these comprise an understanding of the space-time relationships of the regional economy which is the very basis of regional planning.

*(c)* To the study of the physical landscape and its economic significance in changing societies, the geographer adds special attention to the demography of the regional scene; the interplay of natural increase and migration in gross population turnover; the economic and social characteristics of local populations; their local and regional relationships and differing land requirements. Lastly, the geographer emphasizes these spatial studies by his special attention to carto-graphic presentation.

*(d)* The geographer–planner must be capable of applying his discipline to real life. Many academic geographers find difficulty in orienting their work to the specific needs of legislation, case work and realistic plans. Applied geographers must be capable of crossing the threshold into the future and of deep study of existing situations and trends; recognizing their power and the momentum arising from investment in any social and economic infrastructure. They must be ready to forecast how far these trends are susceptible to adjustment with existing or new powers. At the regional planning level, the geographer, sociologist and economist may be more important than others—whose relative significance increases at other levels. Planning in advanced societies is a team activity. Within the team, the geographer is at least as well placed as any by the breadth of his experience and his possession of some knowledge of many of the disciplines involved.

The claims of any specific body for its members alone to have a prescriptive right to all planning is irrelevant; especially as the planning field widens into a comprehensive totality deeply involving economic and social action. The planner 'qualified' before 1960 is out-of-date. The crucial issue is understanding of new methodologies and ability to apply them wisely in team operations. In this all planning disciplines start from scratch. Value comes from experience, in-service training and refresher courses consistent with developing techniques. The recommendations of the Fulton Committee into Civil Service management are equally relevant to planning management.[17]

An all-inclusive institution is required to achieve this; initiating training for new entrants to appreciate the contributions of others; absorbing those already qualified by experience and practical contribution; but concentrating especially on standards and the provision of courses for continuous retraining. Such an institution should represent the best of all participants in the planning process. A *town* planning qualification is clearly out-of-date. Comprehensive, inter-disciplinary planning of town and country, economic-region, city-region and broad structural planning, urgently requires a high-powered and comprehensive Institute of British Planners. Within it, geographer–planners would find their rightfully balanced place, and be able to make the full contribution to planning which their training and experience—and individual personal qualities— deserve.

### NOTES

[1] The views expressed here are purely personal and do not necessarily represent the official view of the Ministry of Housing and Local Government.

[2] *The land of Britain: the report of the Land Utilisation Survey of Britain* (ed. L. D. Stamp) (county volumes and one-inch maps, 1930s–40s). Also L. D. STAMP, *The land of Britain: its use and misuse* (1950).

[3] C. B. FAWCETT, British conurbations in 1921, *Sociological Review* 14 (1922) 111–122; and Distribution of the urban population in Great Britain, 1931, *Geographical Journal* 79 (1932) 100–116.

[4] ROYAL COMMISSION ON THE DISTRIBUTION OF THE INDUSTRIAL POPULATION, *Report* (1940) Cmd. 6153.

[5] COMMITTEE ON LAND UTILISATION IN RURAL AREAS, *Report* (1942) Cmd. 6378.

[6] K. C. EDWARDS and F. A. WELLS, *A survey of the Chesterfield region* (Chesterfield Regional Planning Committee, 1949).

7 F. H. W. GREEN, Urban hinterlands in England and Wales: an analysis of bus services, *Geographical Journal* 116 (1950) 64–81.

8 MINISTRY OF TOWN AND COUNTRY PLANNING (NORTH MIDLAND REGION), *Journey to work survey* (unpublished, 1948).

9 W. I. CARRUTHERS, A classification of service centres in England and Wales, *Geographical Journal* 123 (1957) 371–385; and Service centres in Greater London, *Town Planning Review* 33 (1962) 5–31.

10 *The North East: a programme for regional development and growth* (1963) Cmd. 2206; *The South East study: 1961–81* (1964) Cmd. 2308; *The North West: a regional study* (1965); *The West Midlands: a regional study* (1965).

11 A. G. POWELL, The recent development of Greater London, *Advancement of Science* 17 (1960) 76–86.

12 P. HALL, *London 2000* (1963).

13 P. HAGGETT, *Locational analysis in human geography* (1965).

14 D. E. KEEBLE, Industrial decentralization in the Metropolis, *Trans. Inst. Br. Geogr.* 44 (1968) 1–54.

15 R. E. PAHL, *Urbs in rure* (London School of Economics, 1965).

16 *The future of Development Plans* (Report of the Planning Advisory Group) (1965). *Town and Country Planning Act, 1968* (Part I). *Report of the Royal Commission on Local Government in England, 1966–1969* (1969) (Cmd. 4040) (Redcliffe-Maud Report).

17 *The Civil Service: Report of the Committee, 1966–68* (1968) (Cmd. 3638) (Fulton Report).

# THE BROWN SEAWEED INDUSTRIES
# IN THE BRITISH ISLES

## VALERIE RAMPTON

### INTRODUCTION

For centuries seaweeds have been used by coastal communities as food for man and animals and as manure. These traditional uses are still found in north and west Scotland and western Ireland, but never far from the coast as seaweed is a bulky and heavy commodity. Alongside the traditional uses there are now modern industries—one group using seaweeds as a component of fertilisers and animal feeds, the other extracting alginic acid from the seaweeds for use in a variety of products—and these have spread seaweed utilisation far from the shores.

### THE SEAWEEDS

Seaweeds are those algae growing in salt or brackish water: the part corresponding to the leaf of a flowering plant is known as the frond or lamina, to the stem the stipe, to the roots the holdfast or hapteron, and the term thallus is applied to the whole plant body. Only a few of the larger species are exploited by man, and the most important are *Laminaria cloustoni* and *L. digitata* of the Laminariaceae, or tangle, family and *Ascophyllum nodosum* of the Fucaceae, or rockweed, family. All three are members of the algal class Phaeophyceae, or brown seaweeds. *Laminaria cloustoni* is dark brown and grows up to 12 feet long. The round, rigid, and rough stipe expands abruptly into a large, deeply divided frond. The plant is perennial, but the frond is shed in May each year, and a new one formed. *Laminaria digitata* is similar to *L. cloustoni* in colour and size, but the stipe is oval in cross section, flexible, and smooth, and expands only gradually into a perennial frond. *Ascophyllum nodosum* is brown-yellow and around four feet long. The short stipe gives way to a cylindrical frond showing irregularly dichotomous branching and containing numerous air vesicles. The plant usually bears short lateral deciduous reproductive branches.

### THE DISTRIBUTION OF THE SEAWEEDS IN THE BRITISH ISLES

#### Habitat

The rise and fall of the tide on the shore means that the seaweeds are subjected to continually changing conditions; some species can tolerate prolonged exposure to wind, sun, and rain, others prefer long periods of immersion. The seaweeds are thus zoned at right angles to the slope of the shore. *A. nodosum* is found around mid-tide level, *L. digitata* from low water of neap tides to about 10 fathoms, *L.cloustoni* from low water of spring tides to 15 fathoms. Seaweeds are rare on sandy or muddy shores, and grow best on moderately exposed rocky shores. They grow in greatest abundance where the slope of the shore is gradual as here the algal zones will be widest.

#### Distribution

Figure 1 shows the distribution of harvestable quantities of rockweeds, that is over 10 tons per acre, in Scotland. Most of this is *A. nodosum* but it includes small quantities of *Fucus vesiculosus*, *F. serratus* and *F. spiralis*

233

in the average ratios 100 : 32 : 15 : 13. Also shown are harvestable quantities of Laminarias, that is over five tons per acre. The dominant species is nearly always *L. cloustoni,* occasionally *L. digitata.*[1] The rockweeds are collected where they grow, but the Laminarias are sorted from seaweeds cast on beaches adjacent to the rocky shores. Figure 2 shows the areas in Ireland where *A. nodosum, L. cloustoni,* and *L. digitata* are collected for industrial utilisation.[2]

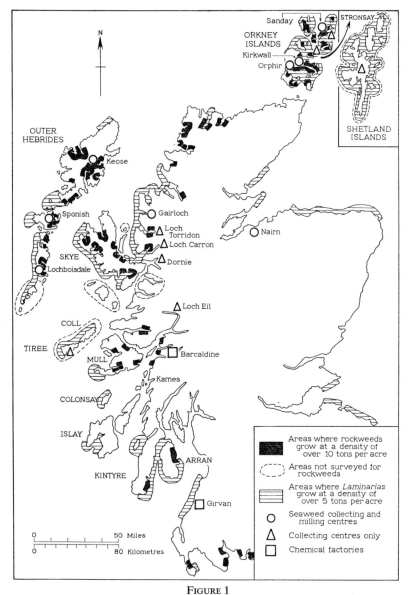

FIGURE 1
Scotland: seaweed harvesting and processing
Based on maps in information from the Scottish Seaweed Research Association

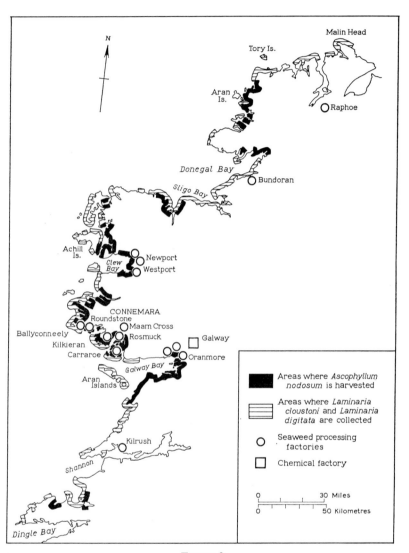

FIGURE 2
Ireland: seaweed harvesting and processing
Based on information from Irish seaweed processors

FERTILISERS AND ANIMAL FEEDS

*The value of seaweeds*

Recent research has shown that as a manure seaweed adds organic matter, minerals, and trace elements to the soil; calcium improves the crumb structure, and hygroscopic particles conserve moisture.[3] It decays rapidly so that nutrients are quickly made available to plants but conversely the effects are of short duration and frequent applications are necessary.

235

In the modern industry dried, milled and ground seaweed meal is mixed with other ingredients as a fertiliser, and recently liquid seaweed extracts, especially Bio and Maxicrop, have become popular.

In animal feeds seaweeds supply carbohydrate, protein, minerals—especially calcium, trace elements—especially iron and iodine, as well as vitamins, especially A, D, and $B_2$. In the modern industry seaweed meal makes up five to 10 per cent of feeds for sheep, cattle, pigs, poultry, and mink.[4]

### History of the industry

Seaweed meal for inclusion in animal feeds was first prepared in the U.S.A. in 1870.[5] During the 1914–18 war attempts were made to establish a similar industry in the British Isles, but it was not until 1948 that the attempts were successful. At about the same time the Scottish Seaweed Research Association (later the Institute of Seaweed Research, closed 1969) was started and one of its purposes was to give advice and technical assistance to those wishing to process seaweed, thus helping the industry to grow. Between 1948 and 1958 nine firms started production: five in Eire at Bundoran, Kilrush, Galway, Ballyconneely and Westport; four in Scotland at Nairn, Kirkwall, Gairloch and Sanday. The Irish firms are still operating, although the Westport factory has moved to Newport, but the Scottish firms were not so fortunate, the Nairn factory closed in 1956 and Kirkwall in 1961, the output of the Gairloch factory was very small, and the Sanday factory moved to Orphir on the Orkney mainland in 1961, but closed in 1962.

Between 1960 and 1965 expansion in Eire was rapid and 12 factories opened, at Roundstone, Carraroe, Oranmore, Westport, Maam Cross, Raphoe, Rosmuck, two at Newport, and one each at Killala, Kenmare and Westport Quay, although these last three closed again in the same period. In Scotland the Orphir firm re-opened under new management, but output was not great.

### The positions of the factories

Scotland

The factories are shown on Figure 1. The Orkney factories were obviously well situated in relation to seaweed supplies but there is no seaweed supply close to Nairn and the factory depended on cast weed brought from Dornie and Lochs Torridon, Carron, and Eil. The Gairloch factory is fairly situated in relation to seaweed supplies but was sited primarily to give out-of-season employment to local salmon fishermen.

Eire

Most of the Irish factories are situated on or close to the coasts where the seaweeds grow most abundantly, and are especially concentrated in Connemara and around Clew Bay. Maam Cross and Raphoe are some distance inland, but here seaweed processing is secondary to other concerns.

### The collection of seaweed

For feeds and fertilisers the factories work with *A. nodosum,* but if this is in short supply other rockweeds or, preferably, the fronds of *L. digitata,* may be used. The rockweeds are cut from the rocks. *L. digitata* is sorted from seaweeds cast on the shore, and is found most frequently after winter storms. The seaweeds are air dried (from 75 to approximately 50 per cent water content) on rocks or walls, then sold to hauliers who convey them to the factories. A few collectors are contracted to a particular firm; most sell to the highest bidder. There are only a few full-time seaweed collectors, most are also farmers. It is estimated that there are over 2,500 collectors in Eire, each, on average, selling 20 tons a year of air-dried seaweed, which provides 30 to 50 per cent of his income.

## The processing and production of seaweed meal

On arrival at the factory the water content of the seaweed must quickly be reduced to 25 per cent to prevent bacterial decay. The drying temperature has to be carefully controlled, as excessive heat alters the chemical composition of the seaweeds, and there is a fire risk, as several firms have found to their cost. After drying, the seaweed can be stored for several weeks. To make meal the seaweed is first chopped to small lengths, then ground to the fine powder required by fertiliser makers and animal food compounders.[6]

In Ireland the number employed in each factory in 1966 was between four and 40. The larger firms maintained employment round-the-clock, throughout the year. Many of the smaller firms, where seaweed processing is usually a subsidiary concern, work short hours, close in winter, and occasionally, when supplies are short, in summer also.

### Eire

In 1958 five firms produced nearly 7,000 tons of meal; in 1964 14 firms produced over 18,000 tons but 20 per cent of this was used for the extraction of alginic acid. In 1962 over 90 per cent of the production was dependent on supplies between Newport and Galway,[7] but this is almost certainly smaller today as with expansion supplies are being sought further afield. In 1964 around 6,000 tons were exported to the United Kingdom, half for use in feeds and fertilisers, the rest for alginic acid extraction. The former has probably increased as seaweed utilisation is now more widespread, the latter decreased as Ireland now has a major alginate factory.

### Scotland

In the mid-1950s production reached 2,000 tons a year, but with factory closures it dropped to 400 tons in 1959. Since then production has been small and erratic.

## Imports of seaweed meal

The U.K. imports most of the seaweed meal it uses. On average up to 90 per cent comes from Eire, up to 20 per cent from Norway, and small amounts from France, South Africa, and other countries. Eire and Norway use more seaweed meal than the U.K. does, and this suggests that there is considerable scope for expansion.

## The advantages of the Irish industry

In Scotland fuel oil, electricity, labour, shipping, and storage costs are all higher than in Eire. Consequently, a ton of seaweed meal costs around £3 more to produce in Scotland than Eire.[8] Other factors contributing to the failure of the Scottish industry are that the kelp industry died out at the beginning of this century, whereas the Irish industry continued until the end of the Second World War, keeping the seaweed harvesting tradition alive; that the early Scottish factories used unsorted cast weed of a variable quality; and that the early establishment of the alginate industry in Scotland meant that later factories could not successfully compete for seaweed supplies.

## ALGINIC ACID AND ALGINATES

### History of the industry

In the eighteenth century unusual trading conditions led to a shortage of soda and potash, thus it became economic to burn seaweed to ash—known as kelp—from which these chemicals could be extracted. When conditions returned to normal, and the Stassfurt mineral deposits were discovered the industry collapsed. There was a small revival in the nineteenth century when seaweeds were the only known source of the newly discovered element iodine, but this likewise collapsed with the discovery of iodates in Chile.

The double collapse brought considerable hardship to western Scotland, especially the Orkney and Outer Hebridean Islands, and western Ireland, where many were dependent on kelp for their livelihood. Attempts were made to find alternative uses for seaweeds and, as a result, in 1881, sodium alginate was discovered, and found to be useful as a textile size, in making jellies, fining spirits, and as an emulsifying agent. E. C. C. Stanford formed the Algin Co. Ltd. to exploit his discovery, but died in 1899 before its full potential was realised. After his death three firms started to use sodium alginate in textile manufacture, and slowly the industry developed.

Cefoil Ltd. was started in 1934 in Kintyre to manufacture alginate films, but during the 1939–45 war was taken over by the Ministry of Supply to provide alginate textiles for camouflage materials. Further factories were set up at Kames, Barcaldine and Girvan, with Cefoil Ltd. as manager. After the war the factories came under the new management of Alginate Industries Ltd., the Kintyre factory closed, Kames became merely a storage depot, but Barcaldine and Girvan were developed as chemical factories.

### The uses of alginates

Alginic acid is a carbohydrate found only in the cell walls of the brown seaweeds and makes up between 15 and 40 per cent of the dry weight—the amount varying between species, stipe or frond, time of year, and other factors.[9] Crude alginic acid is easy to extract, but not to store; but it combines with most metals and organic bases to form stable salts. Sodium alginate is the most widely used—it acts as a thickening, emulsifying, stabilising or deflocculating agent, and can be used for gelling and binding. It is thus used in a variety of products, including sauces, syrups, soups, ice cream, jellies, milk desserts, sausage casing, toothpastes, shampoos, polishes, paints, ceramic glazes, and pharmaceutical tablets. Calcium alginate will form fibres which are soluble in soap and water, an apparent disadvantage which has been put to use in the textile industries where alginate fibres are woven with more delicate fibres to give ease of handling, then washed from the finished product to give a lightweight fabric, or an openwork pattern, which could not be achieved by conventional means. There are many other uses of alginates which cannot be quoted at length.[10]

## The collection and processing of seaweeds

The stipes of *L. cloustoni* contain a particularly high percentage of alginic acid, and are thus favoured for collection. When these are in short supply *A. nodosum* or *L. digitata* are also used. The Laminarias and rockweed are harvested, dried, and processed to meal as described for feeds and fertilisers

## Scotland

It is obviously inconvenient to site large chemical factories, each employing over 200 people, mainly skilled technical staff, and requiring expensive equipment, in remote parts of the British Isles; equally it is uneconomic to transport wet seaweed between 200 and 600 miles directly to the chemical factories. Thus Alginate Industries Ltd. have three stages in the organisation of the industry; collection, air drying and marshalling close to seaweed supplies in the Orkney and Shetland Islands, the Outer Hebrides and Tiree; further drying and milling at intermediate points, at Lochboisdale, Sponish, and Keose in the Outer Hebrides; and chemical extraction on the Scottish mainland, at Barcaldine near Oban, and Girvan, close to convenient services and markets.

## Eire

One of the earliest milling plants to be opened by Alginate Industries Ltd. was at Kilkieran in Connemara in 1946. Air-dried seaweed is collected from the Irish coast between north Donegal and Co. Clare and milled at Kilkieran. Until 1966 the meal was then shipped to Barcaldine or Girvan, but the firm has now opened an alginate factory in Galway. One other firm in Eire, at Ballyconneely, occasionally makes small amounts of alginates.

## England

There are five or six firms in England which extract very small amounts of alginic acid from Norwegian or Irish meal.

## The production of alginates

As over 90 per cent of the British production of alginates comes from one private company it is difficult to learn the total output. A recent estimate puts world production at around 15,000 tons per annum.[11] If earlier trends[12] are being continued the U.S.A. produces about half of this, the U.K. a third to a quarter, and the rest comes mainly from Norway and Japan with smaller quantities from France and Russia. At a selling price of 27s. 6d. per 500 grams for sodium alginate, with reductions for bulk purchase, the industry is probably worth around £3 million to the British Isles. About 70 per cent of the British production is exported throughout the world.[13] In 1969 Alginate Industries Ltd. announced plans to exploit the seaweed resources of the Falkland Islands; they also won the Queen's Award to Industry, for services to exports.

### PROBLEMS OF THE SEAWEED INDUSTRIES

The main problems of the seaweed industries are that seaweeds are zoned on the shores, that they flourish best in areas which frequently experience unpleasant weather conditions, and that the harvesting is entirely manual.

239

*A. nodosum* grows at mid-tide level and can only be harvested for up to six hours around low tide, and often one low tide a day occurs in darkness. The shore is usually uneven, making walking and cutting difficult. The Laminarias grow below low-water mark, and can only be cut from the shore at infrequent exceptionally low tides. In the past, when coastal communities were more dependent on seaweeds, harvesters worked with poles over the sides of boats in shallow water, but there is not enough incentive for this to be done today. Mechanical harvester boats for the Laminarias have been designed and worked, but as yet none has proved to be an economic proposition. The uneven rocky bottom means that machinery is liable to jam, and as the Laminarias grow most abundantly in shallow water navigation is difficult, and there is always the danger of running aground. As the areas to be harvested frequently experience high winds and heavy seas the number of days on which boats can work is severely limited.[14] Lastly, mechanical harvesters do not distinguish between stipes and fronds, nor between species. The crop is more likely to consist of the fronds, as these grow higher on the plants, and this is acceptable for feeds and fertilisers, but it is the stipes which contain the higher percentage of alginic acid.

On account of these difficulties Laminarias are at present sorted from seaweeds cast on the shore, but this also brings problems. Although some communities may know the conditions which lead to casting locally it cannot generally be forecast, and collection cannot be organised in advance. On the other hand, collection must take place as soon as possible after casting, before bacterial decay starts, or the seaweed is removed by a high enough tide. As it is in stormy weather that the laminarias are torn from the rocks and cast on the shores collection is unpleasant, even dangerous. The plants are heavy and wet, and the required species have to be sorted from a tangled mass. Much of the cast weed is lost to industry on account of the uncongenial nature of collection.

In addition to the weather problems already mentioned high relative humidities and frequent rain hinder the air-drying of seaweeds, and encourage decay.

When cutting *A. nodosum* from the rocks the harvesters must take care that at least nine inches of thallus are left above the holdfast, or future crops will be endangered.[15] The crop depends on continued growth from existing plants, and if an area is completely cleared it is several years before it can be harvested again, as *A. nodosum* is rarely a primary coloniser. Experienced harvesters cut in a two- or three-year rotation. At present a parallel problem does not arise with the Laminarias but if mechanical harvesters were widely used similar controls would have to be applied.

Few collectors depend exclusively on seaweed for their income, often it is of very secondary importance, giving little incentive to work in bad weather. Consequently much of the available seaweed is never collected.

### CONCLUSION

It is obvious that the main problems of the seaweed industries are in harvesting. The records of the old kelping industries,[16] and the surveys of the Scottish Seaweed Research Association show that the seaweed reserves of the British Isles are large, but they are not being exploited to the full as not enough is harvested. One answer may be to 'farm' seaweeds. This

# The brown seaweed industries in the British Isles

was tried in the kelping days when large stones for seaweeds to colonise were placed on muddy shores, but this does not at present seem practicable on any but a very small scale. Further incentive to collect could be given by offering a higher price, but this would raise costs without significantly increasing the amount of seaweed collected. The future of the industry may well depend on the development of an effective and economical mechanical harvester.

ACKNOWLEDGMENTS

The research work on which this article is based was carried out at the University of Nottingham from 1963 to 1966 under the joint supervision of Professor K. C. Edwards and Professor C. G. C. Chesters, and with the aid of a Science Research Council Grant. Considerable assistance was given by Mr. E. Booth, formerly of the Institute of Seaweed Research, Inveresk, Midlothian. Many of the facts quoted in the text are from private communications from persons connected with seaweed processing.

NOTES

1 SCOTTISH SEAWEED RESEARCH ASSOCIATION, *Reports on the distribution of rockweeds and sub-littoral seaweeds* (Inveresk, Midlothian, 1947–52); and SCOTTISH SEAWEED RESEARCH ASSOCIATION, *Annual reports* (Inveresk, Midlothian, 1947–52).

2 Information from Irish Seaweed Processors.

3 L. NEWTON, *Seaweed utilisation* (Sampson Low, London, 1951) 55–57; and INSTITUTE OF SEAWEED RESEARCH, *Report on seaweed prospects* (Institute of Seaweed Research, Inveresk, Midlothian, 1956).

4 J. HOIE and F. SANNAN, Further experiments with seaweed meals as supplements to rations for chicks and laying hens, *Abs. 3rd Int. Seaweed Symp.* (Galway, 1958) 48–49; and INSTITUTE OF SEAWEED RESEARCH, *op. cit.* (1956).

5 E. BOOTH, *The production of seaweed meal* (Institute of Seaweed Research, Inveresk, Midlothian, 1962).

6 E. BOOTH, *op. cit.* (1962).

7 INSTITUTE OF SEAWEED RESEARCH, *The seaweed meal industry in Ireland* (Institute of Seaweed Research, Inveresk, Midlothian, 1962).

8 INSTITUTE OF SEAWEED RESEARCH, *op. cit.* (1962).

9 INSTITUTE OF SEAWEED RESEARCH, *op. cit.* (1956).

10 ALGINATE INDUSTRIES LTD., *Alginates* (London); and L. NEWTON, *op. cit.,* 81–96.

11 *The Guardian* (Manchester and London, Tuesday, 3rd December 1968).

12 Private communication from Institute of Seaweed Research; and INSTITUTE OF SEAWEED RESEARCH, *op. cit.* (1956).

13 *The Guardian, op. cit.* (1968).

14 SCOTTISH SEAWEED RESEARCH ASSOCIATION, *op. cit.* (1947–52); and INSTITUTE OF SEAWEED RESEARCH, *op. cit.* (1956).

15 Information from Irish Seaweed Processors.

16 V. E. RAMPTON, Development of the seaweed industries in the British Isles, *Unpublished M.Sc. thesis* (University of Nottingham, 1966) 94–117.

241

# WHERE X, THERE ABC: SOME THOUGHTS UPON A COMPREHENSIVE THEORY OF THE GEOGRAPHY OF PRODUCTION

### E. M. RAWSTRON

The geography of production, which is not synonymous with economic geography, though it often serves as such in practice, deals with the variable productive character of places, be they large or small in area. In one small place employing several thousand people in Nottingham bicycles are made; in another, cigarettes; while yet another, somewhat larger, 'produces' diverse retail services around the city centre. This last is the 'central place' of Nottingham. In one part of the East Midlands there is a much larger place, a sizeable agricultural region, where bulb fields are so closely grouped together, their spatial incidence being so frequent, that they dominate the visual landscape with a blaze of colour in the spring. The spatial incidence of coal mines is frequent, though sub-regionally varied in regularity and size, over the Nottinghamshire and Derbyshire coalfield. Moreover, the pattern of mining has changed through time and is changing even more quickly during the present period than in the past. Knitwear, lace, footwear and engineering factories bespatter some of the urban landscapes of the central East Midlands, and a row of huge power stations flanks the Trent.

These features give a measure of distinctive character to different parts of the East Midlands, and maybe some of them form economic 'stows'[1] therein, so markedly do they locally dominate the economy. To some extent they are interdependent, for there would be no line of power stations without the coal, and no lace without the hosiery that preceded it. But it is not the purpose of this essay to seek a comprehensive theory of the complex of regional and local productive activity. The aim is to ask whether a useful theory can be found that will fit the spatial reality, perceived at any given time, of each class of productive pattern in turn, but which can be applied to all of them treated individually. Can there be a comprehensive theory that will fit the location of the single, large tobacco factory, the multitude of contiguous bulb farms, the 'central retailing place' in every town, the line of large power stations and the clusters of small lace factories?

Much has been, and more will be, written on the topic of the location of productive activity, for it is without doubt interesting as a problem, useful as an adjunct to social and economic policy, and challenging in its complexity and multivariate intractability. My own interest in it derived originally from a case study of electricity production undertaken between 1950 and 1953. It grew later through reading theoretical writings rather than other case-studies, of which in my opinion there is still a great shortage. It has been heightened by the developing interest shown in location by economists and by the increasing controversy between 'optimisers' and 'satisficers'.

## WHERE X, THERE A B C

My own initial approach to the problem of the location of production has been geographically inductive rather than economically deductive. I invert, but nevertheless have long drawn inspiration from, a hypothesis set out in a short article by McCarty[2] in which he discusses the proposition 'where a b c there x'. Where phenomena a b c are found in spatial association, x (the phenomenon under examination) will also be found. In electricity production, however, x being a power station, the spatial association of a b c is not invariably accompanied by the discovery of x. The converse, however, is true, to a tolerance radius of not more than two miles, for the base-load power stations built or enlarged along the Trent between 1948 and the present. The locational tolerance of a large power station is now small and near-optimum locations are discernible. To my recollection only two possible a b c sites remain unoccupied by power. stations on the middle and lower Trent. The site at Holme Pierrepont is one of these.[3]

But methods of, and attitudes to, electricity production have changed through time and vary from one part of the earth's surface to another. X does not remain constant and a b c change too, so the structural composition of the proposition when applied to a given industry is unlikely to be a universal constant in time or space. Nevertheless, 'where x, there a b c' is a helpful beginning, for it sets up the spatial experiment in a form that suits the geographer's method.

When I began writing my first paper[4] for publication I felt inclined to put factors before facts, supposed causes before effects. K. C. Edwards advised me to reverse the order, to take x before a b c. In the electricity industry it is easy to answer the question 'where x?' in quantitative terms of both capacity and output. 'There a b c' was, and remains, less easy. The very word 'there' poses serious problems, for if 'a' represents market, 'b' coal, and 'c' land requirements of site and closely-confined situation, no simple definition of 'there' as a point will serve. *Inter situs* as well as *in situ* relationships are implied. Moreover, 'a, b and c' are each complex divisible phenomena, and probably 'd, e, f and g' at least should be added to the proposition.

### Margin Preferred to Optimum

Although my study of Trent-side power stations yielded clear examples of close approximation to optimum location, examination of electricity production in Britain as a whole, together with subsequent events in electricity itself and subsequent examination of other industries, have made me a confirmed 'marginalist' and 'satisficer'. These two terms, it should be noted, are not exactly synonymous and the word 'satisficer' itself does not appeal to me.[5]

McCarty states, 'The nub of the problem of research procedure seems to lie in finding the best technique for discovering a, b and c'. A suggested solution to this problem is to be found in the second principle in my paper of 1958.[6] The cost structure or, as I would now prefer to put it, the revenue structure of an enterprise should provide the key. One is still so far from gaining access to such data, however, that progress on this tack must appear unbelievably slow to any outsider looking in upon the efforts of economic geographers. But we are not alone in this predicament, for neither the Distribution of Industry Division of the Ministry of Technology nor almost any individual entrepreneur or firm can have precise enough knowledge of the spatial variation in cost or price among the components of revenue structure to do more than guess at the likely precise disposition of optimum locations where profit may be maximised. The best informed

243

are probably the nationalised industries: coal, electricity, gas and steel. And even their locational decisions may rapidly deviate from the optimum soon after they have been made. Such thoughts as these led to the assertion in the final paragraph of my 1958 article that a marginal location theory would prove more useful in the study of real spatial behaviour than an optimum theory.

### THE REVENUE SURFACE

A Nottingham graduate, D. M. Smith, has developed these ideas further.[7] Using a series of simple spatial models he shows how the optimum may be visualised in relation to the margin on a map whose contours express monetary differences rather than those of altitude, barometric pressure or precipitation. One may thus imagine economic surfaces similar in their depiction to those of relief, but, whereas the margin to spatial profitability is always a line or band circumscribing an area, the optimum location where maximum profit can be achieved may turn out to be a point for one industry and a plateau for another. X may be found anywhere within the margin at a given time, while a b c may be deemed to occur in adequate spatial-economic association to satisfy the need for profitability only within the margin. 'There' is intra-marginal and the degree of spatial association among a b c explains the contour pattern within which the margin occurs, but a b c does not explain the detailed choice of locations. One entrepreneur may be satisfied with his recent choice because the locality appeals to his aesthetic or social taste. Without knowing it, he and his shareholders may be forgoing a measure of profit for a benefit he values more highly than money. Another may be obliged to accept a barely viable and even aesthetically—or 'psychically'[8]—unattractive location. It was his father's choice before him, and the decision was originally sound, but the son now lacks the resources and enterprise to change it. Yet another entrepreneur may be going rapidly bankrupt on the optimum pinnacle of a conical profit surface because he is wearying of commerce and no longer has the urge to manage his business efficiently. Another entrepreneur, seeing his profits diminish as the margin approaches through time, may be innovating and changing his range and type of product rather than changing his location.

### CHOICE OF LOCATION WITHIN THE MARGIN

All these, and many more, differing examples are possible and must happen in reality. Thus the variable productive character of places is ever-changing and has to be explained in terms other than those of profit maximisation. Moreover, the spatial margin to profitability serves merely to set the limit to possibility at a given time, for it is determined by the *inter situs* relationships of a b c which, though they restrict the spatial behaviour of enterprises, do not determine the precise site chosen for x. Through time, however, the margin has far greater operational effect than the optimum, for, as the margin moves over the earth's surface, its passing literally *places* some plants out of business or selects for survival from among their successful, productive mutations in much the same way as the movement of climatic margins selects biologically. The evolutionary transformation during economic history of firms in the West Midland conurbation provides many examples of mutation of production in response to spatial changes in revenue surfaces. The productive history of Stanton Ironworks, mentioned below, is probably also an instance of the operation of the same process.

If the spatial-economic margin remains stationary for a sizeable period the spatial optimum may become empirically apparent and plants may tend to concentrate there as growing demand begets increasing supply, but a spatial concentration of similar enterprises is not a sure indication that the optimum has been found. In other words, the dictum 'growth industries demand growth locations' is not the same as saying 'locations where growth is rapid are optimum locations'.

Yet it is the economic geographer's task to try to explain the pattern of production that he finds. The optimum theory will seldom help him, and the margin simply sets a limit to what is possible. What then is to be the approach to understanding locational behaviour within the area contained by the margin? Shackle and Simon[9] examine a similar problem in the context of non-spatial economics, but the most detailed and closely argued statement in economic geography is that of Pred.[10] Deduction, however, rather than induction characterises his theoretical analysis.

Let us return, therefore, to the inductive approach 'where x there a b c' to see if this can be taken further, for the deductive theories propounded by others will have to be tested against real cases and it may be helpful to attempt a theoretical inductive approach with a view ultimately to seeing whether the tunnellers from the deductive side meet those from the inductive side in the middle of the mountain. Both groups may turn out to have been boring in substantially different directions.

If the *inter situs* relationships of a b c are now deemed only to determine operationally where x cannot be rather than where each x is actually to be found—they determine the position of the margin—how can one proceed further without recourse to the findings of economic history and accountancy? Location within the margin satisfies the entrepreneur, but why is Player satisfied with a site in Nottingham and Churchman with one in Ipswich? Why did Wills establish a branch factory in Swindon and why is there no longer a cigar factory in Hankin Street, Hucknall? How did Mackintosh & Co. arise and expand its production of sweet confectionery in Halifax close to the railway station and beneath the glowering escarpment of the Lower Coal Measures? How did Riley, also in the same industry, come to locate one-and-a-half miles away up the gentle slope in the western suburbs of Halifax? What explains the evident success of Percy Shaw, half way up the escarpment at Boothtown, making cats' eyes for the roads of the world? How did William Hollins succeed in Pleasley Vale?[11] Was it location or small size that was primarily responsible for the closure of the Millom iron works? How far does specialisation upon pipe-manufacture and diversification into concrete pipes explain the continued existence of Stanton Iron Works? Perhaps we should seek d, e and f to add to a, b and c, which clearly satisfy or, as the case may be, used to satisfy these enterprises.

### COMMON FACTORS FOUND OPERATING WITHIN THE MARGIN

It seems likely that d, e and f are specific in composition to each of the enterprises named. Yet there may be common factors among them. Place of residence of the founder is likely to prove a recurrent factor. The availability nearby at the right time of a vacant factory or a plot of land for sale is another. Parental backing and range of personal and family contact are others. Imitation and gregariousness among entrepreneurs; Local Authority support; Government location policy; financial takeovers; short- rather than long-term assessments; all these may often be found acting out roles within d, e and f.

There is room for only one example. Eindhoven is now a large city. It was created by N. V. Philips Gloeilampenfabrieken (Philips Electrical), which began producing electric lamps there in 1892. The Philips family were bankers in Zaltbommel on the Waal. When their elder son, Gerard, showed interest and inventiveness in things electrical, they backed him and began a search for a factory. One was soon found in Breda, but a distant cousin, Redelé, who lived in Eindhoven, told them that there was a former buckskin factory, 18 × 20 metres in area and with a 60-horse-power steam engine, standing vacant on a plot of 1,211 square metres in Eindhoven. This building and site seemed *satisfactory*. They looked no farther and, in the course of time, with the business acumen of Anton Philips added to the inventiveness of Gerard, both the enterprise and Eindhoven grew.[12] Neither a b c nor central place theory will adequately explain this spatial-economic event. Only economic historians analysing and assessing the company's minutes, papers and ledgers, will do that.

It appears, therefore, unlikely that any comprehensive theory can yet be adduced to fit the locational patterns of the economy. The optimum theory, being but a special case of the marginal theory and virtually non-operational save as a myth of conventional wisdom, will achieve little in locational analysis for the great majority of industries. The marginal theory is analytically useful: *(a)* through time, since movement of the margin begets both insolvency and innovation; and *(b)* in socio-economic planning, wherein it adds a bloom of theoretical respectability to the sound, grass-roots concept of the footloose or mobile class of enterprise. It tends to weaken such socially harmful notions as that which would have us believe the South East Region to be exclusively the most profitable area for enterprises in the United Kingdom, because entrepreneurs like it and they, of course, know best.

What is needed, if one is to build a comprehensive theory, to understand locational behaviour, and to attempt to guide it effectively, is a more practical approach to spatial analysis. Theory has probably gone far enough, and as far as it usefully can go for the time being without extensive, repetitive testing and concomitant reformulation. With the use of formulae and models alone it will prove hard to progress much beyond the point of perceiving revenue surfaces subject to economic forces of erosion and aggradation and upon which lie mobile margins ever-changing in position and shape, and differing greatly from one kind of enterprise to another. Theoretical progress is baulked because the fund of information about particular cases is too small and fragmentary. Herein the contribution made and yet to be made by economic and social historians is of the utmost importance, for within the margin the findings of business histories, including the hard facts of accountancy, are of great relevance to locational study.

### THE NEED FOR CASE-STUDIES

A deliberate diversion of geographical effort into the history of locational decision-taking—the study of actual cases with the 'marginal–satisficer' theory as a backcloth—is now a most promising direction for research. In the past there were too few economic and social geographers to do more than nibble at this enormous task. Miscellany was the order of the day, and many able students turned their attention away from human geography because it lacked a theoretical regulator to enable the outline of the wood to be distinguished from the trees. Now that we can see the wood more clearly and discern sets of trees within it, it is high time to re-examine the trees themselves. Detailed studies of this kind could very usefully complement the isarithmic findings which must surely follow grid-coordinate analyses of industrial employment which may be used in future demographic censuses. By these twofold means understanding of the variable economic character of places should be greatly enhanced.

## NOTES

[1] D. L. LINTON, The delimitation of morphological regions, *London essays in geography* (eds. L. Dudley Stamp and S. W. Wooldridge) (1951) 199–217.

[2] H. H. McCARTY, An approach to a theory of economic geography, *Econ. Geog.* 30 (1954) 95–101.

[3] E. M. RAWSTRON, Electric power generation, *Nottingham and its region* (ed. K. C. Edwards) (1966) 310–314.

[4] E. M. RAWSTRON, The distribution and location of steam-driven power stations in Great Britain, *Geog.* 36 (1951) 249–262.

[5] The term 'satisficer' is used by A. PRED, Behaviour and location, *Lund Studies in Geography* 27 (1967) and 28 (1969). It derives from the writings of H. A. SIMON, notably *Models of man* (1957), and Theories of decision-making in economics and behavioural science, *Amer. Econ. Rev.* 49 (1959) 253–283.

[6] E. M. RAWSTRON, Three principles of industrial location, *Trans. Inst. Br. Geogr.* 25 (1958) 135–142.

[7] D. M. SMITH, A theoretical framework for studies of industrial location, *Econ. Geog.* 42 (1966) 95–113.

[8] M. L. GREENHUT, *Plant location in theory and in practice* (1956).

[9] G. L. S. SHACKLE, *Decision, order and time in human affairs* (1961); and H. A. SIMON, *op. cit.*

[10] A. PRED, *op. cit.* (1967 and 1969). See also H. W. RICHARDSON, *Regional economics* (1969) 59–105; and M. CHISHOLM, *Geography and economics* (1966) 46–50.

[11] F. A. WELLS, *Hollins and Viyella* (1968).

[12] P. J. BOUMAN, *Anton Philips of Eindhoven* (1958).

# REMOTE SENSING STUDIES IN GEOGRAPHY: A REVIEW

## D. S. SIMONETT

### INTRODUCTION

Recent research in remote sensing by geographers in the United States has ranged widely over topics in rural and urban thematic land use and transportation network mapping, in urban and planning information systems, and in geomorphology, soil and vegetation mapping and hydrology. Most work has been with photographic systems but some has been done with multi-channel scanners and radar. To keep this review brief only selected photographic studies on rural and urban land use, transportation, and spacecraft cartographic mapping are mentioned. Well-illustrated and broader articles to which the reader may refer are those by Lent and Thorley,[1] Colwell,[2] Moore and Wellar,[3] and Moore and Simonett.[4]

Underlying all work in remote sensing has been a concern with improving methods of data collection and with developing ways to answer previously unmanageable scientific and practical problems. Moore and Wellar[5] consider that four criteria are especially pertinent in the evaluation of data obtained by remote sensors, namely: timeliness, flexibility, compatibility, and reliability. The degree to which remote sensors can satisfy these criteria 'more rapidly, accurately, or at lower cost than other available collection methods', will influence their incorporation into geographic data systems.[6]

As work has progressed and we have attempted to answer these questions of timeliness, flexibility, and so on, we have come more and more to realize:

(a) the complexity of the problems being tackled;
(b) the multi-dimensionality which problems acquire by being spread over many environments (an inevitable concomitant of spacecraft sensing);
(c) the necessity for definition and re-definition of problems and aims;
(d) the need critically to scrutinize accepted metrics, procedures, levels of accuracy, and assumptions not only in remote sensing, but in the very problem areas of science and application to which the sensor is addressed;
(e) the errors, and the obscure and many meanings of 'ground truth'; and finally
(f) we have come seriously to question certain tenets of remote sensing.

### CARTOGRAPHY

During the summers of 1967 and 1968 the U.S. National Research Council and the National Aeronautics and Space Administration convened a summer study on space applications. Thirteen panels rendered reports, including one on geodesy and cartography.[7] The panel, in recommending a possible geodetic and cartographic mapping programme using space photography, emphasized that while it is difficult to assess the needs of map users there is general agreement on the need for a synoptic map of the world at a scale of 1 : 1,000,000, for completion of world coverage at a scale of 1 : 250,000 and completion of maps at 1 : 24,000 for areas of special interest. They noted further that maps are three years out of date when they first reach a user's hands, and are revised every five to 10 years for areas most in demand, and 20 to 30 years for other areas. They continued:

> *All* map users agree that the most pressing problem is obtaining *current* map information [panel emphasis]. *Completeness, geometric accuracy, aesthetics, would all be sacrificed for currency. It is precisely in this area that satellite cartography can be most useful* [my emphasis].

To meet the objectives of providing synoptic 1 : 1,000,000, 1 : 250,000 and 1 : 24,000 photo mosaics, and finished maps at the same scales, the satellites would be in a circular sun-synchronous orbit carrying the following cameras:

*(a)* a 150 millimetre focal length, 225 by 225 millimetre format cartographic camera to give a maximum ground resolution of 20 metres with colour film;

*(b)* a 300 millimetre focal length 225 by 370 millimetre format cartographic camera using black and white thin base film, and a maximum ground resolution of 10 metres; and

*(c)* a 600 millimetre focal length, 225 by 460 millimetre format camera, giving 7.5 metres ground resolution.

The final section of the report analyses the costs of the various satellites. Based on 50 per cent usable photography, costs ran about half those for photographs of easily accessible areas in the United States and ranged from one-fifth to one-tenth the cost of Department of Defence photography in other countries.

The whole basis of spacecraft remote sensing has been roundly criticised by Katz on the economics of the satellite photography.[8] The geodesy/cartography panel and Doyle have disagreed with Katz's calculations and assumptions as well as pointing out that with space photography useful products can be made that are totally infeasible with conventional aerial photography.[9] At the time of writing the controversy is still underway and is unresolved.

### THEMATIC LAND USE MAPPING

Thematic land use mapping has long been a concern of geographers and planning agencies. The I.G.U. aim of producing a world land use map at 1 : 1,000,000 and its realisation are, however, widely separated by limitations of accessibility, time, cost, and available data. Spacecraft photographs with resolution of 60 to 120 metres from the Gemini and Apollo series are now being tested by U.S. geographers for land use mapping. These resolutions are of the order of those expected from E.R.T.S. (Earth Resources Technology Satellites) in the early 1970s but are coarser than those desired for large-area land use mapping, for which resolutions should be no poorer than 30 metres and preferably from 10 to 15 metres.

Schwarz *et al.* have shown that very few existing land use maps could be duplicated using spacecraft photography, in part because of shortcomings in spacecraft photography but primarily because of internal inconsistencies in existing land use maps.[10] These inconsistencies arise because thematic maps reflect the peculiarities of their locales and the idiosyncracies of their compilers as well as the diversity of their data sources. The systematic constraint of a single data source restricted to visible phenomena has never applied during their compilation nor has the necessity for developing a classification of general rather than particular application, suitable also for remote sensors, been faced. Schwarz *et al.* also found that variations in the meanings to be attached to photographic tones in different locales forced the land use categories into general groups. Their groups (also those by Thrower and Senger[11]) are very closely related to those set up for the world land use map by the I.G.U. The categories used were: settlement, cultivated, grass, trees, water, brush, bare, ice and snow. Surprisingly detailed large-scale maps frequently use categories as gross as these. Conversely, some land use maps use as many as 30 categories, some of which could not be obtained even with very high resolution aerial photography. The third conclusion they came to was that 'a given resolution does not convey the same information in all environments, that is, information transfer is environmentally modulated'. This conclusion was based upon a study of the number of entities which could be contained within resolution cells of 15, 30, 60, 120 and 300 metres in a variety of environments in central and eastern United States, and other areas. They concluded that a 30 metre resolution would produce an acceptable number of resolution cells containing single rather than multiple entities for much of the world and that 15 metre resolution would be significantly better than 30 metres.

A preliminary report on interpretation of land use, crops, forestry and grazing resources using colour infra-red and multiband photography from the March 1969 Apollo IX space flight has been prepared by R. N. Colwell and associates.[12] General land use mapping was performed, *inter alia,* for the Phoenix area, Arizona, on the Apollo IX photographs but no evaluation of the accuracy of boundaries and units delineated was made. However, studies on crop discrimination based on 'training samples' for interpreters showed that:

> (1) recently cut alfalfa fields are identifiable about 80 per cent of the time, (2) cultivated, but as yet unplanted fields (bare soil) are almost always differentiated from other agricultural features or crops (98–100 per cent), (3) the relative wetness or dryness of unplanted fields is easily detected (86–95 per cent), (4) the continuous cover crops, barley, alfalfa (mature), sugar beets, and wheat are not consistently differentiated from one another, but the groups are easily differentiated from cut alfalfa and bare soil.

A number of illustrations were also given of the improved identification of barley using panchromatic film with a red filter in March, April and May. The principle of using time as a discriminant in crop identification is well established.[13]

Simonett *et al.* examined boundary delineation as a precursor to area typing of an area near Alice Springs, Australia.[14] Two themes were pursued. The first concerns the detection and meaning of boundaries, the second concerns resource confusion and categorisation. They found that space-detected boundaries derived substantially from ground information, that even the smallest pin-pricks of space data related to qualitative changes in the landscape, and that space boundaries were easier to detect than identical boundaries on photo mosaics. Cochrane found that first and second order boundaries—first order boundaries are easily discriminable, second order are intermediate, and third order boundaries are diffuse—without exception were useful indicators of real differences in vegetation and other aspects of the landscape, while third order boundaries were either ecotonal or were transitional in plant density.[15]

Detecting a boundary and knowing that the landscape is somehow different on either side of it is not the same as knowing either the nature or magnitude of that difference, nor is it to be presumed that the boundaries lie at the same level of generalisation. Categorisation of entities on the photograph is also related to this problem of generalisation. In low-level aerial photographs image qualities, such as texture and height, may be used but these are less useful than tone on space photographs, despite the limitations of the latter: similar shades of colour on space photographs will arise from dissimilar mosaics of landscape features, and unlike shades may represent the same combinations. Our experience with space photographs suggests that reconnaissance surveys could use a survey sequence comparable with the following:

*(a)* 50 to 100 feet resolution spacecraft colour infra-red photography;

*(b)* low-altitude 70 millimetre vertical and oblique photography with colour and colour infra-red film obtained by planned flights based on units noted on the space photographs; and

*(c)* ground sampling.

*To summarise:* the advantages of space photography in land use mapping include:

*(a)* the ease of obtaining repetitive cover and the use of time as a discriminant;

*(b)* large areas can be handled on a few photographs, thus much reducing the problems of photography obtained at different times, of 'mosaicking', and of data processing;

*(c)* generalised boundary delineation may be obtained with a high order of reproducibility and fidelity to meaningful boundaries on the ground;

*(d)* a single source of information may be used not subject to the whims of data-collection boundaries, data widely variant in time of collection, prior lumping of data, inconsistent data formats, classifications which are incompatible between collection agencies, etc.; and

*(e)* space photography when available will open the door to new mixes of photographic data for survey purposes. One need not be confined to pan minus blue photographs at a fixed scale.

The present disadvantages are those of:

*(a)* a too-modest resolution;

*(b)* insufficient work on the consistency with which the information can be obtained from place to place and time to time; and

*(c)* the inability to separate entities of similar appearance on the photograph without detailed ground survey. This is, of course, a problem with photographs of any scale.

No attention is given here to the use of multi-channel scanners, radar imaging and infra-red systems in thematic land use mapping. They are reviewed by Simonett.[16]

## TRANSPORTATION ROUTES

It has been suggested that high-altitude aircraft and space photographs may be used for updating maps of transportation networks. The proponents for such a view argue that such photography would permit coverage of large areas while providing current, accurate information on the network. In order to use this photography it is necessary not only consistently to detect the presence of linear elements such as roads, railroads, pipelines, etc., but also consistently to identify and discriminate between them. Pate studied remote sensor applications in urban and regional transportation planning, especially origin and destination surveys.[17] He compared the costs of remote and conventional techniques in planning, survey initiation, data collection, and data handling. For each, the benefits favoured high-altitude aircraft sensing over conventional methods. A systematic study is under way at the University of Kansas on the use of nine space photographs—obtained at different dates—for identifying transportation routes in a nine-county area near Dallas, Texas. Preliminary results indicate that in order consistently to be detected a road plus its shoulder should have a width between one-third to equal that of the photographic resolution, depending on the background.[18]

## URBAN AREA STUDIES

Three major areas have received attention in urban studies using remote sensors, namely, dwelling unit counts, housing quality, and urban land use. The first two require resolutions of the order of 30 centimetres, the third of about one to two metres.

### Dwelling unit estimation

Information on the number of dwelling units and persons per unit area is vital for many planning studies related to urban population densities, journey-to-work problems, and potential land use changes. Binsell used 1 : 5,240 aerial ektachrome photographs to estimate the number of dwelling units in selected areas of Chicago.[19] He used methods established by Green and Hadfield,[20] but added refinements such as

> dwelling unit estimation of small multi-unit residences, dwelling unit estimation with a minimum of field checking, application of correction factors to the data of the original study, and photographic key refinement.

He obtained a total net error of under-estimation of 12.6 per cent in areas covering some 15,000 dwelling units. This was lowered to four per cent and then two per cent by using correction factors, plus improved keys. The final error equals the estimated net error in the United States censuses of 1950 and 1960. These results suggest that the technique should be tried elsewhere and that it may be used to obtain estimates of population density where censuses are not available. However, modifications will be required in each new environment. 'Calibration' of the environment looms as a demanding problem.

### Housing quality surveys

The quality of housing in urban areas is an important aspect of the urban environment. In particular, blighted housing is critical in the ecology of the United States city, for such areas are prime candidates for urban renewal and for re-location of major highways and other facilities. Yet existing field enumeration techniques of housing quality by the Bureau of the Census, the American Public Health Association, and by local city agencies are expensive, time-consuming, and open to criticism on the grounds of non-specificity, subjectivity, the non-additive character of parameters, their unsuitability for application to multi-unit structures, and difficulties of understanding and application.[21]

A series of studies on urban housing quality by Wellar, Moore, Bowden, Mullens, and co-authors, have tested the application of various scales of multiband and colour infra-red photography to delineation of housing quality in Chicago and Los Angeles.[22] Mumbower and Donoghue examined conventional black and white photographs of a dozen United States cities for housing parameters.[23] Moore *et al.* comment that:

> at a non-rigorous level these studies suggest that data relating to many variables included in current field (housing quality) surveys may be collected with comparable accuracy and considerable savings of time and cost using aerial photography. In the light of the urgency expressed for acquiring data on housing conditions for all large urban areas by federal, state, and local agencies it is imperative that these new techniques be subjected to rigorous scientific testing in order to assess their potential quality in housing surveys.[24]

Wellar attempted to discover significant photographic correlates of poor housing quality, using multiband aerial photographs.[25] He developed a procedure he claimed to be rapid, reliable, and an objective source of housing data. He found the most consistent indicators of low-quality housing from the multiband photographs were the presence of litter, garbage, derelict cars, and lumber on weedy, vacant, unlandscaped, crowded lots and the presence of non-residential hazards and nuisances. These criteria were not established by statistical analysis, but by plausible association. Later studies by Mullens[26] and by Moore[27] have provided some statistical verification of Wellar's study.

Bowden used 1 : 60,000 scale colour infra-red photography to study the quality of residential neighbourhoods in 400 census tracts covering the entire range of income levels and housing types in Los Angeles.[28] He compared the classification of residential areas based on the 1960 census with that developed by interpreting the C.I.R. imagery obtained in 1967. In another study in Los Angeles, Mullens[29] used a nine-category set of surrogates of housing quality derived from 1 : 6,000 colour infra-red photography based upon a mixture from those developed by Wellar and by Bowden. His categories were dwelling type (single or multi-unit), vegetation quality, litter, vacant land, land use, location, presence of pools and patios, lot and home size, and street quality and character. He correlated these photographic surrogates with census variables using the Kendall Rank Correlation Technique. Consistently a triplet of variables comprising quality of vegetation plus the presence of litter plus the amount of vacant land served as the best indicators of low housing quality and correlated at values up to 0.86 with census tract data, despite the fact that Mullens' sample was in a very homogeneous area of Los Angeles and did not contain as wide a variation in housing quality as tests such as this require. The surrogate approach needs further testing in other cities to establish the limits of its applicability.

Moore has provided a most useful statistical study on housing characteristics for three study areas of Los Angeles.[30] Patterns of co-variation of housing quality variables at the parcel and block scales were studied along with the potential of photographic sensors for assigning housing to quality classes based on environmental observations only. Principal axis factor analysis showed a structure consistent with the American Public Health Association criteria, and it proved possible to assign quality classes at the block (not parcel) level using observations on environment characteristics only. Whether this situation would apply in other cities is not known. Multiple discriminant function analysis was also applied to the data from the factor analysis. With a much-collapsed matrix the same groupings appeared as with 37 variables devised by the American Public Health Association and the correlations with field enumerated groupings were encouragingly good.

## Urban land use mapping

Urban land use information is needed for a wide range of urban administrative planning and action programmes, and as with data on housing quality, is expensive to obtain, time-consuming, and involves much checking for accuracy. Despite the conventional use of black and white aerial photographs in urban land use mapping many ground surveys are still made, and there have been very few surveys based on balanced use of low and very high altitude colour and colour infra-red aerial photography. Recent studies[18, 31, 33] indicate that much more extensive use could be made of aerial photography and that low, moderate, and high altitude aerial photography are capable of leading to more rapid urban land use mapping than ground techniques.[31]

Bowden constructed a land use map of west and central Los Angeles using high-altitude (1 : 60,000) colour infra-red photography.[32] The maps were constructed entirely from the imagery and ground checks indicate they were more accurate than those compiled by the Los Angeles County Planning Agency during the same year. Both land use maps were completed in two weeks as compared with several months for the Los Angeles County Planning Agency maps.

Hannah predicated a study on three basic questions: can the various land uses be identified as well from remote sensing imagery as from a field survey; can accurate measurements for land use be made; and would the time, cost, and accuracy of accomplishing these studies compare favourably with conventional methods?[33] Asheville, North Carolina, was analysed using colour and false colour photography, the results being compared with a ground-based analysis by a consultant firm for the same area at about the same time the imagery was obtained. Field data were compared against the results obtained from the photographic interpretation. Of 1,713 land use parcels identified on the photography, only 26 were mis-interpreted for a total area of 400 hectares. It was estimated that employing photography the procedure through analysis would cost about $55,000 for Asheville, whereas the conventional field techniques cost $70,000.

### NOTES

[1] J. D. LENT and G. A. THORLEY, Some observations on the use of multi-band spectral reconnaissance for the inventory of wildland resources, *Remote Sensing of Environment* 1(1) (1969) 31–45.

[2] R. N. COLWELL, Aerial photography of the earth's surface, its procurement and use, *Applied Optics* 5(6) (1966) 883–892; and R. N. COLWELL, Remote sensing of natural resources, *Scientific American* 218(1) (1968) 54–69.

[3] E. G. MOORE and B. S. WELLAR, Urban data collection by airborne sensor, *Journal of the American Institute of Planners* 35 (1969) 1–5.

[4] R. K. MOORE and D. S. SIMONETT, Potential research and earth resources studies with orbiting radar: results of recent studies, *American Institute of Aeronautics and Astronautics (A.I.A.A.) Paper No. 67–767* (1967) 1–18.

[5] E. G. MOORE and B. S. WELLAR, *op. cit.* (1969).

[6] B. S. WELLAR, Thermal infrared imagery in urban studies, *Technical Letter NASA–135, NASA Contract No. R–09–020–024* (U.S. Department of Interior, Geological Survey, 1968).

[7] GEODESY/CARTOGRAPHY PANEL, *Useful application of earth-oriented satellites* (National Academy of Science, National Research Council publication, 1969).

[8] A. H. KATZ, Reflections on satellites for earth resource surveys: personal contributions to a summer study, *Publication No. P–3753* (The Rand Corporation, 1969).

9 GEODESY/CARTOGRAPHY PANEL, *op. cit.* (1969); and F. J. DOYLE, Wrong tenor (a reply to A. Katz, Let aircraft make earth-resource surveys, *Astronautics and and Aeronautics* 7(6) (1969) 60–68), *Astronautics and Aeronautics* 7(10) (1969) 78–91.

10 D. E. SCHWARZ, D. S. SIMONETT, G. F. JENKS, and J. R. RATZLAFF, *The construction of thematic land use maps with spacecraft photography* (Department of Geography and Centre for Research in Engineering Science, University of Kansas, Lawrence, Kansas, 1969).

11 N. J. W. THROWER and L. W. SENGER, Land use mapping of the southwestern United States from satellite imagery, (Presented at American Astronautical Society, Las Cruces, New Mexico, 23rd–25th October 1969).

12 R. N. COLWELL, Analysis of earth resources on Apollo 9 photography, *NASA Contract No. NAS 9–9348* (Forestry Remote Sensing Laboratory, University of California, Berkeley, California, 1969).

13 D. H. BRUNNSCHWEILER, Seasonal changes of the agricultural pattern: a study in comparative airphoto interpretation, *Photogrammetric Engineering* 23(1) (1957) 131–139; and E. L. SCHEPIS, Time lapse remote sensing in agriculture, *Photogrammetric Engineering* 34(11) (1968) 1166–1179.

14 D. S. SIMONETT, G. R. COCHRANE, S. A. MORAIN, and D. E. EGBERT, *Environment mapping with spacecraft photography: a central Australian example* (Centre for Research in Engineering Science, University of Kansas, Lawrence, Kansas, 1969).

15 G. R. COCHRANE, Personal communication.

16 D. S. SIMONETT, Land evaluation studies with remote sensors in the infrared and radar regions, *Land Evaluation* (ed. G. A. Stewart) (1968) 349–366.

17 M. PATE, A feasibility study of remote sensor application to urban and regional transportation planning, *Unpublished M.A. thesis* (Graduate School of Planning, University of Tennessee, Knoxville, 1967).

18 D. S. SIMONETT, F. M. HENDERSON, and D. E. EGBERT, On the use of space photography for identifying transportation routes: a summary of problems, *6th Symposium on Remote Sensing of Environment* (University of Michigan, Ann Arbor) (1969) 855-877.

19 R. BINSELL, Dwelling unit estimation from aerial photography, *Technical report prepared under U.S.G.S. Contract No. 14–08–0001–10654* (Department of Geography, Northwestern University, Evanston, Illinois, 1967).

20 N. E. GREEN, Aerial photography in the analysis of urban structure, ecological and social, *Unpublished Ph.D. dissertation* (Department of Sociology, University of North Carolina, Chapel Hill, 1955); and S. M. HADFIELD, *An evaluation of land use and dwelling unit data derived from aerial photography* (Urban Research Section, Chicago Area Transportation Study, Chicago, Illinois, 1963).

21 E. G. MOORE, J. F. BETAK, B. S. WELLAR, and A. S. MANJI, Comments on the definition and measurement of housing quality, *Research Report No. 46* (Department of Geography, Northwestern University, Evanston, Illinois, 1968); and E. G. MOORE, Application of remote sensors to the classification of areal data at different scales: a case study in housing, *Remote Sensing of Environment* (in press).

22 R. K. MOORE and D. S. SIMONETT, *op. cit.* (1967); E. G. MOORE *et al., op. cit.* (1968); E. G. MOORE, *op. cit.* (in press); B. S. WELLAR, Generation of housing quality data from multiband aerial photographs, *Technical Report U.S.G.S. Contract 14–08–0001–10654* (Department of Geography, Northwestern University, Evanston, Illinois, 1967); B. S. WELLAR, Utilization of multiband aerial photographs in urban housing quality studies, *Proceedings of the Fifth Symposium on Remote Sensing of Environment* (University of Michigan, Ann Arbor, Michigan, 1968) 913–926; E. G. MOORE and B. S. WELLAR, Remote sensor imagery in urban research: some potentialities and problems, *Technical Report U.S.G.S. Contract No. 14–08–0001–10654* (Department of Geography, Northwestern University, Evanston, Illinois, 1967); E. G. MOORE and B. S. WELLAR, *Multiband photography and urban data collections: some comments on applied research* (Department of Geography, Northwestern University, Evanston, Illinois, 1968) (mimeographed); L. W. BOWDEN, Southern California regional resources studies in NASA, *Earth Resources Aircraft Program Status Review* I (Manned Spacecraft Centre, Houston, Texas, 1968) 4–1 to 4–29; L. W. BOWDEN, Multi-sensor signatures of urban morphology, function and evolution, *Technical Report No. 2, U.S.D.A. Contract No. 14–08–0001–10674* (Department of Geography, University of California at Los Angeles and Riverside, 1968); and R. H. MULLENS, JR., Analysis of urban residential environments using colour infrared aerial photography, *Status Report III, U.S.D.I. Contract No. 14–08–0001–10674* (Department of Geography, University of California, Los Angeles, 1969).

23 L. E. MUMBOWER and J. DONOGHUE, The use of aerial photography to obtain socioeconomic information: a study of urban poverty, *Photogrammetric Engineering* 33 (1967) 610–618

24 E G. MOORE *et al., op. cit.* (1968).

25 B. S. WELLAR, *op. cit.* (1967) and (1968).

26 R. H. MULLENS JR., *op. cit.* (1969).

27 E. G. MOORE, *op. cit.* (in press).

28 L. W. BOWDEN, *op. cit.* (1968b).

29 R. H. MULLENS JR., *op. cit.* (1969).

30 E. G. MOORE, *op. cit.* (in press).

31 M. PATE, *op. cit.* (1967); R. H. MULLENS JR., *op. cit.* (1969); and B. S. WELLAR, *Hyperaltitude photography as a data base in urban and transportation research* (Department of Geography, Northwestern University, Evanston, Illinois, 1969).

32 L. W. BOWDEN, *op. cit.* (1968b).

33 J. W. HANNAH, A feasibility study for the application of remote sensors to selected urban and regional land use planning studies, *Unpublished M.A. thesis* (Department of Geography, University of Tennessee, Knoxville, Tennessee, 1967).

# LIST OF CONTRIBUTORS

*Mr. F. A. BARNES is Senior Lecturer in Geography, University of Nottingham

Professor K. M. CLAYTON, Dean of the School of Environmental Sciences, University of East Anglia, was formerly Demonstrator, University of Nottingham

*Mr. M. P. COLLINS is Lecturer in Town Planning, University College, London

*Mr. P. DIBB is a Research Fellow, Department of Human Geography, Australian National University, Canberra

*Dr. J. O. N. EZE is Lecturer in Geography, University of Nigeria, Nsukka

*PROFESSOR J. W. FOX is Professor of Geography, University of New England, Armidale, Australia

*Dr. G. JOAN FULLER, now retired, was formerly Senior Lecturer in Geography, University of Nottingham

*Professor B. J. GARNER is Professor of Geography, Geographical Institute, Aarhus University, Denmark

Dr. J. A. GIGGS is Lecturer in Geography, University of Nottingham

*Dr. B. S. HOYLE is Lecturer in Geography, University of Southampton

Professor W. B. JOHNSTON, Professor of Geography and Head of Department, University of Canterbury, New Zealand, was formerly a Lecturer, University of Nottingham

Professor CUCHLAINE A. M. KING is Professor of Physical Geography, University of Nottingham

*Dr. D. R. MILLS, Senior Lecturer in Geography, Ilkley College of Education, was formerly Assistant Lecturer, University of Nottingham

*Dr. P. R. MOUNFIELD, Lecturer in Geography, University of Leicester, was formerly Demonstrator, University of Nottingham

*Professor R. H. OSBORNE is Professor of Economic Geography, University of Nottingham

*Dr. D. C. D. POCOCK, Lecturer in Geography, University of Dundee, was formerly Demonstrator, University of Nottingham

*Professor M. POSNANSKY is Professor of Archaeology, University of Ghana

*Mr. A. G. POWELL is Assistant Chief Planner, Ministry of Housing and Local Government, and Deputy Director, South East Joint Planning Team

*Mrs. VALERIE E. RAMPTON (née Collins), Part-time lecturer, Trent Polytechnic, was formerly Demonstrator in Physical Geography, University of Nottingham

Mr. E. M. RAWSTRON, Reader in Geography, Queen Mary College, London, was formerly Lecturer, University of Nottingham

*Mr. D. N. ROBINSON is W.E.A. Tutor Organiser for South Lindsey

Professor D. S. SIMONETT, Professor of Geography, University of Kansas, was formerly Assistant Lecturer, University of Nottingham

*Dr. D. M. SMITH is Associate Professor, Department of Geography, Southern Illinois University

*Mr. J. M. SMITH is Group Leader (county map and research), Derbyshire County Planning Department

*Mr. L. SPOLTON is Senior Lecturer in Education, University College of Swansea

*Dr. A. STRAW is Senior Lecturer in Geography, University of Sheffield

*Dr. B. J. TURTON is Lecturer in Geography, University of Keele

*Denotes a former student of the Department of Geography, University of Nottingham (or previous University College)*

# LIST OF SPONSORS

Mr. and Mrs. D. J. Ager
Miss R. Aitken
Dr. and Mrs. J. Andrews

Miss M. Ball
Mr. R. J. B. Baker
Professor W. G. V. Balchin
Mr. and Mrs. F. A. Barnes
Professor E. W. Barrington
Mr. N. A. Baynes
Professor S. H. Beaver
Mr. and Mrs. M. Bell (*née* Brindley)
Miss P. M. Bielby
Professor J. H. Bird
Mr. D. J. Blair
Mrs. N. M. Blanchard
  (*nee* Weedon)
Dr. G. T. Bloomfield
Mrs. K. M. Bonniface (*née* Griffin)
Professor A. H. Bour
Mrs. A. Bowley
Mr. H. A. Boyd
Miss E. A. Bradley
Dr. W. G. Briggs
Professor D. K. Britton
Mr. H. J. Brooke
Mr. P. A. Brown
Miss D. Burgess

Mr. A. A. L. Caesar
Professor K. Cameron
Mr. D. J. M. Campbell
Professor Eila M. J. Campbell
Mr. H. Cartwright
Mrs. B. Chamier
Mr. D. P. Church
Dr. Z. Cietak
Professor K. M. and
  Mrs. J. M. Clayton
Dr. and Mrs. J. P. Cole
Professor Monica M. Cole
Mr. M. P. Collins
Miss E. Colthorpe
Miss J. P. Cook
Mr. F. B. J. Coombes
Mr. I. R. Couch
Mr. C. E. Crawford
Professor K. B. Cumberland
Professor F. F. Cunningham

Professor S. Dahl
Dr. F. S. Dainton
Professor H. C. Darby
Professor A. Davies

Mr. and Mrs. J. A. Dawson
Mr. R. Davy
Mr. W. S. Dean
Miss C. Delano Smith
Mrs. M. A. Dennis
Mr. P. Dibb
Professor G. Dix
Dr. and Mrs. J. C. Doornkamp
Mr. and Mrs. J. Douglas
Dr. D. P. Drew
Mr. I. R. Drummond
Mr. N. W. Dunkerley

Professor W. G. East
Mr. R. E. Ebisori
Mr. J. Elliott
Mr. D. M. Ellis
Mr. G. J. Eltringham
Mr. and Mrs. E. W. Entwistle
Mr. A. J. Evans
Dr. S. R. Eyre
Dr. J. O. N. Eze

Mr. J. Farnsworth
Professor C. A. Fisher
Professor W. B. Fisher
Mr. C. T. Forsyth
Dr. F. J. Fowler
Professor J. W. Fox
Mr. T. J. and Mrs. M. L. Freer
Mr. F. Frost
Professor D. W. Fryer
Professor and Mrs. W. R. Fryer
Mr. S. Fullarton
Dr. G. Joan Fuller

Professor B. J. Garner
Geographical Association:
  Derby, Lincoln and
  Nottingham Branches
Geographical Field Group
Geographical Society,
  University of Nottingham
Miss C. M. Gidley
Dr. and Mrs. J. A. Giggs
Dr. P. F. Granger
Miss D. M. Gray
Miss G. Green
Mr. M. W. Gibbs

Dr. Ruth Hannam
Mr. J. A. Harle
Professor C. D. Harris
Mr. D. Harrison
Professor H. C. K. Henderson

Sir Mark Henig
Mr. D. A. Hill
Sir Francis Hill
Mrs. N. Hodgson (*née* Keen)
Mr. W. D. Holmes
Miss J. Hopkinson
Professor J. W. House
Mrs. P. A. Howarth (*née* Moodey)
Mr. L. J. Hughes
Professor J. M. Hunter

Mr. and Mrs. C. A. Inglett
Mr. D. R. Ingram
Dr. J. D. Ives

Mrs. F. Jackson
Miss D. M. Jeffery
Dr. J. R. G. Jennings
Mr. K. E. Johnson

Dr. Joan M. Kenworthy
Kesteven College of Education,
 Department of Geography
Professor Cuchlaine A. M. King
Mr. S. King
Miss S. M. Kirkpatrick
Professor R. Klöpper
Professor L. A. Kosiński

Miss M. Langford
Professor B. W. Langlands
Mr. D. C. Large
Mr. C. M. Law
Professor R. Lawton
Mr. F. L. Lee
Mr. R. H. Lester
Professor S. Leszczycki
Mr. M. Lewis
Miss E. Linnegar
Mr. B. F. Little
Colonel P. H. Lloyd
Miss N. F. Lockton

Mr. P. S. McCullagh
Dr. Kathleen M. MacIver
Mr. and Mrs. J. A. McIver
Mr. and Mrs. N. A. Maddison
Mr. and Mrs. R. Mansfield
 (*née* Williamson)
Professor D. C. Marsh
Mrs. D. E. Masters
Professor W. R. Mead
Mr. G. A. Measures
Mr. W. Middlebrook
Dr. D. R. Mills
Mr. T. M. Milner
Mrs. L. J. Mitchell

Mr. H. A. and Mrs. W. M. Moisley
Mr. F. H. Molyneux
Miss C. Morrison
Mrs. G. H. Morton (*née* Wedlock)
Mrs. S. Morton (*née* Taylor)
Dr. P. R. Mounfield

Mr. K. J. Newman

Sister F. O'Kelly
Mr. J. E. and Mrs. M. J. Old
Professor J. Oliver
Professor M. Ortolani
Professor R. H. Osborne
Mr. F. S. Ottery

Mr. J. C. Pearson
Mr. R. E. Pearson
Professor R. F. Peel
Dr. D. C. D. and
 Mrs. G. M. Pocock
Professor M. Posnansky
Professor N. J. G. Pounds
Mr. A. G. Powell
Dr. B. Proudfoot

Mr. M. A. Raif
Mr. D. J. Rake
Mr. D. G. Rankin
Mr. E. M. Rawstron
Miss J. T. Reekie
Dr. Barbara Reynolds
Miss N. W. Rhodes
Mr. D. and Mrs. E. Riley
Mr. D. N. Robinson
Miss J. Rook
Mr. P. F. Rose
Mr. S. and Mrs. E. Rutherford

Miss C. I. Sansom
Dean N. V. Scarfe
Sir Frederick Scopes
Mr. N. T. Scott
Mrs. P. Searle (*née* Leay)
Mr. I. H. Seeley
Mrs. J. Sellars (*née* Haworth)
Mr. and Mrs. A. L. Semper
Mr. M. Severn
Mr. J. M. Shaw
Mrs. A. J. Shawyer
 (*née* Simmons)
Dr. June A. Sheppard
Mr. R. Shorland-Ball
Mrs. P. M. Simmons (*née* Carroll)
Professor E. S. Simpson
Professor A. E. Smailes
Mr. G. I. Smith

Mr. J. M. Smith
Mr. R. O. Smith
Mr. G. W. Sneesby
Professor A. Sömme
Mr. P. M. Spencer
Mr. L. Spolton
Miss E. M. Steel
Professor R. W. Steel
Mrs. V. Stevens (*née* Deans)
Mr. G. A. Storey
Dr. A. Straw
Mr. F. I. Straw
Mr. J. F. Sugden
Dr. N. Summers
Miss V. A. Sykes

Dr. C. J. Thomas
Miss G. E. Thomas
Mr. G. H. and Mrs. M. L. Thomas
Professor L. Thorpe
Mr. T. M. H. Thorpe
Mr. D. J. Thurgur
Mr. R. F. Tomlinson
Professor C. Troll
Flight-Lieutenant R. Turgoose
Miss J. Twemlow

University of Nottingham:
    Department of Adult Education
    Hugh Stewart Hall Library

Mr. D. Varley
Miss E. C. Vollans

Mr. A. Wadsworth
Dr. K. Warren
Dr. G. T. Warwick
Professor R. S. Waters
Mr. I. G. Weekley
Dr. P. T. Wheeler
Mrs. M. White
Mrs. M. Whittington (*née* James)
Mr. H. L. Widdup
Dr. J. H. Wise
Professor M. J. Wise
Rev. and Mrs. P. P. Wood
Mr. and Mrs. S. T. Wood
Workers' Educational Association,
    East Midlands District
Miss G. M. P. Wortley
Mrs. G. Wraith (*née* Starmer)

Mr. J. R. Young